THE CADWALADR QUESTS

The 11+ and SATs Vocabulary Novel–
a book with a built-in dictionary on every page

THE CADWALADR QUESTS

2

RACE FOR THE GOLD

S. L. AGER

Developmental editor: Anna Bowles
Copyeditor and proofreader: Leonora Bulbeck
Cover design and interior formatting: Mark Thomas / Coverness.com

ISBN 978-1-9993018-2-8 (paperback)
ISBN 978-1-9993018-3-5 (eBook)

Need *The Cadwaladr Quests* in US English? Please visit your local Amazon site for the USA version!

www.slager.co.uk

For all children, regardless of difficult exams

Table of Contents

Preface

This book is the second in the 11+ vocabulary novel series *The Cadwaladr Quests.*

I wrote the first whilst helping my children pass the 11+ and SATs. I aimed to make learning difficult vocabulary easier by including and defining it on the pages of an original and exciting book of fiction.

My daughter was an avid reader, so vocabulary came more naturally to her. My son was the opposite, a reluctant reader. For him, learning vocabulary was dull, especially when set within classic texts.

Many of the words included in this book come from the practice materials we amassed while working towards the 11+ exams and SATs in primary school, as well as Key Stage 3. We worked with both GL and CEM materials.

Of course, no published aids can guarantee that their material will appear on any exam paper, and neither can I. However, considering *The Cadwaladr Quests: Race for the Gold* contains almost 2,000 word definitions and hundreds of corresponding synonyms and antonyms (in a fun story for girls and boys), what does any parent or young reader have to lose?

I hope you enjoy Claire and Ben's gripping journey in the second book of *The Cadwaladr Quests*, but moreover, I hope it helps you and your children with any challenging vocabulary exams they are facing.

How to Use This Book

Treat this book like any other, read it and enjoy it. Its uniqueness is the contextualised, built-in dictionary on every page.

This story has been specially written to help young readers prepare for their 11+, SATs and entrance exams, as well as Key Stage 3. It includes difficult vocabulary embedded in a fun narrative that provides context for the new words and makes them easier to learn and understand.

On every page, key words are in bold, and each has a correlating footnote with a concise definition. The words are defined using the context in which they appear in the text, and definitions are as child-friendly as possible. Chosen key words are defined only once, when they first appear in the story.

Synonyms and antonyms are also provided, although some words do not have antonyms if they do not exist. This book does not aim to replace a dictionary or purport to be one, but dictionaries have been used to check the credibility of each definition.

PS: There are a few Welsh words in the story. To learn how to pronounce them, please visit **slager.co.uk/welsh-words**

Top Tips

- You may find it beneficial to read this book for the first time with an adult, but you and your parents can decide.
- The definitions are included for convenience and to guide the learning, not as a definitive 'must learn' list.
- Chosen key words are defined only once, when they first appear in the story.
- To make learning difficult words easier, try to associate the words with the relevant scene in the book and to picture their meanings.
- Chapter lengths vary, so do not necessarily aim to finish a chapter in each sitting.
- Some pages have more definitions than others to fit in with the storytelling.
- The definitions decrease in the final chapters, enabling the reader to enjoy the ending with minimal interruption to the story.
- Read the book as often as is needed, and continue to use its vast resource of definitions, synonyms and antonyms to reinforce learning.
- The best way to learn new words is to read as widely and with as much variety as possible. Every book is a world of adventure waiting for you to turn to the first page. I hope my books help in this journey of discovery and learning.

Key to Abbreviations of Word Type

(v) verb

(n) noun

(adj) adjective

(adv) adverb

(prep) preposition

(con) conjunction

(int) interjection

(s) synonym

(ant) antonym

The Story So Far

Yesterday, schoolgirl Claire Cadwallader's world changed forever. Her friend Gladys vanished, leaving a mysterious letter saying Claire's sister was in danger and she must catch a train to Bangor to help rescue her. Claire set off, taking Gladys's dog, Jack, with her. Gladys's sister, Anwen, was on the train, and on arrival in Bangor, they left in a pony and **trap**[1] driven by a mysterious man called Gwilym.

Their journey was **hazardous**[2]. When boys on motorbikes chased them, and RAF fighter jets came to the rescue, Claire demanded answers. Many **revelations**[3] **ensued**[4]**.** Gladys, Anwen and Gwilym are Knights Hawk, **hailing from**[5] the **twelfth**[6] century, and Claire, through her **bloodline**[7], shares their same, **significant**[8] **surname**[9], which means 'battle leader'. Claire learned she is a 'Keeper' of the Gwalch Gem bracelet, a powerful **artefact**[10], and if she **subsequently**[11] develops her 'Instinct', she, too, can be knighted and use the **honoured**[12] Welsh version of her name – Cadwaladr.

---

1 **trap** *(n)* two-wheeled carriage pulled by a pony or horse. *(s)* cart, gig, hansom.

2 **hazardous** *(adj)* dangerous. *(s)* risky, perilous, unsafe, precarious. *(ant)* safe, harmless, secure.

3 **revelation** *(n)* a previously unknown fact that has been disclosed (revealed) to others. *(s)* divulgence. *(ant)* concealment.

4 **ensue** *(v)* happen afterwards or as a consequence. *(s)* arise, stem, develop, follow. *(ant)* precede.

5 **hail from** *(v)* originate from. *(s)* come from, have one's roots in, be a native of.

6 **twelfth** *(adj)* occupying position twelve in a sequence.

7 **bloodline** *(n)* a person's ancestors or line of descent.

8 **significant** *(adj)* great or important enough to be worthy of attention. *(s)* notable, meaningful. *(ant)* insignificant.

9 **surname** *(n)* a person's name that is in common with other family members. *(s)* last name. *(ant)* first name.

10 **artefact** *(n)* historical object or article made by a human. *(s)* item, piece, relic.

11 **subsequently** *(adv)* after something has happened. *(s)* later, afterwards. *(ant)* previously.

12 **honoured** *(adj)* regarded with respect. *(s)* reputable, prestigious, esteemed. *(ant)* disreputable.

Gwilym told Claire of the Gwalch Gem bracelet's magical powers, which come from the **coupling**[1] of Welsh gold with an emerald hawk gem, and which **bestows**[2] on the Knights Hawk **benevolent**[3] powers of Instinct and **longevity**[4].

Claire also learned the **tragic**[5] **legend**[6] of Prince Llywelyn, who was tricked long ago by his wife and his brother, Dewi, into killing his **faithful**[7] hound, Gelert, as part of their plan to steal the bracelet. After **seizing**[8] the gem, Dewi, who now calls himself 'the Master', used it to bestow longevity and evil powers on his followers – the Mal-Instinctives.

After searching for years, Gwilym recovered the bracelet, locking it away in a magical glass case in a Manchester museum, where he **vowed**[9] to keep it forever.

Rebecca, Claire's sister, visited that same museum on a school trip and was drugged by Josh Drane, a Mal-Instinctive bent on helping the Master steal the gem.

On arrival at the museum, Claire was surprised to discover the museum's **curator**[10], Robert Evans, is a man she saw on her train journey, a man who, she later learned, is also a Knight Hawk.

Evans and Gwilym set out to protect the Cutter, the only object **capable**[11] of breaking the magical glass case that **houses**[12] the Gwalch Gem bracelet. The Master followed Evans into underground tunnels and stole what he thought was the Cutter. Evans escaped through a **subterranean**[13] tunnel **network**[14].

The Master attacked the glass case with the Cutter, but it did not **yield**[15]. He realised the

---

1 **coupling** *(n)* the pairing of two things. *(s)* linking, combination, merging. *(ant)* separation.

2 **bestow** *(v)* offer or give an honour, gift or right. *(s)* confer, bequeath, grant, donate, present. *(ant)* withdraw.

3 **benevolent** *(adj)* kind and well-meaning. *(s)* altruistic, humane, benign. *(ant)* malevolent, cruel.

4 **longevity** *(n)* long life. *(s)* permanence, durability, endurance, lastingness. *(ant)* impermanence, death.

5 **tragic** *(adj)* causing extreme distress or sorrow. *(s)* dreadful, devastating, woeful. *(ant)* cheerful.

6 **legend** *(n)* story of the past, often fictitious (untrue). *(s)* fable, myth, tale, folklore.

7 **faithful** *(adj)* remaining loyal, steadfast, constant and true. *(s)* dedicated, dependable, reliable. *(ant)* disloyal.

8 **seize** *(v)* forcibly take possession of. *(s)* capture, abduct, hijack, grab, grasp. *(ant)* relinquish, give, return.

9 **vow** *(v)* make a solemn (serious) promise. *(s)* swear, affirm, assure, guarantee, assert, pledge.

10 **curator** *(n)* person who looks after a collection of things or a museum. *(s)* caretaker, warden, supervisor.

11 **capable** *(adj)* able to do something. *(s)* competent, proficient, adequate, apt, effective. *(ant)* incapable.

12 **house** *(v)* provide space for or accommodate (keep in a certain place). *(s)* store, hold, retain. *(ant)* evict, expose.

13 **subterranean** *(adj)* beneath the earth's surface. *(s)* underground, deep, buried. *(ant)* above ground, surface.

14 **network** *(n)* a complex system of something. *(s)* maze, structure, web, arrangement.

15 **yield** *(v)* give way to pressure, arguments or demands. *(s)* cede, succumb, surrender, capitulate. *(ant)* resist.

Knight Hawk Robert Evans had **sabotaged**[1] his plans, and he escaped in his **chauffeur**[2]-driven car.

Claire was left alone to help Rebecca in the museum. She discovered she could hear Josh Drane's thoughts and, seeing her sister in danger, attacked Drane, saving her.

Horrified, Claire saw the glass case appeared ruined. **Astonished**[3], she saw it still held the Gwalch Gem bracelet, and realised the Mal-Instinctives' **quest**[4] had failed. She was **captivated**[5] by the gem until she saw a vision of a man who looked like Gwilym, turning into an emerald and shattering into **smithereens**[6] as a **silhouetted**[7] woman **plucked**[8] the Gwalch Gem from its bracelet. Claire fears this may be a **forewarning**[9] of tragic events to come.

Gwilym entered the museum, posing as a police officer, and **arrested**[10] Drane for drug dealing. He gave Claire a **phoney**[11] ticking off for playing **truant**[12], and another Instinctive, Felicity, **masqueraded**[13] as a **paramedic**[14] and took Rebecca to the hospital, **accompanied**[15] by Claire's father, Vince. Jayne Lewis, her father's new girlfriend, who Claire adores, drove Claire home to her mother. As she was driven home, Claire **contemplated**[16] her life-changing day but said little about it. Claire told Jayne she'd left her school bag in the museum.

Once home, she was relieved to be **reunited**[17] with her mother, Dee, and her brother, Peter. Her father brought Rebecca home from the hospital and told Claire he and Jayne

---

1 **sabotage** *(v)* deliberately damage or prevent something. *(s)* wreck, undermine, spoil, ruin. *(ant)* aid.

2 **chauffeur** *(n)* a person employed to drive a car. *(s)* driver, operator, cab driver. *(ant)* passenger.

3 **astonished** *(adj)* greatly impressed or surprised. *(s)* astounded, amazed, dumbfounded. *(ant)* underwhelmed.

4 **quest** *(n)* long or difficult search for something. *(s)* mission, adventure, crusade, expedition, journey.

5 **captivate** *(v)* attract and capture the interest of. *(s)* fascinate, enchant, charm. *(ant)* repel, bore.

6 **smithereens** *(n)* small pieces. *(s)* bits, fragments, shards, particles, smithers. *(ant)* whole, completeness.

7 **silhouetted** *(adj)* visible as a dark shape or outline. *(s)* contoured, shadowed.

8 **pluck** *(v)* take hold of and quickly remove from. *(s)* pick, pull, tug, grasp, extract, tweak, yank. *(ant)* insert.

9 **forewarning** *(n)* warning of a future danger or problem. *(s)* omen, prediction, portent, sign.

10 **arrest** *(v)* seize and take into custody (jail). *(s)* apprehend, detain. *(ant)* release.

11 **phoney** *(adj)* not genuine (real). *(s)* false, bogus, fake, feigned, spurious. *(ant)* sincere, authentic.

12 **truant** *(n)* a pupil missing school without permission. *(s)* absentee, non-attender, skiver. *(ant)* attendee.

13 **masquerade** *(v)* make a false and deceptive show of pretence. *(s)* impersonate, pose, imitate.

14 **paramedic** *(n)* a person skilled in emergency medical care. *(s)* ambulance attendant, medical technician.

15 **accompany** *(v)* go with someone. *(s)* chaperone, attend, escort. *(ant)* abandon, desert.

16 **contemplate** *(v)* think about. *(s)* ponder, consider, deliberate, reflect on, ruminate on. *(ant)* disregard.

17 **reunite** *(v)* come or get back together. *(s)* reconcile, reunify. *(ant)* split, separate, estrange.

would see her on Sunday for their planned **theatre**[1] visit.

Claire had unanswered questions, so she visited Gladys and Jack. When Claire asked the **whereabouts**[2] of Gladys's cat, Thomas, Gladys told Claire he was **tracking**[3] the Cutter. Gladys also told Claire that the Master was unaware that two halves of the Cutter existed and that the knight Robert Evans had successfully **hoodwinked**[4] him into believing he had the complete Cutter. Evans had **evaded**[5] the Master by **warping**[6] time using a Time-Tangler, **fleeing**[7] with the other half of the Cutter into the tunnel network he had created, but **severely**[8] **depleting**[9] his powers in the **process**[10]. Claire surprised Gladys by telling her Robert Evans had been on the Bangor train.

While Claire slept at home, Evans reached Via-Corp in his quest to deliver his half of the Cutter to its **recipient**[11]. Unknown to Claire, that recipient was Jayne Lewis, and both she and Evans were **exposed**[12] as **potential**[13] **traitors**[14]. Neither of them noticed Thomas, Gladys's soot-black cat, watching the **transaction**[15].

Claire was woken in the early hours of Saturday by a **horrific**[16] nightmare. In it, she saw her father's girlfriend, Jayne, enter the museum and smash the glass case, putting the Gwalch Gem bracelet onto her wrist and taking her school bag. Relieved it was a dream, Claire was soon disappointed when her father called round to cancel the theatre trip, owing to Jayne being called

---

1 **theatre** *(n)* a building or outdoor area in which dramatic performances are given. *(s)* playhouse, auditorium.

2 **whereabouts** *(n)* the place where something or someone is. *(s)* position, location.

3 **track** *(v)* follow the movements or trail of. *(s)* pursue, shadow, stalk, trace, trail, locate. *(ant)* lead, guide.

4 **hoodwink** *(v)* trick or deceive. *(s)* fool, dupe, mislead, bluff.

5 **evade** *(v)* avoid or escape. *(s)* elude, dodge. *(ant)* confront.

6 **warp** *(v)* make abnormal. *(s)* skew, bend, twist, distort.

7 **flee** *(v)* run away. *(s)* depart, escape, vanish, abscond, bolt, fly, leave. *(ant)* linger, remain.

8 **severely** *(adv)* to a great degree. *(s)* seriously, gravely, acutely. *(ant)* slightly, somewhat.

9 **deplete** *(v)* use up. *(s)* exhaust, consume, decrease, expend, drain, lessen, diminish, sap. *(ant)* replenish.

10 **process** *(n)* a series of actions taken to achieve an outcome. *(s)* course, method, proceeding.

11 **recipient** *(n)* a person or thing that receives something. *(s)* receiver, beneficiary, awardee. *(ant)* giver, donor.

12 **expose** *(v)* uncover the true nature of someone or something. *(s)* reveal, unveil. *(ant)* cover, hide.

13 **potential** *(adj)* having the possibility of being. *(s)* possible, budding, prospective, probable. *(ant)* unlikely.

14 **traitor** *(n)* a disloyal person. *(s)* betrayer, turncoat, back-stabber, double-crosser. *(ant)* supporter, loyalist.

15 **transaction** *(n)* an instance of conducting business or a deal. *(s)* exchange, agreement, arrangement.

16 **horrific** *(adj)* causing horror. *(s)* ghastly, horrendous, appalling, dreadful, sickening, gruesome. *(ant)* appealing.

into work because of a **catastrophic**[1] security **breach**[2]. Vince handed Claire her school bag and said Jayne had asked him to give it to her. She was shocked, as this **implied**[3] her dream may not have been so innocent but rather an **omen**[4] of worse things to come. Claire told Gladys of her fears.

Claire went with her best friend, Ben Brady, to watch him in a kung fu competition. During the car journey, his father, John, announced Ben's competition had been cancelled and he'd been called into work to deal with a security breach. Claire realised that was the same reason Jayne had been called into work, and he, too, works for Via-Corp, whose **headquarters**[5] are in Beddgelert, the same place Prince Llywelyn's hound, Gelert, was buried.

Claire now fears that her dream was real and that Jayne Lewis is a Mal-Instinctive. Every part of Claire wants to believe that is not true.

---

1 **catastrophic** *(adj)* extremely unfortunate and damaging. *(s)* disastrous, calamitous, ruinous. *(ant)* beneficial.

2 **breach** *(n)* a break or gap in something, often made by an attacking enemy. *(s)* violation. *(ant)* repair.

3 **imply** *(v)* indicate the truth of. *(s)* mean, signify, hint, signal. *(ant)* declare, spell out.

4 **omen** *(n)* a sign of something to come. *(s)* signal, portent, premonition, prophecy.

5 **headquarters** *(n)* command and control centre of an organisation. *(s)* head office, nerve centre. *(ant)* branch.

SATURDAY

1. Mountain Rescue

Is Jayne Lewis a Mal-Instinctive? Is Jayne Lewis a Mal-Instinctive?

Like an **irksome**[1] pop song, the **intrusive**[2] **earworm**[3] **burrowed**[4] deeper into Claire's brain, **chanting**[5] its **stark**[6], repetitive tune. Her head throbbed. She rested it awkwardly against the Tesla's **rear**[7] window, tempted to bang her skull against the glass to **expel**[8] and **expunge**[9] the **invasive**[10] worm, but its **monotone**[11] **droned**[12] on. *Is Jayne Lewis a Mal-Instinctive?* The smell of the Tesla's **opulent**[13] leather **interior**[14] reminded her of Jayne's **luxurious**[15] four-by-four. Could her dad's girlfriend really be a **hideous**[16] traitor?

Claire had chickened out, **disclosing**[17] nothing of yesterday to Ben. He still thought she'd

---

1 **irksome** *(adj)* irritating. *(s)* annoying, vexing, galling, exasperating. *(ant)* agreeable, pleasant.
2 **intrusive** *(adj)* disturbing and impossible to ignore. *(s)* inescapable, invasive, obtrusive. *(ant)* inconspicuous.
3 **earworm** *(n)* a song or tune that repeats continually in a person's mind.
4 **burrow** *(v)* dig. *(s)* excavate, penetrate, tunnel, probe, bore. *(ant)* withdraw.
5 **chant** *(v)* say or shout repeatedly in a sing-song tone. *(s)* chorus, repeat, carol.
6 **stark** *(adj)* sharply clear. *(s)* crisp, distinct, obvious, sheer, blatant, glaring. *(ant)* indistinct, ambiguous.
7 **rear** *(adj)* placed at the back part of something. *(s)* posterior, hind, aft. *(ant)* front, fore, anterior.
8 **expel** *(v)* force something out. *(s)* exclude, eject, oust, evict, banish. *(ant)* admit.
9 **expunge** *(v)* erase or remove entirely. *(s)* delete, efface, eliminate. *(ant)* preserve.
10 **invasive** *(adj)* intruding undesirably (difficult to ignore). *(s)* intrusive, persistent. *(ant)* non-invasive, restrained.
11 **monotone** *(n)* a continuing, unchanging sound. *(s)* monotony, drone, flatness. *(ant)* variation.
12 **drone** *(v)* speak in a dull or monotonous way. *(s)* murmur, intone, mumble. *(ant)* lilt.
13 **opulent** *(adj)* extremely luxurious or lavish. *(s)* splendid, sumptuous, extravagant. *(ant)* austere.
14 **interior** *(n)* inner part of something. *(s)* inside. *(ant)* exterior, outside.
15 **luxurious** *(adj)* extremely elegant and often expensive. *(s)* opulent, sumptuous, extravagant. *(ant)* meagre.
16 **hideous** *(adj)* extremely unpleasant. *(s)* ugly, revolting, repugnant, appalling, monstrous. *(ant)* attractive.
17 **disclose** *(v)* make known. *(s)* show, reveal, uncover, unveil, divulge, impart, tell. *(ant)* hide, conceal, secrete.

truanted[1] from school to visit a museum, and besides, the Tesla was so quiet John Brady would hear everything. She stared at the various shades of countryside colours, which **gradated**[2] from **rustic**[3] browns to **lush**[4] greens as they headed to Mr Brady's headquarters in Beddgelert.

'How much further, Dad?' asked Ben. 'It's hilly now,' he added, poking his **index finger**[5] into his ear and wiggling it around. 'Your ears popped yet?' he asked Claire, nudging her from her **unsettling**[6] **reverie**[7].

She cracked a weak half smile and stuck a **forefinger**[8] into each ear. Wiggling them hard, she nodded, **feigning**[9] interest. 'Yeah,' she replied, then held her nose, blowing out her cheeks to help pop her ears.

'These roads are narrow, hey, kids?' Mr Brady interrupted, eyeing them both through the rear-view mirror.

Not compared to yesterday's, thought Claire, casting her mind back to the **perilous**[10] journey in the **rickety**[11] trap with Anwen, Gwilym and Jack the dog.

Yesterday, she **mused**[12] in disbelief, **mulling**[13] over Gladys's explanation of 'time-tangling'. It was a complete **cliché**[14], but yesterday felt like a **parallel**[15] life. *Perhaps this is another universe, or maybe it's not happened yet at all.* She almost laughed out loud at the **preposterous**[16] **notion**[17].

---

1 **truant** *(v)* stay away from school without leave or explanation. *(s)* wag, skive, bunk off. *(ant)* attend.

2 **gradate** *(v)* change by gradations or degrees. *(s)* blend, adjust.

3 **rustic** *(adj)* of or relating to the countryside. *(s)* rural, bucolic, pastoral. *(ant)* urban, cosmopolitan.

4 **lush** *(adj)* rich and pleasing to the eye. *(s)* fresh, abundant, profuse, healthy. *(ant)* dull.

5 **index finger** *(n)* the first finger (the one next to the thumb). *(s)* pointer, forefinger, indicator.

6 **unsettle** *(v)* cause to feel anxious. *(s)* bother, upset, disturb, worry, perturb, unnerve. *(ant)* appease, soothe.

7 **reverie** *(n)* a state of being lost in thought. *(s)* daydream, musing, contemplation, fantasy. *(ant)* concentration.

8 **forefinger** *(n)* the first finger (the one next to the thumb). *(s)* pointer, index finger, indicator.

9 **feign** *(v)* simulate or pretend. *(s)* affect, fake, bluff, sham.

10 **perilous** *(adj)* full of extreme risk or danger. *(s)* unsafe, hazardous, treacherous, precarious, chancy. *(ant)* safe.

11 **rickety** *(adj)* likely to collapse, poorly manufactured. *(s)* wobbly, unstable, unsound. *(ant)* reliable, sound.

12 **muse** *(v)* ask oneself in a thoughtful manner. *(s)* think, wonder, ponder, consider, contemplate. (ant) disregard.

13 **mull** *(v)* think about. *(s)* ponder, consider, contemplate, deliberate, muse, reflect, ruminate. *(ant)* disregard.

14 **cliché** *(n)* an expression used by many people. *(s)* banality, saying, stereotype. *(ant)* originality, novelty.

15 **parallel** *(adj)* existing at the same time. *(s)* coexisting, concurrent, simultaneous. *(ant)* divergent.

16 **preposterous** *(adj)* utterly nonsensical. *(s)* stupid, ridiculous, absurd, ludicrous. *(ant)* sensible, reasonable.

17 **notion** *(n)* an idea or something imagined. *(s)* thought, concept, conception.

'OK, guys, nearly there. We're approaching Beddgelert village,' said Mr Brady in his **distinctive**[1] American **accent**[2]. 'It's real **quaint**[3]. Shame it's so chilly; otherwise, you guys could have braved a dip,' he added as they drove alongside a fast-flowing river. 'It's as **shallow**[4] as a **brook**[5] in parts, but you'd freeze today.'

I'd rather not, thank you very much, thought Claire, eyeing the **ominous**[6] sky and angry-looking clouds gathering above the snow-capped mountains. She'd never been keen on getting wet.

Beddgelert. Claire tried to remember how Anwen, Gladys's sister, had **pronounced**[7] it yesterday.

As if reading her thoughts, Mr Brady asked, 'Are you guys familiar with Beddgelert's legend? That's Gelert's **supposed**[8] grave way over there. You can come down later. It's not too far.'

Before Ben could answer, Claire **blurted**[9] a clumsy, 'Yeah, I read it somewhere. It's dead boring. Summat about a Welsh prince who accidentally killed his dog. Are we nearly there yet, Mr Brady?'

'Yes, Claire, not much further,' he answered.

The Tesla glided through the **picturesque**[10] village and joined a tarmac road that **tapered**[11] to a single lane, leaving behind empty cafes, **lonesome**[12]-looking gift shops and a **plethora**[13] of grey stone cottages.

---

1 **distinctive** *(adj)* standing out because of a specific characteristic. *(s)* distinguishing, peculiar. *(ant)* indistinct.
2 **accent** *(n)* pronouncing of language in a way that is distinctive. *(s)* pronunciation, intonation.
3 **quaint** *(adj)* attractive or pleasingly old-fashioned. *(s)* picturesque, appealing, charming. *(ant)* ordinary, modern.
4 **shallow** *(adj)* having little depth. *(s)* depthless. *(ant)* deep.
5 **brook** *(n)* a small stream. *(s)* streamlet, rill, rivulet, runnel, beck.
6 **ominous** *(adj)* indicating imminent misfortune. *(s)* threatening, warning. *(ant)* unthreatening, auspicious.
7 **pronounce** *(v)* sound out. *(s)* say, speak, utter, enunciate, articulate. *(ant)* mispronounce.
8 **supposed** *(adj)* assumed to be true. *(s)* presumed, claimed, apparent, alleged. *(ant)* real.
9 **blurt** *(v)* say something suddenly and without consideration. *(s)* announce, exclaim, cry, utter.
10 **picturesque** *(adj)* visually attractive. *(s)* quaint, charming, delightful, scenic, pleasing. *(ant)* unattractive.
11 **taper** *(v)* narrow, diminish or reduce in thickness towards one end. *(s)* contract, decrease. *(ant)* thicken, expand.
12 **lonesome** *(adj)* remote and unfrequented. *(s)* solitary, forlorn, desolate. *(ant)* frequented, crowded.
13 **plethora** *(n)* a large or excessive amount of something. *(s)* abundance, myriad. *(ant)* lack, dearth, deficiency.

Ubiquitous[1] countryside stretched out before them, but its **terrain**[2] became **steeper**[3], **barren**[4] and **bleak**[5], **akin**[6] to **moorland**[7] in parts. Claire spotted a **lone**[8] **chestnut**[9] horse nibbling for grass in a bare, muddy field. She pictured the Welsh mountain pony Lady, who had pulled them along in the trap with such **courage**[10] yesterday.

Me, possibly becoming a Knight Hawk, she thought. It sounded **ludicrous**[11]. *How the heck will I explain this to Ben? He'll think I'm* ***insane***[12].

The horrific dream that had **roused**[13] Claire this morning still haunted her. She refused to believe Jayne, her dad's amazing girlfriend, was a traitor, a Mal-Instinctive. Jayne would never hurt her or her dad, Vince, in that way, would she? Claire couldn't believe Mr Evans, the museum curator, was a Knight Hawk, and she struggled to shake the **unease**[14] that had **niggled**[15] her from the moment she'd clapped eyes on him when she'd caught the train to Bangor with Jack yesterday.

'Hey, Dad, is my skateboard in the **boot**[16]?' Ben asked in his Mancunian-American **twang**[17].

'Yeah, son. I threw in a couple of your decks and the snowboarding gear for tomorrow's lesson. Save me packing it tonight.'

'Claire, you sure you don't want to come boarding with us tomorrow? Oh no, sorry, I forgot. You're at the theatre with your dad, right?' said Ben, shaking his head.

---

1 **ubiquitous** *(adj)* present everywhere. *(s)* abundant, omnipresent, pervasive. *(ant)* absent, limited, rare, scarce.
2 **terrain** *(n)* a stretch of ground or its features. *(s)* area, land, environment, territory, setting, shape.
3 **steep** *(adj)* sharply rising or falling. *(s)* sheer, bluff, precipitous, vertical, vertiginous. *(ant)* gentle, gradual.
4 **barren** *(adj)* (of land) producing little or no vegetation. *(s)* arid, austere, bare, bleak, deserted. *(ant)* productive.
5 **bleak** *(adj)* stark and not encouraging or favourable. *(s)* unwelcoming, austere, desolate. *(ant)* appealing.
6 **akin** *(adj)* similar in character. *(s)* related, close, comparable. *(ant)* unlike, dissimilar.
7 **moorland** *(n)* a large area consisting of moors (uncultivated, open upland).
8 **lone** *(adj)* having no companions (company). *(s)* individual, solitary, single, alone, solo. *(ant)* accompanied.
9 **chestnut** *(adj)* deep reddish-brown like the colour of a chestnut. *(s)* rusty, coppery.
10 **courage** *(n)* the ability to do something frightening. *(s)* bravery, pluck, valour, audacity. *(ant)* cowardice.
11 **ludicrous** *(adj)* so foolish, stupid or unreasonable as to be amusing. *(s)* absurd, farcical, comical. *(ant)* sensible.
12 **insane** *(adj)* foolish, mad and irrational. *(s)* crazy, idiotic, irresponsible, senseless. *(ant)* sensible, rational.
13 **rouse** *(v)* cause to stop sleeping. *(s)* wake, waken, awaken. *(ant)* lull, calm.
14 **unease** *(n)* want or lack of ease. *(s)* anxiety, angst, apprehension, dread, foreboding, jitters. *(ant)* calmness, ease.
15 **niggle** *(v)* slightly irritate. *(s)* bother, trouble, worry, annoy. *(ant)* ease, alleviate, appease.
16 **boot** *(n)* storage space in an automobile (often at the rear). *(s)* trunk.
17 **twang** *(n)* a distinctive manner of pronunciation. *(s)* sound, accent, diction, articulation.

She nodded and said, 'Yeah,' her answer too **upbeat**[1]. She hated herself for lying to her best friend. Anyway, she didn't want to snowboard again. She'd hurt her backside so much last time, she'd **waddled**[2] like a duck for a week.

Claire stared at the bag lying by her feet.

Why, and how, did Jayne return to the museum last night to collect it?

No matter how much Claire tried to forget the **grim**[3] scene she had **witnessed**[4] yesterday, it still sickened her. The image of Gwilym in the cracked glass case, turning into emerald and shattering into smithereens. *What did that* ***grisly***[5] *vision mean? Will something dreadful happen to the Knights Hawk if the Gwalch Gem is separated from the magical gold bracelet, just like the image in the scene?* Claire was sure the man **depicted**[6] in that terrifying **portrayal**[7] of death had been Gwilym, the leader of the Knights Hawk.

'You OK, Claire?' Ben's eyes **scrutinised**[8] hers.

'Yeah, just tired after yesterday.' At least that wasn't a fib; Ben knew her too well to **dupe**[9] him for long.

Preoccupied[10], she muttered something about how peaceful the landscape looked. In truth, she was **rehearsing**[11] the explanations of yesterday she would give Ben the minute his dad was out of **earshot**[12]. The **nausea**[13] surfacing in her **gut**[14] was not a **consequence**[15] of travel sickness.

---

1 **upbeat** *(adj)* cheerful. *(s)* optimistic, positive, confident, hopeful. *(ant)* negative, pessimistic, cynical.

2 **waddle** *(v)* walk with a clumsy swaying motion. *(s)* toddle, wobble, totter, sway. *(ant)* stride, glide.

3 **grim** *(adj)* worrying or unpleasant. *(s)* frightful, sinister, terrible. *(ant)* pleasant.

4 **witness** *(v)* see something happen. *(s)* observe, view, watch, perceive, eyeball, notice. *(ant)* ignore, overlook.

5 **grisly** *(adj)* causing disgust or horror. *(s)* abominable, appalling, ghastly, frightful, hideous. *(ant)* delightful.

6 **depict** *(v)* represent in some form. *(s)* portray, show, describe, paint, picture, illustrate. *(ant)* misrepresent.

7 **portrayal** *(n)* a vivid depiction of something or someone. *(s)* representation, picture, rendering, sketch.

8 **scrutinise** *(v)* look, inspect or examine closely and thoroughly. *(s)* study, search, survey, analyse. *(ant)* glance.

9 **dupe** *(v)* deceive and trick. *(s)* fool, hoodwink, mislead, cheat, delude, beguile, bamboozle, con.

10 **preoccupied** *(adj)* engrossed in thought or mentally distracted. *(s)* absorbed, concerned. *(ant)* unconcerned.

11 **rehearse** *(v)* practise or prepare (sometimes mentally). *(s)* recite, list, review, repeat, iterate. *(ant)* improvise.

12 **earshot** *(n)* the distance within which one can hear or be heard. *(s)* close range, hearing, range.

13 **nausea** *(n)* a feeling of sickness. *(s)* queasiness, biliousness, revulsion. *(ant)* wellness.

14 **gut** *(n)* the belly or stomach. *(s)* tummy, tum, insides, abdomen, intestines.

15 **consequence** *(n)* a result or effect. *(s)* outcome, upshot, repercussion, product. *(ant)* cause.

After Beddgelert village disappeared behind them, the **stealthy**[1] Tesla powered up through the **meandering**[2] lane, managing its steep **incline**[3] with ease. As if **conjured**[4] by the magic of **ancient**[5] **rituals**[6], **mighty**[7] stacks of **monolithic**[8] **slate**[9]-coloured rock **jutted**[10] **incongruously**[11] from the sides of sloping hills. Gushing streams slashed through open moorland. Gone were the **patchwork**[12] fields **hemmed**[13] in by yellow **gorse**[14] hedges and grey **drystone**[15] walls.

'Hey, Dad, where are your headquarters? How do they build stuff up here?' Ben laughed, **peering**[16] upwards out of the window.

'Oh, it's tucked away in an **ingenious**[17] spot,' his dad replied. 'David Lewis, our **founder**[18], is a **stickler**[19] for security and **privacy**[20], but then he has to be in his line of work – **artificial intelligence**[21] and **data**[22] storage.'

Claire's ears pricked up as her stomach **clenched**[23], not because of excitement but because of shock and dread. The name he'd just mentioned, Lewis, was the same surname as Jayne's.

---

1 **stealthy** *(adj)* done so as not to be seen or heard. *(s)* quiet, cautious, covert, surreptitious. *(ant)* blatant, overt.
2 **meandering** *(adj)* following a winding, twisting course. *(s)* zigzagging, bendy, curvy, twisty, snaky. *(ant)* straight.
3 **incline** *(n)* a slope. *(s)* gradient, pitch, ascent, rise, cant. *(ant)* decline.
4 **conjure** *(v)* make something appear unexpectedly or from nowhere. *(s)* summon, raise, rouse. *(ant)* dispel.
5 **ancient** *(adj)* in existence for a long time. *(s)* early, antique, olden, obsolete, archaic. *(ant)* contemporary, new.
6 **ritual** *(n)* relating to or done as a religious or solemn rite. *(s)* ceremony, observance, sacrament, practice.
7 **mighty** *(adj)* strong and powerful, especially due to size. *(s)* forceful, huge, almighty. *(ant)* weak, insignificant.
8 **monolithic** *(adj)* formed of a single very large block of stone.
9 **slate** *(n)* grey, green or bluish-purple rock that can be split easily into thin layers.
10 **jut** *(v)* protrude (stick out from). *(s)* poke out, project, extend, overhang. *(ant)* indent, depress, recede.
11 **incongruously** *(adv)* in a way that is out of keeping. *(s)* oddly, inappropriately. *(ant)* appropriately.
12 **patchwork** *(n)* a thing composed of many different parts or sections. *(s)* assortment, jumble, medley.
13 **hem** *(v)* surround and restrict. *(s)* enclose, border, edge.
14 **gorse** *(n)* spiky, yellow-flowered shrub.
15 **drystone** *(adj)* (of a stone wall) built without using mortar.
16 **peer** *(v)* look with concentration. *(s)* stare, scrutinise, gaze, scan, focus, examine, study, rake. *(ant)* glance.
17 **ingenious** *(adj)* clever, inventive and original. *(s)* innovative, smart, enterprising, creative. *(ant)* ignorant.
18 **founder** *(n)* a person who sets up something. *(s)* originator, creator, initiator.
19 **stickler** *(n)* someone who believes something should be done properly. *(s)* perfectionist, fusspot. *(ant)* neglecter.
20 **privacy** *(n)* the state of being free from observation and disturbance. *(s)* privateness, seclusion, isolation. *(ant)* publicity.
21 **artificial intelligence** *(n)* computer technology that simulates intelligent behaviour.
22 **data** *(n)* information collected for use. *(s)* statistics, facts, figures, numbers, documents, records.
23 **clench** *(v)* contract or tighten. *(s)* constrict, tense, cramp. *(ant)* relax.

Surely that's a **coincidence**[1], Claire thought. *It must be.*

The same **debilitating**[2] fear she had suffered yesterday **paralysed**[3] her again. Claire **yearned**[4] to have Jack by her side. She missed his doggy smell and **wiry**[5] coat, but **moreover**[6], his unfailing **loyalty**[7]. He was clearly a dog with Instinct, perhaps a Knight Hawk even.

'Not long now,' said Mr Brady as the **responsive**[8] Tesla picked up speed on a straighter, wider stretch. 'You guys hungry yet? There's a superb twenty-four-hour, **subsidised**[9] restaurant at work. David Lewis is **renowned**[10] for his **philanthropy**[11] and staff relations, although people rarely get to meet him – he's a **reclusive**[12] kinda guy.'

Most days, Claire would have perked up at the sound of **gourmet**[13] food, but today, even promises of **culinary**[14] delights didn't tempt her. Her usual **voracious**[15] **appetite**[16] had vanished.

'That sounds ace. I'm starved.' Ben looked straight at Claire, an **expectant**[17] **expression**[18] on his face.

'Er, yeah, me too,' she answered, her tone **unconvincing**[19].

Ben's eyes narrowed. 'You sure you're OK?' he whispered.

---

1 **coincidence** *(n)* something that seems to happen by chance. *(s)* accident, fluke, luck, quirk, fate. *(ant)* plan.

2 **debilitating** *(adj)* tending to weaken or hinder. *(s)* incapacitating, draining, enervating. *(ant)* invigorating.

3 **paralyse** *(v)* cause to become unable to act or function properly. *(s)* disable, incapacitate. *(ant)* mobilise.

4 **yearn** *(v)* really want something. *(s)* long, ache, pine, crave, desire, hanker, thirst. *(ant)* reject, abjure.

5 **wiry** *(adj)* resembling wire in texture or form. *(s)* coarse, rough, bristly, scratchy. *(ant)* soft, sleek, smooth.

6 **moreover** *(adv)* even more so, as a further matter. *(s)* in addition, furthermore, also.

7 **loyalty** *(n)* the quality of giving constant support. *(s)* faithfulness, allegiance, reliability, devotion. *(ant)* disloyalty, treachery.

8 **responsive** *(adj)* reacting speedily. *(s)* active, reactive, receptive. *(ant)* sluggish, unresponsive.

9 **subsidise** *(v)* pay some of the cost to keep prices low for customers. *(s)* sponsor, fund, finance, back, assist. *(ant)* defund.

10 **renowned** *(adj)* known or talked about widely. *(s)* famous, eminent, esteemed. *(ant)* obscure, unknown.

11 **philanthropy** *(n)* the act of helping others, especially by donating money. *(s)* benevolence, charity. *(ant)* miserliness.

12 **reclusive** *(adj)* avoiding the company of others. *(s)* solitary, isolated, withdrawn, antisocial. *(ant)* sociable.

13 **gourmet** *(adj)* of high quality and prepared by an expert. *(s)* luxurious, opulent, decadent. *(ant)* poor.

14 **culinary** *(adj)* relating to cooking. *(s)* gastronomic, dietary.

15 **voracious** *(adj)* having a large appetite. *(s)* gluttonous, greedy, ravenous. *(ant)* full, sated, satiated.

16 **appetite** *(n)* an impulse to eat. *(s)* hunger, desire.

17 **expectant** *(adj)* eagerly waiting for something. *(s)* anticipative, awaiting. *(ant)* unexpectant, uninterested.

18 **expression** *(n)* look that conveys (shows) a certain emotion. *(s)* face, appearance, air.

19 **unconvincing** *(adj)* unable to persuade someone that something is true. *(s)* unbelievable. *(ant)* convincing, believable.

'Yeah. I'm a bit carsick. Don't tell your dad. It's **embarrassing**[1],' she lied, again.

Suddenly the car swung in a sharp **veer**[2] to the right, **careering**[3] across the narrow road. Mr Brady stiffened, **grappling**[4] with the Tesla's steering wheel while **simultaneously**[5] hitting the brakes. Claire froze. A weakness **pervaded**[6] her muscles, **sapping**[7] their strength.

'What's happening, Dad?' asked Ben in an **anxious**[8] tone.

'I suspect a tyre's blown,' Mr Brady answered, **wrestling**[9] back control of the Tesla. 'Hear that flapping sound? My guess is it's shredded.'

While guiding the Tesla to an **undignified**[10] stop in a tiny lay-by, Mr Brady's voice remained calm, his **demeanour**[11] **unflustered**[12].

As the car **halted**[13], Claire breathed again. She glanced through the window to her right, then to her left, and back through the rear screen, battling to **conceal**[14] her **anxiety**[15].

'That was close!' she said, her **senses**[16] **heightened**[17].

'They build these cars to **withstand**[18] more than a blown tyre,' Mr Brady **reassured**[19] her. 'Although I wouldn't want to test it at super-high speeds,' he added with a light laugh as he opened his door and stepped outside to inspect the damage.

---

1 **embarrassing** *(adj)* causing awkwardness or shame. *(s)* humiliating, mortifying, degrading. *(ant)* dignifying.

2 **veer** *(v)* suddenly change direction. *(s)* turn, depart, deviate, diverge, divert, swerve.

3 **career** *(v)* move in a quick, uncontrolled manner. *(s)* hurtle along, race, tear, gallop, dash, rush. *(ant)* dawdle.

4 **grapple** *(v)* engage in a struggle. *(s)* wrestle, fight, battle, tussle, scuffle. *(ant)* surrender.

5 **simultaneously** *(adv)* at the same time, all together. *(s)* concurrently, instantaneously. *(ant)* separately.

6 **pervade** *(v)* spread throughout, be present and apparent. *(s)* permeate, infiltrate, encompass. *(ant)* evacuate.

7 **sap** *(v)* gradually weaken, erode, destroy or deplete power. *(s)* drain, debilitate, reduce. *(ant)* bolster.

8 **anxious** *(adj)* feeling uneasy about uncertainty. *(s)* worried, apprehensive, edgy, fretful. *(ant)* calm, carefree.

9 **wrestle** *(v)* force or fight by grappling (tussling). *(s)* struggle, brawl, battle, scuffle, scramble.

10 **undignified** *(adj)* lacking a composed manner or style (dignity). *(s)* unseemly, shameful, unbecoming. *(ant)* dignified.

11 **demeanour** *(n)* outward bearing or behaviour. *(s)* appearance, attitude, disposition, air, character, conduct.

12 **unflustered** *(adj)* self-controlled. *(s)* unruffled, composed, unperturbed, cool. *(ant)* flustered.

13 **halt** *(v)* stop abruptly. *(s)* still, pull up, hold up, stall. *(ant)* go, start.

14 **conceal** *(v)* hide or disguise. *(s)* screen, shroud, cloak, cover, camouflage, obscure, veil. *(ant)* reveal, uncover.

15 **anxiety** *(n)* worried and nervous feeling. *(s)* apprehension, unease, disquiet. *(ant)* calmness, reassurance.

16 **sense** *(n)* a faculty of the body that perceives the external environment. *(s)* awareness, ability, perception.

17 **heighten** *(v)* increase. *(s)* intensify, strengthen, amplify, enhance. *(ant)* lessen, reduce.

18 **withstand** *(v)* stay unaffected by. *(s)* resist, combat, fight, repel, defy. *(ant)* succumb to, yield to, capitulate to.

19 **reassure** *(v)* remove doubt and fear. *(s)* assure, comfort, soothe, cheer. *(ant)* discourage, unnerve, alarm.

'You sure you're OK?' Ben asked Claire again. 'Still carsick?'

'Yeah, but I'll be fine once we get there.'

To Claire, nothing felt fine. Everything felt wrong: the last-minute change of **venue**[1] for Ben's **martial**[2] arts **tournament**[3], its **subsequent**[4] cancellation, Jayne's theatre trip **postponement**[5], John Bracy and Jayne Lewis both being called into Via-Corp's headquarters at Beddgelert, and even worse, David Lewis, the founder of Via-Corp, having the same surname as Jayne. The sum of all these parts left Claire with a **portentous**[6] sense of doom. Her stomach **squirmed**[7] like a snake pit.

'Kids, I'm afraid we're going nowhere fast. Both front tyres have blown.' Mr Brady sat back in the driver's seat. 'I'll call Tesla, but I doubt they'll **deploy**[8] their recovery vehicles out here. We'll need a local place. I'll call Via-Corp too; they can send a car to collect us.'

'OK, Dad,' said Ben. 'Can we get out for a minute, please? Claire needs fresh air,' he added, glancing at Claire's **ashen**[9] face.

'Sure, but stay close. My guess is Via-Corp will show up soon.'

'Cool,' said Ben. 'Come on, Claire, let's get out.'

Claire pressed the button to unbuckle her seat belt, but nothing happened.

'What's up?' asked Ben, getting out of the car and heading around to her.

'My seat belt's stuck,' she answered, **jabbing**[10] repeatedly at the release **mechanism**[11].

'Hey, your hands are trembling,' **observed**[12] Ben. 'What's up?'

'It's 'cause I feel sick,' she answered too quickly, avoiding Ben's eyes. 'Maybe something broke

---

1 **venue** *(n)* place where something (an event) happens. *(s)* site, location, setting, spot, ground.

2 **martial** *(adj)* relating to fighting (or war). *(s)* military, warlike, combative, belligerent. *(ant)* civilian, peaceable.

3 **tournament** *(n)* a series of contests with multiple contestants. *(s)* competition, series, event.

4 **subsequent** *(adj)* occurring after something in time. *(s)* ensuing, following, later. *(ant)* antecedent, prior, former.

5 **postponement** *(n)* the action of delaying something. *(s)* deferral, suspension.

6 **portentous** *(adj)* of or like a portent (sign of something bad). *(s)* ominous, threatening, fateful. *(ant)* trivial.

7 **squirm** *(v)* wriggle or twist nervously. *(s)* writhe, turn, jiggle, fidget, flail. *(ant)* relax.

8 **deploy** *(v)* use for a purpose. *(s)* employ, utilise, call on, exploit.

9 **ashen** *(adj)* pale because of shock, fear or illness. *(s)* wan, pasty, pallid, sallow, ghostly, ashy, grey. *(ant)* rosy.

10 **jab** *(v)* poke roughly or quickly. *(s)* prod, dig, stab, push, nudge.

11 **mechanism** *(n)* a system of parts working together in a machine, tool or apparatus. *(s)* device, contraption.

12 **observe** *(v)* remark perceptively. *(s)* note, comment, mention, state, announce. *(ant)* ignore, overlook.

when the tyres blew,' she grumbled, still struggling with the **jammed**[1] **restraint**[2].

'Dad, we can't release Claire's seat belt.'

Mr Brady was a few metres away, making calls.

'Dad, she's stuck fast.'

Mr Brady **gesticulated**[3], signalling he'd be there soon.

The seat belt was jammed so tight Claire fought to move. 'So much for this **posh**[4], **expensive**[5] car,' she said. 'Exploding tyres, and now I'm trapped in the daft thing!'

Claire's laugh was light-hearted, but beneath her **veneer**[6], her heart hammered so hard she feared it might stop. She sat **ensnared**[7] in the back of a top-of-the-range Tesla on a mountainside in North Wales, convinced this was something to do with the Mal-Instinctives and Dewi – the one they called 'the Master'. After playing that name over and over in her mind, it now sounded **absurd**[8]. *I'm sure* Doctor Who *has a baddy called the Master*, she thought, trying to **quash**[9] her racing thoughts. Her mouth felt as **coarse**[10] as **sandpaper**[11]; it was so dry she struggled to speak.

'Is your dad coming? Can he hurry?' she snapped, her words a command. 'I hate this! I'm **claustrophobic**[12]!' **Evidently**[13], crawling through **numerous**[14] tiny, dark tunnels yesterday had failed to cure her **irrational**[15] fear of **confined**[16] spaces.

Still tugging at the **taut**[17] belt, she thought of yesterday when she'd turned that rusty old key in

---

1 **jammed** *(adj)* stuck. *(s)* frozen, lodged, wedged, fast, fixed, glued, trapped. *(ant)* free, loose.

2 **restraint** *(n)* a device that limits movement. *(s)* harness, seat belt.

3 **gesticulate** *(v)* use gestures (movements) to communicate. *(s)* wave, signal, motion, indicate.

4 **posh** *(adj)* elegant or luxurious and stylish. *(s)* superior, snobbish, grand, upmarket. *(ant)* downmarket, common.

5 **expensive** *(adj)* costing a lot of money. *(s)* dear, costly, pricey, steep. *(ant)* inexpensive, cheap.

6 **veneer** *(n)* the outside layer or appearance of. *(s)* front, facade, mask, guise, show. *(ant)* inside, interior.

7 **ensnare** *(v)* catch or seize as though in a trap. *(s)* capture, entangle, snare, trap, enmesh. *(ant)* release.

8 **absurd** *(adj)* something ridiculous or very unreasonable. *(s)* ludicrous, preposterous, farcical. *(ant)* sensible, reasonable.

9 **quash** *(v)* put an end to. *(s)* suppress, quell, repress, crush, curb, overwhelm, defeat, conquer. *(ant)* allow.

10 **coarse** *(adj)* rough or hard, bristly. *(s)* wiry, scratchy, prickly, hairy, shaggy, abrasive. *(ant)* smooth, sleek, silky.

11 **sandpaper** *(n)* paper with a rough surface, used for smoothing other surfaces.

12 **claustrophobic** *(adj)* fearful of enclosed spaces.

13 **evidently** *(adv)* it would seem that. *(s)* apparently, seemingly. *(ant)* implausibly.

14 **numerous** *(adj)* many. *(s)* frequent, plentiful, abundant, various, copious, several, diverse. *(ant)* few, one.

15 **irrational** *(adj)* without logic or reason. *(s)* unfounded, unreasonable, illogical. *(ant)* rational, logical, reasonable.

16 **confined** *(adj)* very small or restricted. *(s)* cramped, constricted, limiting. *(ant)* open, roomy.

17 **taut** *(adj)* tight, with no slack. *(s)* stretched, strained, rigid, stressed. *(ant)* slack, loose.

the lock beneath the police station. *Why can't I open this now?* she asked herself, **yanking**[1] at the belt with **frustration**[2]. *I don't have any Instinct*, she **admonished**[3] herself **bitterly**[4]. *It's nonsense!*

'Calm down. My dad's coming now,' said Ben.

'Oh, thank goodness!' replied Claire.

'Hey, Dad, it is stuck,' **reiterated**[5] Ben. 'Look,' he said, tugging harder at the **immobile**[6] seat belt.

'Ben, watch out! You're gonna choke me!' spluttered Claire.

'Sorry, buddy,' said Ben.

'Let me look closer, Claire,' suggested Mr Brady, his voice **soothing**[7]. 'I'm sure we can fix this,' he added, **furrowing**[8] his **brow**[9] as he inspected the seat belt. Ben stood behind him, **craning**[10] his neck to see.

'Push your shoulders and back into the seat as hard as you can,' Mr Brady instructed.

Claire pushed her **torso**[11] into the Tesla's leather.

'Bit further. I need you to create some **slack**[12],' he added.

'That won't be easy with my **barrel**[13] belly,' joked Claire, though she meant it. 'They don't call me "Choccy **Eclair**[14]" at home for nothing.' She **self-consciously**[15] sucked in her stomach and pushed back harder into the seat, holding her breath.

As Claire's face reddened, Mr Brady angled the seat belt a fraction outwards and upwards, as

---

1 **yank** *(v)* pull with a sudden, hard movement. *(s)* tug, jerk, wrench, heave, haul. *(ant)* push, shove.

2 **frustration** *(n)* an upset or annoyance. *(s)* aggravation, irritation, exasperation. *(ant)* success, satisfaction.

3 **admonish** *(v)* reprimand (tell off) firmly. *(s)* warn, advise, reproach, chide, caution, rebuke. *(ant)* allow, praise.

4 **bitterly** *(adv)* in a bitter (harsh or resentful) way. *(s)* cruelly, sullenly, ruefully, sourly. *(ant)* gently, sweetly, pleasantly.

5 **reiterate** *(v)* say again for emphasis or clarity. *(s)* repeat, restate, recap, retell.

6 **immobile** *(adj)* not moving. *(s)* motionless, static, unmoving, still. *(ant)* mobile, moving.

7 **soothing** *(adj)* gently calming or quietening. *(s)* relaxing, reassuring, comforting, consoling. *(ant)* aggravating, exacerbating.

8 **furrow** *(v)* line with grooves or wrinkles. *(s)* crinkle, crease, pucker, crumple. *(ant)* smooth.

9 **brow** *(n)* area on the head comprising (consisting of) the forehead and temples.

10 **crane** *(v)* stretch one's body or neck to see something. *(s)* outstretch, extend, stick out. *(ant)* retract, shrink.

11 **torso** *(n)* the trunk (body without head or limbs) of a human. *(s)* upper body.

12 **slack** *(n)* part of a rope or line that is held loosely. *(s)* play, give, looseness.

13 **barrel** *(n)* a cylindrical container usually wider around the middle. *(s)* cask, butt, keg, vat, tub, drum.

14 **eclair** *(n)* an oblong choux dough pastry filled with cream and topped with icing. *(s)* cake, bun.

15 **self-consciously** *(adv)* done with excessive awareness of oneself. *(s)* shyly, insecurely. *(ant)* confidently, assuredly.

if weighing up the **pivot**[1] point where it might **relent**[2] and yield its grip.

Just as Claire felt she might explode, the belt's pressure **eased**[3]. With a huge **exhalation**[4] of relief, she began to wriggle out of it. The belt remained stuck in its **clasp**[5], but Mr Brady had somehow created enough room for her to escape its clutches.

'Phew! Thanks, Mr Brady.'

'Now that was a close shave,' joked Mr Brady with an **ambiguous**[6] laugh. 'I thought we might have to leave you here.'

'Huh, that's funny,' **retorted**[7] Claire, **confused**[8] at the unsettling tone in Mr Brady's voice, and not finding any of it **remotely**[9] funny.

'What's happening, Dad? Are Via-Corp sending a car?'

'Yes, son, they'll arrive soon. A local recovery company will fit new front tyres, but they'll have to take the car away. We can't leave it **stranded**[10] here. They're heading up from the village now.'

'OK, cool. How long will they take to fix them? Don't forget my gear is in the back.'

'Depends if they have the right tyres, I guess. Let's hope they source them soon. Don't bet on it though, not after Lady Luck's unfavourable treatment of us today,' his dad said with a **wry**[11] smile.

I doubt any of this is bad luck, thought Claire **cynically**[12]. She stretched out her legs and rubbed her shoulder where the seat belt had **chafed**[13] it.

'Hey, Dad, can you get my decks from the boot, please? We might get a chance to use them today.'

---

1 **pivot** *(n)* the point that something balances on or turns around.
2 **relent** *(v)* give in to something. *(s)* capitulate, acquiesce, surrender, yield, concede, weaken. *(ant)* stand firm.
3 **ease** *(v)* become less severe or slacken. *(s)* lessen, reduce, diminish. *(ant)* increase, tighten.
4 **exhalation** *(n)* a release of air from the lungs (a breath out). *(s)* sigh. *(ant)* inhalation.
5 **clasp** *(n)* a device that fastens things together. *(s)* catch, clip, fastener, buckle.
6 **ambiguous** *(adj)* open to misinterpretation. *(s)* unclear, vague, equivocal. *(ant)* clear, definite, unambiguous.
7 **retort** *(v)* say something in answer to a remark. *(s)* reply, snap, counter, retaliate, riposte, bite back.
8 **confused** *(adj)* bewildered or perplexed. *(s)* puzzled, baffled, mystified, bamboozled. *(ant)* enlightened, clear.
9 **remotely** *(adv)* in the smallest degree. *(s)* in the least bit, at all, one bit. *(ant)* completely, entirely.
10 **stranded** *(adj)* left without the means (capability) to leave. *(s)* trapped, stuck, marooned. *(ant)* rescued.
11 **wry** *(adj)* (of the face) twisted to express disappointment or annoyance. *(s)* unimpressed, vexed. *(ant)* pleased, impressed.
12 **cynically** *(adv)* in a cynical (distrustful or disbelieving) way. *(s)* suspiciously, sceptically. *(ant)* trustfully, naively.
13 **chafe** *(v)* make sore by rubbing. *(s)* abrade, irritate, scour.

Before Claire could say, 'No, thanks; I don't need one,' Mr Brady had reached into the boot and handed her a skateboard.

'Here are the helmets too,' he added, passing one to each of the kids.

'Really? Do I have to wear one? They're **unsightly**[1],' Ben **whined**[2].

'Yes, you do!' answered his dad. 'Especially if you have Claire skating with you. What on earth would Dee say if Claire **sustained**[3] a **concussion**[4], or worse?' he added.

If only you had any idea what I went through yesterday, thought Claire. She tucked the sticker-**adorned**[5] skateboard under one arm and plonked the helmet onto her head. *I bet I look ridiculous*, she thought as it wobbled.

'Ben, you know I'm hopeless at anything with the word *boarding* in it,' she hissed under her breath. 'Don't expect me to carry this thing around all day and wear your stupid pink helmet just 'cause you reckon it's a cool colour,' she grumbled.

'Why not? It matches your cheeks now,' Ben joked, flashing his broadest white smile at her. 'Come on, dude!' he chuckled, **mustering**[6] his strongest American accent. 'I'll teach you how to do an **ollie**[7].'

'An ollie?' she replied. 'Are you kidding? I can't even stand up on the daft **contraption**[8]!' she **scoffed**[9].

'Oi, you two, Laurel and Hardy!' joked Mr Brady **affectionately**[10]. 'Looks like the recovery truck is here to rescue the Tesla.'

'No prizes for guessing which one of the comedy **duo**[11] I am,' laughed Claire, forcing her cheer. 'Being compared to Oliver Hardy is the closest I'll get to doing an ollie today.' She patted

---

1 **unsightly** *(adj)* not pleasing to look at. *(s)* unattractive, ugly, disagreeable. *(ant)* pleasant, attractive.

2 **whine** *(v)* complain in a petulant way. *(s)* moan, whinge, grouch, gripe. *(ant)* compliment.

3 **sustain** *(v)* suffer or undergo (an injury or other discomfort). *(s)* experience, endure.

4 **concussion** *(n)* brain injury resulting in confusion and sometimes loss of consciousness.

5 **adorn** *(v)* make more attractive or beautiful. *(s)* decorate, embellish, ornament, enhance. *(ant)* strip.

6 **muster** *(v)* summon up (a response, attitude or feeling). *(s)* gather, collect, rally, raise, call on. *(ant)* disperse.

7 **ollie** *(n)* (in skateboarding and snowboarding) a jump performed by pushing the foot down on the tail of the board.

8 **contraption** *(n)* an unnecessarily complicated, badly made or unsafe thing. *(s)* gadget, device, gubbins.

9 **scoff** *(v)* speak in a mocking or derisive way. *(s)* ridicule, deride, sneer at. *(ant)* praise, respect.

10 **affectionately** *(adv)* in an affectionate (kind or fond) way. *(s)* warmly, amicably. *(ant)* coldly.

11 **duo** *(n)* two people, especially in a performance. *(s)* couple, pair, duet.

her **rotund**[1] stomach. She and Ben often watched old black-and-white movies with Mr Brady – he loved **slapstick**[2] comedy.

A **gnarled**[3] pickup truck rumbled towards them, **spewing**[4] out **plumes**[5] of dark smoke **amid**[6] clouds of **toxic**[7] diesel **fumes**[8]. Claire coughed, waving away the smoke as it pulled up behind the **stricken**[9] Tesla. A round-faced man, built like a barrel and wearing greasy **overalls**[10], **heaved**[11] himself from the driver's seat and **stomped**[12] over to the waiting threesome, an oil-stained hand **thrust**[13] out before him.

'Geraint the Garage at your service!' the man announced, in such a strong **accent**, Claire only just caught what he said. Even though she'd **encountered**[14] Welsh accents all day yesterday, it still sounded **alien**[15] to her ears.

As they shook hands, Geraint appeared capable of wresting Mr Brady's arm from its **socket**[16]. Claire couldn't help noticing Geraint's oil-stained **meat hook**[17] of a hand and Mr Brady's **manicured**[18] fingers, the **latter**[19] never having seen the sun or done a day's **manual**[20] labour.

---

1 **rotund** *(adj)* plump. *(s)* chubby, dumpy, portly, round, stout. *(ant)* thin, slender, skinny.

2 **slapstick** *(n)* comedy based on clumsiness and humiliation.

3 **gnarled** *(adj)* battered and misshapen, usually with age. *(s)* contorted, deformed. *(ant)* straight, smooth.

4 **spew** *(v)* expel or pour out rapidly. *(s)* eject, emit, spout, spurt, gush, flow, stream, spill. *(ant)* dribble, trickle.

5 **plume** *(n)* a long puff of smoke. *(s)* trail, cloud, curl, spiral, column.

6 **amid** *(prep)* surrounded by, in the middle of. *(s)* among, within, amidst, between, during. *(ant)* outside.

7 **toxic** *(adj)* poisonous. *(s)* noxious, dangerous, harmful, unsafe, injurious. *(ant)* non-toxic, harmless, safe.

8 **fume** *(n)* a gas or vapour that is harmful to breathe in. *(s)* exhaust, smoke.

9 **stricken** *(adj)* gravely affected by a disagreeable feeling or unwanted condition. *(s)* afflicted, affected. *(ant)* unaffected.

10 **overalls** *(n)* one-piece garment (clothing) worn over ordinary clothes. *(s)* coveralls, all-in-one.

11 **heave** *(v)* lift or drag with great effort. *(s)* haul, lug, hoist, heft.

12 **stomp** *(v)* tread heavily. *(s)* stamp, clump, plod, clomp, trudge. *(ant)* tiptoe.

13 **thrust** *(v)* move or extend forcefully. *(s)* shove, propel, drive.

14 **encounter** *(v)* meet unexpectedly. *(s)* face, confront, run into, come across. *(ant)* avoid.

15 **alien** *(adj)* from elsewhere. *(s)* unfamiliar, unusual, foreign, incongruous, strange. *(ant)* familiar, usual.

16 **socket** *(n)* a hollow that something fits into or revolves within. *(s)* opening, niche.

17 **meat hook** *(n)* pejorative (unpleasant) term for a person's hand. *(s)* fist.

18 **manicured** *(adj)* trimmed and neatly maintained. *(s)* cut, shaped. *(ant)* overgrown, unkempt.

19 **latter** *(n)* the second mentioned of two people or things. *(s)* last. *(ant)* former.

20 **manual** *(adj)* involving or relating to the hands. *(s)* physical, hand-operated. *(ant)* automatic, mechanical.

Strangely, it left her with an odd **sensation**[1], one she failed to **fathom**[2]: the same **queasy**[3] sort of unease she'd experienced too often yesterday. However, what **perturbed**[4] her most was the fact that this uneasy feeling was directed towards Mr Brady, her best friend's dad. Dismissing the thought, she plonked the skateboard onto the ground and followed the men over to inspect the Tesla's tyres.

'Blimey O'Reilly!' **exclaimed**[5] Geraint in his **barely**[6] **decipherable**[7] accent. ''Ave you **savaged**[8] these tyres? What the 'eck did you drive across? Two running chainsaws and a smashed-up greenhouse?' He glanced around the **vicinity**[9] as if looking for **incriminating**[10] **evidence**[11]. 'You ain't gonna be driving this car anywhere today.'

'That's the mystery,' replied Mr Brady. 'I didn't see anything sharp on the road. Perhaps the tyres are **defective**[12]. The car's not a year old yet,' he added. 'It's a Via-Corp company vehicle, so I'll report this.'

Claire and Ben searched, hunting for clues as to what might have **annihilated**[13] the Tesla's front tyres, but they, too, found no evidence.

'Well, if you can't find anything, it's gotta be a fault,' said Geraint. 'I'd get onto this fancy-schmancy Tesla firm right away and tell 'em Geraint the Garage is fixing it for 'em,' he added **emphatically**[14]. 'I don't trust these **newfangled**[15], battery-operated cars. Gimme a good old dirty diesel any day, something you can get your 'ands **grimy**[16] on and fix with tools, not with a ruddy

---

1 **sensation** *(n)* a physical feeling or perception. *(s)* sense, impression, awareness.
2 **fathom** *(v)* comprehend after much thought. *(s)* understand, grasp, perceive. *(ant)* misunderstand.
3 **queasy** *(adj)* feeling slightly sick (nauseous) or uneasy. *(s)* odd, unsettled, troubled. *(ant)* well, untroubled.
4 **perturb** *(v)* make uneasy or anxious. *(s)* worry, concern, upset. *(ant)* reassure, calm.
5 **exclaim** *(v)* cry out suddenly. *(s)* blurt, proclaim, declare, shout, call, yell. *(ant)* whisper, mutter.
6 **barely** *(adv)* only just, almost not. *(s)* hardly, narrowly, scarcely. *(ant)* easily, amply, fully, profusely.
7 **decipherable** *(adj)* able to be understood or identified. *(s)* fathomable, discernible. *(ant)* unclear, unintelligible.
8 **savage** *(v)* attack. *(s)* maul, bite, mutilate, lacerate, mangle. *(ant)* nurture, tend, care for.
9 **vicinity** *(n)* surrounding or nearby areas. *(s)* proximity, propinquity, locale. *(ant)* distance.
10 **incriminate** *(v)* make someone seem guilty of a crime. *(s)* implicate, blame, accuse. *(ant)* acquit, vindicate, exonerate.
11 **evidence** *(n)* facts or information presented to support the truth. *(s)* proof, confirmation, corroboration.
12 **defective** *(adj)* faulty or flawed. *(s)* broken, inoperative, malfunctioning. *(ant)* working, perfect.
13 **annihilate** *(v)* destroy completely. *(s)* obliterate, eliminate, exterminate, kill. *(ant)* create, build.
14 **emphatically** *(adv)* in an emphatic (clear and forceful) way. *(s)* vehemently, ardently, vigorously. *(ant)* tentatively.
15 **newfangled** *(adj)* recently created or overly modern. *(s)* novel, advanced. *(ant)* old-fashioned, dated.
16 **grimy** *(adj)* covered with grime. *(s)* dirty, grubby, filthy, stained, soiled. *(ant)* clean.

computer! And self-driving, what's that nonsense all about, eh? What's the point of 'avin' a car if you can't drive the ruddy thing yourself?'

'I hear you, Mr … er, Geraint,' replied Mr Brady, shooting a glance over at Claire and Ben, who were **stifling**[1] chuckles. 'You have a **valid**[2] point,' he agreed in a **faux**[3] **grave**[4] tone.

'Right, then! I'll 'oist this useless 'eap onto my truck and get it sorted for you.' Geraint handed an oil-**soiled**[5] business card over to Mr Brady. 'Stick your number on there, an' I'll call you when it's ready. Don't be bothering with them texts or social **medium**[6], or whatever it's called, apps or something. I don't use 'em. It's good old-fashioned conversation for me,' he said as he readied the **winch**[7] on the back of his truck.

'Come on, Lily, you lazy lump!' Geraint commanded out of the blue. 'Stop **shirking**[8]! Get your backside out of the truck, and give me a hand with this 'eap o' metal.'

To Claire's surprise, a youngish girl, **hitherto**[9] concealed in the truck's cab, stepped out, pulled a baseball cap low over her brow and joined Geraint at the rear of the recovery vehicle. The girl was anything but a 'lump'. Claire observed she was **petite**[10], **nimble**[11] and, from what Claire **glimpsed**[12] of her under the baseball cap, pretty.

'My **idle**[13] daughter, Lily,' mumbled Geraint in a **dismissive**[14], **gruff**[15] voice as he continued his work.

---

1 **stifle** *(v)* restrain a reaction or stop oneself acting on an emotion. *(s)* suppress, repress, curb. *(ant)* encourage.

2 **valid** *(adj)* grounded in fact or reason. *(s)* logical, sound, rational, justifiable. *(ant)* invalid.

3 **faux** *(adj)* not genuine. *(s)* false, fake, pretend, imitation, unreal. *(ant)* authentic, genuine.

4 **grave** *(adj)* serious or solemn. *(s)* sombre, sober, thoughtful, unsmiling, stony, gloomy. *(ant)* cheerful, upbeat.

5 **soil** *(v)* make dirty. *(s)* foul, sully, muddy, stain, spot. *(ant)* cleanse.

6 **medium** *(n)* a means of communication. *(s)* channel, method, way, forum, avenue.

7 **winch** *(n)* a device for hauling or lifting using rope or cable wrapped around a rotating drum, powered by a motor or crank.

8 **shirk** *(v)* neglect or avoid work or responsibility. *(s)* dodge, evade, skive, duck. *(ant)* embrace, pursue.

9 **hitherto** *(adv)* until this point. *(s)* previously, formerly, beforehand, yet, before, thus far. *(ant)* henceforth.

10 **petite** *(adj)* attractively small and dainty. *(s)* slight, elfin, delicate, diminutive, little, tiny. *(ant)* large, bulky.

11 **nimble** *(adj)* light and quick in movement. *(s)* agile, sprightly, lithe, deft, lissom. *(ant)* awkward, clumsy.

12 **glimpse** *(v)* view something quickly or partially. *(s)* peep, peek, glance. *(ant)* stare.

13 **idle** *(adj)* not inclined to work. *(s)* lazy, indolent, slothful, work-shy. *(ant)* industrious, hard-working, diligent.

14 **dismissive** *(adj)* showing something is unworthy of consideration. *(s)* indifferent, unconcerned. *(ant)* interested.

15 **gruff** *(adj)* rough and deep (voice), or abrupt in manner. *(s)* brusque, curt, surly, stern, blunt. *(ant)* friendly.

'Hello, Lily.' Mr Brady flashed a **charming**[1] smile in the girl's direction.

Lily didn't speak but dipped a slight nod at Mr Brady.

Daughter? thought Claire. *She's his daughter? He's the lump, not her!*

'Hey, was that thunder just then?' asked Ben, picking up the skateboard Claire had dumped near the Tesla in the **vain**[2] hope of leaving it there.

'I dunno. The sky's getting darker though,' Claire said, looking upwards, causing the pink helmet to fall off her head.

'That ain't thunder,' answered Lily as Claire bent to pick up the helmet.

She sounds like her dad, thought Claire, straightening up to face Lily and wondering how old she might be.

'See, did you hear it?' Ben pointed to the sky. 'Thunder, in the distance.'

'It ain't thunder,' Lily reiterated in the same bored tone she'd used the first time.

'What is it, then?' asked Ben.

'It's the fighters,' mumbled Lily as she inspected a shiny **spanner**[3].

'Fighters?' **remarked**[4] Ben.

'Yeah, more junk flying around and **polluting**[5] our skies with noise and fumes,' Geraint the Garage **chimed**[6] in, **contradicting**[7] his earlier comments about preferring dirty diesel. 'Damn filthy 'eaps of winged metal! **Scandalous**[8]!'

'Really?' replied Claire, taken immediately back to yesterday, in Anglesey, when the RAF Hawk had zoomed into view, its noise deafening, frightening the **pursuing**[9] Mal-Instinctives away from Gwilym's pony and trap.

'Yep, they practise low-level flying up here in the mountains. Makes 'em better pilots,

---

1 **charming** *(adj)* very pleasant or attractive. *(s)* appealing, charismatic, delightful, pleasing. *(ant)* unattractive.

2 **vain** *(adj)* producing no result. *(s)* useless, pointless, futile, worthless. *(ant)* productive, successful.

3 **spanner** *(n)* a tool for turning nuts and bolts.

4 **remark** *(v)* notice, say, or regard (look at) with attention. *(s)* comment, observe, state, utter.

5 **pollute** *(v)* contaminate with hazardous substances. *(s)* poison, taint, foul, dirty. *(ant)* purify, clean.

6 **chime** *(v)* join in a conversation. *(s)* say, interrupt, comment, contribute, add.

7 **contradict** *(v)* deny the truth, assert the opposite. *(s)* oppose, counter, dispute, refute. *(ant)* agree, confirm.

8 **scandalous** *(adj)* unacceptably bad. *(s)* shocking, monstrous, outrageous. *(ant)* praiseworthy, acceptable.

9 **pursue** *(v)* chase or follow. *(s)* hunt, trail, track, tail, shadow, hound, seek, trace, stalk. *(ant)* guide, lead.

apparently[1], Lily said, her tone still disinterested.

'Wow!' **enthused**[2] Ben. 'I hope we get to see one up close. How cool would that be?' He turned to Claire with his huge **pearly**[3] grin.

'So cool,' replied Claire **glibly**[4], meaning the complete opposite.

'Hey, guys, that was a Via-Corp **colleague**[5] on the phone,' interrupted Mr Brady. 'A car will be here in five, so grab your stuff from the Tesla before Geraint **hoists**[6] it onto his truck.' He swiped his finger across his phone.

Drawn again to his long, **slender**[7], almost-**feminine**[8] fingers, Claire was reminded, creepily, of Jayne's perfectly manicured hands. Perturbed, she went to grab her school bag from the car's **footwell**[9] and slung it onto her shoulder.

Why did Jayne return for my bag last night? she thought. *How could she have even entered the closed museum?* It **flummoxed**[10] her. Although Claire had found nothing **awry**[11] when she'd repacked her bag this morning, everything still felt wrong.

Suddenly, from nowhere, a **fleeting**[12] black shadow darted across the ground beneath them, followed by an **ear-splitting**[13] boom. Claire, Ben and even Mr Brady jumped so much they practically **collided**[14].

'Yikes! What in the heavens was that?' exclaimed Mr Brady, patting his chest above his heart.

---

1 **apparently** *(adv)* as far as one knows or can see. *(s)* supposedly, seemingly, evidently. *(ant)* implausibly.

2 **enthuse** *(v)* express with delight, interest or approval. *(s)* rave, gush, effuse, acclaim. *(ant)* lament, denounce.

3 **pearly** *(adj)* like a pearl in lustre or colour. *(s)* shimmery, milky, shiny. *(ant)* dull, lustreless.

4 **glibly** *(adv)* in a glib (easy) manner. *(s)* urbanely, neatly, smoothly, slickly, casually. *(ant)* inarticulately.

5 **colleague** *(n)* a person who one works with. *(s)* associate, workmate, co-worker.

6 **hoist** *(v)* lift with effort (often with pulleys or ropes). *(s)* heave up, raise, elevate. *(ant)* lower.

7 **slender** *(adj)* slim and graceful. *(s)* lean, willowy, trim, lithe, svelte. *(ant)* big, chubby, firm, heavy, plump, fat.

8 **feminine** *(adj)* having qualities associated with a woman. *(s)* womanly, womanlike, ladylike. *(ant)* masculine.

9 **footwell** *(n)* a space in front of a seat to place one's feet in.

10 **flummox** *(v)* perplex or bewilder. *(s)* baffle, confound, puzzle, mystify, bemuse. *(ant)* clarify, demystify.

11 **awry** *(adj)* out of the ordinary. *(s)* amiss, wrong, untoward. *(ant)* right, in order.

12 **fleeting** *(adj)* lasting for a very short time. *(s)* brief, momentary, sudden, transitory. *(ant)* lasting, permanent.

13 **ear-splitting** *(adj)* very loud. *(s)* deafening, piercing, booming. *(ant)* quiet, soft, low.

14 **collide** *(v)* come into contact with (usually forcefully). *(s)* bump, impact, crash, hit, ram, knock. *(ant)* miss.

Ben looked **utterly**[1] **bewildered**[2], but Claire knew what it was.

'See? See what I mean? Scared you lot 'alf to death, didn't it?' shouted an **overzealous**[3] Geraint the Garage. 'Those ruddy nuisances, noisy, filthy flying pests,' he **declaimed**[4], pausing his work to gesticulate **furiously**[5] at the now-empty sky. 'I'd shoot the damn things down if I could!' he **ranted**[6].

'Ahhh, yes. How could I forget the **Mach Loop**[7]?' Mr Brady rubbed his ears **ruefully**[8].

'What did you say, Dad?' asked Ben.

'Yeah, they're flyin' the Mach Loop all right.' It was **laid-back**[9] Lily who replied. 'Mmm, that was a bit of an odd one though,' she puzzled, removing her baseball cap, staring skywards and **ruffling**[10] her short copper-coloured hair.

'What do you mean?' asked Claire. 'Why was it odd?' She shuddered as if something **elusive**[11] had crawled over her skin, leaving goosebumps in its **wake**[12].

Lily replaced her cap and pulled it down over her eyes. 'It's odd,' she **drawled**[13], ''cause that was an RAF Tornado.'

Claire waited, her **apprehensive**[14] gaze attempting to **locate**[15] Lily's **evasive**[16] eyes, shielded by

---

1 **utterly** *(adv)* to an extreme degree. *(s)* absolutely, completely, totally, entirely. *(ant)* somewhat, partly.

2 **bewildered** *(adj)* perplexed or confused. *(s)* baffled, bemused, mystified, confounded, discombobulated. *(ant)* enlightened.

3 **overzealous** *(adj)* too zealous (keen). *(s)* enthusiastic, eager, spirited, intense. *(ant)* apathetic, uninterested.

4 **declaim** *(v)* speak as if giving a speech. *(s)* pronounce, preach, lecture, spout.

5 **furiously** *(adv)* in a furious (energetic) manner. *(s)* energetically, feverishly, frantically. *(ant)* slowly, calmly.

6 **rant** *(v)* speak or shout in a lengthy and passionate way. *(s)* bluster, yell, bellow, rage, go on. *(ant)* sweet-talk.

7 **Mach Loop** (the Machynlleth Loop) valleys in Wales, notable for their use as low-level training areas for fast jet aircraft.

8 **ruefully** *(adv)* in a rueful (regretful or sorrowful) way. *(s)* sheepishly, agonisingly, dolefully. (ant) blissfully, joyfully.

9 **laid-back** *(adj)* easy-going and relaxed. *(s)* casual, informal, nonchalant. *(ant)* edgy, uptight, tense.

10 **ruffle** *(v)* mess up something or someone's hair. *(s)* tousle, disarrange, dishevel, mess. *(ant)* smooth, straighten.

11 **elusive** *(adj)* hard to catch or find. *(s)* evasive, slippery, shifty, intangible. *(ant)* accessible.

12 **wake** *(n)* disturbed air or water following behind something. *(s)* aftermath, trail, path, track, furrow, wash, train.

13 **drawl** *(v)* speak in a slow, idle way. *(s)* drone, draw out. *(ant)* gabble, gush.

14 **apprehensive** *(adj)* worried that something bad will happen. *(s)* alarmed, anxious, concerned. *(ant)* confident, calm.

15 **locate** *(v)* find the exact position or place of. *(s)* track down, detect, establish, discover, pinpoint. *(ant)* lose.

16 **evasive** *(adj)* tending to avoid, hard to catch. *(s)* elusive, avoiding, dodging. *(ant)* direct, frank.

the cap. Trying her best to sound **nonchalant**[1], **summoning**[2] her **breeziest**[3] tone, Claire asked, 'Odd? Why?'

Lily didn't answer. She continued to help her father setting up the winch, seeming to mull over Claire's question **interminably**[4].

Patience not being one of Claire's **fortes**[5], she blurted again, 'What do you mean, odd?' Her tone was so **abrupt**[6] Mr Brady's eyebrows shot upwards.

With a **languid**[7] movement, Lily put down her spanner, turned to face Claire and drawled, 'It's odd 'cause that stunning machine was a Tornado GR4, and I'm gonna miss 'em now they're **put out to grass**[8].' Her blue eyes **bored**[9] into Claire's.

What? thought Claire as the first stabs of **panic**[10] **inflicted**[11] their pain.

'Spit it out, then, **lass**[12]! What is it you're wanting to say?' snapped Geraint the Garage. 'Now you know why we **dubbed**[13] 'er "Lazy Lily",' he **mocked**[14], looking over at the onlooking, expectant threesome.

For such a **lithe**[15]-looking girl, Lily reacted at the speed of a **sloth**[16]. 'The reason it's odd,' she responded finally, 'is those little beauties ain't supposed to be **frequenting**[17] our Welsh skies any more.'

---

1 **nonchalant** *(adj)* casual and relaxed. *(s)* cool, calm, untroubled, unruffled, blasé. *(ant)* nervous, concerned.

2 **summon** *(v)* try to produce from within oneself. *(s)* call, muster, rouse, find, mobilise, rally. *(ant)* suppress.

3 **breezy** *(adj)* relaxed and cheerily brisk. *(s)* carefree, airy, jaunty. *(ant)* uptight.

4 **interminably** *(adv)* in an interminable (endless) way. *(s)* ceaselessly, continually, eternally, forever.

5 **forte** *(n)* a great strength, something one excels at. *(s)* strong suit, speciality, thing. *(ant)* weakness, failing.

6 **abrupt** *(adj)* brief, almost rude. *(s)* brusque, curt, sharp, terse. *(ant)* polite, unhurried.

7 **languid** *(adj)* lacking quickness of movement. *(s)* unhurried, relaxed, unenergetic. *(ant)* energetic.

8 **put out to grass** (v) force someone or something to retire.

9 **bore** *(v)* drill a hole into (often used figuratively). *(s)* stare, pierce, penetrate, burrow, mine.

10 **panic** *(n)* uncontrollable anxiety or fear. *(s)* fright, dread, alarm, consternation, horror. *(ant)* calm, self-control.

11 **inflict** *(v)* cause or impose pain or suffering. *(s)* enforce, wreak, exact, perpetrate, force. *(ant)* relieve, remit.

12 **lass** *(n)* a girl or young woman. *(s)* miss, lassie, young lady. *(ant)* lad.

13 **dub** *(v)* give a nickname to. *(s)* designate, entitle, call, label, name, term, tag, style, knight.

14 **mock** *(v)* tease or make fun of. *(s)* ridicule, deride, scorn, insult, taunt. *(ant)* praise, compliment, flatter.

15 **lithe** *(adj)* (especially of the body) thin, supple and graceful. *(s)* agile, fit, nimble. *(ant)* dumpy, chubby, stiff.

16 **sloth** *(n)* a slow-moving mammal from Central and South America that hangs from the branches of trees using its claws.

17 **frequent** *(v)* visit often. *(s)* attend regularly, revisit.

'Oh my word! Stop being so **cryptic**[1] and just tell us,' snapped Claire, so **aggressively**[2] even Ben's eyebrows now shot skywards.

'Yeah, sure, hold your horses, missus,' Lily drawled. 'It's odd 'cause in February the Tornado GR4s took their final ride. The RAF **decommissioned**[3] them in favour of the Typhoon,' she finished, turning back to her spanner.

The blood drained from Claire's face. She rubbed at her right eye, trying to conceal its nervous twitching as, in a **quavering**[4] voice, she muttered, 'Ben, give me that daft thing. I'll carry it.'

Snatching the skateboard from Ben, Claire fought to regain some **semblance**[5] of calm. She dropped the deck onto the road, prodding at it with her foot, feigning interest to buy herself time.

Lily had said the Tornado had been 'decommissioned'. Claire knew *exactly* what that meant, because Gladys had told her yesterday – 'no longer in service'. The RAF Hawk and the yellow Sea King helicopter that had saved their bacon were both retired from service. Gladys had **explicitly**[6] told her, the only pilots left flying this class of aircraft were Knights Hawk. So *who* was commanding this retired Tornado just minutes ago, and more importantly, *why*? It had to have been a Knight Hawk.

'Right, come on, you guys.' Mr Brady nodded at Ben and Claire. 'Go wait over there. Let these **seasoned**[7] **mechanics**[8] do their work. I can hear a car approaching; it's probably for us.'

Claire **clocked**[9] the throaty growl of the powerful car before it came into view, rounding the snaking bend. She immediately recognised the **sleek**[10] black Bentley with its **iconic**[11] 'B' **nestled**[12]

---

1 **cryptic** *(adj)* having a mysterious or obscure (unclear) meaning. *(s)* enigmatic, puzzling. *(ant)* straightforward.

2 **aggressively** *(adv)* done in an aggressive (forceful) way. *(s)* violently, belligerently, vigorously. *(ant)* gently.

3 **decommission** *(v)* withdraw (remove) from service. *(s)* mothball, retire, discharge. *(ant)* introduce, activate.

4 **quaver** *(v)* shake or tremble. *(s)* quiver, warble, tremor, flinch, flutter. *(ant)* steady.

5 **semblance** *(n)* the outward appearance of something. *(s)* approximation, show, pretence. *(ant)* reality.

6 **explicitly** *(adv)* in an explicit (definite) way. *(s)* openly, clearly, obviously, unequivocally. *(ant)* ambiguously.

7 **seasoned** *(adj)* experienced and accustomed to certain conditions. *(s)* veteran, expert. *(ant)* inexperienced.

8 **mechanic** *(n)* a worker who repairs and maintains vehicles, machinery and engines.

9 **clock** *(v)* notice or watch. *(s)* see, note, perceive, discern, detect. *(ant)* overlook, ignore.

10 **sleek** *(adj)* smooth and shining. *(s)* glossy, glistening, polished, glassy. *(ant)* dull, rough, coarse.

11 **iconic** *(adj)* of or relating to an icon (something or someone worthy of admiration). *(s)* emblematic. *(ant)* obscure.

12 **nestle** *(v)* be situated. *(s)* lie, hide, shelter, settle, huddle, burrow.

between the silver wings above the criss-crossed front **grille**[1]. The **emblem**[2] was unmistakable, as was the stunning car that cruised towards them, commanding the **entire**[3] carriageway of the narrow mountain pass. Claire had always **harboured**[4] a secret **penchant**[5] for **prestige**[6] cars.

'Wow!' Ben let out a long, low whistle. 'I hope *that's* our ride,' he cried, beaming as the supercar approached.

'I wish!' laughed Mr Brady.

With **longing**[7] looks, Claire and Ben stared at the car as it slowed to pass the **marooned**[8] onlookers, its growl **diminishing**[9] to a purr as it glided past them. Although they craned their necks to see inside, the Bentley's blacked-out windows prevented them.

'Blimey, how can the driver see the road?' asked Ben. 'Even the windscreen is tinted,' he remarked as the car picked up speed and disappeared around the mountain bend.

'D-L-one,' Claire mouthed to herself. DL1. Why did that **exorbitantly**[10] priced and rare number plate **rankle**[11] her so much?

'That was the boss's car.' Mr Brady chuckled at the kids. '*That* was *not* our ride, but I am wondering where ours is.'

Geraint finished securing the Tesla onto his truck and waddled over to the waiting party, nodding his **bulbous**[12] head, which **aptly**[13] accompanied the **smug**[14] smile on his face. 'See, now

---

1 **grille** *(n)* wire mesh or metal bars placed in front of something for protection or ventilation.

2 **emblem** *(n)* distinctive symbol of an organisation. *(s)* badge, representation, mark, sign, image.

3 **entire** *(adj)* whole or complete. *(s)* total, full. *(ant)* fractional, partial.

4 **harbour** *(v)* hold a thought or feeling in the mind. *(s)* nurture, foster, entertain.

5 **penchant** *(n)* a liking for something. *(s)* fondness, preference, affection, weakness. *(ant)* aversion, dislike.

6 **prestige** *(n)* something that inspires extensive admiration and respect.

7 **long** *(v)* have a strong wish or desire. *(s)* crave, yearn, hunger, pine, ache, wish, hanker.

8 **maroon** *(v)* trap in an inaccessible place. *(s)* strand, leave, abandon, desert, forsake. *(ant)* reclaim.

9 **diminish** *(v)* become or make less. *(s)* reduce, decrease, lessen, wane. *(ant)* increase.

10 **exorbitantly** *(adv)* of or in an exorbitant (excessively high) manner. *(s)* overly, unduly, remarkably. *(ant)* moderately.

11 **rankle** *(v)* cause ongoing irritation. *(s)* bother, annoy, upset, nark. *(ant)* please, gratify.

12 **bulbous** *(adj)* round, fat or bulging. *(s)* rotund, spherical, swollen, bloated.

13 **aptly** *(adv)* in an apt (suitable) manner. *(s)* appropriately, fittingly, pertinently. *(ant)* inappropriately.

14 **smug** *(adj)* having an overly high opinion of oneself. *(s)* self-satisfied, superior, complacent. *(ant)* humble, modest.

that was a *real* car. A **classy**[1] piece of **engineering**[2] sits under 'er **bonnet**[3], not like the useless stack of rechargeable batteries under yours!' Geraint waved at the Tesla. ''E's a flash so-and-so though, that one,' he ranted, barely pausing for breath. ''E doesn't send it to me for **servicing**[4]. Must reckon I ain't good enough for the likes of 'im,' he added, ending his **diatribe**[5] with a **disgruntled**[6] grunt.

'I'm sure that's not the case,' replied Mr Brady, his tone **diplomatic**[7] and **conciliatory**[8]. 'Your service **thus far**[9] is excellent.'

Geraint puffed out his **portly**[10] chest, stuck his nose in the air and said, 'Right, then. Me an' Lazy-Lump Lily 'ere'll be off now. 'Ope your lift comes soon, else you'll catch a nasty chill up 'ere,' he finished, turning on his heel and **trundling**[11] off to his truck with not a hint of concern for the stranded party.

'Dad, Claire and I are starving. When's our ride getting here?' whined Ben, spluttering as Geraint's truck left amid plumes of **noxious**[12] fumes.

Most **uncharacteristically**[13], hunger was the furthest thing from Claire's mind.

'Benjamin, you are NOT starving,' replied his dad. 'I *will* call again though,' he added. 'I guess everyone's busy trying to **patch**[14] this security breach.'

There's that security breach *phrase again*, thought Claire.

Just as Mr Brady went to press dial on his phone, the distant sound of a car's engine cut through the silent mountain air.

---

1 **classy** *(adj)* having sophistication and style. *(s)* superior, high-class, elegant. *(ant)* inferior, cheap.

2 **engineering** *(n)* branch of technology for the design, building and use of engines, machines and structures.

3 **bonnet** *(n)* liftable canopy covering the engine of a vehicle.

4 **servicing** *(n)* routine maintenance or repair work on a vehicle. *(s)* repairs, aftercare, upkeep.

5 **diatribe** *(n)* a bitter and strong verbal attack. *(s)* harangue, tirade, criticism. *(ant)* compliment.

6 **disgruntled** *(adj)* displeased or angry. *(s)* aggrieved, discontented, dissatisfied. *(ant)* pleased, contented.

7 **diplomatic** *(adj)* showing tact (diplomacy) and sensitivity (feeling). *(s)* tactful, politic, discreet. *(ant)* tactless.

8 **conciliatory** *(adj)* likely or intended to calm. *(s)* peacemaking, appeasing, pacifying. *(ant)* antagonistic.

9 **thus far** *(adv)* up to now. *(s)* hitherto, to this point, so far.

10 **portly** *(adj)* large, fat or overweight. *(s)* round, corpulent, chubby, tubby, heavy. *(ant)* slim, slender, skinny.

11 **trundle** *(v)* move slowly and heavily. *(s)* trudge, plod, slog, traipse, wander. *(ant)* sprint.

12 **noxious** *(adj)* harmful, poisonous or unpleasant. *(s)* toxic, deadly, lethal, foul. *(ant)* harmless, pleasant.

13 **uncharacteristically** *(adv)* in an uncharacteristic (unusual) way. *(s)* strangely, unexpectedly. *(ant)* typically.

14 **patch** *(v)* fix or strengthen something. *(s)* mend, repair, cover. *(ant)* damage, weaken.

'Ah, this might be for us.' Mr Brady popped his phone back into his pocket and tilted his head towards the approaching sound.

'Hope so,' said Ben. 'I'm getting cold now too.'

Claire rolled her eyes at him. 'Check you've got your stuff,' she said, 'and quit whining.'

A surprised and now-**biddable**[1] Ben **duly**[2] followed her.

Thankfully, the oncoming car slowed and pulled into the lay-by where they waited.

'Hey, John. How are you? I'm sorry I kept you guys waiting so long,' said a young woman jumping out of the car and holding out her hand to Mr Brady. 'It's been **manic**[3] panic at work!' she added. She had an American accent. 'I came as soon as possible. You must be Ben and Claire. John told me you were with him when he called.' She shook their hands. 'I'm Cristy Grant. So pleased to meet you. I'll pop the **trunk**[4], and you can throw your gear in there,' she said, pressing a button on the key **fob**[5] in her hand.

Claire noticed Cristy's hair was the same colour and style as Jayne's. She was tall and slim too.

Why do Americans call the boot a trunk? Claire asked herself **rhetorically**[6] as she placed her belongings into the boot of the car, Ben following suit.

Mr Brady placed his jacket on top and slammed the boot shut.

'Hop in,' Cristy **chirped**[7] with a cheery **lilt**[8]. 'Let's get you up to Via-Corp.'

Claire and Ben were climbing into the car when something stopped Claire in her tracks.

'What's up?' asked Ben.

'Can you hear that?' Claire replied.

'No. What?' Ben's face creased with confusion.

'That sound. Shush and listen.' Claire put her finger to her lips.

In the near distance, but gradually getting louder, was the clip-clop of metal on the tarmac, a sound Claire recognised from yesterday.

---

1 **biddable** *(adj)* ready to accept and carry out instructions. *(s)* obedient, amenable, pliant. (ant) disobedient.

2 **duly** *(adv)* as is required. *(s)* fittingly, correctly, aptly. (ant) improperly.

3 **manic** *(adj)* incredibly busy. *(s)* frenzied, feverish, hectic, intense. (ant) calm.

4 **trunk** *(n)* (US English) storage space in an automobile (often at the rear). *(s)* boot.

5 **fob** *(n)* an object on a key ring.

6 **rhetorically** *(adv)* in a rhetorical (not seeking information) way.

7 **chirp** *(v)* speak cheerfully. *(s)* cheep, squeak, twitter, pipe, sound, tweet. *(ant)* lament, groan.

8 **lilt** *(n)* characteristic rise and fall of the voice. *(s)* cadence, intonation, accent, tone, rhythm. *(ant)* monotone.

'What is it?' repeated Ben, but Claire didn't answer.

'Come on, kids, get in! We need to go right now!' Mr Brady's tone sounded **irate**[1], but Claire didn't move. Coming up from the bend where the Bentley had disappeared, and heading towards them at a fast trot, was a pony and trap.

'Dad! You gotta see this before we go,' exclaimed Ben. 'Look, it's a real horse and cart,' he said, pointing at the pony as it approached in the distance.

In the half-light of the **murky**[2] grey day, Claire couldn't make out the pony's colour at first, but as it neared, its unmistakable rich chestnut tone shone, its cream-coloured mane **billowing**[3] in the wind.

'You gotta snap a picture of this, Dad. We don't have many horses in Manchester,' **pleaded**[4] Ben as Mr Brady turned to see.

Claire's eyes remained fixed on the rapidly approaching trap.

'It is charming,' said Mr Brady. 'But get in now. We're leaving.' His tone was suddenly **acerbic**[5] and out of character.

As the trap **clattered**[6] past them, the **ruddy**[7]-faced driver, with hands the size of shovels, **doffed**[8] his worn **tweed**[9] cap. He swiftly replaced it, growled 'Yarrhhh' to the pony and sped away without a backward glance. All the while, a small, scruffy white dog with black and tan patches remained **steadfastly**[10] perched by his side, his proud, upright head **surveilling**[11] all from his position at the **helm**[12] of the rickety old trap.

It was Gwilym and Jack, being pulled along by Lady.

---

1 **irate** *(adj)* very angry. *(s)* furious, incensed, mad, enraged, fuming, infuriated, livid. *(ant)* calm.

2 **murky** *(adj)* gloomy and dark. *(s)* dim, shadowy, sombre, dreary, dingy, obscured. *(ant)* bright, light, clear.

3 **billow** *(v)* inflate and move outwards. *(s)* undulate, wave.

4 **plead** *(v)* make an emotional appeal. *(s)* beg, beseech, implore, supplicate, request. *(ant)* offer.

5 **acerbic** *(adj)* (of speech) direct and sharp. *(s)* cutting, caustic, biting, harsh. *(ant)* mild, kind.

6 **clatter** *(v)* make a continuous rattling sound. *(s)* clack, clank, jangle, clash, bump, hurtle, clang.

7 **ruddy** *(adj)* having a reddish colour of the face. *(s)* blooming, florid, flush, rosy, bronzed. *(ant)* pale.

8 **doff** *(v)* remove (clothing). *(s)* raise, lift, shed, take off. *(ant)* don.

9 **tweed** *(n)* a rough cloth (originating from Scotland) flecked with colours.

10 **steadfastly** *(adv)* in a steadfast (firm) way. *(s)* unwaveringly, persistently, staunchly. *(ant)* weakly, irresolutely.

11 **surveil** *(v)* keep under surveillance (watch closely). *(s)* observe, monitor, inspect.

12 **helm** *(n)* a position of leadership (at the front of). *(s)* command, reins, controls.

2. The Mountain Lair

Although it had been **mere**[1] minutes, Claire had no **recollection**[2] of getting into Cristy's car. Since Gwilym, Jack and Lady had trotted past, her mind had gone blank. She'd not heard Mr Brady's third **prompt**[3]. Only when he had walked over and tapped her arm had she responded and climbed into the car.

'You still sick?' Ben whispered to Claire. 'You're green. You gonna **barf**[4]?'

'Shut up, will you?' she hissed, hating biting at her best friend but needing time. 'I *will* **puke**[5] if you keep reminding me to!' she snapped, turning her head away to face the window.

She wasn't sure how long they'd been in the car, but they had climbed uphill the whole time. Her ears hurt. The adults' voices drifting from the front seats sounded **muffled**[6] and distant. Gwilym and Jack were here in Snowdonia, which both comforted and terrified her. Why were they here? Something was wrong. She felt sure it wouldn't be long before she discovered what.

As the car climbed, the sky darkened. Patches of grimy, melting snow lay in **mounds**[7] along the edges of the mountain road, **accumulating**[8] in size and **stature**[9]. Space between the **spindly**[10]

---

1 **mere** *(adj)* having no greater extent than, barely. *(s)* meagre, measly, only, sheer.

2 **recollection** *(n)* the act of remembering something. *(s)* memory, remembrance. *(ant)* amnesia.

3 **prompt** *(n)* an encouragement to say or do something. *(s)* reminder, cue.

4 **barf** *(v)* vomit (be sick). *(s)* puke, throw up, chunder, spew, retch, gag, heave, regurgitate, disgorge.

5 **puke** *(v)* vomit (be sick). *(s)* barf, throw up, chunder, spew, retch, gag, heave, regurgitate, disgorge.

6 **muffled** *(adj)* not loud due to being obstructed or muted in some way. *(s)* stifled, faint, soft. *(ant)* loud.

7 **mound** *(n)* a heap or large amount of something. *(s)* pile, stack, accumulation, collection.

8 **accumulate** *(v)* build up. *(s)* multiply, amass, increase, accrue. *(ant)* dissipate.

9 **stature** *(n)* height. *(s)* tallness, loftiness, build, size.

10 **spindly** *(adj)* tall or long and thin. *(s)* twiggy, spindling, insubstantial. *(ant)* sturdy, stout.

evergreen[1] trees widened as they were replaced by grey slate. A still, **eerie**[2] mist hung in the air, hugging the distant mountains, slicing them in two to reveal just their bases and peaks. No animals grazed. The landscape was too **exposed**[3] and steep, even for a mountain goat.

'Hey, Dad, how much snow do they get up here?' Ben asked. 'Looks like they've had a fair fall.'

'We're high now,' replied his dad, 'so you'll see quite a bit. Via-Corp welcomes the snow. It adds another layer of security to the compound,' he added.

The compound, thought Claire. *Sounds more like a prison.*

Claire chewed at her thumbnail, peering out of the window and straight down the mountain. Her stomach **lurched**[4]. Sitting on the car's left afforded her the stunning view of the **majestic**[5] Snowdonia mountain range but also the **sheer**[6] drop down it. They snaked around the **precipitous**[7] bends with sometimes less than a metre between the car's tyres and the cliff edge; she **loathed**[8] it.

'Ben, why didn't you sit on this side? You're used to these winding roads from your drives to the French Alps. I can't stand these drops,' she whined, her nausea now **genuine**[9].

'We'll be fine,' Ben replied. 'There's no snow on the road. That's when it gets **hairy**[10].'

'Great,' Claire replied, with more than a hint of **sarcasm**[11].

Just then tiny little flakes, like **motes**[12] of dust, began to whirl around the car.

'It's snowing now though!' remarked Ben. 'Look, Dad, snow!'

'Yeah, son, a little. I doubt it will stick,' replied his dad.

That's all we need, thought Claire.

'Mr Brady, why are there no signs on this road?' asked Claire.

---

1 **evergreen** *(adj)* relating to a plant that keeps green leaves all year round. *(ant)* deciduous.

2 **eerie** *(adj)* strange and scary. *(s)* spooky, creepy, weird, uncanny, peculiar, paranormal. *(ant)* normal, earthly.

3 **exposed** *(adj)* bared to the elements (weathered). *(s)* unprotected, open, unsheltered. *(ant)* sheltered.

4 **lurch** *(v)* move in an abrupt, unsteady or uncontrolled way. *(s)* jerk, lean, reel, falter.

5 **majestic** *(adj)* showing or having magnificent beauty or size. *(s)* awesome, epic, splendid. *(ant)* pathetic, pitiful.

6 **sheer** *(adj)* so steep as to be perpendicular or nearly so. *(s)* vertical, precipitous, sharp. *(ant)* gentle, moderate.

7 **precipitous** *(adj)* steep, sheer or high. *(s)* abrupt, dizzying, lofty, vertical, arduous. *(ant)* gentle, flat, gradual.

8 **loathe** *(v)* feel intense dislike or disgust for. *(s)* hate, despise, abhor, detest, disdain, scorn. *(ant)* adore, love.

9 **genuine** *(adj)* real, truthful or sincere. *(s)* honest, authentic, veritable. *(ant)* insincere, false, bogus.

10 **hairy** *(adj)* difficult and alarming. *(s)* risky, dangerous, perilous, hazardous. *(ant)* safe.

11 **sarcasm** *(n)* use of irony (opposite) to mock or convey dislike. *(s)* derision, scorn, disdain. *(ant)* flattery.

12 **mote** *(n)* a tiny piece of something. *(s)* particle, speck, spot, grain, fleck, mite.

'This **access**[1] is private,' Cristy answered for him. 'No outside vehicles use this pass. Via-Corp built it.'

Claire caught Cristy's eye in the rear-view mirror and quickly looked away.

'Why all the privacy?' asked Claire.

'Via-Corp **trades**[2] in AI and **secure**[3] data,' said Mr Brady. 'Few folks know the company is here. If it weren't for this **critical**[4] issue today, you guys wouldn't be visiting,' he added.

'But didn't you say the headquarters are on the **outskirts**[5] of Beddgelert village?' asked Claire, knowing she sounded too **inquisitive**[6].

'They are,' he replied, 'at least the part we want folks to see. You kids lucked out today. You'll see the *other* HQ. HQ2.'

'That's why it took me so long to reach you,' said Cristy. 'I've come down from HQ2. We **desperately**[7] need your father up there, Ben, so you guys get to have a **peek**[8] too – of certain parts, that is.'

'Sorry, you won't be able to explore the quaint village today,' apologised Mr Brady.

'Okay,' said Ben. 'Dad, you've never mentioned HQ2 before now.'

'Exactly,' replied Mr Brady. 'Exactly.'

'WOW!' Ben cried.

'What? What is it?' asked a jumpy Claire.

'Look!' said Ben. 'Look at the snow now!'

Claire was speechless. Snowflakes the size of two-pound coins now fell in **mesmerising**[9] swirls around the car, their **density**[10] increasing by the second.

'What the heck?' she said, turning towards Ben. 'I've never seen such heavy snow.'

---

1 **access** *(n)* the means to advance towards or enter a place. *(s)* entry, entrance, approach.

2 **trade** *(v)* buy and sell things. *(s)* deal, market, peddle, flog, tout.

3 **secure** *(adj)* sure to stay safe. *(s)* guarded, invulnerable, protected. *(ant)* insecure, vulnerable.

4 **critical** *(adj)* potentially disastrous. *(s)* serious, grave, dangerous, perilous. *(ant)* safe.

5 **outskirts** *(n)* outer parts of a town or city. *(s)* bounds, border, edge, suburbs, fringes, peripheries. *(ant)* centre.

6 **inquisitive** *(adj)* curious about other people's affairs. *(s)* interested, intrigued, prying. *(ant)* uninterested.

7 **desperately** *(adv)* in a desperate (urgent) way. *(s)* vitally, critically, acutely. *(ant)* non-urgently.

8 **peek** *(n)* a quick or secretive look. *(s)* peep, glance, glimpse, gander. *(ant)* stare, gaze.

9 **mesmerising** *(adj)* holding the complete attention of. *(s)* hypnotic, captivating, enthralling, spellbinding. *(ant)* boring.

10 **density** *(n)* a substance's compactness. *(s)* thickness, solidity, bulk, substance, mass.

Cristy had switched on her windscreen wipers and slowed the car. **Visibility**[1] had **dramatically**[2] **decreased**[3]. Claire was sure the back of the car had slid as they rounded the last **hairpin bend**[4].

'This sure is **dense**[5] now,' said Cristy, leaning towards the windscreen.

Claire sat as still and upright as an on-duty meerkat. She realised she was **grinding**[6] her teeth and stopped.

'Man, I don't know about skateboarding. I might get to use my snowboard though!' laughed Ben.

For the first time, Claire wanted to swipe at Ben.

A **pang**[7] of guilt stabbed her. Ben was **irritating**[8] her, but it wasn't his fault. He didn't know what she'd been through yesterday. *What is happening?* The **maelstrom**[9] of thoughts careering through her mind added to her **impending**[10] sense of **foreboding**[11]. She **surreptitiously**[12] rubbed at her **twitching**[13] eye and wiped the beads of sweat from her top lip. How would she tell Ben about yesterday?

'Guys, when we arrive, there will be security processing,' said Mr Brady. 'We'll arrange passes to the **recreational**[14] areas; you can hang around there and wait for me. Don't worry, that will include the restaurant too, and our rec areas are pretty entertaining,' he added.

'Dad, we're gonna need chains if this continues,' said Ben, peering out of the window.

'Chains?' asked Claire, screwing up her face.

---

1 **visibility** *(n)* the degree to which something can be seen. *(s)* observability. *(ant)* opacity.

2 **dramatically** *(adv)* in a dramatic (powerful) way. *(s)* greatly, radically, noticeably, severely. *(ant)* modestly.

3 **decrease** *(v)* become smaller or fewer. *(s)* lessen, reduce, dwindle, diminish, decline, subside. *(ant)* increase.

4 **hairpin bend** *(n)* a sharp bend in a road that turns the road in the opposite direction.

5 **dense** *(adj)* tightly compacted. *(s)* heavy, thick, concentrated. *(ant)* thin, light.

6 **grind** *(v)* rub together. *(s)* grate, gnash, scrape.

7 **pang** *(n)* a sudden painful feeling or emotion. *(s)* twinge, stab, ache.

8 **irritate** *(v)* make annoyed or slightly angry. *(s)* aggravate, bother, vex, exasperate. *(ant)* soothe, pacify, appease.

9 **maelstrom** *(n)* confused movement or tumult. *(s)* commotion, turmoil, disorder, chaos.

10 **impending** *(adj)* about to happen. *(s)* imminent, looming, approaching, threatening, brewing. *(ant)* receding.

11 **foreboding** *(n)* a bad feeling about something. *(s)* apprehension, dread, misgiving. *(ant)* confidence.

12 **surreptitiously** *(adv)* in a surreptitious (secret) way. *(s)* furtively, slyly, covertly. *(ant)* overtly, openly.

13 **twitch** *(v)* jerk, tremble or quiver lightly and involuntarily (without will). *(s)* spasm, convulse.

14 **recreational** *(adj)* relating to enjoyment. *(s)* fun, relaxing, entertaining. *(ant)* working, boring.

'Hey, don't worry, Claire,' Cristy chimed in. 'The car has four-wheel drive; we should make it without them.'

'Chains?' Claire mouthed to Ben, shaking her head.

'Snow chains, to stop us sliding back down the hill,' muttered Ben.

'Great!' said Claire, her sarcasm **blatant**[1].

The snow fell so heavily now, the tarmac was invisible. Within minutes the landscape had **transformed**[2] from a bleak grey to pure white. Cristy's driving slowed to a crawl, and **despite**[3] the four-wheel drive, the car was sliding. Anxiety hung in the air.

'Dad, *do* we need snow chains?' Ben **persisted**[4].

Claire recognised the concern in his voice. *He's scared. If Ben's scared, this is serious.*

'We should make it without chains, son,' replied Mr Brady. 'It's a few more bends now, and then we reach a **plateau**[5],' he added.

'Plateau?' mouthed Claire to Ben.

'A level area,' he whispered.

Claire wondered where Gwilym, Jack and Lady were in this **treacherous**[6] weather. She'd left Manchester just hours before and was now almost stuck on a Welsh mountain. After **toying**[7] with asking Mr Brady to call her mum, she decided against it. Her dad's visit this morning felt like **aeons**[8] ago. Thoughts of her dad brought Jayne back into her mind with a **jarring**[9] **jolt**[10]. Her awful dream flooded back. No matter how hard she pushed it away, telling herself it wasn't real, it returned like a **persistent**[11] toothache.

The car slowed to a limp. The engine was making strange noises, and Cristy struggled to

---

1 **blatant** *(adj)* done openly and without shame. *(s)* obvious, overt, flagrant. *(ant)* subtle, inconspicuous.

2 **transform** *(v)* markedly change something. *(s)* alter, modify, convert, remodel, revamp. *(ant)* preserve, sustain.

3 **despite** *(prep)* in spite of, regardless of. *(s)* even though, even with, undeterred by. *(ant)* because of.

4 **persist** *(v)* continue stubbornly or repeat insistently. *(s)* carry on, push, persevere. *(ant)* stop, yield.

5 **plateau** *(n)* a level area of high ground. *(s)* upland, table, highland, mesa. *(ant)* mountain.

6 **treacherous** *(adj)* presenting hidden or unforeseen dangers. *(s)* hazardous, precarious, perilous. *(ant)* safe.

7 **toy** *(v)* consider an idea or proposal casually or indecisively. *(s)* contemplate, ponder, muse. *(ant)* decide.

8 **aeon** *(n)* an indefinite and long time. *(s)* age, yonks, eternity, forever. *(ant)* moment, jiffy, flash.

9 **jarring** *(adj)* causing physical impact or vibration. *(s)* shaking, jolting, rattling, disturbing. *(ant)* gentle.

10 **jolt** *(n)* a forceful movement or shock. *(s)* bump, lurch, impact, jerk.

11 **persistent** *(adj)* continuing firmly or over a prolonged period. *(s)* tireless, unrelenting. *(ant)* irresolute, fleeting.

drive. Visibility was practically zero.

'Keep moving,' said Mr Brady, his voice calm. 'If you lose **momentum**[1], you'll lose grip. Maintain a slow speed and brake only if necessary. I'll drive if you prefer, but it's best not to stop,' he finished.

Claire's fingers gripped the edge of her seat so hard they lost their colour.

Out of nowhere, blinding headlights **dazzled**[2] them. Cristy hit the brakes, causing the car's rear to swing close to the sheer mountain drop. Claire shrieked and Ben's caramel-coloured skin turned ashen. Their car, as if in slow motion, began sliding backwards towards the sheer drop.

'Dad!' shrieked Ben.

Mr Brady had grabbed the steering wheel from a shocked Cristy and gently **engaged**[3] the car's handbrake. After an interminable wait, they eventually came to an unsteady stop. The oncoming car had **streaked**[4] past them.

'Shall I drive the rest of the way?' said Mr Brady, opening his door to swirls of snow. 'You slide across this side, Cristy,' he added as though nothing hazardous had just occurred.

'John, I didn't see the car until we nearly hit it. They didn't even slow down,' she added with a catch in her voice.

'Don't worry,' Mr Brady reassured her. 'That was a Via-Corp vehicle and driven way too fast. I'll check the **logs**[5] when I get a chance and speak with the driver. Now, scooch across here and I'll hop in,' he said, jumping out of the passenger door.

Cristy wriggled across to the passenger seat, turned to Ben and Claire, and said, 'Sorry, kids.'

Mr Brady opened the driver's door and flopped onto the seat, scattering snow from his shoulders and hair. 'It's pretty bad out there. We'd better move, or we might need to call on Geraint again.'

*Does he ever get **flustered**[6]?* thought Claire.

---

1 **momentum** *(n)* the impetus (speed) gained by a moving object. *(s)* force, motion, thrust. *(ant)* inertia.

2 **dazzle** *(v)* (of a light) blind temporarily. *(s)* daze, overwhelm, stun.

3 **engage** *(v)* put into use. *(s)* employ, enlist, appoint, involve, draw from. *(ant)* disengage.

4 **streak** *(v)* move quickly in a specific direction. *(s)* race, speed, fly, charge, shoot. *(ant)* dawdle.

5 **log** *(n)* an official record. *(s)* register, logbook, diary, chronicle.

6 **flustered** *(adj)* agitated and confused. *(s)* unsettled, alarmed, disconcerted, perturbed. *(ant)* calm.

'Dad, how much further is it?' asked Ben anxiously as his dad started the car and pushed the lever forward into drive.

'Not far, son, almost there.'

With a creaking crunch, the car edged a few centimetres forward, its wheels spinning in **protest**[1] before they finally gained some semblance of **purchase**[2] on the snow and picked up speed.

'Phew!' said Ben to Claire.

'Phew indeed,' she replied.

This was Claire's first experience of nature's **wrath**[3]. They travelled little as a family, and **torrential**[4] rain was as risky as it got in Manchester. It rarely snowed, and when it did, it was not like this.

'I never realised snow could be so terrifying,' Claire said, turning to Ben with a warm smile to **make amends**[5]. She'd been so mean to him today; the guilt was killing her. 'Not a **flapper**[6], your dad,' Claire whispered to Ben. 'Does he ever lose his cool?'

'Only when I'm cheeky,' Ben chuckled. 'But no, he's not. He leaves that to Mum. You OK?' he asked, his brows **knitted**[7] together.

'Feeling sick,' she said, and meant it.

They both turned to their **respective**[8] windows. Everywhere was white.

The car **inched**[9] up the steep **gradient**[10], sliding around the tight, winding turns.

'Guys, last bend now,' Mr Brady said.

It was Claire who said 'Phew!' this time, smiling with **sheer**[11] relief. 'Oh, wow!' she remarked, peering through the window as the snow seemed to ease a little.

---

1 **protest** *(n)* an expression of disapproval, disagreement or objection. *(s)* complaint, fuss. *(ant)* approval.

2 **purchase** *(n)* a firm contact or grip. *(s)* grasp, hold, clasp, leverage, foothold. *(ant)* release.

3 **wrath** *(n)* anger. *(s)* fury, rage, outrage, annoyance, vexation. *(ant)* happiness.

4 **torrential** *(adj)* (of rain) falling quickly. *(s)* heavy, severe, copious, relentless. *(ant)* light.

5 **make amends** *(v)* make up for a misdeed. *(s)* compensate, recompense, repay.

6 **flapper** *(n)* someone who panics.

7 **knit** *(v)* unite (come together). *(s)* meet, merge, meld. *(ant)* separate.

8 **respective** *(adj)* separate, not shared. *(s)* different, individual. *(ant)* same.

9 **inch** *(v)* move along carefully and slowly. *(s)* ease, budge, edge, shuffle, creep, crawl. *(ant)* rush, leap.

10 **gradient** *(n)* degree of steepness. *(s)* incline, pitch, angle, leaning.

11 **sheer** *(adj)* unrestricted. *(s)* pure, utter, absolute, total, downright, outright, unmitigated. *(ant)* restricted.

'Pretty, isn't it?' said Cristy, speaking for the first time since almost colliding with the oncoming vehicle.

'It's perfection!' said Claire, **awestruck**[1].

After limping around the final bend, the road opened into what Claire could only imagine **resembled**[2] the most **idyllic**[3], **quintessential**[4] **Alpine**[5] village. They drove beneath a huge, weathered archway. Each **strut**[6] stood carved **entirely**[7] from **stout**[8] tree trunks, which held up the crooked arch and a **kitsch**[9] painting of the **scenery**[10], announcing, 'Welcome to Via-Corp Village'.

Wooden **chalets**[11] dotted the gently sloping hills, the narrow road slicing this **idyll**[12] in two. A blanket of powdery snow transformed the landscape into a **panoramic**[13] picture postcard.

Shame it melts, thought Claire.

'Dad, is *this* your HQ2?' asked Ben, his eyes widening. 'It's like a ski **resort**[14].'

'Well, sort of, son. Many **permanent**[15] **employees**[16] live here. Via-Corp provides **accommodation**[17] as part of their **salary**[18] – if they work on the compound, that is.'

'Compound? It's gorgeous up here, but *compound* sounds like a prison,' Claire observed, admiring the **vista**[19].

---

1 **awestruck** *(adj)* filled with or revealing awe. *(s)* astonished, staggered, rapt, overwhelmed. *(ant)* unimpressed.

2 **resemble** *(v)* have a similar appearance to or qualities in common with. *(s)* approximate, echo. *(ant)* differ.

3 **idyllic** *(adj)* extremely happy, peaceful or picturesque. *(s)* blissful, wonderful, heavenly. *(ant)* bad, nightmarish.

4 **quintessential** *(adj)* the most perfect or representative. *(s)* model, classic, essential, typical. *(ant)* poor, average.

5 **Alpine** *(adj)* typical of the Alps or other high mountains. *(s)* mountainous.

6 **strut** *(n)* a bar made to resist pressure in a framework. *(s)* support, beam, lintel.

7 **entirely** *(adv)* completely. *(s)* wholly, absolutely, totally, fully. *(ant)* slightly, partially.

8 **stout** *(adj)* heavily built. *(s)* strong, solid, big, sturdy, robust, heavy-duty. *(ant)* flimsy, thin, slight.

9 **kitsch** *(adj)* of poor taste but often appreciated for it. *(s)* tacky, cheap, tasteless. *(ant)* tasteful.

10 **scenery** *(n)* natural and picturesque features of a landscape. *(s)* surroundings, backdrop, setting, panorama.

11 **chalet** *(n)* a wooden house in the traditional style of the Alps. *(s)* cabin, lodge.

12 **idyll** *(n)* a happy, tranquil or picturesque place or time. *(s)* paradise, utopia. *(ant)* hell.

13 **panoramic** *(adj)* (of view) wide, sweeping. *(s)* extensive, commanding, scenic. *(ant)* narrow.

14 **resort** *(n)* holiday or recreation place. *(s)* spot, centre, retreat, haunt.

15 **permanent** *(adj)* lasting or intended to last indefinitely. *(s)* constant, perpetual, persistent. *(ant)* temporary.

16 **employee** *(n)* a paid worker. *(s)* member of staff, job holder, workman. *(ant)* employer.

17 **accommodation** *(n)* where a person can live or lodge (stay). *(s)* dwelling, housing, living quarters, residence.

18 **salary** *(n)* a person's income (regular pay) from employment (work). *(s)* wages, earnings, remuneration.

19 **vista** *(n)* a lovely view. *(s)* panorama, outlook, scene, landscape, perspective.

'Can we take a photo, Dad?' interrupted Ben.

'No! No pictures at all!' replied Mr Brady in the **sternest**[1] voice Claire had ever heard him use.

'Oh, OK,' replied Ben, looking **abashed**[2]. 'Sorry I asked.'

Mr Brady's **barbed**[3] tone silenced both the kids. They glanced at each other, their eyebrows raised.

'Photography isn't **permitted**[4] up here,' added Cristy, her tone conciliatory. 'Your dad's **abiding**[5] by the rules, Ben. He's a **senior**[6] **executive**[7], so he must lead by example,' she finished. 'To answer your question, Claire, we folks **refer**[8] to HQ2 as "the compound".'

I wonder why, thought Claire.

The excitement of arriving in a winter wonderland had **distracted**[9] Claire from the **dilemma**[10] of telling Ben about yesterday.

'I'm gutted my snowboarding gear is stuck in the back of the Tesla,' said Ben, **marvelling**[11] at the falling snow's **persistence**[12].

Claire rolled her eyes and smiled at her friend.

'Son, there are no lifts. You'd have to **hike**[13] to catch a hill,' replied his dad.

'Well, we won't be skateboarding anywhere in this, will we?' said a disappointed Ben.

Phew! thought Claire, yet again.

'I wouldn't be too sure, son,' teased Mr Brady. 'Our recreational **facilities**[14] are not too **shabby**[15].'

---

1 **stern** *(adj)* serious and strict. *(s)* severe, firm, formidable, dour, uncompromising. *(ant)* cheerful, lenient.

2 **abashed** *(adj)* embarrassed, ashamed or disconcerted. *(s)* humiliated, deflated, mortified. *(ant)* undaunted.

3 **barbed** *(adj)* (of a remark) hurtful. *(s)* prickly, spiked, spiky. *(ant)* gentle, kind.

4 **permit** *(v)* allow to do something. *(s)* approve, authorise, let, sanction, consent, OK, facilitate. *(ant)* forbid.

5 **abide** *(v)* follow or accept. *(s)* adhere to, stick to, observe, comply with. *(ant)* flout, reject, disobey.

6 **senior** *(adj)* high in rank or status. *(s)* top, superior, high-ranking. *(ant)* junior.

7 **executive** *(n)* senior manager in a business. *(s)* chief, head, principal, director.

8 **refer** *(v)* describe or denote something as. *(s)* signify, mean, indicate, allude, imply, state.

9 **distract** *(v)* draw away someone's attention. *(s)* sidetrack, preoccupy, disturb. *(ant)* focus, concentrate.

10 **dilemma** *(n)* a difficult situation where a decision must be made. *(s)* predicament, plight. *(ant)* breeze, cinch.

11 **marvel** *(v)* be filled with amazement and wonder. *(s)* admire, gape, stare, applaud. *(ant)* deride, disregard.

12 **persistence** *(n)* the act of continuing despite difficulty. *(s)* tenacity, perseverance, resolve. *(ant)* feebleness.

13 **hike** *(v)* walk vigorously or for recreation. *(s)* climb, trek, tramp, slog, ramble, stroll.

14 **facility** *(n)* space provided for a specific purpose. *(s)* amenity, establishment, centre.

15 **shabby** *(adj)* poor. *(s)* seedy, scruffy, dingy, slummy, grubby, neglected. *(ant)* smart, upmarket

he added, winking at Cristy, who smiled back.

'Almost there now,' chirped Cristy.

If I hear that once more …! Claire was itching to get out – the **novelty**[1] of the snow had lost its **appeal**[2], and she was hungry now. 'Can we grab some grub when we get there?' she whispered **sidelong**[3] to Ben. *I could tell him everything while we eat.*

What on earth? Claire turned to Ben, her eyes as wide as saucers.

The car faced a wall of grey rock, the road ending where the mountainside rose. Mr Brady swiped a manicured finger across his phone's screen, then placed it on the **dashboard**[4]. **Precisely**[5] ten seconds later, like a scene from a James Bond movie, a **vast**[6] **swathe**[7] of rock slowly but smoothly slid sideways, revealing the mouth of an **enormous**[8] black tunnel.

After yesterday's crawling through tunnels with Gwilym, Claire feared she might **vomit**[9] from panic. Ben squealed in delight. Cristy smiled and Mr Brady said nothing. He drove the car into the tunnel's entrance, then stopped and switched off the headlights. The car's engine cut out.

'Quiet, kids' was all he said.

Surrounded by darkness, they sat in silence.

Claire felt sure everyone in the car could hear her heart **pounding**[10].

Unexpectedly, white lights shone from beneath the car, **illuminating**[11] it so brightly Claire **squinted**[12]. Then the car **revolved**[13], the lights beneath it creating a laser effect. They shone in

---

1 **novelty** *(n)* a new, unusual or original object or experience. *(s)* newness, originality, freshness. *(ant)* familiarity.

2 **appeal** *(n)* attraction or interest. *(s)* allure, charm, magnetism. *(ant)* repulsion.

3 **sidelong** *(adv)* directed sideways. *(s)* indirectly, obliquely, surreptitiously. *(ant)* directly.

4 **dashboard** *(n)* a panel in front of a driver or pilot that contains controls.

5 **precisely** *(adv)* in a precise (exact) way. *(s)* meticulously, absolutely, strictly, just, without doubt. *(ant)* vaguely.

6 **vast** *(adj)* large or immense. *(s)* enormous, broad, extensive, colossal, huge, gigantic. *(ant)* small, insignificant.

7 **swathe** *(n)* a wide strip or area of something. *(s)* band, track, belt.

8 **enormous** *(adj)* large in size or quantity. *(s)* giant, massive, colossal, vast, huge, immense. *(ant)* tiny, minute.

9 **vomit** *(v)* be sick. *(s)* regurgitate, disgorge, retch, gag, heave, spew, puke, barf. *(ant)* swallow.

10 **pound** *(v)* throb or beat strongly. *(s)* thump, hammer, pulse, pump.

11 **illuminate** *(v)* light up. *(s)* brighten, lighten, irradiate, illume. *(ant)* darken, dim.

12 **squint** *(v)* look with one's eyes screwed up or partly closed. *(s)* scan, peer, peek, glance.

13 **revolve** *(v)* move in circles. *(s)* rotate, spin, whirl, pirouette.

blinding straight lines, **pivoting**[1] and swirling as though searching. A strange **metallic**[2] clanging sound accompanied the light show, and the car shuddered. The sound reminded Claire of an ankle MRI scan she'd had in hospital. On completion of a three-hundred-and-sixty-degree turn, the revolving **ceased**[3]. They were in some form of holding area, as it seemed sealed. A hissing sound followed by a whoosh saw the entire **chamber**[4] fill with something that resembled steam. **Yelping**[5], Claire **recoiled**[6] from the window.

'It's OK, nearly done,' said Mr Brady, his voice **silky**[7] smooth.

As the **substance**[8] cleared, Claire pressed her nose against the car's window. The lasers stilled, and their stark brightness dimmed to a warm **hue**[9]. She stared at the cave's ceiling and dark **crags**[10]. They peered back, their surfaces lined, ominous and old, like the **wrinkles**[11] of ancient folks' faces. Their **malformed**[12] expressions were **inscribed**[13] and **charted**[14] into **multiple**[15] maps of blue-black **crannies**[16], lumps and bumps. **Prehistoric**[17] metallic **streaks**[18] **traced**[19] the rock's history, as if **woven**[20] throughout old skin and shiny veins. The **dome**[21]-shaped area where they

---

1 **pivot** *(v)* turn as if on a pivot (central point). *(s)* rotate, revolve, spin, swivel, whirl, pirouette.
2 **metallic** *(adj)* relating to or resembling something metal. *(s)* metal-like. *(ant)* non-metallic.
3 **cease** *(v)* stop, end or finish. *(s)* conclude, terminate, halt, pause, quit, discontinue. *(ant)* start, continue.
4 **chamber** *(n)* compartment or private room. *(s)* cubicle, space, cell.
5 **yelp** *(v)* make a short, sharp cry, especially of pain or alarm. *(s)* squeal, squeak, wail, yell.
6 **recoil** *(v)* suddenly spring or flinch back in horror or disgust. *(s)* withdraw, retreat, dodge. *(ant)* confront.
7 **silky** *(adj)* (of voice or manner) smooth and pleasing. *(s)* suave, charming, soft. *(ant)* rude, coarse.
8 **substance** *(n)* a kind of matter. *(s)* stuff, material, medium.
9 **hue** *(n)* colour, tone or shade. *(s)* complexion, aspect, tinge, tint.
10 **crag** *(n)* a steep or rugged wall of rock. *(s)* cliff, bluff, precipice, scarp.
11 **wrinkle** *(n)* lines or folds. *(s)* crease, furrow, crinkle, rumple, pucker.
12 **malformed** *(adj)* poorly formed. *(s)* misshapen, distorted, deformed, contorted.
13 **inscribe** *(v)* carve or write on something. *(s)* etch, engrave, cut, chisel, score.
14 **chart** *(v)* record, make a map of. *(s)* plot, delineate, sketch, graph, represent.
15 **multiple** *(adj)* numerous and usually varied. *(s)* many, various, legion, manifold, different. *(ant)* few, one, same.
16 **cranny** *(n)* a little, narrow space or opening. *(s)* gap, niche, crevice, crack, cleft, split. *(ant)* closure.
17 **prehistoric** *(adj)* relating to the time prior to written records. *(s)* ancient, primeval, primal, early. *(ant)* modern.
18 **streak** *(n)* a thin line or mark on something. *(s)* band, strip, smudge, smear, stroke, stripe.
19 **trace** *(v)* follow the course or history of something. *(s)* chart, outline, record.
20 **weave** *(v)* interlace thread to form cloth (past participle: woven). *(s)* intertwine, interweave. *(ant)* unravel.
21 **dome** *(n)* a rounded space forming part of a structure. *(s)* arched roof, rotunda, mound, hemisphere.

waited stood carved from the rock. *The car is sitting on a* ***turntable***[1], thought Claire.

Then, just as the entrance had revealed itself earlier, the solid rock wall before them slid sideways to show a thick **pane**[2] of glass, beyond which stood rows and rows of cars.

Mr Brady started the car engine and, as **blithely**[3] as if he was leaving a supermarket car park, said, 'All done.'

Another ten seconds passed, and the glass sheet moved aside, slotting **flush**[4] into its **housing**[5]. Mr Brady drove into a **humongous**[6] car park. Hundreds of vehicles stood lined up in neat rows, ordered by size, colour and model, parked like rows of **dominoes**[7].

'The boss likes order,' said Mr Brady, smiling at the **wonderstruck**[8] kids through the rear-view mirror.

More like ***obsessive-compulsive disorder***[9], thought Claire as they drove around the **perimeter**[10] of the **immaculate**[11] car park.

'Row one zero eight; model, Ford; colour, **azure**[12] blue,' Cristy said to Mr Brady, who **promptly**[13] headed to the **allocated**[14] parking space, slotting between lines of blue Fords **identical**[15] to Cristy's.

Claire and Ben clocked each other, raising their eyebrows even higher.

'Weird!' whispered Ben.

Mr Brady swung the car into the space and, as the engine cut, said, 'All set?'

---

1 **turntable** *(n)* a circular platform that revolves.

2 **pane** *(n)* a sheet of glass in a door or window. *(s)* panel, windowpane.

3 **blithely** *(adv)* in a blithe (carefree) manner. *(s)* casually, carelessly, unthinkingly. *(ant)* anxiously, warily.

4 **flush** *(adv)* so as to be level or even with another surface. *(s)* flatly, smoothly. *(ant)* unevenly, irregularly.

5 **housing** *(n)* rigid, protective casing. *(s)* case, covering, encasement.

6 **humongous** *(adj)* huge. *(s)* immense, enormous, prodigious, colossal. *(ant)* tiny, minute.

7 **domino** *(n)* any of twenty-eight small rectangular pieces marked with zero to six spots, used in the game dominoes.

8 **wonderstruck** *(adj)* struck with a feeling of delight or wonder. *(s)* dumbfounded, flabbergasted. *(ant)* underwhelmed.

9 **obsessive-compulsive disorder** *(n)* a mental disorder where a person's thoughts drive them to repeat actions.

10 **perimeter** *(n)* the boundary of an area. *(s)* circumference, border, periphery, edge. *(ant)* centre.

11 **immaculate** *(adj)* without flaw or mistake. *(s)* impeccable, faultless, pristine, perfect, spotless. *(ant)* defective.

12 **azure** *(adj)* blue in colour like a clear sky.

13 **promptly** *(adv)* in a prompt (immediate) manner. *(s)* swiftly, rapidly, straight away, hastily. *(ant)* slowly.

14 **allocate** *(v)* distribute (share out). *(s)* assign, allot, administer.

15 **identical** *(adj)* similar in every way. *(s)* equal, indistinguishable, duplicate, alike, like, matching. *(ant)* different, separable.

His casual air **bemused**[1] Claire. They'd just braved a tyre blowout and a **blizzard**[2], and had now entered an underground **lair**[3] using what appeared to be laser security **technology**[4], yet he was acting as though they'd parked up at Lidl. *Maybe he's just a supercool guy.*

Claire scrutinised him as Cristy said, 'Thanks for coming to the rescue, John. I was spooked back there.'

Mr Brady nodded at Cristy and then said, 'I've popped the trunk. You guys in the back go get your things. I'm real late, so hurry.'

He's just too cool, thought Claire, unbuckling her seat belt and getting out of the car.

'Crikey, my legs are stiff,' she said to Ben, who didn't seem to be suffering from the same problem. He was irritatingly fit.

'Now *you* quit your moaning,' he teased.

'**Touché**[5],' she laughed, walking to the boot of the car and grabbing her coat and bag. The sight of her school bag stopped her laughter in its tracks. Who had put it outside her dad's front door, and why?

'Ben, grab my jacket, please,' called Mr Brady.

'This place is mind-boggling,' said Ben.

'Have you got your decks, kids?' shouted Mr Brady.

'Really, Dad?' questioned a hopeful Ben.

'Really!' he replied. 'And hurry!'

Claire stuffed her coat into her bag, slung it over her shoulder, and snatched a skateboard and the pink helmet from Ben.

'Really?' she said, screwing up her face at Ben.

'Really!' Ben laughed. 'You never know, you might enjoy it.'

'Reckon?' she scoffed.

They crossed the car park, which was also carved out of the rock, but it was supported by

---

1 **bemuse** *(v)* confuse or muddle. *(s)* bewilder, perplex, flummox, stump. *(ant)* enlighten.

2 **blizzard** *(n)* an intense snowstorm. *(s)* white-out, snow blast.

3 **lair** *(n)* a place where a wild animal lives, secret hideaway. *(s)* den, warren, hole, hideout.

4 **technology** *(n)* equipment developed from the practical application of scientific knowledge.

5 **touché** *(int)* used to recognise a good or clever point made in a discussion.

prominent[1] metal **girders**[2]. It was **essentially**[3] a **gigantic**[4] cave but had a super-high-tech **vibe**[5] to it. Air-conditioned warmth **enveloped**[6] them, and the **atmosphere**[7] crackled as if charged with electricity. The lighting was **phenomenal**[8]. Sparkling **specks**[9] dotted the entire ceiling, **mimicking**[10] stars, twinkling in **intermittent**[11] **sequences**[12] like Christmas lights. As they walked towards what looked like a lift, the floor lit up beneath every footstep, illuminating the **pedestrians**[13]' exact pathway. Both kids looked **rapt**[14]. Mr Brady and Cristy grinned at each other.

'Dad, I had no idea your HQ was soooo cool,' marvelled Ben. 'And this is just the *car park*! It's like a movie set.'

'I'm not here too often,' replied his dad. 'I'm usually in Beddgelert village. It's a touch more **pedestrian**[15] down there!' he laughed.

They reached a slate-grey metal door fitted into the rock. There was no control panel, no button to press to open it. Mr Brady placed his palm against the sleek metal and leaned close, looking into what Claire thought was a spyhole, like the one in their front door at home.

The metal door slid open, and they **traipsed**[16] into a lift. There was no numbering system, nothing in the lift, bar more metal, soothing lighting and **cheesy**[17] lift music. *Maybe the boss has a sense of humour*, Claire thought, listening to it.

---

1 **prominent** *(adj)* readily perceptible. *(s)* conspicuous, noticeable, discernible. (ant) inconspicuous.

2 **girder** *(n)* a strong beam used for building. *(s)* rafter, strut, joist, lintel, bar, crossbeam.

3 **essentially** *(adv)* in essence (used to emphasise the basic nature of something). *(s)* fundamentally, inherently, principally.

4 **gigantic** *(adj)* great in extent or size. *(s)* enormous, huge, extensive, vast. *(ant)* tiny.

5 **vibe** *(n)* the atmosphere or feel of a place. *(s)* impression, sense, flavour, overtone.

6 **envelop** *(v)* surround completely. *(s)* enclose, enfold, enwrap, blanket, swaddle, swathe, cloak, encompass.

7 **atmosphere** *(n)* the tone, mood or ambience. *(s)* impression, feeling, air, character.

8 **phenomenal** *(adj)* exceptionally good. *(s)* remarkable, impressive, prodigious, outstanding. (ant) ordinary.

9 **speck** *(n)* tiny dot or particle. *(s)* fleck, spot, pinprick, speckle. (ant) mass.

10 **mimic** *(v)* resemble or imitate (copy or behave like). *(s)* mirror, impersonate, simulate. (ant) differ from.

11 **intermittent** *(adj)* not continuous or regular. *(s)* irregular, sporadic, random. *(ant)* steady, constant.

12 **sequence** *(n)* the order in which things follow each other. *(s)* series, chain, succession, course.

13 **pedestrian** *(n)* a person on foot. *(s)* walker, stroller, rambler.

14 **rapt** *(adj)* fascinated by what one sees or hears. *(s)* riveted, captivated, mesmerised. *(ant)* uninterested, inattentive.

15 **pedestrian** *(adj)* lacking excitement. *(s)* uneventful, plodding, commonplace, dull. *(ant)* exciting.

16 **traipse** *(v)* move reluctantly or in a tired manner. *(s)* trudge, plod, lumber, amble.

17 **cheesy** *(adj)* low in quality. *(s)* tacky, trashy, poor. *(ant)* classy, tasteful.

'Rec,' Mr Brady said in an **assertive**[1] tone but to no one in particular.

The door slid closed, and to Claire's surprise, the lift moved downwards. It was a smooth, **plush**[2] lift, not like those in the flats where her friends lived – they often got stuck and stank of wee.

Ben's grin was akin to an upturned banana. Claire smiled back at him. He was such an **easy-going**[3], **optimistic**[4] friend, her *best* friend.

Momentarily[5] **awash**[6] with **gratitude**[7], she was comforted by a warm sensation. *I'm so lucky to have Ben*, she thought as the lift dived deeper and deeper. It was so smooth Claire didn't realise they'd stopped until the door glided open to reveal an **underwhelming**[8], empty room.

'Security,' said Cristy, smiling at the kids. 'Out you get.'

Mr Brady **focused**[9] on his phone.

'Claire, hands on there,' said Cristy, pointing at the wall.

Claire plonked the skateboard and helmet on the floor and placed both palms flat against the wall. To her surprise, the moment they touched the cool surface, it lit up, and a warm, tingling sensation ran through her fingers. For a fleeting moment, the **internal**[10] structure of her hand was **discernible**[11]; then the backlight was **extinguished**[12].

'Now your eyes here,' said Cristy, pointing to another panel.

Claire focused her eyes upwards towards the panel, resting her chin on a cup-like **receptacle**[13] for support, and heard a slight whir.

---

1 **assertive** *(adj)* having a positive and forceful personality. *(s)* confident, bold, assured. *(ant)* passive, retiring, meek.

2 **plush** *(adj)* expensive and luxurious. *(s)* deluxe, lavish, posh, swanky, swish, lush. *(ant)* spartan, cheap.

3 **easy-going** *(adj)* tolerant and relaxed in manner. *(s)* mellow, placid, lenient. *(ant)* tense, intolerant.

4 **optimistic** *(adj)* positive and hopeful about the future. *(s)* cheery, sanguine, confident. *(ant)* pessimistic, gloomy.

5 **momentarily** *(adv)* for a moment in time. *(s)* fleetingly, briefly, temporarily. *(ant)* indefinitely, permanently.

6 **awash** *(adj)* flooded or covered with. *(s)* oversupplied, swamped, inundated, overflowing. *(ant)* dry, deficient.

7 **gratitude** *(n)* quality of being thankful and showing appreciation. *(s)* thanks, gratefulness. *(ant)* ingratitude.

8 **underwhelm** *(v)* fail to make a favourable impact. *(s)* disappoint, dismay, displease. *(ant)* impress.

9 **focus** *(v)* pay attention to or concentrate on. *(s)* look, fix, pinpoint. *(ant)* ignore.

10 **internal** *(adj)* relating to the inside. *(s)* interior, inner. *(ant)* external, outer.

11 **discernible** *(adj)* able to be recognised, seen or found out. *(s)* noticeable, visible, detectable. *(ant)* imperceptible.

12 **extinguish** *(v)* cause to stop shining. *(s)* put out, douse, snuff out. *(ant)* light.

13 **receptacle** *(n)* a hollow object for containing something. *(s)* holder, container, vessel.

'One last thing, finger in here, please,' said Cristy, waving her hand at the wall. 'Print upwards, like so.' She **demonstrated**[1] in the air to Claire.

'Where do I put it?' asked Claire, glancing at Ben, who watched **engrossed**[2] – it was his turn next.

'Ah, I see,' said Claire, putting her finger into a small opening that had appeared in the wall. A squirt of icy liquid to her fingertip surprised her. 'Ouch! I didn't see that coming,' she yelped at Ben, who'd jumped backwards. A small dot of blood had appeared on the end of her finger. 'I **assumed**[3] it was taking my prints,' said Claire, **affronted**[4].

'Now, press your finger on that glass panel there,' pointed Cristy.

Claire pressed her finger with the blob of blood onto the glass. There was an **immediate**[5] beep, and Cristy said **matter-of-factly**[6], 'You're done, Claire. Ben, your turn.'

Claire sucked her sore finger as she watched Ben go through the same **procedure**[7]. *Is this even **legal**[8]?* Claire asked herself. Had she known what was coming, she would have refused.

A beep from the machine signalled Ben was done, and Mr Brady looked up, slipping his phone back into his pocket. 'OK, guys, let's go. Just one final step,' he said. 'Place your palm on the reader and look into the **retinal**[9] **scanner**[10].'

They each took their turn. A **sturdy**[11], well-**camouflaged**[12] but incongruously **rudimentary**[13] door clunked **ajar**[14] on its **hinges**[15]. It was unlike the smooth, gliding doors hitherto. It was even

---

1 **demonstrate** *(v)* practically explain or show something. *(s)* display, illustrate, exhibit.
2 **engross** *(v)* capture all the attention or interest of. *(s)* engage, rivet, captivate, enthral. *(ant)* bore.
3 **assume** *(v)* suppose something to be the case without prior proof. *(s)* presume, think, believe. *(ant)* doubt.
4 **affront** *(v)* offend. *(s)* insult, slight, hurt, wound, mortify. *(ant)* compliment.
5 **immediate** *(adj)* happening or done at once. *(s)* instant, instantaneous. *(ant)* delayed.
6 **matter-of-factly** *(adv)* in a practical and unemotional manner. *(s)* straightforwardly, sensibly. *(ant)* emotionally.
7 **procedure** *(n)* a series of actions done in a particular order. *(s)* routine, system, process, practice.
8 **legal** *(adj)* allowed by law. *(s)* legitimate, lawful, permitted, valid. *(ant)* illegal, criminal.
9 **retinal** *(adj)* relating to a means of identifying a person from the distinctive patterns of blood vessels in their retina.
10 **scanner** *(n)* a device used to identify, read, monitor or examine something.
11 **sturdy** *(adj)* strong and solidly built. *(s)* robust, durable, substantial, rugged, muscular, burly. *(ant)* weak, frail.
12 **camouflage** *(v)* hide or disguise by means of camouflage. *(s)* conceal, mask. *(ant)* reveal, show.
13 **rudimentary** *(adj)* basic in form. *(s)* primitive, crude, unsophisticated, simple. *(ant)* sophisticated.
14 **ajar** *(adj)* slightly open. *(s)* agape, unclosed, cracked, unfastened. *(ant)* closed, shut.
15 **hinge** *(n)* movable joint or mechanism that a gate or door is hung upon. *(s)* link, pivot.

thicker than the cell doors Claire had encountered yesterday, below the Manchester police station.

'Let's get you guys food first,' Mr Brady said, pushing the heavy door open into a dark corridor. As Mr Brady stepped into it, lights flickered on just above his head to show the way forward. 'We light only when necessary,' he said. 'The compound saves energy and recycles waste.'

The corridor was short, **sterile**[1] and, when lit, bright. They reached another solid door at the end. Mr Brady held his palm against an **adjacent**[2] panel, and this door clunked ajar.

'Welcome to Via-Corp,' he said.

Claire's jaw dropped in **wonderment**[3], not because of the striking surroundings, not because they were underground, **encompassed**[4] by rock, metal and **fortified**[5] glass, but because **striding**[6] towards them, dressed in a perfectly **tailored**[7] **ivory**[8] trouser suit and **killer**[9] heels, was her dad's girlfriend, Jayne Lewis.

---

1 **sterile** *(adj)* totally clean. *(s)* sterilised, disinfected, hygienic. *(ant)* dirty, septic, infected.

2 **adjacent** *(adj)* next to or adjoining. *(s)* beside, neighbouring, alongside, joining. *(ant)* remote from, distant from.

3 **wonderment** *(n)* awed respect or admiration. *(s)* awe, amazement, astonishment. *(ant)* indifference.

4 **encompass** *(v)* surround, enclose or hold within. *(s)* circle, envelop, contain, hold, wrap, swathe. *(ant)* exclude.

5 **fortified** *(adj)* strengthened against attack. *(s)* reinforced, braced, toughened, hardened. *(ant)* weakened.

6 **stride** *(v)* walk in long marching steps. *(s)* tread, stomp, pace, pound, stamp. *(ant)* dawdle, drag, shuffle.

7 **tailored** *(adj)* made to fit exactly. *(s)* custom, smart, fitted, stylish, elegant, designed. *(ant)* misadjusted.

8 **ivory** *(adj)* creamy-white like ivory (tusk of an elephant). *(s)* off-white, cream, blonde.

9 **killer** *(adj)* impressive. *(s)* excellent, effective, cool. *(ant)* naff, poor, ordinary.

3. The Rec Rooms

'Claire, darling, what a tiny world!' Jayne wrapped her silky arms around Claire, enveloping her in an **intoxicating**[1] **customised**[2] **fragrance**[3]. 'I had no idea your friend here was John Brady's boy,' she **gushed**[4]. 'Not until Cristy **relayed**[5] today's tale. What a coincidence.' Jayne released her grip on Claire.

Claire was **reeling**[6], **rendered**[7] shocked and speechless at seeing Jayne.

'John,' said Jayne, **proffering**[8] her manicured hand.

'Jayne,' he replied, shaking it.

'It's been too long,' she said. 'Good to have you back.'

'Yes, ma'am. Good to be back.' Mr Brady flashed his toothy white smile.

Ma'am? thought Claire, pulling a face. *Look at him, all googly-eyed at Jayne.* Claire suspected her thoughts were **unwarranted**[9], but Mr Brady's **suave**[10] moves niggled her. She watched him **fawning**[11] over Jayne and narrowed her eyes, glaring at him. *I'll read your mind like I did Josh*

---

1 **intoxicating** *(adj)* exciting or exhilarating. *(s)* appealing, delightful, enlivening, thrilling, rousing. *(ant)* boring.

2 **customise** *(v)* modify (change) to suit specific tastes or needs. *(s)* personalise, tailor. *(ant)* generalise.

3 **fragrance** *(n)* a pleasant smell. *(s)* scent, perfume, bouquet, aroma, cologne, eau de toilette. *(ant)* stench.

4 **gush** *(v)* speak or write quickly and enthusiastically. *(s)* enthuse, effuse, pour, babble, admire. *(ant)* drawl.

5 **relay** *(v)* receive and pass on messages or information. *(s)* deliver, communicate, convey. *(ant)* withhold.

6 **reel** *(v)* feel bewildered and shocked. *(s)* falter, lurch, wobble, shake, spin, stagger. *(ant)* steady, stabilise.

7 **render** *(v)* cause to become. *(s)* make, leave.

8 **proffer** *(v)* put forward or hold out to someone. *(s)* offer, extend, tender, volunteer, give. *(ant)* withdraw.

9 **unwarranted** *(adj)* not justified, having no basis in fact. *(s)* groundless, unfounded, baseless. *(ant)* warranted, justified.

10 **suave** *(adj)* confident and elegant. *(s)* smooth, polished, refined, debonair, sophisticated. *(ant)* awkward.

11 **fawn** *(v)* flatter and give excessive attention to. *(s)* court, pander, cajole, crawl, grovel, butter up. *(ant)* belittle.

Drane's yesterday, she thought. **Mortified**[1], she immediately blushed at her **absurdity**[2] and looked away. *I'm losing the plot*, she **chided**[3] herself, **crestfallen**[4]. She'd had no **inkling**[5] of mind reading since hearing Drane's horrid voice in her head yesterday.

'Claire, did your father hand over your bag this morning?' asked Jayne.

Claire **tensed**[6], pulling the bag's shoulder strap into view and revealing it, but Jayne continued to speak.

'Your father said someone returned your bag after you forgot it yesterday. I told him you would need it for school on Monday.'

Someone? thought Claire, shocked. It was difficult for her to conceal her frown, but being **polite**[7], she forced a smile.

'I'm so sorry for postponing tomorrow's theatre trip. I promise I'll make it up to you,' said Jayne, a regretful expression **flitting**[8] across her face. 'Let me begin *right* now. You need a feast and to enjoy our rec facilities.'

Had her dad said the note left with her bag was from Jayne? Claire was pretty sure he had, but Jayne's remark had thrown her. She must ask him as soon as she could.

With a **haughty**[9] wave, Jayne **beckoned**[10] to Cristy. 'Accompany Claire and Ben to the **VIP**[11] restaurant, full **complimentary**[12] menu, and add access-all-rec-areas passes.' She didn't say please.

No mistaking who's in charge here, thought Claire.

'John, follow me,' Jayne commanded, and marched away.

'See you later, kids,' said Mr Brady, winking and pulling a faux afraid face at them before following Jayne.

---

1 **mortified** *(adj)* embarrassed or ashamed. *(s)* humiliated, degraded, shamed, humbled. *(ant)* pleased, gratified.

2 **absurdity** *(n)* something ridiculous or very unreasonable. *(s)* illogicality, irrationality. *(ant)* logic, sensibleness.

3 **chide** *(v)* tell off, rebuke or scold. *(s)* chastise, berate, reprimand, reproach, reprove. *(ant)* praise, applaud.

4 **crestfallen** *(adj)* sad, disappointed, low in confidence. *(s)* downcast, despondent, disconsolate. *(ant)* upbeat.

5 **inkling** *(n)* a suspicion or vague knowledge. *(s)* idea, hint, sense, notion, impression. *(ant)* certainty.

6 **tense** *(v)* become rigid, usually from anxiety. *(s)* tighten, brace, stiffen. *(ant)* relax.

7 **polite** *(adj)* showing respectful and considerate behaviour. *(s)* civil, courteous, deferential. *(ant)* rude, aloof.

8 **flit** *(v)* move swiftly. *(s)* dart, dip, flicker, sweep, fly, skim, flutter, flash. *(ant)* dawdle.

9 **haughty** *(adj)* high in one's own estimation. *(s)* arrogant, superior, disdainful, conceited. *(ant)* modest, humble.

10 **beckon** *(v)* make a gesture with the hand, arm or head to instruct someone. *(s)* attract, signal, sign.

11 **VIP** *(n)* very important person. *(s)* celebrity, name, personality, star. *(ant)* nobody.

12 **complimentary** *(adj)* given free. *(s)* gratis, courtesy, on-the-house. *(ant)* chargeable.

'I didn't know your dad's girlfriend worked with my dad,' whispered Ben as they followed Cristy.

'Me neither,' said Claire.

'I think she's his boss,' added Ben. 'She's scary. Man, this place is something else!' he marvelled, **pirouetting**[1] on his heel, wide-eyed.

'It's OK,' replied Claire, subdued.

'Smile, **misery guts**[2]!' said Ben. 'What's up? This place is **radical**[3].' He skipped along behind Cristy.

Claire **conceded**[4]: the place was **spectacular**[5]. They'd exited the last corridor into a **gargantuan**[6] cave **constructed**[7] entirely from rock, metal and glass. **Transparent**[8] **tubular**[9] walkways **suspended**[10] in the air carried people across and around the open **cavern**[11]. Glass panels surrounded the entire perimeter, housing people in hollowed-out office pods, workspaces expertly carved into the bare rock. **Trendy**[12] employees of all ages swiped at touch screens and tapped away on tiny keyboards. They bustled like worker bees, as if their **sole**[13] **objective**[14] was to provide for their queen.

'Hungry, guys?' asked Cristy.

'Starved!' replied Ben.

'Then follow me,' she answered with a wave of her hand.

'Don't look down,' Ben said. 'It's freaky.'

---

1 **pirouette** *(v)* perform a pirouette. *(s)* twirl, whirl, spin, rotate, turn, circle.

2 **misery guts** *(n)* miserable or discontented person. *(s)* spoilsport, killjoy, grump, grouch.

3 **radical** *(adj)* (informal) very good. *(s)* excellent, cool, sick, wicked. *(ant)* rubbish, uncool, cheesy.

4 **concede** *(v)* admit defeat. *(s)* acknowledge, accept, recognise, allow, capitulate, quit, cede. *(ant)* deny, fight.

5 **spectacular** *(adj)* beautiful and striking. *(s)* eye-catching, arresting, breathtaking, glorious. *(ant)* dull.

6 **gargantuan** *(adj)* huge. *(s)* large, enormous, massive, colossal, mammoth, vast, immense, gigantic. *(ant)* tiny.

7 **construct** *(v)* make or build. *(s)* erect, establish, create, assemble, fabricate, raise. *(ant)* demolish, destroy.

8 **transparent** *(adj)* can be seen through. *(s)* see-through, clear, translucent. *(ant)* opaque, blocked, cloudy, dark.

9 **tubular** *(adj)* made from a tube or tubes. *(s)* cylindrical, tube-like.

10 **suspend** *(v)* hang from or over something. *(s)* swing, dangle.

11 **cavern** *(n)* a large cave. *(s)* cavity, hollow, dugout, grotto, underground chamber.

12 **trendy** *(adj)* up to date or fashionable. *(s)* modish, popular, contemporary, hip, cool, chic. *(ant)* unfashionable.

13 **sole** *(adj)* one and only. *(s)* singular, solitary, single, individual, lone, solo. *(ant)* numerous, many.

14 **objective** *(n)* something aimed at. *(s)* goal, intention, intent, purpose, aim, object, ambition.

Of course, Claire immediately looked and then wished she hadn't. They'd stepped onto a tubular walkway. Nothing but glass separated them from the ground metres below.

'I hate heights!' moaned Claire. *And tunnels.* There was no handrail; only sleek glass surrounded them. Akin to a hall of mirrors, the walkway swam before her eyes. She blinked hard, but her **vertigo**[1] persisted. Pressing her hand against the glass sides to steady herself, and almost dropping the skateboard and helmet, she left a trail of greasy palm prints behind her.

As the transparent tube led onto a metal platform, they **alighted**[2] to face another **robust**[3] glass **barrier**[4]. Cristy held her palm over a panel in the adjacent rock, and in silence, the sheet glass slid away. It separated them from what appeared to be more-normal surroundings – a **partially**[5] lit corridor.

'This way, guys,' said Cristy, walking into the long corridor lined with doorways. 'That's what we call the Hive back there. The rest of the compound isn't so spectacular. Choose a door,' Cristy suggested. She grinned, nodding towards the long rows of identical flush-fitting doors **uniformly**[6] fitted along both sides of the corridor.

'Sorry?' asked a **perplexed**[7] Claire, squinting in Ben's direction. The long line of doors reminded her of the prison cells again.

'Pick a door,' Cristy repeated, smiling. 'Ben, you go first.'

Ben walked ahead, then back towards Cristy and Claire.

'I can't choose. They're the same,' he said, **dithering**[8].

'For pity's sake, Ben! This one!' Claire barked, pointing to the closest.

'A palm on the panel, an eye to the scanner,' said Cristy.

'Really?' said Claire, hesitating.

'Go ahead,' said Cristy. 'Either palm, either eye.'

---

1 **vertigo** *(n)* whirling sensation. *(s)* dizziness, giddiness.

2 **alight** *(v)* descend from something. *(s)* dismount, disembark, exit. *(ant)* embark.

3 **robust** *(adj)* healthy and strong. *(s)* vigorous, tough, hardy, stout, sturdy, powerful. *(ant)* weak, feeble.

4 **barrier** *(n)* an obstacle to prevent movement through or across. *(s)* obstruction, boundary, limit.

5 **partially** *(adv)* to a partial (limited) extent. *(s)* partly, somewhat, moderately. *(ant)* completely, totally.

6 **uniformly** *(adv)* in a uniform (constant) manner. *(s)* consistently, systematically, identically. *(ant)* inconsistently.

7 **perplexed** *(adj)* completely confused. *(s)* baffled, confounded, foxed, flummoxed, bemused. *(ant)* enlightened.

8 **dither** *(v)* act indecisively or waver between. *(s)* hesitate, dally, dawdle, teeter, vacillate, fluctuate. *(ant)* decide.

As if fearing **electrocution**[1], Claire placed a **tentative**[2] right palm on the panel beside the door. She leaned her left eye in towards the retinal scanner. That warm sensation tingled through her hand again, accompanied by a slight whir. Then the door slid silently sideways.

'What the …?' exclaimed Claire.

Seeing Claire's face fall, Cristy said, 'That's so **typical**[3]. Sorry, you chose the skate park, Claire. These doors conceal different rec rooms. You'll have a blast today, guys.'

'Man, how cool is this?' said Ben, **barging**[4] past Claire and stepping into the vast, **bustling**[5] room.

Loud music **blared**[6] and a deep **bass**[7] **resonated**[8]. **Funky**[9] young people whooshed around a half-pipe. They scooted across bowls and rails, jumping and grabbing their boards.

'You have an indoor skate park?' shouted Ben above the noise. Ben's eyes scanned the whole room, his face beaming.

Are they on their lunch hour? thought Claire, thinking how her mum grabbed a pasty from Greggs on hers.

'We do,' answered Cristy. 'Go put your gear in a locker. You can skate later, once you've eaten.' She winked at a **grateful**[10] Claire.

I like Cristy, Claire decided. *She's cool. She's OK.*

'Ben, you can choose another rec door later,' Cristy said as they left. 'That door at the end is the VIP restaurant, and we're in for a real treat there,' she finished, striding ahead and lighting their way.

Claire felt like Alice trapped down the rabbit hole. **Nevertheless**[11], the **imminent**[12] promise

---

1 **electrocution** *(n)* injury or death caused by electric shock.

2 **tentative** *(adj)* done without confidence. *(s)* cautious, hesitating, faltering, reluctant, unsure. *(ant)* sure, certain.

3 **typical** *(adj)* characteristic of something. *(s)* regular, normal, standard. *(ant)* atypical, aberrant.

4 **barge** *(v)* move forcefully or roughly. *(s)* rush, charge, burst, surge, push, shove, jostle, elbow. *(ant)* pull, glide.

5 **bustling** *(adj)* (of a place) full of people and activity. *(s)* busy, vibrant, hectic, lively. *(ant)* deserted, empty.

6 **blare** *(v)* make a loud sound. *(s)* boom, roar, blast, bellow. *(ant)* murmur, whisper.

7 **bass** *(n)* the low-frequency output of an audio system.

8 **resonate** *(v)* (of a sound) cause to prolong, echo or resound. *(s)* reverberate, vibrate, oscillate.

9 **funky** *(adj)* stylish and contemporary. *(s)* trendy, hip, fly, fashionable, supercool. *(ant)* old-fashioned, outmoded, square.

10 **grateful** *(adj)* feeling or showing appreciation for something. *(s)* thankful, glad, appreciative. *(ant)* ungrateful.

11 **nevertheless** *(adv)* all the same. *(s)* however, even so, nonetheless.

12 **imminent** *(adj)* about to happen. *(s)* pending, expected, looming, forthcoming, likely, immediate. *(ant)* remote.

of food distracted her as she followed Cristy along the corridor. Facing the **furthermost**[1] door, Cristy performed the **obligatory**[2] palm–eye **routine**[3], and it slid sideways.

The **divine**[4] **aroma**[5] hit Claire's nostrils at once. A **heavenly**[6] mixture of roasting meats, baking bread and pastries swirled in the air. The room was so **tranquil**[7] her stomach growled above the silence. Claire and Ben exchanged excited glances as they crossed the **threshold**[8] into the quiet, luxurious surroundings. Tables adorned with crisp white cloths and **arrays**[9] of glassware and **cutlery**[10] sat dotted at **discreet**[11] distances apart. **Classical**[12] music drifted through the air, fittingly loud enough to please but not to disturb.

'Cristy, isn't this a bit posh for us?' whispered Claire, suddenly anxious.

'Absolutely not,' replied Cristy. 'You're as welcome as any guest of Via-Corp. We don't **discriminate**[13] on grounds of age, **attire**[14] or **wealth**[15].' She **gestured**[16] towards the diners in the room.

Claire glanced around, relieved the **clientele**[17] wasn't all men in stuffy suits and ties. Folks of all ages and outfits dined. Many were young, dressed like Claire and Ben, in jeans, hoodies and trainers, as though they'd just left the skate park too.

'Coolio,' Claire mumbled to Ben, relaxing **a tad**[18] and following Cristy and a waiter to their table.

---

1 **furthermost** *(adj)* situated at the greatest distance from some point. *(s)* furthest, last. *(ant)* nearest.

2 **obligatory** *(adj)* required or expected. *(s)* essential, compulsory, mandatory. *(ant)* optional, voluntary.

3 **routine** *(n)* a regular sequence of actions. *(s)* pattern, practice, drill, regime, method, formula, plan.

4 **divine** *(adj)* incredibly pleasing. *(s)* delightful, beautiful, ravishing, exquisite, dazzling. *(ant)* unsatisfactory.

5 **aroma** *(n)* distinctive, typically pleasant smell. *(s)* bouquet, scent, perfume. *(ant)* stench, stink, reek.

6 **heavenly** *(adj)* of heaven. *(s)* divine, stellar, saintly, blessed. *(ant)* hellish, unbearable.

7 **tranquil** *(adj)* calm. *(s)* quiet, serene, peaceful, restful. *(ant)* busy, noisy.

8 **threshold** *(n)* a doorway or other point of entrance.

9 **array** *(n)* a significant display or range of something. *(s)* selection, arrangement, group. *(ant)* individual, one.

10 **cutlery** *(n)* utensils (items) used for eating and serving food. *(s)* knives, forks, spoons.

11 **discreet** *(adj)* showing prudence and restraint. *(s)* restrained, judicious, considerate. *(ant)* indiscreet.

12 **classical** *(adj)* representing a long-established, proven style. *(s)* traditional, orthodox. *(ant)* new, novel.

13 **discriminate** *(v)* judge or treat unfairly. *(s)* show prejudice, disfavour, victimise.

14 **attire** *(n)* clothes. *(s)* clothing, dress, outfit, apparel, garb, garments, wardrobe.

15 **wealth** *(n)* money or possessions. *(s)* riches, means, affluence, fortune. *(ant)* poverty.

16 **gesture** *(v)* move (usually the head or hand) to express something. *(s)* gesticulate, signal, nod.

17 **clientele** *(n)* customers. *(s)* patronage, consumers.

18 **a tad** *(adv)* by a small amount or extent. *(s)* a touch, somewhat, slightly. *(ant)* profoundly, considerably.

'Let me.' The waiter smiled, pulling out Claire's chair. She yanked her backpack from her shoulders and dropped it beside her. It hit the **marble**[1] floor with an unexpected metallic clunk.

Huh? thought Claire, pulling the handle to straighten up her bag. *What was that sound?*

She sat and took the menu proffered by the waiter, then bent to pick up her school bag again. 'Need a tissue.' She waved one apologetically, then, with a purpose, dropped her bag back onto the floor. *Clunk!*

Ben and Cristy studied their menus **intently**[2]. Claire's sat on the table; she had barely glanced at it.

'Claire, what you gonna have?' Ben asked, looking **enthusiastic**[3].

'You guys have the younger-persons' menu, but you can check out the adult version if you like, although I suspect you'll prefer the food on yours,' Cristy said, smiling at the waiter, who nodded in **accord**[4].

Claire tried to concentrate, but the menu's contents hardly **registered**[5].

'I'll have the Monster Welsh Beefburger with fat cheese fries and all the **trimmings**[6], please,' said Ben, licking his lips.

'Claire?' asked Cristy.

'Oh, um, that sounds ace. I'll have the same, please.' Claire had no clue what she'd agreed to order. 'Cristy, where are the loos?' Claire asked. 'I'm bursting.'

'Over there, to the right.' Cristy gestured, waving her menu towards the toilets.

'Thanks.' Claire swooped up her bag and made a **beeline**[7] for the loos.

Once there, Claire barely noticed the lavish opulence of the bathroom: its **exquisitely**[8] **blended**[9] toiletries, the fluffy Egyptian cotton towels adorning the washbasins, and the

---

1 **marble** *(n)* polished (shined) limestone (a type of rock), often used decoratively.
2 **intently** *(adv)* in an intent (eager) way. *(s)* closely, keenly, earnestly, attentively. *(ant)* casually, absently.
3 **enthusiastic** *(adj)* eager. *(s)* keen, excited, fervent, animated, exuberant. *(ant)* apathetic, indifferent.
4 **accord** *(n)* agreement. *(s)* harmony. *(ant)* disagreement, discord.
5 **register** *(v)* make an impression (mark) on one's mind. *(s)* enter, penetrate, sink in. *(ant)* erase.
6 **trimmings** *(n)* extras that accompany a meal. *(s)* accompaniments, garnish, frills.
7 **beeline** *(n)* a direct route between two places.
8 **exquisitely** *(adv)* in an exquisite (perfect and beautiful) way. *(s)* flawlessly, supremely, elegantly. *(ant)* crudely.
9 **blend** *(v)* mix together. *(s)* combine, unite, join, incorporate. *(ant)* clash.

decadent[1] heated toilet seats. She locked herself in a cubicle and **rifled**[2] through her school bag, her heart pounding her ribs. She threw her crumpled coat onto the floor and continued emptying the bag's contents. Claire had checked her bag this morning, and like then, it now revealed nothing untoward, just the usual **miscellany**[3] she'd packed after her dad had given it back to her. She dropped it once more. *Clunk!* There was that metallic sound again as the bag hit the marble tiles.

Ah, the hidden zip pocket, I always forget that. I bet it's coins I ***stashed***[4] *away to buy sweets,* thought Claire, relieved. Scooping up the bag, she located the tucked-away zip hidden from view. Tugging hard at it, she tried to open the zip, but its teeth caught the lining. 'Argh!' she growled, pulling harder both ways, but it didn't budge.

Perched on the loo seat, Claire turned the bag inside out for a better view and began teasing the **fabric**[5] out of the zip's teeth. With tentative wiggles, she eased open the zip, one tooth at a time. Recoiling, she dropped the bag. Another clunk.

'No way! No way!' she whispered to herself, over and over.

Her hands shook violently, her breath coming in rapid bursts.

'No way!' she repeated, **hyperventilating**[6].

Claire stared at the backpack and its **discarded**[7] contents, **strewn**[8] across the cubicle floor. She reached for the bag and, trembling, placed it **gingerly**[9] onto her lap, taking out the coins that were indeed partly **culpable**[10]. However, the source of her intense **consternation**[11] wasn't the coins. It was the item that had clunked against the floor that paralysed her now.

She lifted the golden piece from the zip pocket and held it in her palm. It was heavier than

---

1 **decadent** *(adj)* luxurious and self-indulgent (spoiling oneself). *(s)* hedonistic, deluxe. *(ant)* restrained.

2 **rifle** *(v)* search through something in a hasty way. *(s)* hunt, rummage, scour, rake.

3 **miscellany** *(n)* a group or mixture of different items. *(s)* assortment, collection, array, variety. *(ant)* uniformity.

4 **stash** *(v)* keep in a hidden place. *(s)* hide, conceal, stow, secrete, hoard. *(ant)* reveal, unpack.

5 **fabric** *(n)* cloth. *(s)* fibre, material, textile, drapery.

6 **hyperventilate** *(v)* breathe rapidly in an anxious or excited way. *(s)* overbreathe, pant, gasp. *(ant)* suffocate.

7 **discarded** *(adj)* thrown aside, as no longer useful or desirable. *(s)* abandoned, dumped, ditched. *(ant)* retained.

8 **strew** *(v)* scatter or spread things untidily. *(s)* throw, cast, distribute, toss, litter. *(ant)* gather, assemble.

9 **gingerly** *(adv)* in a careful manner. *(s)* cautiously, delicately, tentatively, warily, gently. *(ant)* boldly, rashly.

10 **culpable** *(adj)* deserving of the blame. *(s)* guilty, responsible, accountable, liable, answerable. *(ant)* innocent, blameless.

11 **consternation** *(n)* a feeling of dismay or worry, distress, perturbation, angst, trepidation. *(ant)* satisfaction.

it looked. Claire stared, almost afraid to inspect it. It appeared to have lost its **allure**[1] since she'd seen it in the cracked glass case yesterday, its **spirit**[2] and **verve**[3] dead. That made complete sense, because the stunning piece now sitting in her palm no longer housed the **unique**[4] hawk-shaped emerald, the Gwalch Gem. It was gone.

1 **allure** *(n)* a mysterious fascination or attraction. *(s)* magnetism, charm, appeal. *(ant)* repulsion.

2 **spirit** *(n)* a prevalent quality or attitude. *(s)* essence, substance.

3 **verve** *(n)* enthusiasm. *(s)* spirit, vigour, energy, vitality, zest, zeal.

4 **unique** *(adj)* unlike anything else. *(s)* exclusive, distinctive, particular, individual, one-off. *(ant)* common.

4. Plastic Palm Print

'Claire, you OK? You look like you've seen a ghost,' Cristy asked.

'Seems I didn't just *feel* travel sick,' said Claire, sitting back at the table.

'Oh no! You barfed?' asked Ben through a mouthful of food.

'I was thinking about a search party,' said Cristy.

'I'm OK,' said Claire. 'Just needed a minute.'

'That reminds me,' said Cristy. 'Here, take my spare cell phone. I doubt you'll need it, but press any number, and you'll come straight through to me. I'll **override**[1] my retinal ID while you guys are here, or the phone won't **function**[2] correctly,' she added, handing Claire an ultra-slim, **unbranded**[3] mobile. 'To switch it on, just look at it.'

Ben, meanwhile, stuffed his face with olives, **crudités**[4] and bread. Claire's appetite had vanished. The waiter glided over and placed an oversized plate of food in front of her.

'Thank you,' she said.

'Claire, you can put your bag on the floor and eat something,' said Cristy in a concerned voice.

'Sorry,' replied Claire. 'I'm still feeling icky. I doubt I'll manage this lot.'

'I will!' said Ben, attacking his burger **voraciously**[5].

Claire put the phone into her bag and placed it on the floor, gripping it tightly between her

---

1 **override** *(v)* cancel the action of. *(s)* interrupt, revoke, suspend. *(ant)* permit, allow, clear.

2 **function** *(v)* work in a specific way. *(s)* operate, run, perform. *(ant)* malfunction.

3 **unbranded** *(adj)* (of a product) without a brand name. *(s)* unlabelled. *(ant)* branded, labelled.

4 **crudités** *(n)* raw vegetables often served with a sauce (dip).

5 **voraciously** *(adv)* in a voracious (greedy) manner. *(s)* ravenously, insatiably, hungrily. *(ant)* contentedly.

feet. She poked her food with her fork and **gnawed**[1] at a few chips, but with her current lack of appetite, they tasted like **sawdust**[2].

What do I do now? Claire's mind whirled.

Gladys's words struck her again: *Cadwaladr will watch over you.*

What if Gwilym dies? What if he's already dead? she thought, remembering the **gruesome**[3] scene in the glass **cabinet**[4] and her dream once more. *Did Jayne put the bracelet in my bag, or was it perhaps Mrs Evans? Who else could have put it there? What if Jack's dead, and Gladys too?*

'I'm sorry, but I've got to revisit the loo,' said Claire, grabbing her bag.

'Shame to leave these,' said Ben nonchalantly, tucking into Claire's fries.

Claire locked herself into a cubicle again and sat on the loo, her thoughts racing.

OK. OK. What can I do? she asked herself.

She reached into her bag and took out the Gwalch Gem bracelet, carefully wrapping it in toilet paper before zipping it away into her coat pocket. She folded her coat and placed it into her bag, did a wee and left the restroom, forgetting to wash her hands.

'Sorry,' Claire said with a half smile, returning to the table. 'I'm better now,' she lied.

'Shall we get you something else?' asked Cristy. 'Your burger's cold, and Ben's **demolished**[5] your fries,' she joked with a look of feigned **admonishment**[6].

'Could I get a takeaway sandwich, please?' asked Claire.

'Sure,' replied Cristy, beckoning to the waiter.

'What would you like?' Cristy asked.

'What is there?' asked Claire.

'Pretty much whatever you imagine would fit between two pieces of bread,' laughed Cristy.

'Cucumber butty, then, please. No butter,' said Claire.

'What? Just boring cucumber?' quizzed an astonished Ben.

---

1 **gnaw** *(v)* chew persistently. *(s)* bite, nibble, champ, chomp, masticate, munch, crunch.

2 **sawdust** *(n)* powdery particles produced by the sawing of wood.

3 **gruesome** *(adj)* causing horror. *(s)* grisly, hideous, ghastly, fearful, macabre. *(ant)* pleasant.

4 **cabinet** *(n)* a unit for storing or displaying articles. *(s)* case, cupboard, dresser, closet, chest, locker, container.

5 **demolish** *(v)* (of food) eat quickly. *(s)* guzzle, devour, gobble, wolf down. *(ant)* pick, nibble.

6 **admonishment** *(n)* a reprimand or warning. *(s)* rebuke, scolding, chiding, reproach. *(ant)* praise.

'Something **bland**[1], nothing fatty,' Claire added, pointing to her stomach **solemnly**[2] and trying her **utmost**[3] to appear normal. Food was the last thing she wanted right now.

The waiter cleared their plates and returned with a lavish pudding for Ben and a cling-film-wrapped package for Claire.

'Thanks,' Claire said gratefully, placing the sandwich into her bag. 'I'm feeling so much better now. I can't wait to see which rec room door Ben chooses,' she added with a wide grin, and **shuffled**[4] forward to the edge of her chair, her shiny enthusiasm totally phoney.

'I'm stuffed,' said Ben, spooning in his sticky toffee pudding and Welsh vanilla ice cream. 'No way I can skate yet, so I'd better choose a less energetic door,' he said, laughing.

'Greedy piglet!' said Claire.

'OK, there's no bill to pay, so I'm off to the bathroom. Two ticks,' said Cristy, pushing back her chair and heading off.

'That was amazing,' said Ben, leaning back and patting his taut stomach. 'Honestly, I can't move. I need an old-man snooze,' he said.

'You can sleep tonight,' Claire **insisted**[5]. 'I want to see those other rec rooms,' she added, standing up and fixing her backpack over both shoulders.

'Hark at you!' said Ben. 'Miss I'm Fine Now.'

Claire felt guilty for giving Ben such mixed messages, but she must act fast. The gemless bracelet was in her bag, and she wasn't about to wait around to see if her **premonition**[6] of Gwilym shattering would come true.

'Ready, you guys?' asked Cristy, striding back over to them. She left a **hefty**[7] **tip**[8] on the table and beckoned the kids to follow her. 'Back to "Door or No Door",' Cristy giggled.

Cristy opened the sliding door using the palm reader, and they left the restaurant into the light-up-as-you-walk corridor.

---

1 **bland** *(adj)* lacking flavour or interest. *(s)* flavourless, insipid, tasteless, dull. *(ant)* tasty, interesting.

2 **solemnly** *(adv)* in a solemn (honest) way. *(s)* formally, sincerely, earnestly. *(ant)* insincerely.

3 **utmost** *(n)* the most extreme extent or amount. *(s)* greatest, best, supreme, maximum, uttermost. *(ant)* least.

4 **shuffle** *(v)* shift one's position. *(s)* budge.

5 **insist** *(v)* demand forcefully without allowing refusal. *(s)* command, assert, urge.

6 **premonition** *(n)* a feeling that something is about happen. *(s)* forewarning, intuition, hunch.

7 **hefty** *(adj)* large. *(s)* big, sizable, ample, substantial. *(ant)* little, paltry.

8 **tip** *(n)* money given in thanks for a service. *(s)* gratuity, gift, reward.

'OK, Ben. Eyes on the prize,' said Claire. 'Which door is it going to be?' she asked, giving him a playful prod. 'And don't choose the skate park,' Claire added, rolling her eyes upwards.

'Ip dip doo, doggy did a poo,' laughed Ben.

'You're kidding me!' said Claire.

'Only joking!' he teased. 'This one,' he said, beaming at Cristy.

'Go on, then, Ben,' said Cristy. 'Open it.'

Ben pressed his palm against the panel and looked into the scanner, and sure enough, the door slid sideways.

'Yes!' shouted Ben.

The door opened to reveal a **myriad**[1] of flashing machines. Pinball tables and driving arcades stood amongst rows of giant screens. People balanced on **elevated**[2] platforms, wearing **futuristic**[3] **virtual-reality**[4] masks, their heads pivoting, **immersed**[5] in their imaginary digital worlds.

'Wow! I'm so gonna work here when I'm older,' remarked Ben.

'OK, guys. I'm responsible for you two,' said Cristy. 'Strictly speaking, this room is off-limits to **minors**[6], but I'm trusting John Brady's boy,' she **declared**[7] with a wink at Ben. Cristy glanced at her watch. 'I must join the team for a while. You guys have rec and restaurant access only, so you can go eat more, if you can fit it in, Ben,' she finished.

'Cristy, can you come in with us for a minute or two?' asked Claire, appearing **intimidated**[8].

'Sure,' replied Cristy, smiling. 'Let me show you how a couple of things work.'

'Can we play pinball first? I kind of know that,' asked Claire, heading over to a flashing machine.

'Sure,' replied Cristy.

'Can you remind me how to do it?' asked Claire.

Ben had wandered elsewhere.

---

1 **myriad** *(n)* extremely great number. *(s)* multitude, mass, crowd, horde. *(ant)* handful.

2 **elevated** *(adj)* raised or in a higher position. *(s)* heightened, lifted, hoisted, aloft. *(ant)* lowered, dropped.

3 **futuristic** *(adj)* involving or having modern technology or design. *(s)* innovative, revolutionary. *(ant)* outdated.

4 **virtual reality** *(n)* computer-generated, interactive, three-dimensional imagery that is often viewed with a helmet or mask.

5 **immerse** *(v)* involve oneself deeply in. *(s)* absorb, engross, engage, occupy, steep. *(ant)* withdraw, remove.

6 **minor** *(n)* a person who is below the age of full legal responsibility. *(s)* child, youth, adolescent. *(ant)* adult.

7 **declare** *(v)* say in a serious and clear manner. *(s)* proclaim, announce, state, assert, affirm. *(ant)* withhold.

8 **intimidate** *(v)* force or frighten into submission. *(s)* threaten, bully, menace, overawe. *(ant)* assure.

Cristy rested both palms on the pinball machine, **sizing it up**[1], then **depressed**[2] the side buttons, aggressively shooting the white ball up into the **obstacle**[3] course.

'You press these buttons, which pull on the flaps, and keep going, so your ball doesn't fly into the **gully**[4],' laughed Cristy, but she was taking her game seriously.

'Wow, you're good,' remarked Claire, wide-eyed.

'**Misspent**[5] youth,' Cristy laughed, again.

'Claire, Claire, you gotta see this VR stuff!' cried Ben, running over and pointing at someone whose face was **shrouded**[6] in a black helmet.

'OK. I'll be over with you and Darth Vader in a second,' laughed Claire, with her **customary**[7] eye roll, as he disappeared back to the VR machines.

'Ahhh, it got me!' laughed Cristy, flicking the flippers with **indignation**[8]. 'Time for me to go,' she said, slapping her palms onto the machine.

'I'll see you both later,' said Cristy, with a wave in Ben's direction.

'Yeah, see you later,' said Claire, removing her backpack and checking where Ben was.

Shielding the pinball machine so no one else could use it, Claire opened her bag, **casually**[9] took out the cucumber sandwich and carefully unwrapped it. She scanned the room, leaned against the machine and took a bite. She hated cucumber **with a vengeance**[10], but it had been the safest bet. Risking any grease on the inside of the cling film would have **defeated**[11] the object of her plan. She bent and slid the other half of the **insipid**[12] sandwich underneath the pinball machine, out of view. She turned around and fiddled with the flippers, **retching**[13] as she

---

1 **size up** *(v)* form a vague judgement of something or someone. *(s)* suss out, inspect, examine, scrutinise.

2 **depress** *(v)* pull or push into a lower position. *(s)* activate, press, operate. *(ant)* lift.

3 **obstacle** *(n)* something that obstructs progress or blocks the way. *(s)* barrier, hurdle. *(ant)* asset, aid.

4 **gully** *(n)* a channel (groove). *(s)* trench, cut, gutter, flume, depression.

5 **misspent** *(adj)* spent wastefully. *(s)* wasted, squandered, profitless. *(ant)* profitable, fruitful.

6 **shroud** *(v)* envelop or cover to prevent from being seen. *(s)* conceal, mask, hide, veil, swathe. *(ant)* reveal.

7 **customary** *(adj)* usual or typical. *(s)* expected, habitual, characteristic. *(ant)* unusual, uncharacteristic.

8 **indignation** *(n)* anger caused by something unfair. *(s)* resentment, distress, discontent. *(ant)* contentment.

9 **casually** *(adv)* in a casual (relaxed and informal) manner. *(s)* nonchalantly, informally. *(ant)* formally.

10 **with a vengeance** *(adv)* with intensity (force, strength). *(s)* vigorously, powerfully, fiercely. *(ant)* mildly.

11 **defeat** *(v)* beat in a conflict. *(s)* conquer, vanquish, pulverise, overpower. *(ant)* lose to.

12 **insipid** *(adj)* lacking flavour. *(s)* tasteless, bland, unflavoured, unpalatable. *(ant)* tasty.

13 **retch** *(v)* make the motion and sound of vomiting. *(s)* reach, heave, gag, convulse.

swallowed down the sandwich.

After checking the coast was clear, Claire opened out the cling film, gently shaking it to rid it of crumbs. She laid it flat on top of the pinball machine, taking care to handle only its four corners. This was a long shot but the only one she had; she must get a **decent**[1] print from the machine first time.

To prevent **contamination**[2] from her hands, Claire put on her school gloves, gently smoothing the plastic onto the glass, trying not to wrinkle it further. Then she flipped it over, keeping it flat, and placed it into the top of her bag. She removed her gloves and shoved them into her jeans pocket. Claire put on her backpack and headed over to Ben.

'Come on,' she said. 'We're leaving.'

'Why?' replied Ben, shocked. 'We've only just got here,' he protested.

'Come on!' she said, tugging at his hoody.

'You wanna try another door?' he asked.

'Sort of,' she replied.

They reached the games room door.

'Who does the palmy–eye thing?' asked Ben. 'Do we both do it?'

'I dunno,' she said. 'Give it a go.'

Ben **did the honours**[3], and the door slid open.

'Why all this security stuff?' asked Ben. 'Not that great if one of us can open doors for the other,' he remarked.

'Mmm,' murmured Claire. 'We're in the rec area though, aren't we? We've got access here. Who knows what it's like elsewhere?'

'True,' said Ben. 'Fancy the skate park again?'

'I do not!' said Claire, her tone **emphatic**[4]. 'Follow me!' Claire didn't know where she was going, but the lifts were a good place to start, if they could find one.

'These lights are a real pain,' she moaned as they walked along the rec area corridor. 'Why can't they switch on and stay lit?'

---

1 **decent** *(adj)* of a satisfactory standard. *(s)* reasonable, adequate, acceptable. *(ant)* unsatisfactory.

2 **contamination** *(n)* the act of polluting or infecting. *(s)* spoiling, soiling, dirtying, poisoning. *(ant)* purification.

3 **do the honours** *(v)* carry out a social obligation. *(s)* oblige. *(ant)* disobey.

4 **emphatic** *(adj)* expressing something explicitly and firmly. *(s)* forcible, forceful, vehement, direct. *(ant)* tentative, hesitant.

'Are you gonna choose a door, Moaning Minnie?' said Ben.

'I have,' replied Claire. 'That one at the end, up there.' She pointed to the opposite end of the corridor as it lit up.

'We can't use that. It won't open,' said Ben. 'Doesn't it lead back into the Hive?' he asked.

'Yep,' said Claire, 'it does.'

Ben followed her, looking bewildered.

'What *are* you doing?' he asked once they'd reached the end of the corridor. Claire was kneeling and opening her backpack. She took out the piece of cling film so carefully, as if it might explode, and laid it on the floor beside her.

'Getting us out of rec prison so I can help my friends,' she replied.

'What?' asked Ben, his face screwed up.

Claire didn't answer but laid her bag face down, flat on the floor. She picked up the cling film and laid it out on the back of her bag. Her heart thumped. If someone came now, it would **scupper**[1] them. Claire could spin a quick **yarn**[2], but it would be difficult to hide the cling film without ruining it.

Ben watched, **agog**[3]. 'What on earth are you doing?'

'Shush!' she commanded, fishing a glove from her pocket and laying it next to the cling film. She stared at both objects, her eyes narrowing, her lips pressed together.

'Is it big enough?' she asked herself, picking up the glove and wriggling her hand into it. Then, with precise movements, she spread her fingers and pressed her palm onto the cling film.

'Ben,' she said, making him jump, 'wrap the **excess**[4] cling film up and around the back of my hand so it meets, so you are sticking it into place on the back of the glove. Do you get what I mean?' she asked as he stood in puzzled silence. 'Do you get it?' she barked.

'Yeah! Yeah, I think so,' he said, kneeling by the bag. 'I think so.'

'Be careful,' she warned. 'You rip it; you ruin it.'

Ben's hands trembled as he picked up both sides of the **flimsy**[5] plastic and lifted them up and

---

1 **scupper** *(v)* prevent from working or succeeding. *(s)* ruin, wreck, foil, spoil, stymie. *(ant)* help, facilitate.

2 **yarn** *(n)* a far-fetched story. *(s)* tale, lie, anecdote, alibi, line. *(ant)* truth.

3 **agog** *(adj)* keen or curious. *(s)* impatient, excited, eager, intrigued. *(ant)* uninterested.

4 **excess** *(adj)* exceeding what is necessary. *(s)* surplus, extra, redundant, spare. *(ant)* insufficient.

5 **flimsy** *(adj)* light and easily damaged. *(s)* insubstantial, fragile, delicate, slight. *(ant)* substantial, robust.

over the back of her gloved hand to join them together.

'I hope it reaches,' said Claire, 'or it won't stick. You're aiming to create a kind of **mitten**[1] from the plastic, which fits over the glove.'

'Yeah, got it,' said Ben, his face fixed in **concentration**[2] as he fiddled with the **fragile**[3] plastic.

'Yes!' he said, **triumphantly**[4] sticking the pieces of plastic together on the back of her hand.

'Now, take the flappy extra bit underneath my fingers and fold it over them so it makes a plastic mitten.'

'Like this?' asked Ben.

'Perfect,' she said, lifting her hand to inspect it. 'Fits like a glove!' she laughed, but inside she prayed her **jury-rigged**[5] **invention**[6] would work.

Claire got to her feet. The corridor behind them was in complete darkness; only where they stood was lit. Although darkish, she was sure Via-Corp digitally recorded everything. This whole place was like one **colossal**[7] computer.

'Ben, you wear my backpack for a bit. I can't put it on. I don't want to ruin this,' she said, waving her plastic-coated hand. 'Here goes,' she said, placing the cling film mitten onto the palm reader. She felt sure it took longer, but the door slid open to reveal another thick glass panel and the Hive on the other side of it.

'**Bingo**[8]!' Claire muttered.

'What's going on?' whispered Ben. 'You're scaring me.'

'I'm trying something,' Claire replied, praying Cristy's greasy palm print on the cling film would be enough to get them through the glass barrier before them and into the Hive. 'I'm not sure it will work,' she said just as the glass panel swooshed sideways. They both stepped out onto the metal ledge.

---

1 **mitten** *(n)* a glove with one section for the thumb, and another for the four fingers.

2 **concentration** *(n)* the act of focusing all attention. *(s)* application, awareness, attentiveness. *(ant)* inattention.

3 **fragile** *(adj)* easily broken or damaged. *(s)* delicate, flimsy, brittle, breakable, weak. *(ant)* sturdy, robust.

4 **triumphantly** *(adv)* in a triumphant (joyful after winning) manner. *(s)* gleefully, successfully, victoriously. *(ant)* hopelessly.

5 **jury-rigged** *(adj)* makeshift. *(s)* make-do, crude, rough, unrefined. *(ant)* refined.

6 **invention** *(n)* something made for the first time. *(s)* innovation, creation, contrivance.

7 **colossal** *(adj)* exceptionally large or great. *(s)* gargantuan, immense, huge, mammoth. *(ant)* little, small.

8 **bingo** *(int)* used to express pleasure at a sudden favourable outcome or event.

'Pull up your hood,' she said, lifting hers. 'Then we'll look like everyone else working here. Now, where are the lifts?'

5. Telling Ben

'What's happening? You're *really* scaring me,' Ben whispered.

They strode **purposefully**[1] through the glass walkway but with heads down.

'Best not to **skulk**[2]. Act **confidently**[3],' Claire said. 'Pretend to chat with me and smile.'

'I *am* trying to chat!' replied Ben. 'Tell me what's happening.'

'You won't believe me,' she replied.

'Try me,' he insisted, his voice pleading. 'You're a different person today. You're doing my head in!'

'OK! OK! Let's get through this part first though. Can you spot a lift?' Claire asked.

'I think there's one over there, where we came in with my dad.'

'Were there lifts on the other side of the security room?' **queried**[4] Claire.

'Oh yes, there were!' said Ben.

'They can't be too far away, then; should be on the same side,' said Claire. 'Let's head that way.'

A passing employee raised his eyes from his phone and nodded at them.

'We're so gonna get busted,' Ben said once he'd walked past.

'I know,' replied Claire.

They stepped out of the glass tube, onto a metal platform and then onto another transparent walkway, heading to a lower level.

'These suspended tube-ways freak me out,' whispered Claire. 'There's a lift down there, on

---

1 **purposefully** *(adv)* in a purposeful (determined) way. *(s)* firmly, steadfastly, resolutely. *(ant)* aimlessly, irresolutely.

2 **skulk** *(v)* move furtively and stealthily, not wanting to be seen. *(s)* lurk, prowl, loiter. *(ant)* appear, materialise.

3 **confidently** *(adv)* in a confident (certain) manner. *(s)* assuredly, positively. *(ant)* timidly, meekly.

4 **query** *(v)* question. *(s)* enquire, ask, probe, grill, quiz, interrogate. *(ant)* answer.

that level. What do you reckon?'

'Worth a try,' he said. 'But what *are* we doing?'

'Trying to save my uncle,' she replied.

'What?' he exclaimed. 'Uncle? I didn't even know you *had* an uncle.'

'Me neither, not until yesterday,' she said. 'I didn't skip school to go to that museum. I got a train to Wales with Jack to meet Gladys.'

'Gladys? What's Gladys got to do with this? What are you on about?' asked Ben, his face **incredulous**[1].

'I hope it's a lift, and I hope we can open it,' said Claire, distracted, as they stepped off the glass onto metal again. 'Stand here. Shield my glove from the worker bees' view,' she said, referring to the employees behind glass in their hollowed-out-of-rock offices. Nobody looked the least bit concerned about Claire and Ben's presence. Claire placed her gloved palm to the panel, and the door moved sideways to reveal the inside of a lift.

'Thank goodness on both counts. Come on,' she said as the door closed behind them, to the sounds of familiar cheesy music.

'How come it's opening without doing the eye thing?' asked Ben.

'Cristy **disabled**[2] her retinal ID when she gave me her phone in the restaurant,' said Claire. 'To turn the phone on, I just have to look at it, so I guess it works with my ID now.'

'David Lewis,' Claire ordered, remembering Mr Brady had said 'Rec' to the lift earlier, but this time the lift remained **stationary**[3]. 'Jayne Lewis,' she tried, but nothing.

'Do something!' **implored**[4] Ben.

Claire's face burned. 'Boss!' she blurted, trying the **epithet**[5] Mr Brady had used, and thankfully, the lift began gliding downwards.

'What do you mean, you got a train to Wales to meet Gladys?' asked Ben, picking up the conversation where he'd left off.

---

1 **incredulous** *(adj)* not able to believe, unbelieving. *(s)* sceptical, doubtful, unconvinced. *(ant)* believing.

2 **disable** *(v)* render (put) out of action. *(s)* incapacitate, debilitate, immobilise, cripple. *(ant)* enable.

3 **stationary** *(adj)* not moving. *(s)* still, motionless, stopped, immobile, halted. *(ant)* moving.

4 **implore** *(v)* plead or beg desperately. *(s)* beseech, pray, entreat, appeal. *(ant)* offer.

5 **epithet** *(n)* a descriptive name used instead of a real name. *(s)* nickname, name, title, tag, description.

'That's just the **small fry**[1],' answered Claire. 'An RAF fighter jet **escorted**[2] us, and I flew back home in a helicopter, which landed at Old Trafford,' she said **flippantly**[3]. 'Oh, and this will make you die! I think I can mind-read, at least sometimes.'

'Have you gone mad?' asked Ben.

'Nope! All true! It sounds mega **far-fetched**[4], I know, but it's true. Even crazier is Gladys isn't from Lancashire; she's Welsh, *but* she's a Welsh knight.'

'You've defo lost it,' remarked Ben, shaking his head **vigorously**[5].

'She's been alive since the *twelfth century*. Her brother – I'm not sure if he's her real brother – Gwilym, is my so-called *uncle*, and he's a knight too, a Knight Hawk. He's their leader.'

With his mouth **agape**[6], Ben's face **portrayed**[7] a picture of shock and **incredulity**[8].

'Then there's this magical bracelet,' she said, eyeing her backpack, which was still on Ben's shoulders. 'The bracelet has untold powers, stuff I don't understand. Honestly, Ben, they can even mess up *time* with it. Prince Llywelyn used it to give his loyal knights long life – longevity, I think it's called – but the thing is, I think the bracelet might be killing the knights now.' She stopped, out of breath.

Ben didn't speak; he stared at her, his eyes confused with astonishment and disbelief.

'Ben, you trust me, right? Everything's true, and there's more, much more. That's why we're here now, because of the Master.'

'The Master, a prince and a magical bracelet?' said Ben, crinkling up his face and shaking his head.

'I'll prove it to you later, but I think there are cameras everywhere. The Master is a complete **lunatic**[9], and I have a **hunch**[10] who he might be,' said Claire.

---

1 **small fry** *(n)* unimportant people or things. *(s)* trivia, trifles, subordinates, small-timers. *(ant)* bigwigs, essentials.

2 **escort** *(v)* accompany (go with) someone somewhere. *(s)* shepherd, chaperone, lead, direct. *(ant)* abandon.

3 **flippantly** *(adv)* in a disrespectful or unserious way. *(s)* frivolously, offhandedly, jokingly, cheekily. *(ant)* seriously.

4 **far-fetched** *(adj)* unlikely. *(s)* implausible, unconvincing, dubious, doubtful. *(ant)* credible, likely.

5 **vigorously** *(adv)* with vigour (energy). *(s)* energetically, forcefully, strongly, boldly. *(ant)* sluggishly, feebly.

6 **agape** *(adj)* (of the mouth) wide open in shock or awe. *(s)* open, awestruck, yawning. *(ant)* shut, clenched.

7 **portray** *(v)* represent or describe something in a certain way. *(s)* depict, show, reveal. *(ant)* obscure.

8 **incredulity** *(n)* refusal to believe something. *(s)* doubt, disbelief, distrust, cynicism. *(ant)* credulity, belief.

9 **lunatic** *(n)* a person showing a wayward state of mind. *(s)* maniac, loony, nutter, nutcase.

10 **hunch** *(n)* an intuitive feeling or idea. *(s)* impression, suspicion, guess, inkling, notion. *(ant)* certainty.

'You're freaking me out,' said Ben.

'*He* freaks *me* out,' replied Claire, remembering the Master's **frenzied**[1] **pummelling**[2] of the exhibition case with the Cutter as he tried to break the glass. She shuddered.

'Who is this *Master*?' Ben asked as the lift came to a stop and the door slid open.

'I suspect he's *the boss*,' she replied.

'The boss?' asked Ben.

'Yes, *your* dad's boss, David Lewis.'

As the name Lewis left her lips, Claire's heart **heaved**[3] with a **tangible**[4] ache. Jayne Lewis's surname sounded less **coincidental**[5] by the minute.

'*Really?*' asked Ben, his expression a mix of incredulity and fear.

'Hi!' said a bearded young man casually as he stepped past them and into the lift.

Claire nodded back politely and beckoned to Ben with a raised eyebrow and **tilt**[6] of her head. The lift had opened into a bright **reception**[7] space that, although bustling with people, **exuded**[8] an eerie hush. Silent employees glided across the **polished**[9] marble floor, carrying slim devices. Claire noticed they had more **formal**[10] dress than those in the Hive, and their **cutting-edge**[11] haircuts fell into expensively **chic**[12] lines. No ordinary desk **hosting**[13] a **dazzling**[14] **receptionist**[15] waited to greet them. Nothing but a bank of thin screens perched like black **flamingos**[16] on long

---

1 **frenzied** *(adj)* uncontrolled or abnormally excited. *(s)* fraught, frantic, wild, hectic, feverish. *(ant)* calm.

2 **pummelling** *(n)* the act of striking repeatedly with the fists. *(s)* beating, thrashing, bashing, pounding, battering.

3 **heave** *(v)* rise and fall. *(s)* churn, swell, roll. *(ant)* still, steady.

4 **tangible** *(adj)* able to be perceived by touch. *(s)* real, physical, palpable, material. *(ant)* intangible.

5 **coincidental** *(adj)* occurring by chance. *(s)* accidental, random, fortuitous, fluky. *(ant)* intentional.

6 **tilt** *(n)* a leaning movement. *(s)* nod, inclination, tip, dip, bob.

7 **reception** *(n)* an area in a building where people are greeted. *(s)* welcome desk, front desk.

8 **exude** *(v)* display an emotion or quality strongly and openly. *(s)* radiate, convey, ooze, emit. *(ant)* absorb.

9 **polished** *(adj)* rubbed or cleaned until shiny. *(s)* lustrous, shining, glossy, bright. *(ant)* dull, tarnished.

10 **formal** *(adj)* official in attitude or appearance. *(s)* conventional, stiff, prim. *(ant)* informal, unconventional.

11 **cutting-edge** *(adj)* the latest or most advanced. *(s)* leading, innovative, progressive. *(ant)* old-fashioned.

12 **chic** *(adj)* stylishly fashionable. *(s)* elegant, smart, dapper, dashing, tasteful. *(ant)* unfashionable.

13 **host** *(v)* provide a place or facilities for. *(ant)* exclude.

14 **dazzling** *(adj)* amazing or overwhelming due to an impressive quality. *(s)* stunning, beautiful. *(ant)* boring.

15 **receptionist** *(n)* a person who greets and helps visitors, guests and clients. *(ant)* guest, client, visitor.

16 **flamingo** *(n)* a tall pink bird that stands and eats in water.

slim stands, presenting various flashing **motifs**[1], stood between them and beyond.

'Come on,' Claire muttered, pushing her gloved hand deeper into her hoody pocket, now feeling **conspicuous**[2] in her casual clothes.

'I've no idea how long this cling film contraption will work,' she whispered to Ben, reading the instructions **scrolling**[3] up on the various screens.

'They're **virtual**[4] receptionists,' said Ben. 'Look, your dad's girlfriend's name is right there.' He pointed, touching the screen.

That **fretful**[5] pang at the mention of Jayne tugged at Claire's chest again.

'Hi. My name is Stephanie,' said the image of a woman on the screen. 'How may I help you today?'

'What have you done?' Claire whispered.

'She's CGI. Don't worry,' he replied.

'Don't prod anything else,' Claire hissed. 'Find one that says "David Lewis".'

'Why do you think he's this *Master* guy?' whispered Ben.

'The number plate on his Bentley,' replied Claire. 'I suspect Dewi is a Welsh version of the name David.'

'Who's Dewi?' asked Ben.

'The Master,' replied Claire. 'I think he's David Lewis in public, Dewi to his friends, and the Master to his **minions**[6].'

Sophisticated[7] employees approached the banks, swiping screens as they confirmed next meetings with the virtual assistants. Claire and Ben turned their backs, **furtively**[8] continuing to search adjacent screens for the boss's name.

'It's here,' whispered Ben, pointing instead of touching this time.

---

1 **motif** *(n)* image or design. *(s)* pattern, logo, shape, emblem.

2 **conspicuous** *(adj)* attracting attention. *(s)* noticeable, visible, discernible. *(ant)* inconspicuous.

3 **scroll** *(v)* (of text or graphics) move on a screen. *(s)* rise, fall, shift, slide.

4 **virtual** *(adj)* simulated by a computer. *(s)* unreal, not real, computer-generated. *(ant)* real, physical.

5 **fretful** *(adj)* irritated or distressed. *(s)* uneasy, unsettled, miserable, upset, stressed. *(ant)* relaxed, happy.

6 **minion** *(n)* an underling or follower. *(s)* lackey, stooge, hanger-on, servant. *(ant)* peer.

7 **sophisticated** *(adj)* having experience of life, fashion and culture. *(s)* classy, refined. *(ant)* unrefined, naive.

8 **furtively** *(adv)* in a furtive (secret or sneaky) manner. *(s)* stealthily, clandestinely, covertly. *(ant)* openly, overtly.

Claire hoped and prayed Cristy was senior, like Ben's dad, and that her security **clearance**[1] reflected that position and would let them through.

'Touch it. I can't,' commanded Claire, her eyes **swivelling**[2] **tellingly**[3] towards the pocket concealing her gloved hand.

'Hello. My name is Scarlet. How may I help you today?' asked the assistant.

'Hello. My name is Cristy,' replied Claire, **inadvertently**[4] imitating the voice's **synthetic**[5] **cadence**[6]. 'I have a **classified**[7] document delivery for David Lewis.' Claire mustered her most adult voice.

'Surname, please,' asked the artificial intelligence.

'Grant,' replied Claire, relieved that she'd remembered Cristy's surname.

'Please place your palm on the screen,' said Scarlet with an **unctuous**[8] **simulated**[9] smile.

Claire removed her gloved right hand from her hoody pocket and, trying not to **dislodge**[10] the flimsy plastic, tentatively placed it onto the screen. Her heart hammered as she held her breath.

'Please enter, Ms Grant. Follow the **personalised**[11] green lighting situated at your feet, and you will reach Mr Lewis's assistant's office.'

Claire glanced at her feet. A narrow but bright strip of tiny emerald-green lights **embedded**[12] in the floor twinkled in an alluring, **hypnotic**[13] sequence. She nodded to Ben, and they both walked beyond the bank of screens, following the electronic guideline below them.

'That was easy,' said Claire to Ben, a tone of **pride**[14] in her voice.

---

1 **clearance** *(n)* official authorisation. *(s)* sanction, approval, consent, permission. *(ant)* veto, ban.

2 **swivel** *(v)* turn around a point. *(s)* rotate, pivot, spin.

3 **tellingly** *(adv)* in a telling (revealing) way. *(s)* decisively, dramatically, energetically, forcefully. *(ant)* weakly, feebly.

4 **inadvertently** *(adv)* in an inadvertent (unintended) manner. *(s)* accidentally, unwittingly. *(ant)* purposely.

5 **synthetic** *(adj)* not real. *(s)* simulated, manufactured, artificial, fake. *(ant)* real, genuine, natural.

6 **cadence** *(n)* the sound and rhythm of a voice. *(s)* tempo, inflection, modulation, measure, beat.

7 **classified** *(adj)* officially secret. *(s)* confidential, restricted, private. *(ant)* public, open.

8 **unctuous** *(adj)* overly nice. *(s)* fawning, crawling, obsequious, insincere. *(ant)* blunt, no-nonsense.

9 **simulated** *(adj)* produced by computer modelling software. *(s)* artificial, imitation, mock. *(ant)* real.

10 **dislodge** *(v)* force or knock out of position. *(s)* displace, move, shift.

11 **personalised** *(adj)* produced for one's requirements. *(s)* individualised, customised, tailored. *(ant)* generalised.

12 **embedded** *(adj)* fixed into surrounding mass. *(s)* inserted, implanted, sunken, inlayed. *(ant)* protruding.

13 **hypnotic** *(adj)* making one feel sleepy (soporific). *(s)* mesmerising, rhythmic, repetitive. *(ant)* invigorating.

14 **pride** *(n)* feeling of satisfaction. *(s)* enjoyment, pleasure, fulfilment, gratification, joy. *(ant)* shame.

*

Close by, in a **suite**[1] of **palatial**[2] private rooms, the tall, **impeccably**[3] attired man ran his fingers through his thick, dark hair. He gently patted the breast pocket of his Savile Row suit. The purpose-built metal box containing what he now knew was only half of the Cutter rested there.

He sat crossed-legged, his arms outstretched on a **sumptuous**[4] deep-purple **velvet**[5] sofa edged with throne-worthy gold **tassel**[6] trim. He faced a broad, ultra-thin graphene screen. From this **vantage**[7] point, he had watched Claire's every move since she had entered Beddgelert, and wherever possible, he had listened to her every word.

'Her **arrogance**[8] **divulges**[9] her **ignorance**[10],' he said to a blonde woman who stood observing, his accent **subtly**[11] Welsh. 'Does she believe she **saunters**[12] about my **realm**[13] at will? Does she believe **unfettered**[14] access to my **domain**[15] is on account of her **ingenuity**[16]?' he scoffed.

The woman remained silent and **expressionless**[17].

'The **foil**[18] in losing the Cutter yesterday is **attributed**[19] to the **guileful**[20] knight Robert Evans – of that I am sure – but this **hubristic**[21] pup will lead us to him eventually.'

---

1 **suite** *(n)* a set of rooms. *(s)* living quarters, apartment, flat.

2 **palatial** *(adj)* like a palace in splendour and capacity. *(s)* grand, luxurious, deluxe, sumptuous. *(ant)* modest, humble.

3 **impeccably** *(adv)* in an impeccable (perfect) way. *(s)* flawlessly, faultlessly. *(ant)* poorly.

4 **sumptuous** *(adj)* splendid and expensive-looking. *(s)* luxurious, lavish, plush, extravagant, grand. *(ant)* meagre.

5 **velvet** *(n)* fabric woven from silk, cotton or nylon with a dense, short pile on one side.

6 **tassel** *(n)* a bunch of hanging threads fastened together at one end and attached to things for decoration.

7 **vantage** *(n)* a position or place offering the best view. *(s)* viewpoint, angle, stance.

8 **arrogance** *(n)* an exaggerated sense of one's importance. *(s)* big-headedness, conceit, pride. *(ant)* humility.

9 **divulge** *(v)* make known. *(s)* disclose, reveal, show, exhibit, tell, confess. *(ant)* conceal, hide, protect.

10 **ignorance** *(n)* lack of awareness or knowledge. *(s)* inexperience, innocence, stupidity. *(ant)* cognizance, awareness.

11 **subtly** *(adv)* in a subtle (understated) way. *(s)* faintly, softly, vaguely. *(ant)* obviously.

12 **saunter** *(v)* walk in a slow and relaxed manner. *(s)* stroll, amble, wander, mosey, dawdle. *(ant)* hurry, hasten.

13 **realm** *(n)* area of responsibility or rule. *(s)* kingdom, domain, monarchy, empire, dominion, jurisdiction.

14 **unfettered** *(adj)* not restricted or inhibited. *(s)* free, unchecked, unbridled. *(ant)* fettered, restricted.

15 **domain** *(n)* an area governed by a specific ruler. *(s)* kingdom, empire, dominion, estate.

16 **ingenuity** *(n)* the quality of being creative and clever. *(s)* inventiveness, resourcefulness. *(ant)* ignorance.

17 **expressionless** *(adj)* not conveying any emotion on the face. *(s)* unresponsive, deadpan. *(ant)* expressive.

18 **foil** *(n)* a setback. *(s)* defeat, loss, conquest, beating, vanquishment. *(ant)* success, victory.

19 **attribute** *(v)* see something as being the result of something else. *(s)* credit, assign, accredit. *(ant)* disconnect.

20 **guileful** *(adj)* cunning (sly). *(s)* crafty, clever, shrewd, wily, tricky. *(ant)* guileless, innocent.

21 **hubristic** *(adj)* overly proud or self-assured. *(s)* cocky, conceited, arrogant, overconfident. *(ant)* cautious, humble, meek.

The blonde woman nodded, coolly gathering her hair and moving it off her shoulder.

'I am sure you are correct, sir,' the woman eventually responded. 'If I might suggest, sir, you may benefit from some **recuperation**[1]. Sleep has **eluded**[2] you for days. I can **monitor**[3] the girl now she is here and rouse you should the need **arise**[4].'

The man uncrossed his legs and **raked**[5] his fingers through his hair again.

'Shall I bring you a **draught**[6] of **chamomile**[7] tea, sir? It will help you sleep.'

He lay back into the opulent sofa, stretching out his long, slim legs before him.

The woman waited.

'Perhaps you are right,' he eventually answered. 'Bring the tea.'

The woman lowered her head, turned and left. She entered a richly stocked **adjoining**[8] kitchen and removed a **delicate**[9] white **china**[10] cup and saucer from a sleek, glossy cupboard. She broke the seal on a **sachet**[11] of fresh dried chamomile tea flowers and scooped them into a **spherical**[12] **mesh**[13] **infuser**[14], allowing it to snap shut once she'd filled it with the perfumed **blooms**[15].

Placing the sphere into the cup and dangling its delicate chain over the rim, she held the cup up to a slim metal tube and pressed a button. Steam hissed and spat from the tap until the spherical steeper rested, **submerged**[16], in the boiling liquid.

As the woman watched the clear liquid transform into a pale **ochre**[17] yellow, she smiled,

---

1 **recuperation** *(n)* recovery from exertion or ailment. *(s)* improvement, convalescence, rejuvenation. *(ant)* deterioration.

2 **elude** *(v)* avoid or escape. *(s)* evade, dodge, flee, circumvent, foil, outrun, thwart. *(ant)* embrace, pursue.

3 **monitor** *(v)* observe and review, watch over. *(s)* check, supervise, control, scrutinise. *(ant)* ignore, mismanage.

4 **arise** *(v)* become evident or emerge. *(s)* appear, surface, occur, transpire. *(ant)* end, disappear.

5 **rake** *(v)* scrape or scratch in a sweeping motion. *(s)* comb, scour.

6 **draught** *(n)* liquid with medicinal properties. *(s)* medicine, dose, dosage, potion, elixir.

7 **chamomile** (n) an aromatic European plant that produces white and yellow flowers.

8 **adjoining** *(adj)* joined with or next to. *(s)* neighbouring, adjacent, connecting. *(ant)* separate, detached.

9 **delicate** *(adj)* fine in structure or easily broken. *(s)* dainty, frail, fragile, breakable. *(ant)* strong, durable.

10 **china** *(n)* fine white ceramic (made from clay) material.

11 **sachet** *(n)* a small packet with something sealed inside. *(s)* wrapper, package, envelope.

12 **spherical** *(adj)* like a sphere (round). *(s)* globular, rotund, circular, orbicular, bulbous. *(ant)* flat.

13 **mesh** *(n)* material made of a network of thread or wire. *(s)* lattice, webbing.

14 **infuser** *(n)* small mesh container that holds leaves to steep (soak) in liquid.

15 **bloom** *(n)* a flower. *(s)* blossom, flowering, blossoming.

16 **submerged** *(adj)* located below the surface of something. *(s)* immersed, plunged, sunken. *(ant)* surfaced.

17 **ochre** *(n)* a red or yellow pigment (natural colouring).

reached into her jacket pocket and took out a small glass **vial**[1]. Removing its snug cap, she angled the vial over the cup. With her forefinger, she tapped the vial once, and a **minuscule**[2] drop of clear liquid plopped out into the cup. The woman replaced the cap and slipped the vial back into her jacket pocket. Timing the **brew**[3] for precisely three minutes – a second longer, and he would complain it was **bitter**[4] – she removed the mesh sphere from the cup, **meticulously**[5] **ensuring**[6] there were no unwanted splashes in the saucer, picked up the **beverage**[7] and left the kitchen.

'Your tea, sir,' she said.

He beckoned to a glass side table that stood next to the sofa's curled arm. The woman placed the tea down and stepped discreetly away. The man said nothing. She knew he would drink soon – he **despised**[8] **tepid**[9] tea. She stood stock-still, as if waiting for further instruction from her master. The man picked up the cup and saucer, took a tentative sip, then smacked his tongue against the roof of his mouth with a loud, **unsavoury**[10] click.

A minute twitch of the woman's mouth was the only sign she had **flinched**[11].

'Perfect!' he barked. 'You may leave. I will **retire**[12] to my chambers. Do not lose sight of the girl.'

With **diffidence**[13], the woman bowed her head, turned on her heel and left the room, smiling to herself as she did so.

---

1 **vial** *(n)* a small cylindrical glass container. *(s)* ampoule, phial, bottle, flask.

2 **minuscule** *(adj)* incredibly small. *(s)* tiny, minute, microscopic, infinitesimal, diminutive. *(ant)* gigantic, vast.

3 **brew** *(n)* cup of tea or coffee. *(s)* drink, beverage.

4 **bitter** *(adj)* not sweet. *(s)* sour, tart, biting, pungent. *(ant)* sweet.

5 **meticulously** *(adv)* in a meticulous (careful and thorough) way. *(s)* diligently, scrupulously. *(ant)* carelessly.

6 **ensure** *(v)* make certain. *(s)* guarantee, assure, safeguard, confirm, warrant, protect. *(ant)* undermine, weaken.

7 **beverage** *(n)* any drink, but not usually water unless it is bottled. *(s)* libation, potable, potation.

8 **despise** *(v)* look down upon, view with contempt. *(s)* hate, detest, loathe, spurn, deride. *(ant)* love, admire.

9 **tepid** *(adj)* slightly warm. *(s)* lukewarm, warmish, mild, temperate. *(ant)* cold, icy, boiling.

10 **unsavoury** *(adj)* unpleasant. *(s)* disagreeable, distasteful, unattractive. *(ant)* pleasant, attractive, agreeable.

11 **flinch** *(v)* shy away from instinctively. *(s)* move, withdraw, twitch, recoil, start, baulk, wince. *(ant)* stand firm.

12 **retire** *(v)* go to bed. *(s)* turn in, call it a day, hit the hay. *(ant)* get up, wake up.

13 **diffidence** *(n)* modesty or shyness. *(s)* humility, timidity, meekness. *(ant)* confidence.

6. The Glass Staircase

Claire and Ben had followed their line of twinkly green lights past the bank of touch screens and beyond security. Although **marginally**[1] less impressive than the Hive, their surroundings, carved from the ubiquitous rock, were modern and tasteful in a way that only **oodles**[2] of money delivered. The **memorable**[3] space was **innovatively**[4] designed to showcase only rock, metal and glass.

Silent employees glided alongside Claire and Ben, following their lines of twinkling guides, which glimmered in subtly personalised hues along the floor. They sailed from place to place like well-dressed robots, reading and swiping devices. Many wore earbuds, like high-tech earrings, their faces frozen in concentration.

'These people don't look real,' whispered Ben.

'They're probably not!' replied Claire. 'Don't look at them.'

Once past security, the rock walls had gradually widened, increasing as they walked, like the expanding mouth of a giant **funnel**[5]. As Claire and Ben progressed, the space opened dramatically onto a **cavernous**[6] work floor, which Claire **gauged**[7] was roughly the size of two football pitches. In parallel lines, rows of glass cubicles, their size and shape identical, housed Via-Corp employees.

---

1 **marginally** *(adv)* in a marginal (slight) way. *(s)* minutely, minimally, somewhat, insignificantly. *(ant)* substantially.

2 **oodles** *(n)* a large amount. *(s)* lots, tons, heaps, loads, masses. *(ant)* a smattering.

3 **memorable** *(adj)* worthy of remembrance or noting. *(s)* unforgettable, noteworthy, notable. *(ant)* ordinary.

4 **innovatively** *(adv)* in an innovative (original) way. *(s)* creatively, inventively, ingeniously. *(ant)* unoriginally.

5 **funnel** *(n)* a tube that is wide at the top and tapers to the bottom. *(s)* pipe, conduit, channel.

6 **cavernous** *(adj)* like a cavern (large cave). *(s)* vast, spacious, capacious, roomy, yawning. *(ant)* small, cramped.

7 **gauge** *(v)* measure or estimate the amount of. *(s)* judge, assess, evaluate, determine, calculate.

'The boss likes order,' whispered Claire, **emulating**[1] precisely Mr Brady's earlier comments.

'There's only one person in each cube,' replied Ben in a whisper. 'That's so weird. They look like caged animals.'

'They must be soundproofed. That's why it's deathly quiet and we can hear the electricity hum,' replied Claire.

'Probably so visitors can't hear them scream,' said Ben, looking like he meant it.

'No wonder they call it the compound,' said Claire.

Neither of them raised their voices above a whisper.

'Isn't it weird that no one has stopped us, or even looked at us?' asked Ben. 'There must be cameras everywhere. Something's out of whack. Why does no one seem to care we're here?'

Claire didn't answer, stubbornly refusing to accept his suggestion. She longed to believe her bravery and loyalty, as well as her **fledgling**[2] Instinct, had brought them this far. Gwilym had said those **attributes**[3] would develop her Instinct – it wasn't free. They could not train her. Earning the **honour**[4] of becoming a Knight Hawk and **adopting**[5] the **authentic**[6] Welsh name Cadwaladr was her responsibility. 'Trust your Instinct,' Gladys had said, and that was what she was doing.

'Nobody is stopping us, because Cristy has the highest level of security clearance here. Like I said before, she switched off her retinal ID, or the spare phone she gave us wouldn't work,' replied Claire, jutting out her chin at a **wilful**[7] angle. 'That's why we can use just her palm print to open doors.'

'OK,' said Ben. 'I trust you, but this stuff is hard to **digest**[8]. I wonder where my dad is,' he added, a worried edge **quivering**[9] in his voice. 'I think we should go find him.'

I wonder too, thought Claire. *I don't trust him.*

---

1 **emulate** *(v)* copy the actions of. *(s)* imitate, reproduce, match, mimic, mirror, echo, rival. *(ant)* differ from.

2 **fledgling** *(adj)* inexperienced or underdeveloped (still learning). *(s)* emergent, budding, novice. *(ant)* expert.

3 **attribute** *(n)* a feature or quality seen as a characteristic. *(s)* trait, element, aspect, part, quirk, feature, mark.

4 **honour** *(n)* high respect. *(s)* esteem, distinction, privilege, kudos, prestige, credit, importance. *(ant)* disgrace.

5 **adopt** *(v)* take up. *(s)* use, follow, assume, acquire. *(ant)* abandon.

6 **authentic** *(adj)* genuine, original or traditional. *(s)* valid, accurate, real, legitimate. *(ant)* false, fake.

7 **wilful** *(adj)* intending to do as one wants. *(s)* headstrong, stubborn, obstinate, defiant. *(ant)* amenable, biddable.

8 **digest** *(v)* understand. *(s)* absorb, comprehend, assimilate, grasp, consider. *(ant)* misunderstand.

9 **quiver** *(v)* tremble or shake. *(s)* shiver, quaver, shudder, vibrate, quake, tremor. *(ant)* steady, still.

'Wow! Look ahead, up there,' Claire whispered, ignoring Ben's suggestion of finding Mr Brady. 'Look at the ceiling.'

Ben was staring, his mouth **gaping**[1] open.

About twenty-five metres ahead, suspended from the rock ceiling, was a **stupendous**[2] circular glass **construction**[3]. Its flat base and smooth, curved sides were **opaque**[4]. It reminded Claire of a **hovering**[5] giant flying saucer she'd seen in a sci-fi movie. A **hauntingly**[6] beautiful metal-and-glass staircase, fitting for a modern-day fairy tale, **spiralled**[7] down from its centre, curving in a **sweeping**[8], **graceful**[9] **helix**[10]. Metallic lighting shone subtly from beneath its **curvaceous**[11] **treads**[12], its source ingeniously invisible.

'The **diameter**[13] of that flying saucer thing must be twenty metres, and floor-to-ceiling depth, at least ten. It's awesome,' remarked Ben.

'What's holding it up?' asked Claire. 'It looks like it's floating in the air.'

'It's **moulded**[14] and **fused**[15] into the cave's rock. Look at the top bit. The staircase is **helical**[16]. That's why it sweeps round like that,' said Ben, drawing the shape in the air with his hand. 'No support strut in the middle to spoil it.'

---

1 **gape** *(v)* be or become wide open. *(s)* part, split, separate, divide, yawn. *(ant)* close, shut.

2 **stupendous** *(adj)* incredibly impressive. *(s)* astounding, astonishing, remarkable. *(ant)* unremarkable.

3 **construction** *(n)* a structure or building. *(s)* assembly, edifice, development, build.

4 **opaque** *(adj)* not able to be seen through. *(s)* cloudy, hazy, filmy. *(ant)* transparent.

5 **hover** *(v)* remain in one place in the air. *(s)* hang, float, drift. *(ant)* descend, ascend.

6 **hauntingly** *(adv)* in a poignant (moving) or evocative (powerful) manner. *(s)* touchingly, emotively, powerfully.

7 **spiral** *(v)* wind continuously. *(s)* coil, twirl, swirl, snake, twist.

8 **sweeping** *(adj)* extending in a continuous curve (curved and long). *(s)* wide, full, broad. *(ant)* narrow.

9 **graceful** *(adj)* having grace, elegance and poise (not stiff and ungainly). *(s)* agile, nimble, fluid. *(ant)* clumsy.

10 **helix** *(n)* a spiral or coiled form. *(s)* corkscrew, twirl, twist, whirl, whorl, loop.

11 **curvaceous** *(adj)* pleasingly curved. *(s)* curvy. *(ant)* straight.

12 **tread** *(n)* the upper surface of a step.

13 **diameter** *(n)* a straight line passing through the centre of a circle (or a sphere). *(s)* width, span, breadth.

14 **moulded** *(adj)* formed or cast into a shape using malleable (bendable) material. *(s)* fashioned, shaped, sculpted.

15 **fused** *(adj)* combined to form one thing. *(s)* merged, melded, amalgamated, blended, joined. *(ant)* separate.

16 **helical** *(adj)* having the shape of a helix. *(s)* spiral.

'OK, brainbox,' said Claire. 'No guesses where our green fairy lights lead to, then,' she added, nodding towards the floor. 'That's gotta be David Lewis's office, or should I call him Dewi? Come on.'

'No way am I walking up that staircase, like Prince Charming,' said Ben. 'No way!'

'Really?' Claire answered, her face **indignant**[1] but not shocked by his refusal.

'Really,' he replied with an **adamant**[2] look that Claire knew well.

'I'll do it on my own, then, chicken,' said Claire, trying to save face and **pursing**[3] her lips into an **obstinate**[4] shape.

'Claire, you'll stick out like a snowboarder in a bunch of old-age skiers if you climb that staircase. You'll totally get busted.'

'Ha ha! You have such great similes!' **quipped**[5] Claire, her tone sarcastic and a bit too loud. She was **miffed**[6].

'Shush!' said Ben, frowning hard and pulling a face at her.

But their line of flashing guide lights led straight to the base of the heavenly looking staircase, which fast approached.

'I mean it, Claire. I'm not going up those shiny stairs,' reiterated Ben.

'I know. You've made *that* **abundantly**[7] clear,' she replied, her tone sarcastic again. 'Am I **underdressed**[8] for my grand entrance?' she quipped, again, attempting another lame **jest**[9], but beneath her **brash**[10] exterior, her stomach churned and her hands shook. She tried her utmost to keep her fear from Ben but realised she was coming across as plain mean.

'You'd better **mosey**[11] about, looking **officially**[12] occupied, then,' said Claire, conceding. 'This

---

1 **indignant** *(adj)* anger or annoyance at what is perceived as unfair. *(s)* offended, disgruntled, irate. *(ant)* content.

2 **adamant** *(adj)* unwavering. *(s)* firm, resolute, unshakeable, stubborn. *(ant)* unsure, wavering.

3 **purse** *(v)* (of the lips) press together. *(s)* pucker, tighten, compress, pout.

4 **obstinate** *(adj)* stubbornly unwavering. *(s)* wilful, headstrong, unyielding, inflexible. *(ant)* compliant, amenable.

5 **quip** *(v)* make a witty (humorous) remark. *(s)* joke, wisecrack, retort, banter, jest, jibe.

6 **miffed** *(adj)* a little annoyed. *(s)* peeved, irritated, vexed, riled, cross. *(ant)* happy, content.

7 **abundantly** *(adv)* extremely. *(s)* very, especially, exceedingly. *(ant)* scarcely.

8 **underdressed** *(adj)* dressed too informally or simply for a specific event or setting. *(ant)* overdressed.

9 **jest** *(n)* a joke. *(s)* quip, pun, gag, witticism, crack, wisecrack.

10 **brash** *(adj)* cocky and overbearing. *(s)* arrogant, cheeky, brazen, pushy, impudent. *(ant)* self-effacing, mild.

11 **mosey** *(v)* move in a relaxed manner. *(s)* amble, meander, linger, loiter. *(ant)* hurry.

12 **officially** *(adv)* in an official (formal) way. *(s)* authoritatively, properly, correctly. *(ant)* unofficially, informally.

may take a while,' she added, her voice shaky, her tongue sticking to the roof of her mouth as she hoped and prayed Ben would have a change of heart and join her.

'I'll wait right here,' said Ben, sounding like his dad.

Claire **cringed**[1] at the thought of Mr Brady, but they'd reached the foot of the stairs, and now wasn't the time to question why.

'Here goes. Don't **stray**[2] far, buddy,' she said, forcing a **bold**[3] tone and trying to ignore her eye, which twitched with **telltale**[4] fear.

'I'm going nowhere,' said Ben. 'I'll keep watch down here. Go, girl,' he said with an **encouraging**[5] but **nervy**[6] grin.

Unaccustomed[7] to **leadership**[8], Claire tried to **comprehend**[9] their **emerging**[10] **role reversal**[11]. Why should Ben believe her **risible**[12] tale and blindly follow her? Why should he risk anything for her without proof? She couldn't blame him, yet a **palpable**[13] hurt **plagued**[14] her, for she was sure of one thing: she knew **unequivocally**[15] that *she* would *never* have left Ben behind.

Be brave, she told herself. *This is your test, your task. This is not Ben's fault. He's innocent.*

Again she pictured Gwilym's horrific image, **metamorphosing**[16] into emerald and shattering into thousands of pieces. She prayed that hadn't really happened. She thought of Gladys and Anwen and Owain. Would they all die too? Even worse, were they already dead? What if Thomas

---

1 **cringe** *(v)* shiver inwardly with embarrassment or disgust. *(s)* wince, squirm, blush, recoil.

2 **stray** *(v)* move away aimlessly. *(s)* drift, wander, roam, meander. *(ant)* stay, remain.

3 **bold** (adj) lacking fear. *(s)* confident, courageous, brave, daring, intrepid, valiant, undaunted. *(ant)* timid, scared.

4 **telltale** *(adj)* suggesting or betraying something. *(s)* revealing, indicative, meaningful. *(ant)* uninformative.

5 **encouraging** *(adj)* persuasive or supportive. *(s)* reassuring, helpful, positive. *(ant)* dissuasive, discouraging.

6 **nervy** *(adj)* nervous. *(s)* alarmed, agitated, anxious, edgy, stressed, apprehensive. *(ant)* calm.

7 **unaccustomed** *(adj)* not used to or familiar with. *(s)* untuned, unfamiliar, unacquainted. *(ant)* accustomed.

8 **leadership** *(n)* the action of leading. *(s)* guidance, control, direction, authority, influence. *(ant)* following.

9 **comprehend** *(v)* understand. *(s)* follow, get, realise, fathom, grasp, twig. *(ant)* misunderstand, misinterpret.

10 **emerging** *(adj)* becoming apparent (clear or evident). *(s)* unfolding, transpiring, arising. *(ant)* disappearing.

11 **role reversal** *(n)* a situation where roles are exchanged. *(s)* swap, switch.

12 **risible** *(adj)* so ridiculous (silly) as to make one laugh. *(s)* absurd, comical, droll, ludicrous. *(ant)* serious.

13 **palpable** *(adj)* so intense as to seem almost tangible (real). *(s)* obvious, profound, substantial. *(ant)* intangible.

14 **plague** *(v)* cause continual distress to. *(s)* afflict, torture, torment, beleaguer, harass. *(ant)* soothe, support.

15 **unequivocally** *(adv)* in an unequivocal (certain) manner. *(s)* absolutely, definitely, undeniably. *(ant)* questionably.

16 **metamorphose** *(v)* change. *(s)* mutate, transmute, alter, transfigure. *(ant)* remain.

and Jack *were* Knights Hawk? They were so clever they might be. She shivered, **envisioning**[1] the animals suffering the same unthinkable **fate**[2] as Gwilym. That was **catalyst**[3] enough; no longer **procrastinating**[4], she stepped beyond the blinking emerald lights and, as if fearing it might **devour**[5] her whole, placed one foot onto the first step of the broad, shining stairs.

Gulping down the lump **constricting**[6] her throat, Claire cast a weak smile back in Ben's direction. She turned back, and peering up the **magnificent**[7], curling staircase towards the opaque base of the circular **elevation**[8], she wiped a **stray**[9] tear on the sleeve of her grubby hoody. Her right hand still wore the cling film mitten, so she placed her left onto the cold metal **banister**[10] that followed the staircase's **sublime**[11] curve.

Don't look back. Don't look back. This was today's 'stay **sane**[12]' **mantra**[13]. She mouthed it every sparkling step she trod.

Puffing and **puce**[14], she'd barely **ascended**[15] a third of the exquisite staircase, its gentle **elegance**[16] **belying**[17] its steep pitch, when she paused for breath.

The endless rows of glass cubicles, each housing a lone worker, lay beneath her. Claire glanced in Ben's direction but couldn't see him. She scanned the **locale**[18], instant panic rising. Then she glimpsed his mop of caramel-tipped hair bobbing above her backpack.

---

1 **envision** *(v)* picture as a future likelihood. *(s)* imagine, visualise, envisage.

2 **fate** *(n)* a future outcome that is out of one's control. *(s)* destiny, upshot, fortune, luck, lot.

3 **catalyst** *(n)* something or someone that causes an event to begin. *(s)* spur, spark. *(ant)* inhibitor.

4 **procrastinate** *(v)* delay doing something. *(s)* stall, put off, hesitate, dither, waver. *(ant)* do, finish.

5 **devour** *(v)* eat quickly or totally absorb. *(s)* consume, engulf, gobble, overwhelm. *(ant)* reject, abstain from.

6 **constrict** *(v)* make narrower. *(s)* tighten, compress, contract, choke. *(ant)* dilate, expand.

7 **magnificent** *(adj)* spectacular, impressive and awesome. *(s)* superb, superlative, brilliant. (ant) unimpressive.

8 **elevation** *(n)* a high position, or an entity in such a place.

9 **stray** *(adj)* random or on its own. *(s)* unexpected, chance, lone, single.

10 **banister** *(n)* safety barrier on a staircase. *(s)* rail, railing.

11 **sublime** *(adj)* of great beauty or excellence. *(s)* moving, uplifting, superb, heavenly. *(ant)* inferior, poor.

12 **sane** (adj) of sound (balanced) mind. *(s)* rational, sensible, sober, stable, lucid, logical. (ant) insane.

13 **mantra** (n) a repeated statement. *(s)* chant, saying, slogan.

14 **puce** (adj) dark red or purple-brown in colour.

15 **ascend** *(v)* go up or climb up. *(s)* mount, scale, rise. *(ant)* descend, drop.

16 **elegance** (n) style and grace. *(s)* refinement, sophistication, finesse. (ant) inelegance.

17 **belie** (v) fail to give an accurate impression of. *(s)* contradict, distort, misrepresent. (ant) reveal, testify to.

18 **locale** (n) a place. *(s)* area, location, locality, setting, position.

I forgot to get my backpack from him. He's got the bracelet, she thought, a shot of fear firing through her, but she couldn't go back now.

Gathering herself for the continuing climb, she **swore**[1] to make more effort in PE lessons. For support, Claire grasped the **glinting**[2] handrail again, hoisting herself up.

The stairs' **substantial**[3] treads glinted a **glacial**[4] blue. Claire wondered if the treads were crystal, they were so accurately cut and angled; nothing would surprise her in this place. Money was evidently no object here.

As if ascending into an alien unknown, she stared at the flying saucer's base. It was constructed from metal and glass, and its opaque panes rendered it **resolutely**[5] private.

I bet they're watching me, she thought, staring up at the gigantic sphere.

She looked back down again for Ben's bobbing head. He was fiddling with something, but she couldn't make out what. She was too high, about two-thirds of the way up the climb. Clueless as to what to expect when she reached the top, she continued as Cristy Grant, an **imposter**[6].

She looked up at the glass **creation**[7], which grew vast as she neared it.

Finding the **fortitude**[8] to continue, she stole one last glance at Ben, but something caught her eye, someone she recognised. She froze.

It can't be, she thought, squinting hard in disbelief.

Overcome[9] by a sudden **disorientating**[10] sensation, she clung to the handrail, a ringing in her ears. She was so high up, even trying to **descend**[11] the stairs in fours wouldn't give her enough time. Screaming would be **futile**[12]. Her vision blurred, but through the **haze**[13], she recognised the

---

1 **swear** *(v)* promise (past tense: *swore*). *(s)* vow, affirm, proclaim, attest, declare.

2 **glint** (v) reflect light in small flashes. *(s)* gleam, shimmer, wink, sparkle, twinkle.

3 **substantial** *(adj)* of largish size, importance or worth. *(s)* considerable, sizeable, ample. *(ant)* small, minor.

4 **glacial** *(adj)* like a glacier. *(s)* icy, wintry, cold. *(ant)* warm.

5 **resolutely** *(adv)* in a resolute (deliberate) manner. *(s)* purposefully, decidedly. *(ant)* irresolutely, half-heartedly.

6 **imposter** *(n)* someone pretending to be someone else to deceive others. *(s)* phoney, charlatan.

7 **creation** *(n)* something that has been made. *(s)* construction, design, building.

8 **fortitude** *(n)* courage (bravery) when faced with difficulty. *(s)* mettle, resilience, nerve, pluck, valour. *(ant)* weakness.

9 **overcome** *(adj)* overwhelmed or moved emotionally. *(s)* gripped, seized, affected, disturbed. *(ant)* underwhelmed.

10 **disorientating** *(adj)* confusing. *(s)* perplexing, bewildering, unsettling, discombobulating. *(ant)* orientating.

11 **descend** *(v)* move or fall downwards. *(s)* plunge, dip, swoop, dive, plummet. *(ant)* ascend, climb.

12 **futile** *(adj)* useless and pointless. *(s)* fruitless, vain, unsuccessful, ineffective, ineffectual, wasted. *(ant)* useful.

13 **haze** *(n)* blur or mist. *(s)* fog, obscurity, fuzziness, cloudiness. *(ant)* clarity, clearness.

smugness of the **youth**[1] who peered straight up at her. She watched from on high as the youth, with an unknown **accomplice**[2], **hustled**[3] Ben into an empty cubicle, its glass door sliding closed behind them.

Ben had struggled, but with a hand across his mouth, they had **jostled**[4] him away. Craning his neck, he locked on to her terrified gaze, his expression pleading with her.

Endeavouring[5] to regain some **composure**[6], Claire **scurried**[7] down the stairs, her eyes fixed on Ben, who, now inside the soundproofed cube, battled to free himself from his **captors**[8]. Although he was fit, **agile**[9] and an **adept**[10] martial artist, Claire knew Ben's skills **paled**[11] in comparison to this Mal-Instinctive's capabilities.

Yet somehow Ben had wriggled his hand free and was waving **frantically**[12] at her. He shook his pinched forefinger and thumb as though writing in mid-air. Claire struggled to **interpret**[13] the sign. Horrified, she watched as the taller youth quashed Ben's fleeting **liberty**[14], yanking and twisting his arm high behind his back. Claire gasped, **vicariously**[15] sharing in Ben's agony.

'You'll pay for that, Rat-Boy!' she shouted, gesticulating at the soundproofed cube, a flash of anger **igniting**[16] into **rage**[17].

As if hearing Claire's words, Josh Drane **smirked**[18] up at her and thrust Ben's arm further up

---

1 **youth** *(n)* young person. *(s)* teenager, adolescent, junior, youngster, juvenile. *(ant)* adult, old person.

2 **accomplice** *(n)* a person who helps another commit a crime. *(s)* co-conspirator, collaborator, abettor.

3 **hustle** *(v)* push roughly. *(s)* shove, jostle, bump, manhandle.

4 **jostle** *(v)* push, bump or elbow something. *(s)* collide with, knock, shove, manhandle, shoulder.

5 **endeavour** *(v)* attempt with effort. *(s)* aim, bid, strive, struggle, undertake. *(ant)* quit.

6 **composure** *(n)* feeling of being calm and in control. *(s)* self-control, serenity, tranquillity, poise. *(ant)* agitation.

7 **scurry** *(v)* move quickly with short, hurried steps. *(s)* dash, dart, scamper, scuttle, hasten. *(ant)* saunter, amble.

8 **captor** *(n)* one who takes a prisoner by force. *(s)* detainer, capturer, jailer, keeper. *(ant)* liberator.

9 **agile** *(adj)* able to move easily and quickly. *(s)* nimble, spry, responsive, swift, lithe, lively. *(ant)* sluggish, stiff.

10 **adept** *(adj)* highly skilled or proficient (good) at something. *(s)* competent, adroit, consummate. *(ant)* inept.

11 **pale** *(v)* seem or become inferior. *(s)* diminish, fade, lessen, reduce. *(ant)* intensify, strengthen.

12 **frantically** *(adv)* in a frantic (fearful) way. *(s)* desperately, madly, uncontrollably. *(ant)* calmly.

13 **interpret** *(v)* understand the meaning of. *(s)* construe, untangle, comprehend, decipher. *(ant)* misinterpret.

14 **liberty** *(n)* freedom. *(s)* independence, autonomy. *(ant)* constraint, subjugation.

15 **vicariously** *(adv)* in a vicarious (imagined through the feeling or actions of another) way. *(s)* indirectly. *(ant)* directly.

16 **ignite** *(v)* arouse. *(s)* trigger, spark, kindle, stir up, agitate. *(ant)* dampen.

17 **rage** *(n)* extreme anger. *(s)* wrath, fury, indignation, outrage.

18 **smirk** *(v)* smile, but in a smug, conceited or silly way. *(s)* grin, sneer, leer, simper.

his back. He then languidly waved his hand in the air, and the transparent cube's glass switched to a misty grey **opacity**[1], as if someone had pulled down all the blinds at once.

'That's it!' she snapped, **bolting**[2] down the stairs, almost forgetting she still wore the precious cling film mitten.

At the foot of the stairs, aware of the **probing**[3] looks from the **android**[4]-like employees, she placed her right hand into her pocket, slowed and strode past rows of glass cells towards Ben's. It was further than it had appeared from above and **indistinguishable**[5] at ground level amongst the uniform rows. Although she had been convinced of its **location**[6] a moment ago, now it wasn't where she'd thought it was. None of the nearby cells was opaque, and none imprisoned Ben. All she saw was Via-Corp employees.

Panic **surged**[7]. Like **coordinates**[8] on a **grid**[9], she should have counted the cubes. **Distraught**[10], she couldn't find Ben, and fearing imminent arrest, she'd failed her best friend. No **shepherding**[11] lights blinked beneath her trainers now. Sweat prickled on her neck as she patrolled the maze in a **fervent**[12] search for Ben. Drane must have known the view from above **yielded**[13] a very different landscape from that on the ground. She was lost, as was Ben. But *worse*, and **unbeknown**[14] to him, *Ben* was carrying the Gwalch Gem bracelet in Claire's bag on his back. She had lost that too.

---

1 **opacity** *(n)* the quality of not being transparent (see-through). *(s)* cloudiness, murkiness, obscurity. *(ant)* transparency.

2 **bolt** *(v)* move or run suddenly. *(s)* sprint, dash, dart, hurtle. *(ant)* linger.

3 **probing** *(adj)* enquiring closely (nosy). *(s)* invasive, prying, personal, impertinent. *(ant)* restrained, discreet.

4 **android** *(n)* a robot that looks human. *(s)* cyborg, clone, drone. *(ant)* human.

5 **indistinguishable** *(adj)* not able to be understood as different. *(s)* identical, duplicate. *(ant)* distinctive, dissimilar.

6 **location** *(n)* specific position or place. *(s)* site, setting, scene, locality, whereabouts, situation, spot, area.

7 **surge** *(v)* increase suddenly and with more power. *(s)* outpour, rise, gush, heave, course. *(ant)* decline, ebb.

8 **coordinate** *(n)* a group of numbers used to indicate a position.

9 **grid** *(n)* lines crossing each other to form squares or rectangles. *(s)* matrix, network.

10 **distraught** *(adj)* extremely worried and upset. *(s)* distressed, hysterical, fraught, desperate. *(ant)* calm, serene.

11 **shepherd** *(v)* guide. *(s)* usher, direct, steer, lead, marshal, escort, accompany.

12 **fervent** *(adj)* displaying intense feeling. *(s)* impassioned, passionate, ardent, vehement, sincere. *(ant)* apathetic.

13 **yield** *(v)* provide or produce. *(s)* give, offer, bear, supply.

14 **unbeknown** *(adj)* not known. *(s)* unperceived, unrecognised, undetected. *(ant)* known, perceived, recognised.

7. Glass Cages

Still searching in vain, Claire paused as she happened upon a **quartet**[1] of empty cubes, wrestling to **corral**[2] her wild thoughts. It was as though Ben had vanished. He *had* been signalling to her; she was sure of it. But in her bewildered state, she had no idea what he'd meant. She must find him. Ben had her backpack, the bracelet and their one means of contacting Cristy – the phone.

She **fruitlessly**[3] scanned the room, wishing Gwilym or Jack would appear yet knowing they wouldn't. As if pressed by cruel thumbs, her eyes strained against the glare of **oppressive**[4] lights, and her head pounded with an **intensifying**[5] thump. Like melting ice, her **confidence**[6] trickled away, as if **evaporating**[7] into the perfectly air-conditioned **atmosphere**[8].

Claire leaned heavily against one of the glass workspaces. She **slumped**[9] into a squat, resting her head in her hands, grappling for answers. In **despair**[10], she thought of the Knights Hawk, trying to **recall**[11] Gwilym's and Gladys's wise words.

Just as she had shone through for Rebecca yesterday, she must now persist for Ben. She must

---

1 **quartet** *(n)* a group of four things or people.

2 **corral** *(v)* gather together. *(s)* assemble, herd, confine, collect, capture, group.

3 **fruitlessly** *(adv)* in a fruitless (pointless) way. *(s)* unsuccessfully, uselessly, futilely, ineffectually. *(ant)* fruitfully, effectively.

4 **oppressive** *(adj)* harsh and overwhelming. *(s)* overpowering, relentless, severe. *(ant)* gentle, lenient.

5 **intensify** *(v)* become more intense (stronger). *(s)* rise, boost, increase, strengthen. *(ant)* abate, lessen.

6 **confidence** *(n)* a feeling of self-assurance and belief in oneself. *(s)* certainty, faith, trust. *(ant)* uncertainty.

7 **evaporate** *(v)* cease to exist, melt away. *(s)* vanish, end, disappear, dissolve, vaporise. *(ant)* appear, solidify.

8 **atmosphere** *(n)* the air in a certain place. *(s)* ether.

9 **slump** *(v)* sink or fall heavily and wearily. *(s)* flop, slouch, sag, droop, hunch. *(ant)* straighten, rise.

10 **despair** *(n)* loss or lack of hope. *(s)* distress, anguish, pain, desperation. *(ant)* joy, hope.

11 **recall** *(v)* bring something back into one's mind. *(s)* remember, recollect, reminisce. *(ant)* repress, forget.

overcome[1] failure and **forge**[2] a way forward; there was no turning back.

Her chest hurt, and tears threatened again, but **inhaling**[3], she closed her eyes, adopted an awkward lotus position and fought to still her mind. She'd witnessed Ben **meditating**[4] before his kung fu competitions, sometimes, annoyingly so, ignoring her on their car journeys. Now she copied him. What she lacked, though, was the luxury of time.

Breathe. Breathe, she urged herself. *Empty your mind. Open your senses. Banish negativity; welcome positivity.*

Claire counted to ten. She **duelled**[5] with her straying thoughts, playing tug of war and **hauling**[6] them back each time they wandered from the anchor she pictured – Ben. Seeing only her friend, and breathing from the pit of her stomach, she focused, **limiting**[7] her senses to nothing but Ben.

With each softening breath, a surprising **serenity**[8] **soothed**[9] her, a state she would have scoffed at **prior to**[10] this, blatantly **disregarding**[11] Ben's **respect**[12] for the ancient **Shaolin**[13] practice. But yesterday's **supernatural**[14] revelations had transformed that **entrenched**[15] **bias**[16] forever. Never would she **judge**[17] with a closed mind again, because through the thickening **tranquillity**[18], she began to hear his voice.

Claire, where are you? Please help me! Where are you?

---

1 **overcome** *(v)* deal with a problem successfully. *(s)* master, control, conquer, crush. *(ant)* fail, surrender.

2 **forge** *(v)* form or make. *(s)* build, establish, devise, invent. *(ant)* destroy.

3 **inhale** *(v)* breathe in. *(s)* suck in, respire, smell, gulp, snort, sniff, gasp. *(ant)* exhale, breathe out.

4 **meditate** *(v)* silently focus one's mind for a time. *(s)* contemplate, reflect.

5 **duel** *(v)* fight. *(s)* battle, clash, combat, contend, joust. *(ant)* surrender.

6 **haul** *(v)* drag or pull with force or effort. *(s)* tow, lug, heave, yank, wrench. *(ant)* push, shove.

7 **limit** *(v)* restrict (prevent from obtaining or achieving more than). *(s)* curb, cap, restrain. *(ant)* increase.

8 **serenity** *(n)* the state of being calm. *(s)* peace, tranquillity, quiet, composure. *(ant)* anxiety, agitation.

9 **soothe** *(v)* gently calm or quieten. *(s)* allay, alleviate, assuage, mollify, console. *(ant)* aggravate, exacerbate.

10 **prior to** *(prep)* before or previous to. *(s)* in advance of, earlier than, ahead of. *(ant)* later than, after.

11 **disregard** *(v)* ignore. *(s)* overlook, neglect, snub, slight. *(ant)* regard, admire.

12 **respect** *(n)* admiration (love). *(s)* awe, appreciation, regard, recognition. *(ant)* disdain, disregard.

13 **Shaolin** *(n)* martial art styles or schools developed by the monks of the Shaolin Temple in China.

14 **supernatural** *(adj)* inexplicable in scientific terms. *(s)* paranormal, mystical, ghostly, uncanny. *(ant)* natural.

15 **entrenched** *(adj)* well-established and difficult to change. *(s)* ingrained, unshakeable, firm. *(ant)* superficial.

16 **bias** *(n)* prejudice (opinion not based on fact). *(s)* bigotry, predisposition, partiality. *(ant)* fairness, objectivity.

17 **judge** *(v)* form an opinion (view) about. *(s)* believe, think, conclude, decide, deduce.

18 **tranquillity** *(n)* the quality or state of being tranquil. *(s)* calm, serenity, peacefulness, lull. *(ant)* turmoil, agitation.

'Ben,' she whispered.

More gold is needed. What are they talking about? Who is Evans?

Claire was listening to Ben's **chaotic**[1] thoughts, or perhaps it was his voice. She didn't care which, or how; she could hear him, and that was all that mattered.

I hope she finds them. I hope she finds the marks. Where are they taking me? Claire, bring my dad.

Then, abruptly, silence.

Claire didn't move, terrified that if she did, his voice wouldn't return.

Breathe. Breathe, she repeated, picturing Ben again while fighting to maintain her composure. *Ben, Ben*, she chanted, but she heard no more. He was gone.

I must get back to those stairs. I'll never find him down here.

Claire leaped to her feet, needing a high vantage point to spot Ben's cube. Her one hope of finding him was from the glittering staircase. However, no illuminated foot guide would escort her back through the maze. She'd lost sight of it a while back. Dewi's flying saucer would offer a landmark to the stairs, and **regardless**[2] of the risk of potential capture, she headed straight for it, praying she wasn't too late.

As Claire dodged workers, she avoided eye contact and their distracting twinkling guides. Moving as **inconspicuously**[3] as possible, she focused on the landmark that would lead her back to the stairs. Although she sweated, she concealed her gloved hand in her hoody pocket and marched, as the crow flies, towards what she suspected was Dewi's office – the flying saucer.

Taken aback, she slowed. A faint **waft**[4] of **beguiling**[5] fragrance had caught her unawares. *Was that Jayne's perfume?* Alarmed, she glanced around for the source, relieved to see only unfamiliar faces.

While trying to ignore the employees' flashing guides, a sequence of hypnotic **violet**[6] lights

---

1 **chaotic** *(adj)* in a state of confusion and disorder. *(s)* muddled, haywire, messy, untidy. *(ant)* orderly.

2 **regardless** *(adv)* not caring about the circumstances or outcomes. *(s)* anyway, nevertheless.

3 **inconspicuously** *(adv)* in an inconspicuous (unnoticeable) manner. *(s)* discreetly. *(ant)* conspicuously, overtly.

4 **waft** *(n)* a gentle movement or current of air. *(s)* blow, wave, breath, puff, gust, draught.

5 **beguiling** *(adj)* charming, often in a misleading way. *(s)* enchanting, captivating, bewitching. *(ant)* unappealing.

6 **violet** *(adj)* bluish-purple in colour. *(s)* lilac, lavender.

drew her gaze to the **elegantly**[1] **shod**[2] feet of a young woman. Claire was about to look away, but something small lying on the floor by an empty cubicle caught her eye. Moving to one side, she bent to tie up an imaginary loose trainer lace. Surreptitiously, and shuffling closer to the cubicle, she **squatted**[3], shielding the **article**[4] from view with her bottom. Using her left hand, not having dared to remove the cling film glove **lest**[5] she tear it, she picked up the item.

'Yes!' she mouthed, **retrieving**[6] what she hoped was Cristy's mobile phone, pocketing it as she stood. While she couldn't be confident it was Cristy's until she switched it on, if it was, then Ben had left it there for Claire to find.

Claire scanned the **immediate**[7] floor and **proximate**[8] glass cubes. Two cubicles stood empty. She **sidled**[9] up to them, aiming her gaze towards the floor and base of the **vacant**[10] offices. Ben had signalled to her, and if he'd dropped this phone with **intent**[11], then she aimed to miss no further clues.

She **racked her brains**[12]. He'd been fiddling around with something before Drane had **accosted**[13] him. What had it been? What was in her school bag?

She ran through a list in her head.

My pencil case! My pencil case was in my bag from yesterday. I left it there this morning. He was signalling 'pinch and rest' when he waved at me, like holding a pen. He must have written something somewhere.

Claire hoped she was right. Acting relaxed, she cast more **covert**[14] glances around the bases

---

1 **elegantly** *(adv)* in an elegant (stylish) manner. *(s)* attractively, gracefully, tastefully. *(ant)* poorly.

2 **shod** *(adj)* outfitted with shoes.

3 **squat** *(v)* crouch down with bent knees. *(s)* cower, bend, hunch, stoop, hunker. *(ant)* stand, straighten.

4 **article** *(n)* an item or object. *(s)* piece, thing, entity, commodity, artefact, thingamajig, stuff.

5 **lest** *(con)* with the intention of preventing or to avoid the risk of. *(s)* in case, for fear that.

6 **retrieve** *(v)* bring or get something back. *(s)* reclaim, fetch, recover, rescue, salvage.

7 **immediate** *(adj)* next to or nearest in space or time. *(s)* direct, near, close, nearby. *(ant)* distant, far.

8 **proximate** *(adj)* close by. *(s)* immediate, near, adjacent, nearby. *(ant)* far, distant.

9 **sidle** *(v)* walk in a furtive (secretive) or timid (shy) manner. *(s)* sneak, creep, slink, slip, edge. *(ant)* stride.

10 **vacant** *(adj)* (of a place) not occupied. *(s)* bare, deserted, empty, clear, unfilled, unoccupied. *(ant)* occupied.

11 **intent** *(n)* purpose or intention. *(s)* resolve, determination.

12 **rack one's brains** *(v)* try hard to remember something. *(s)* concentrate, focus, think back.

13 **accost** *(v)* approach and speak to someone aggressively. *(s)* confront, corner, waylay, collar. *(ant)* avoid.

14 **covert** *(adj)* not openly displayed or acknowledged. *(s)* secret, underground, concealed. *(ant)* obvious, overt.

of the empty cubicles, searching inside and outside for clues from Ben.

What would he use? What would he do? She bent to inspect something.

'Hello. Are you all right down there?' enquired a perfectly **groomed**[1] young woman. She hugged a thin tablet device to her chest, her feet **straddling**[2] a line of twinkling **crimson**[3] lights.

'Um, yes, thanks. Dropped my phone,' said Claire with a **spurious**[4] smile, grabbing it from her pocket. Claire's pulse rocketed, but the woman just nodded and walked onwards.

Claire exhaled. Her clammy right hand was sweating and squelched in her pocket. This was no place for winter gloves **swathed**[5] in plastic, and she doubted her **makeshift**[6] **gizmo**[7] would perform its wonders again.

As Claire pressed the phone back into her jeans pocket, she caught sight of something. She **stooped**[8], dismissing it at first, but after spitting on her finger and rubbing it, she realised the **significance**[9] – she couldn't **erase**[10] the mark. Splodged **indelibly**[11] on the **pristine**[12] glass of a cubicle, in an almost-**illegible**[13] **scrawl**[14], was the letter C. It was **daubed**[15] in candy-pink ink, and she **possessed**[16] the exact same shade in her pencil case – a Sharpie. Claire owned most of their rarer shades. Ben had used his guile to leave a trail, which she dearly hoped didn't end here.

Claire glanced over her shoulder and placed her gloved hand up to the ID panel, **willing**[17]

---

1 **groom** *(v)* prepare the appearance of something. *(s)* dress, brush, preen, primp, smarten. *(ant)* dishevel.
2 **straddle** *(v)* spread the legs wide apart (either side of something). *(s)* bestride, span, sprawl.
3 **crimson** *(adj)* deep, rich purplish-red colour. *(s)* ruby, scarlet, rouge, carmine, cherry, cerise.
4 **spurious** *(adj)* outwardly false (not real). *(s)* phoney, bogus, fake, feigned, pretend. *(ant)* real, genuine.
5 **swathe** *(v)* wrap in multiple layers. *(s)* bind, swaddle, envelop, shroud. *(ant)* unwrap.
6 **makeshift** *(adj)* acting as a temporary or make-do measure. *(s)* pretend, improvised, crude. *(ant)* permanent.
7 **gizmo** *(n)* a gadget or novel device. *(s)* contraption, widget, contrivance, thingamajig.
8 **stoop** *(v)* bend one's head or body forward and downwards into a hunch. *(s)* crouch, slouch. *(ant)* straighten.
9 **significance** *(n)* meaning or idea. *(s)* import, implication, relevance.
10 **erase** *(v)* remove or rub out. *(s)* expunge, obliterate, delete, eradicate, eliminate, destroy. *(ant)* preserve.
11 **indelibly** *(adv)* in an indelible (cannot be removed) way. *(s)* permanently, forever, eternally, everlastingly.
12 **pristine** *(adj)* unspoiled. *(s)* spotless, immaculate, perfect, flawless. *(ant)* dirty, sullied.
13 **illegible** *(adj)* unable to be read. *(s)* unreadable, scrawled, unintelligible, scribbled. *(ant)* legible, clear.
14 **scrawl** *(n)* careless writing. *(s)* scribble, squiggle, doodle.
15 **daub** *(v)* smear, coat or paint in a clumsy way. *(s)* smudge, plaster, stain, cover, slop, splatter. *(ant)* clean.
16 **possess** *(v)* have or own a characteristic or thing. *(s)* acquire, occupy, carry, obtain, maintain. *(ant)* lack.
17 **will** *(v)* want something to happen. *(s)* long, wish, desire, yearn, pray.

the door to open and praying she wouldn't be **apprehended**[1]. With tangible relief, and both wishes **granted**[2], she stepped into the glass cube. The flush door pane glided shut behind her, **skimming**[3] her backside. With a **start**[4], Claire leaped forward into the glass office. The cube was soundproofed and **deceptively**[5] spacious; it was as if she had **donned**[6] noise-cancelling headphones.

Surrounded by identical cubes housing **slick**[7] workers, Claire worked. She moved about the space, feigning purpose for the employees but with her eyes peeled for further clues of Ben. **Stumped**[8], she searched **clandestinely**[9], trying to avoid outside attention. How had Ben and his **assailants**[10] vanished?

She gazed up through the glass ceiling at the **infinite**[11] blue lights, shining like **implanted**[12] stars. Jewels dotted into the crags and **fissures**[13] of the cave's rock ceiling, their allure was **incomparable**[14]. It was as though part of an **unsullied**[15] midnight sky had been plucked from its precise location and replaced above this subterranean city. But now wasn't the time to admire the **architecture**[16]; she must locate Ben.

Subterranean! Claire's attention fell to her feet. *Tunnels!* Those words **induced**[17] a shudder

---

1 **apprehend** *(v)* take into custody. *(s)* bust, catch, seize, capture, nab. *(ant)* release.

2 **grant** *(v)* allow or give. *(s)* accord, award, assign, bestow. *(ant)* deny.

3 **skim** *(v)* pass over (a surface) nearly or lightly touching it. *(s)* glide, graze, brush, glance.

4 **start** *(n)* a jerk or jump of alarm. *(s)* jolt, flinch, twitch, wince, spasm.

5 **deceptively** *(adv)* in a deceptive (misleading) way. *(s)* dishonestly, deceivingly, spuriously. *(ant)* truly, honestly.

6 **don** *(v)* put on or get dressed in. *(s)* throw on, slip on, change into, wear. *(ant)* take off, remove.

7 **slick** *(adj)* impressive and efficient. *(s)* deft, smooth, skilful, adroit. *(ant)* amateurish, clumsy.

8 **stump** *(v)* cause to be at a loss. *(s)* baffle, bewilder, confuse, confound, mystify. *(ant)* clarify, explain.

9 **clandestinely** *(adv)* in a clandestine (secretive) manner. *(s)* covertly, stealthily, surreptitiously. *(ant)* overtly.

10 **assailant** *(n)* a person who physically harms or attacks another. *(s)* assaulter, aggressor, opponent. *(ant)* ally.

11 **infinite** *(adj)* never-ending or impossible to calculate. *(s)* unlimited, endless, boundless. *(ant)* finite, limited.

12 **implant** *(v)* insert or fix into. *(s)* embed, insert, lodge, bury, install. *(ant)* remove, extract.

13 **fissure** *(n)* narrow opening, split or crack. *(s)* crevice, chink, cleft, rift, slit, fracture, breach. *(ant)* closure.

14 **incomparable** *(adj)* without an equal. *(s)* unmatched, matchless, unrivalled. *(ant)* ordinary.

15 **unsullied** *(adj)* not spoiled or made impure. *(s)* untainted, perfect, pure, clean, untarnished. *(ant)* tarnished.

16 **architecture** *(n)* the design and construction of buildings. *(s)* composition, style, formation.

17 **induce** *(v)* bring about. *(s)* cause, prompt, generate, activate. *(ant)* prevent.

of **claustrophobia**[1]. Being inside and below a mountain was **grim**[2] enough, but the thought of **slithering**[3] through **dank**[4], insect-**riddled**[5] burrows, like yesterday, **provoked**[6] immediate nausea. Yesterday's taste of **mouldy**[7] soil and crawling amongst **hordes**[8] of bugs flooded back; a foreboding sense of **déjà vu**[9] **prevailed**[10]. She shuddered again. If Drane had vanished, then Claire **surmised**[11] he must have used tunnels.

A **solitary**[12], **minimalistic**[13] metal desk, more like a **lectern**[14], stood centre stage in the glass cube, an ultra-thin screen suspended above it. Claire peeked at her fellow co-workers, waving at screens in their silenced cells. To appear **industrious**[15], she motioned her hand towards her screen in a **re-enactment**[16] of their movements. All the while, she protected her gloved hand and **scoured**[17] for clues from Ben. **Despondent**[18] and fearful, she plucked Cristy's mobile from her back pocket.

Should I call Cristy? she thought, feeling downright **dispirited**[19]. *What on earth would I tell her?*

She flipped the phone over and over in her hand, torn between calling Cristy and recalling

---

1 **claustrophobia** *(n)* extreme fear of confined (small) spaces. *(ant)* agoraphobia.

2 **grim** *(adj)* forbidding or unattractive. *(s)* bleak, miserable, wretched, dismal, joyless. *(ant)* attractive, joyful.

3 **slither** *(v)* move over a surface with a twisting or oscillating motion. *(s)* crawl, slide, glide, slip, wriggle.

4 **dank** *(adj)* cold and damp. *(s)* musty, humid, clammy, unaired, moist, fusty, soggy, wet. *(ant)* warm, dry.

5 **riddle** *(v)* fill with something (often undesirably so). *(s)* infest, pervade.

6 **provoke** *(v)* deliberately cause or stimulate something (often unwelcome). *(s)* aggravate, incite. *(ant)* allay.

7 **mouldy** *(adj)* covered with a fungal growth (mould) that causes decay. *(s)* rotten, festering. *(ant)* fresh, new.

8 **horde** *(n)* a large group of people. *(s)* crowd, throng, mass, gathering, mob, host, multitude. *(ant)* few, one.

9 **déjà vu** *(n)* a feeling of having already experienced or seen something. *(s)* recollection, recognition, familiarity.

10 **prevail** *(v)* gain influence or become dominant. *(s)* persist, hold sway, abound, predominate. *(ant)* vanish.

11 **surmise** *(v)* suppose to be true with little or no evidence. *(s)* guess, deduce, infer, conclude. *(ant)* know.

12 **solitary** *(adj)* isolated or secluded, existing alone. *(s)* individual, single, remote. *(ant)* accompanied.

13 **minimalistic** *(adj)* simple and unadorned. *(s)* plain, basic, modest, stark. *(ant)* fancy, elaborate.

14 **lectern** *(n)* a tall stand to hold up notes or a book to read from while standing.

15 **industrious** *(adj)* hard-working and diligent. *(s)* conscientious, untiring, busy, assiduous. *(ant)* lazy, indolent.

16 **re-enactment** *(n)* the acting out of a past event. *(s)* repetition, imitation, recreation. *(ant)* original.

17 **scour** *(v)* look or search thoroughly. *(s)* scrutinise, study, review, inspect, read, revise, rifle. *(ant)* overlook.

18 **despondent** *(adj)* feeling low from loss of hope. *(s)* downcast, crestfallen, discouraged. *(ant)* hopeful.

19 **dispirited** *(adj)* having lost hope and eagerness. *(s)* disheartened, crestfallen, discouraged, disconsolate. *(ant)* heartened.

Gwilym's words of **wisdom**[1]: *Your Instinct will* **evolve**[2] *and* **thrive**[3] *if you work for it and deserve it, but moreover, when you* need *it.*

Well, she *needed* it now, and it eluded her. 'Battle leader!' she scoffed out loud at the **translation**[4] of Cadwaladr. 'I couldn't lead a dog to a bone,' she **ridiculed**[5] herself, **berating**[6] herself as she leaned both elbows onto the metal lectern.

Defeated, she put down the phone and examined her gloved hand. The cling film clung, just about hanging on. Her hand sweated, irritating her skin; she yearned to tear the glove off. She'd lost the Gwalch Gem bracelet. The Master's **thuggish**[7] right-hand man had **abducted**[8] Ben. Both **catastrophes**[9] were down to her **ineptitude**[10]. Mr Brady would be furious. She was in a complete fix. If she left this cube, where would she go? Her glove **conveyed**[11] little life; it might not open this cube. In a **dire**[12] **predicament**[13], she knew she must call Cristy and involve Mr Brady. She had no choice.

To disguise her searching from the Via-Corp clones, Claire lifted her hand, concealing it in front of the suspended screen. As she readied to remove the glove and call Cristy, her hand brushed the screen, and startling her, its **interface**[14] sprang into life. Astonished, Claire lowered her hand and glanced around the cube. No one in the **encircling**[15] offices **batted**[16] an eyelid.

The screen displayed, 'Hello, Ms Grant.'

---

1 **wisdom** *(n)* the quality of having experience or good judgement. *(s)* intelligence, insight. *(ant)* foolishness.

2 **evolve** *(v)* develop gradually over time. *(s)* grow, change, progress, advance, thrive, flourish. *(ant)* regress.

3 **thrive** *(v)* do well. *(s)* flourish, grow, prosper, advance, succeed, blossom. *(ant)* wither, decline, deteriorate.

4 **translation** *(n)* the act of changing one language into another. *(s)* conversion, interpretation. *(ant)* original.

5 **ridicule** *(v)* subject to unpleasant language or behaviour. *(s)* mock, humiliate, deride, tease, scorn. *(ant)* praise.

6 **berate** *(v)* criticise or scold (tell off). *(s)* rebuke, slate, censure, chide, revile, lambaste. *(ant)* praise.

7 **thuggish** *(adj)* characterised by bad or brutal behaviour. *(s)* yobbish, rough, violent. *(ant)* gentle.

8 **abduct** *(v)* take away by force. *(s)* kidnap, seize, capture. *(ant)* release.

9 **catastrophe** *(n)* a terrible event. *(s)* disaster, crisis, calamity, tragedy, blow, shock. *(ant)* salvation.

10 **ineptitude** *(n)* lack of know-how, skill and ability. *(s)* incompetence, incapacity. *(ant)* competence.

11 **convey** *(v)* communicate or make known. *(s)* give, transmit, exude, broadcast. *(ant)* obscure, conceal.

12 **dire** *(adj)* serious or urgent. *(s)* terrible, dreadful, appalling, frightful. *(ant)* mild, good.

13 **predicament** *(n)* difficult or embarrassing situation. *(s)* dilemma, crisis, plight. *(ant)* walkover, doddle.

14 **interface** *(n)* a program or device enabling a user to communicate with a computer.

15 **encircle** *(v)* form a circle around. *(s)* ring, surround, enclose, encompass.

16 **bat** *(v)* (of eyelashes) open and close in fluttering movements. *(s)* flicker, blink, flap, wink.

Waving Cristy's greasy palm print before the screen had **activated**[1] it. Claire's heart hammered as she skimmed its words: 'Welcome to **efficiency**[2] cube 118. Please select your atmosphere and **ambience**[3].'

Efficiency cube, that's ***novel***[4]*!*

As an **Egyptologist**[5] might handle **priceless**[6] **papyrus**[7], Claire **methodically**[8] rewrapped the **ailing**[9] plastic around her glove and inched it back onto her hand. She'd thought her **handiwork**[10] only opened doors. The sweaty mitt would now stay **in situ**[11] until it failed.

A series of prompts appeared on the screen under the respective menus: 'Atmosphere' and 'Ambience'.

Zero evidence of mouse-clicking existed here. Everyone just waved at screens, so Claire pointed at the first menu. She wiggled her cling-film-coated finger, and sure enough, a drop-down list appeared. Claire skimmed the screen again, but what she required evaded her.

She waved at 'Ambience', and down dropped its choices: '**Hospitable**[12]', '**Genial**[13]', 'Welcoming'. Claire knew what she wanted but couldn't find it. This was her only chance, so she continued **browsing**[14].

'Privacy', she waved her finger over it. 'Bingo!' she shouted, regretting the volume, then smiling to herself with relief. She was, after all, in a **hermetically**[15] sealed glass box. She stared at the drop-down list, wanting to get this right. Not convinced she knew the word's meaning but

---

1 **activate** *(v)* make active. *(s)* operate, start, trigger, initialise, animate. *(ant)* deactivate, switch off.

2 **efficiency** *(n)* maximum productivity with minimum waste. *(s)* competence, proficiency. *(ant)* inefficiency.

3 **ambience** *(n)* the character of a place. *(s)* mood, feel, climate, tone, air, vibe.

4 **novel** *(adj)* unusual or new. *(s)* different, unfamiliar, peculiar, unprecedented, curious. *(ant)* normal, familiar.

5 **Egyptologist** *(n)* a person who studies the history and language of ancient Egypt.

6 **priceless** *(adj)* so precious that a value cannot be put on it. *(s)* invaluable, rare, high-priced. *(ant)* worthless.

7 **papyrus** *(n)* sheets made in ancient Egypt from a tall water plant and used for writing and painting on.

8 **methodically** *(adv)* in a methodical (systematic) way. *(s)* coherently, carefully, precisely. *(ant)* randomly.

9 **ailing** *(adj)* in poor condition or health. *(s)* weak, infirm, indisposed, feeble, frail. *(ant)* well, strong, fit.

10 **handiwork** *(n)* something made or done by someone. *(s)* design, creation, work, craft, action.

11 **in situ** *(adv)* in the appropriate place or position. *(s)* in place.

12 **hospitable** *(adj)* welcoming and friendly. *(s)* congenial, sociable, cordial, warm, open, kind. *(ant)* inhospitable.

13 **genial** *(adj)* cheerful and friendly. *(s)* mild, cordial, affable, warm, amiable, congenial. *(ant)* unfriendly, cold.

14 **browse** *(v)* look through in a leisurely way. *(s)* read, peruse, scan, skim.

15 **hermetically** *(adv)* in a hermetic (airtight) manner. *(s)* imperviously. *(ant)* porously.

using a process of **elimination**[1], she decided on 'Opaque'. Biting her lip, she waved her finger at it.

'YES!' she shouted, pumping her left fist in the air, **mindful**[2] of the glove on her right. Her view to the **exterior**[3] **hub**[4] had become partially **obscured**[5] by misty glass – from outside, she would be invisible. Without **prying**[6] eyes, she could search the cube **diligently**[7].

'Mustn't forget that,' she said, squeezing Cristy's phone into her back pocket.

Tunnels, she thought, **surveying**[8] the slate floor beneath her feet. They must have descended, or she would have seen them leave the cube from the staircase. Either that, or they *really had* vanished. However, if *time-tangling* was real, she'd rule nothing out. Now was not the time for **complacency**[9].

The floor **comprised**[10] robust square **slabs**[11]. Beginning in one corner, Claire knelt. **Systematically**[12], working in rows, she searched for clues of Ben. Lest she miss any, she traced her finger along each **grout**[13] line before inspecting the tile's surface. If Ben had marked the glass on the outside of a cube, then he'd be able to mark inside too, unless they had **confiscated**[14] the Sharpie first.

'Ouch!' she yelled, not realising kneeling could induce such pain, but crawling on a bare slate floor was **excruciating**[15]. With just a few slabs left to inspect, Claire's **pessimism**[15] **escalated**[17]. As

---

1 **elimination** *(n)* the exclusion of something. *(s)* eradication, removal, riddance. *(ant)* inclusion.

2 **mindful** *(adj)* aware. *(s)* conscious, attentive, knowledgeable, observant. *(ant)* heedless, ignorant, careless.

3 **exterior** *(adj)* situated outside. *(s)* outer, external. *(ant)* interior.

4 **hub** *(n)* a centre of activity. *(s)* heart, core, focus, middle. *(ant)* periphery.

5 **obscured** *(adj)* concealed, not able to be seen. *(s)* hidden, veiled, covered, blocked, unclear. *(ant)* clear, distinct.

6 **prying** *(adj)* looking or enquiring too closely. *(s)* inquisitive, curious, probing. *(ant)* disinterested.

7 **diligently** *(adv)* in a diligent (careful) way. *(s)* conscientiously, meticulously, attentively. *(ant)* carelessly.

8 **survey** *(v)* look closely at or examine. *(s)* study, inspect, analyse, assess, evaluate, consider. *(ant)* overlook.

9 **complacency** *(n)* a smug feeling of satisfaction with oneself. *(s)* smugness, conceit, pride. *(ant)* dissatisfaction.

10 **comprise** *(v)* be made up or consist of. *(s)* include, contain, involve, compose, encompass. *(ant)* exclude.

11 **slab** *(n)* a thick slice of stone. *(s)* piece, hunk, wedge, block.

12 **systematically** *(adv)* in a systematic (according to a plan or system) way. *(s)* methodically, consistently. *(ant)* haphazardly.

13 **grout** *(n)* a paste or mortar (like concrete) used for filling gaps in between tiles. *(s)* filler.

14 **confiscate** *(v)* take ownership with authority. *(s)* seize, commandeer, appropriate. *(ant)* return.

15 **excruciating** *(adj)* very painful. *(s)* searing, agonising, harrowing. *(ant)* painless.

16 **pessimism** *(n)* an inclination to believe or see the worst aspects of something. *(s)* cynicism, gloom. *(ant)* optimism, faith.

17 **escalate** *(v)* increase quickly. *(s)* intensify, heighten, spiral, accelerate, soar, rocket, surge. *(ant)* drop.

she paced around the perimeter, she found no sign of Ben, but he was **resourceful**[1]. He would have left something for her, somewhere.

Claire stepped back to the lectern and waved her plastic-coated palm to rouse the **dormant**[2] screen. She couldn't kick her way out of this dilemma or read someone's mind, like yesterday. With all options now **exhausted**[3], she'd reached a dead end. Flicking through the various menus again, and at her lowest **ebb**[4], Claire **grudgingly**[5] accepted the **prospect**[6] of calling Cristy. Then something beneath the 'Exit efficiency cube' menu on the screen caught her attention. She mouthed the word 'Basement.' There it was, 'Exit via basement', **emblazoned**[7] on the screen.

A triumphant wave rose and fell through her. Claire pointed her plastic finger at the three words and waited. Nothing. What was she missing? On double-checking the menu, she had chosen the only **apt**[8] option, 'Exit via basement'. Then, with **devastating**[9] **realisation**[10], her heart fell. It was the palm print; it wasn't working.

Feeling hollow, she checked the glove's plastic covering. It was still **intact**[11] and accurately fitted. She pulled its **cuff**[12] lower over her wrist and pointed at the three words, to no **avail**[13]. Attempting various hand angles, she waved furiously at the screen, but nothing.

Oversized tears sprang to her eyes, blurring her vision. With a heart-rending sob, she pulled off the **ineffectual**[14] glove, **hurled**[15] it at the screen and **bawled**[16] like a frustrated baby.

---

1 **resourceful** *(adj)* able to overcome difficulties. *(s)* capable, ingenious, quick-witted. *(ant)* unimaginative.

2 **dormant** *(adj)* temporarily inactive. *(s)* sleeping, resting, quiet, latent, idle, inert, quiescent. *(ant)* active.

3 **exhausted** *(adj)* completely depleted. *(s)* used up, consumed, spent, drained. *(ant)* replenished.

4 **ebb** *(n)* a point of decline or a worsened state. *(s)* deterioration, degeneration. *(ant)* ascent, upswing.

5 **grudgingly** *(adv)* in a grudging (reluctant) manner. *(s)* unwillingly, resentfully, loathingly. *(ant)* willingly.

6 **prospect** *(n)* a future or anticipated event. *(s)* thought, vision, idea, contemplation.

7 **emblazon** *(v)* display or depict on something. *(s)* present, show, exhibit. *(ant)* hide, conceal.

8 **apt** *(adj)* suitable for a particular purpose. *(s)* appropriate, fitting, relevant. *(ant)* inappropriate.

9 **devastating** *(adj)* destructive, causing grief or shock. *(s)* harmful, distressing, detrimental. *(ant)* constructive.

10 **realisation** *(n)* the act of becoming aware that something is a fact. *(s)* understanding, comprehension. *(ant)* ignorance.

11 **intact** *(adj)* not impaired or damaged. *(s)* complete, whole, unbroken, together, unharmed. *(ant)* broken.

12 **cuff** *(n)* the part of a sleeve around the wrist, where the material is often turned back.

13 **avail** *(n)* benefit or use. *(s)* advantage, reward, purpose, gain, profit, help, boon, edge. *(ant)* uselessness.

14 **ineffectual** *(adj)* not producing a desired effect. *(s)* unsuccessful, inefficient, ineffective. *(ant)* effective.

15 **hurl** *(v)* impel or throw with force. *(s)* fling, heave, lob, launch, pitch, dash, fire. *(ant)* hold, catch.

16 **bawl** *(v)* cry or shout noisily. *(s)* howl, wail, sob, weep, blubber, blub, roar, bellow. *(ant)* whisper.

Several minutes passed before her **hysteria**[1] **subsided**[2], and Claire regained a **modicum**[3] of calm composure. She glanced at the **trashed**[4] plastic, the **static**[5] causing it to cling to the screen. Feeling **isolated**[6], and with **insurmountable**[7] guilt at having failed Ben and Gwilym, she dried her eyes on her sleeve and reached for the phone wedged in her back pocket.

'What!' Claire dropped the phone as though she'd picked up a poo. As she bent to **retrieve** it, she stared at what had caused her to drop it so suddenly. **Dumbfounded**[8], she **gawked**[9], **oscillating**[10] between **elation**[11] and terror. A dim yellow light glowed from a gap that had **materialised**[12] between the slate slabs. Taking a wary step forward, she peered into the **crevice**[13]-like opening. Her stomach lurched. She knew what was next: a hole and what looked like a **primitive**[14] ladder fixed to the side of a deep **shaft**[15], followed by endless darkness.

With an impending sense of déjà vu, Claire knelt, peeking into the **abyss**[16]. A waft of dank air hit her nostrils, a smell she remembered well. It conjured the promise of **retaliatory**[17] bites from the indignant insects upon whose **dwellings**[18] she was about to **wreak**[19] **havoc**[20] and **annihilation**[21]. For she was sure of one thing: that ladder led to tunnels suited only for crawling.

---

1 **hysteria** *(n)* extreme emotion or excitement. *(s)* hysterics, frenzy, wildness, panic, irrationality. *(ant)* calmness.

2 **subside** *(v)* become less severe or intense. *(s)* diminish, ease, abate, calm, lull, relent. *(ant)* increase.

3 **modicum** *(n)* a small amount. *(s)* degree, scrap, touch, dash, tinge, dab, snippet.

4 **trash** *(v)* damage. *(s)* destroy, wreck, ruin, mar, spoil, total, vandalise.

5 **static** *(n)* (static electricity) a motionless electric charge that can cause sparks or attraction between two objects.

6 **isolated** *(adj)* set apart. *(s)* separated, solitary, lonely, secluded, friendless. *(ant)* integrated.

7 **insurmountable** *(adj)* too great to overcome. *(s)* invincible, impossible, unbeatable. *(ant)* easy, surmountable.

8 **dumbfound** *(v)* greatly astonish. *(s)* stagger, startle, amaze, flabbergast, confound, stupefy. *(ant)* underwhelm.

9 **gawk** *(v)* stare stupidly. *(s)* gape, gaze, gawp, rubberneck, ogle, goggle, watch. *(ant)* glance, ignore.

10 **oscillate** *(v)* vary (change), swing back and forth. *(s)* vacillate, alternate, undulate.

11 **elation** *(n)* great happiness. *(s)* ecstasy, bliss, enthusiasm, euphoria, exhilaration, glee, joy. *(ant)* despair, misery.

12 **materialise** *(v)* appear. *(s)* emerge, arrive, arise, occur, manifest, develop, evolve. *(ant)* disappear, evaporate.

13 **crevice** *(n)* narrow opening or crack (especially in rock). *(s)* gap, fissure, cleft, fracture, cranny. *(ant)* ridge.

14 **primitive** *(adj)* very basic. *(s)* crude, rough, simple, elementary, makeshift, rudimentary. *(ant)* sophisticated.

15 **shaft** *(n)* a long, narrow hole that gives access to a mine. *(s)* bore, borehole, mineshaft, tunnel, passage.

16 **abyss** *(n)* a deep hole or chasm. *(s)* gorge, canyon, fissure, rift, pit, depth, void.

17 **retaliatory** *(adj)* characterised by wanting revenge. *(s)* vengeful, punitive, revengeful, retaliative.

18 **dwelling** *(n)* a house, flat or other place of residence. *(s)* home, accommodation, abode, lodging, habitat.

19 **wreak** *(v)* cause. *(s)* create, inflict, engender, unleash, bestow.

20 **havoc** *(n)* destruction. *(s)* damage, devastation, disaster, ruin, catastrophe. *(ant)* peace.

21 **annihilation** *(n)* total destruction. *(s)* demolition, decimation, elimination, eradication. *(ant)* creation.

*

Alone, the woman studied the screen, her **countenance**[1] **impassive**[2] and hard. Her **astute**[3] eyes followed Claire's every move inside the cube. Impatient and unmoved, she had observed Claire's weeping, her **maternal**[4] instincts **indifferent**[5] to such displays of emotion.

Amused[6], and with **scorn**[7], she had watched Claire **painstakingly**[8] peel off her precious piece of plastic, which had *oh-so* ***fortuitously***[9] landed with pinpoint **accuracy**[10] on the screen, **ergo**[11] **triggering**[12] the opening. At least that was what the **gullible**[13] girl thought.

Little did Claire know that to this woman, she was a mere **pawn**[14] in her **menacing**[15] game, an **unremarkable**[16] and biddable piece, a **lowly**[17] counter **sacrificed**[18] to ensure the queen cornered her king – in **checkmate**[19].

---

1 **countenance** *(n)* a person's expression or face. *(s)* features, look, appearance.

2 **impassive** *(adj)* not feeling or showing emotion. *(s)* inexpressive, unrevealing, expressionless. *(ant)* expressive.

3 **astute** *(adj)* able to quickly assess and turn to one's advantage. *(s)* sharp, shrewd, cunning. *(ant)* dim-witted.

4 **maternal** *(adj)* relating to motherhood. *(s)* motherly, nurturing, loving, protective.

5 **indifferent** *(adj)* having no interest. *(s)* casual, apathetic, uninterested, unconcerned. *(ant)* concerned.

6 **amused** *(adj)* finding something funny. *(s)* entertained, pleased, tickled, charmed. *(ant)* bored, displeased.

7 **scorn** *(n)* open contempt (dislike). *(s)* disdain, derision, mockery, ridicule, sarcasm, sneering. *(ant)* admiration, respect.

8 **painstakingly** *(adv)* done in a painstaking (careful) way. *(s)* thoroughly, diligently, meticulously. *(ant)* carelessly.

9 **fortuitously** *(adv)* in a fortuitous (by chance) way. *(s)* luckily, serendipitously, accidentally. *(ant)* intentionally.

10 **accuracy** *(n)* correctness or precision. *(s)* certainty, skill, exactness, exactitude, mastery. *(ant)* inaccuracy.

11 **ergo** *(adv)* for that reason. *(s)* therefore, hence, consequently, as a result, thus.

12 **trigger** *(v)* cause something to function or set off. *(s)* start, activate, spark, initiate, fire. *(ant)* halt.

13 **gullible** *(adj)* easily persuaded to believe something. *(s)* trusting, naive, impressionable. *(ant)* cynical, suspicious.

14 **pawn** *(n)* a chess piece of the smallest value, used figuratively to indicate a person exploited for someone else's purposes.

15 **menacing** *(adj)* threatening or dangerous. *(s)* ominous, intimidating, sinister, fearsome. *(ant)* reassuring.

16 **unremarkable** *(adj)* not interesting or surprising (not noteworthy). *(s)* ordinary, average. *(ant)* extraordinary.

17 **lowly** *(adj)* low in importance or rank. *(s)* humble, ordinary, simple, plain, common, poor. *(ant)* noble.

18 **sacrifice** *(v)* give up something for the sake of others. *(s)* surrender, forgo, forfeit, cede. *(ant)* keep, obtain.

19 **checkmate** *(n)* (in chess) when a player's king is attacked and cannot escape. Used figuratively to indicate a last defeat.

8. A Knight's Demise

Letting go of Claire would be difficult.

In the **solitude**[1] of his ancient mountain **hideaway**[2], **sequestered**[3] from man, Gwilym Cadwaladr closed his **weary**[4] eyes. He struggled to clear his head and focused his thoughts on finding Claire. **Envisaging**[5] the **emergent**[6] Instinctive, he located her in his mind – a blurry image. Distant and fuzzy, her silhouette was now weakening with each passing second, and although Gwilym still heard her voice, he feared the potential loss of its sound.

The fledgling Instinctive battled alone in the modern-day castle of Prince Llywelyn's traitorous brother, Dewi. A subterranean **fortress**[7] camouflaged beneath nature's **formidable**[8] and **unsurpassed**[9] **defences**[10] – mountains. Here the Master masqueraded as the **philanthropic**[11] **entrepreneur**[12] David Lewis.

Now, as Gwilym's strength **dwindled**[13], so did his connection to Claire. He would soon lose

---

1 **solitude** *(n)* the state or quality of being alone. *(s)* isolation, seclusion, loneliness. *(ant)* company.

2 **hideaway** *(n)* a retreat or a place used for hiding from people. *(s)* refuge, hideout, sanctuary, bolthole.

3 **sequester** *(v)* keep apart or hide away from. *(s)* isolate, seclude, cloister, segregate. *(ant)* reveal, integrate.

4 **weary** *(adj)* extremely tired. *(s)* exhausted, fatigued, drained, whacked, shattered. *(ant)* fresh, refreshed.

5 **envisage** *(v)* form a mental picture of. *(s)* imagine, envision, visualise, picture, foresee.

6 **emergent** *(adj)* coming into being or prominence. *(s)* arising, dawning, emerging, fledgling. *(ant)* mature.

7 **fortress** *(n)* a fortified military stronghold. *(s)* fort, fortification, castle, keep, tower.

8 **formidable** *(adj)* respected and feared. *(s)* intimidating, forbidding, daunting, alarming. *(ant)* weak, non-threatening.

9 **unsurpassed** *(adj)* superior to everything else. *(s)* unrivalled, unequalled, matchless. *(ant)* eclipsed, inferior.

10 **defences** *(n)* means of defending against attack. *(s)* protection, fortification, security. *(ant)* offences.

11 **philanthropic** *(adj)* desiring to help others by giving. *(s)* charitable, generous, humanitarian. *(ant)* miserly, mean.

12 **entrepreneur** *(n)* a person who establishes a business. *(s)* speculator, magnate, tycoon.

13 **dwindle** *(v)* become smaller. *(s)* decrease, decline, abate, fade, diminish, reduce, disappear. *(ant)* increase.

her, her **hazy**[1] outline **ebbing**[2] and **flowing**[3], fading along with his powers. **Mercifully**[4], he still heard **vague**[5] thoughts, but as he was unable to help her whilst he **degenerated**[6] at such pace, she was now alone.

Unless Claire retrieved more magical Welsh gold, Gwilym Cadwaladr **foresaw**[7] no **favourable**[8] outcome to this dire **plight**[9]. He feared an **inevitable**[10] fate might soon **befall**[11] the Knights Hawk. The only explanation for their failing health was a parting of the Gwalch Gem from the Welsh gold bracelet. Someone, or something, had split them.

The Knights Hawk were fortunate to be alive. As **predicted**[12] by the Shaolin masters centuries ago, had the bracelet's gold and gem been separated sooner, whilst at its full, early **potency**[13], the knights would have shattered into **shards**[14] of emerald.

Just as the pairing of the Gwalch Gem and Welsh gold had given the Knights Hawk **prodigious**[15] powers, its separation would bring their **ultimate**[16] **demise**[17]. Mercifully, the passing of time would now *give* them time. If more Welsh gold could be added to the bracelet, then the knights would **rejuvenate**[18], but only if the bracelet became whole again would the knights live on.

The bracelet, like the knights, possessed longevity, not **immortality**[19]. Unknown to its new,

---

1 **hazy** *(adj)* vague or difficult to see. *(s)* unclear, indistinct, faint, dim, indefinite. *(ant)* clear, defined.
2 **ebb** *(v)* (of a quality or emotion) gradually lessen. *(s)* decrease, diminish, dwindle, wane. *(ant)* flow, increase.
3 **flow** *(v)* proceed or produce continuously and effortlessly. *(s)* arise, ensue, continue. *(ant)* ebb, trickle.
4 **mercifully** *(adv)* fortunately. *(s)* thankfully, luckily, happily. *(ant)* unfortunately.
5 **vague** *(adj)* unclear. *(s)* indistinct, hazy, cloudy, fuzzy, misty, blurred, blurry. *(ant)* clear, precise.
6 **degenerate** *(v)* decline physically, mentally or morally. *(s)* deteriorate, slip, slide, worsen, sink. *(ant)* improve.
7 **foresee** *(v)* see something coming before it happens (past tense: foresaw). *(s)* predict, forecast, prophesy.
8 **favourable** *(adj)* good or advantageous. *(s)* beneficial, helpful, conducive, auspicious. *(ant)* disadvantageous.
9 **plight** *(n)* a difficult or dangerous situation. *(s)* trouble, predicament, difficulty, mess, bind.
10 **inevitable** *(adj)* certain to happen. *(s)* inescapable, sure, unpreventable, necessary. *(ant)* avoidable, uncertain.
11 **befall** *(v)* happen to someone. *(s)* strike, hit, overtake, come upon.
12 **predict** *(v)* say or guess that something will happen in the future. *(s)* foresee, forecast, expect, anticipate.
13 **potency** *(n)* the power of something to impress or influence. *(s)* strength, force, vigour, might. *(ant)* impotence.
14 **shard** *(n)* a piece of something broken, creating sharp edges or fragments. *(s)* sliver, splinter, spike.
15 **prodigious** *(adj)* remarkably or impressively great. *(s)* extraordinary, exceptional, impressive. *(ant)* average.
16 **ultimate** *(adj)* final. *(s)* eventual, concluding, last. *(ant)* first.
17 **demise** *(n)* downfall or death. *(s)* ruin, end, failure, collapse, expiry, departure. *(ant)* ascent, birth.
18 **rejuvenate** *(v)* make better, younger or livelier. *(s)* renew, restore, revive, revitalise. *(ant)* age, suppress.
19 **immortality** *(n)* eternal life. *(s)* deathlessness, everlastingness, perpetuity. *(ant)* mortality.

unwelcome Keeper, centuries of use had taken their **toll**[1] on its power, weakening its strength. Whoever had stolen the bracelet would have experienced **bitter**[2] disappointment in expecting its power to equal that at its **genesis**[3]. Perhaps because of this realisation, in a fit of rage, the **pilferer**[4] had **wrenched**[5] the Gwalch Gem from the Welsh gold, triggering the slow demise of the Knights Hawk.

Like a snake's **venom**[6], thoughts of Dewi **infiltrated**[7] Gwilym's brain. The Knights Hawk and Mal-Instinctives had **acquired**[8] their immense powers, both good and evil, from the same source – the magical **combination**[9] of Welsh gold and the Gwalch Gem.

Only Gwilym knew its deepest secrets, for he had risked his life to mine the gold in a **bygone**[10] era. He understood its **properties**[11], which they must now **replenish**[12] lest the Knights Hawk **perish**[13].

But who had taken the gem from the gold? Who had portrayed such **audacity**[14], perhaps **jeopardising**[15] their own life in doing so? Not even the highest-**ranking**[16] Mal-Instinctive would know the risks of dividing gem and gold. Dewi, Llywelyn's younger brother, was **rash**[17] and hot-

---

1 **toll** *(n)* the adverse (unfavourable) effect of something. *(s)* harm, damage, detriment, injury. *(ant)* benefit.
2 **bitter** *(adj)* painful or unpleasant to accept or contemplate. *(s)* acrimonious, harsh, upsetting. *(ant)* agreeable.
3 **genesis** *(n)* origin. *(s)* root, beginning, start, commencement, birth, inception. *(ant)* finish, end.
4 **pilferer** *(n)* someone or something that steals. *(s)* thief, burglar, robber, larcenist, plunderer.
5 **wrench** *(v)* twist or pull suddenly. *(s)* jerk, jolt, yank, wrest, tug, heave.
6 **venom** *(n)* a poisonous substance created by animals. *(s)* toxin, poison.
7 **infiltrate** *(v)* gain access to or pass into unobtrusively. *(s)* invade, penetrate, enter.
8 **acquire** *(v)* obtain (get) or buy something. *(s)* secure, gain, attain, take, achieve, receive. *(ant)* lose, relinquish.
9 **combination** *(n)* a mixing of things that remain individually distinct. *(s)* arrangement, grouping. *(ant)* division.
10 **bygone** *(adj)* from an earlier time. *(s)* past, former, ancient, departed, antiquated. *(ant)* present.
11 **property** *(n)* a feature or characteristic. *(s)* attribute, trait, peculiarity, quality.
12 **replenish** *(v)* restore. *(s)* replace, restock, recharge, reload. *(ant)* exhaust, empty.
13 **perish** *(v)* die, especially suddenly. *(s)* expire, succumb, decease, depart, fade, pass away. *(ant)* live, survive.
14 **audacity** *(n)* boldness. *(s)* daring, bravery, fearlessness, recklessness. *(ant)* timidity.
15 **jeopardise** *(v)* put into a dangerous situation. *(s)* risk, endanger, threaten, imperil. *(ant)* safeguard.
16 **rank** *(v)* have a position in a scale of something or organisation. *(s)* rate, grade, place, class.
17 **rash** *(adj)* acting without consideration of the outcome. *(s)* hasty, reckless, impetuous, impulsive. *(ant)* careful, prudent.

headed, but surely, even *he* would **baulk**[1] at entering such **uncharted**[2] **territory**[3]. Contemplating such a **calamity**[4] was **insanity**[5], but someone *had* **ventured**[6] to this edge and leaped off, and he suspected who that someone might be.

As time slipped by, Gwilym struggled to maintain any view of Claire. While he was faced with such **exertion**[7], his remaining powers would soon be depleted. Critically, he must allocate his **sapping** energy **sagely**[8], to hearing her thoughts.

She was afraid and alone, without her friend Ben and the Gwalch Gem bracelet. The girl no longer had the luxury of time to develop her Instinct, something he had declared to Claire yesterday. Unbeknown to her, his assistance was lost, but his faith in Claire remained. Her Instinct ran deep. Her bravery and **integrity**[9] **underpinned**[10] her decisions. With each **minor**[11] **triumph**[12], he believed her confidence and Instinct would **flourish**[13].

His **conviction**[14] must not **waver**[15]. His future rested with her – the unknighted Instinctive. Had Claire already earned that honour and taken the knighted Welsh name Cadwaladr, she would be suffering the same **wretched**[16] fate as the Knights Hawk. She, too, would be dying.

---

1 **baulk** *(v)* hesitate or be unwilling. *(s)* recoil, resist, refuse, cringe, flinch. *(ant)* proceed, accept, advance.

2 **uncharted** *(adj)* not surveyed or mapped. *(s)* unexplored, unknown, unresearched, undiscovered. *(ant)* charted.

3 **territory** *(n)* a field of experience, knowledge or activity. *(s)* area, domain, sphere, arena.

4 **calamity** *(n)* a disastrous event. *(s)* catastrophe, tragedy, blight, distress, misery, blow. *(ant)* blessing.

5 **insanity** *(n)* extreme foolishness. *(s)* stupidity, idiocy, folly, lunacy, silliness. *(ant)* sense.

6 **venture** *(v)* take a risky course of action. *(s)* dare, brave, presume.

7 **exertion** *(n)* mental or physical effort. *(s)* action, toil, labour, hard work. *(ant)* ease, rest, inaction.

8 **sagely** *(adv)* in a sage (profoundly wise) way. *(s)* shrewdly, prudently, astutely, cleverly, carefully. *(ant)* unwisely.

9 **integrity** *(n)* soundness of moral principle. *(s)* truthfulness, honour, reliability. *(ant)* dishonesty, corruption.

10 **underpin** *(v)* form the basis of. *(s)* nurture, promote, develop, foster. *(ant)* hinder, impede.

11 **minor** *(adj)* not important. *(s)* small, slight, unimportant, insignificant. *(ant)* major, important.

12 **triumph** *(n)* a victory. *(s)* achievement, win, success, conquest. *(ant)* defeat, loss.

13 **flourish** *(v)* grow or develop rapidly and successfully. *(s)* succeed, thrive, prosper, bloom. *(ant)* deteriorate.

14 **conviction** *(n)* a firmly held opinion or belief. *(s)* confidence, sureness, certainty. *(ant)* doubt.

15 **waver** *(v)* become weaker or falter. *(s)* fluctuate, change, hesitate, dither, shake, vary. *(ant)* continue, persist.

16 **wretched** *(adj)* extremely unhappy or unfortunate. *(s)* miserable, desolate, dejected, abject. *(ant)* happy.

9. The Abyss

Claire **hovered**[1] over the edge of the abyss, contemplating the unknown. She had lost Ben and the bracelet. Both catastrophes were her fault – she should never have left either alone.

She perched above the small opening, dangling both legs over it. To test the flimsy-looking ladder, she kicked at the top of it. Would it hold? The ladder appeared newish – odd, given it was attached to the side of a **musty**[2] shaft. Beyond two metres, the **excavation**[3] was **ebony**[4] black. She had no idea of its depth or to where it led.

She stared down, dreading the descent and wanting her mum. Since leaving home earlier, she'd barely thought about her family. Guilt **engulfed**[5] her. Hitherto preoccupied with Ben, she'd not considered them.

How was Rebecca after yesterday's **humiliating**[6] **ordeal**[7] in the museum, when Josh Drane had taken her **hostage**[8] and drugged her? And her mum, Dee, who had no idea of the real reason Claire had been there – to stop the Master from stealing the Cutter. Both sisters had **traumatised**[9] Dee yesterday, and now Claire was here, in hot water again but alone this time.

Dee despised Jayne, dubbing her 'Princess Jayne' and blaming her for their marriage

---

1 **hover** *(v)* remain in one place indecisively. *(s)* linger, loiter. *(ant)* commit.

2 **musty** *(adj)* having a stale, mouldy, or damp and dank smell. *(s)* stuffy, fusty, rank, fetid. *(ant)* fresh.

3 **excavation** *(n)* a site that has been dug out or unearthed. *(s)* hole, pit, hollow, shaft.

4 **ebony** *(n)* wood from a tropical tree that is very dark brown or black in colour.

5 **engulf** *(v)* sweep over or surround completely. *(s)* envelop, overtake, overwhelm, swamp, inundate, immerse.

6 **humiliating** *(adj)* making someone feel foolish or ashamed. *(s)* mortifying, humbling, disgraceful. *(ant)* aggrandising.

7 **ordeal** *(n)* a prolonged and horrid experience. *(s)* test, trial, tribulation, trauma, affliction, nightmare. *(ant)* joy.

8 **hostage** *(n)* someone unwillingly held to be exchanged for something else. *(s)* captive, detainee. *(ant)* captor.

9 **traumatise** *(v)* subject to lasting shock from bad experience or injury. *(s)* devastate, torment. *(ant)* soothe.

breakdown, but Claire found that hatred impossible to emulate. Throughout her parents' separation, Jayne had been nothing but kind, diplomatic and helpful towards Claire, and there were two sides to every story, not just Dee's **skewed**[1] version.

Claire thought of her dad, Vince, and how happy he and Jayne were. Although she **empathised**[2], Claire struggled to see the downside. Jayne had helped Claire with homework and other, more **personal**[3] **affairs**[4]. Claire tried to **conclude**[5] right there that Jayne *must* be innocent in all this. Jayne's job at Via-Corp *must* be sheer coincidence, right? Via-Corp was internationally renowned, and her disturbing dream *must* have been just that – an **angst-ridden**[6] nightmare.

This new-found conviction in Jayne bestowed Claire with more self-belief. In need of light, she stared at the phone's dark screen and waited. Within seconds, the face recognition booted up the phone, just as Cristy had promised. 'Thank you! Thank you, Cristy,' said Claire, swiping **deftly**[7] around the screen. She found the torch – it would drain the battery rapidly, so she must use it wisely.

With the sweaty glove and tattered cling film retrieved and in her back pocket, Claire knelt, her backside and feet facing the hole. She **clutched**[8] the phone in one hand, terrified it would **plummet**[9] down the shaft.

With one palm flat beside her knee, Claire steadied herself and inched back towards the hole. She'd never done this before, refusing point-blank to climb anything in the school gym, protesting her fear of heights. Without a handrail, even climbing *onto* this **precarious**[10] ladder, with one hand, would be trickier than she had thought.

As the phone was in one hand, shuffling back a tad more, now on 'all threes', she turned her head to gauge the distance to the top rung. She could see it, but the largish gap between that

---

1 **skewed** *(adj)* altered to be unfair or untrue. *(s)* distorted, biased, slanted, misrepresentative, contorted. *(ant)* fair, accurate.

2 **empathise** *(v)* understand another's feelings. *(s)* identify, sympathise, comprehend, share.

3 **personal** *(adj)* affecting or belonging to a certain person (yours). *(s)* own, private, intimate, special. *(ant)* public.

4 **affairs** *(n)* business or matters of importance. *(s)* concerns, dealings, activities, undertakings.

5 **conclude** *(v)* decide on or judge something by reasoning. *(s)* deduce, infer, determine, surmise. *(ant)* reject.

6 **angst-ridden** *(adj)* deeply anxious about oneself. *(s)* worried, fretful, fearful. *(ant)* easy-going, relaxed.

7 **deftly** *(adv)* in a deft (skilful) manner. *(s)* adeptly, nimbly, dextrously, adroitly. *(ant)* clumsily, slowly.

8 **clutch** *(v)* grab or grasp something tightly. *(s)* hold, grip, seize, clench, grapple. *(ant)* release, let go.

9 **plummet** *(v)* fall or drop straight down at high speed. *(s)* dive, tumble, crash, decrease. *(ant)* climb, rise.

10 **precarious** *(adj)* not safely held, likely to fall or collapse. *(s)* insecure, risky, unsafe, wobbly. *(ant)* secure, safe.

rung and the opening posed an issue. She would need two hands to steady herself. She must either descend into darkness blind or put the makeshift torch between her teeth. It proved an easy decision. Clenching Cristy's phone between her **incisors**[1], she edged back on all fours, all the while checking over her shoulder for a glimpse of the first rung. Her hands grappled for purchase on the edge of the slab, but her nails just scraped along the slate, setting her teeth on edge.

Exasperated[2], she flopped forward onto her stomach, **winding**[3] herself. The phone shot from her mouth, skidding across the cube. Flat out, she **grimaced**[4] at the handset, which had **ricocheted**[5] off the glass and landed out of reach.

I can't even mess up gracefully, she thought, slithering forward commando-style to retrieve the phone. Then it dawned on her: if she wriggled backwards until her **midriff**[6] hung over the opening, then bent her knees, she might get one foot onto the too-low first rung of the ladder. It was worth a try. She dearly hoped she'd fit through the tight opening.

With stretched fingertips, Claire teased Cristy's phone into her grasp and reversed towards the hole. Glancing back, she moved her feet then legs over the opening. With both shins suspended above the gap, Claire clenched the phone between her teeth and slithered towards the target. Centimetres at a time, she inched her torso back until her legs **protruded**[7] straight over the opening. Her hoody rode up into an irritating **ruffle**[8] around her midriff, **impeding**[9] her movements.

Claire swung her heels up to her backside and, balancing like a see-saw, grabbed at the top rung with one hand and pushed a knee onto a lower bar. She balanced precariously, the phone and her heart in her mouth, and grabbed at the ladder as her other knee found a rung. **Teetering**[10],

---

1 **incisor** *(n)* a sharp tooth at the front of the mouth.

2 **exasperated** *(adj)* irritated greatly. *(s)* agitated, frustrated, annoyed, infuriated, incensed. *(ant)* pleased.

3 **wind** *(v)* cause breathing difficulty due to exertion or an impact to the stomach.

4 **grimace** *(v)* make an ugly, twisted expression on one's face. *(s)* scowl, frown, smirk, pout. *(ant)* smile, grin.

5 **ricochet** *(v)* rebound or echo off a surface, fly around. *(s)* reverberate, bounce, reflect.

6 **midriff** *(n)* the front area between the chest and the waist. *(s)* middle, belly, midsection.

7 **protrude** *(v)* extend above or beyond a surface (stick out). *(s)* poke, jut, project. *(ant)* withdraw.

8 **ruffle** *(n)* a piece of material gathered into folds.

9 **impede** *(v)* delay or prevent by obstructing. *(s)* handicap, block, hamper, hinder, bar. *(ant)* facilitate, clear.

10 **teeter** *(v)* be unable to decide between things or actions. *(s)* waver, vacillate, falter, see-saw. *(ant)* decide.

Claire took a moment, clinging on to familiarise herself with this new position.

Without **gagging**[1] or wetting it too much, Claire pushed the phone as far into her mouth as she could, the bright beam of the torch now slicing through the blackness below. She clung on for dear life and withdrew a knee from the rung, locating a thin support for her foot. Once steadier, she repeated the **manoeuvre**[2] with the other leg. Claire waited, perched on the ladder, hugging it, not entirely sure it would hold her weight but relieved that it did.

This unique vantage point must not be wasted. Claire glanced around the opening for clues of Ben but saw nothing. She lowered her hands a rung. Then, one **limb**[3] at a time, she stepped down. As she gripped the ladder and twisted her neck, she used the phone to scan the hole's dirty sides. Inspecting it proved fruitless. There were only the rock and support struts, which prevented this **monstrous**[4] pit from **imploding**[5].

Had Ben ever been here? Fear that she may never find him paralysed her. How long before the phone died? Climbing down would be risky. She may not return, and **rot**[6] here, already **conveniently**[7] buried in bug-ridden soil, her family never knowing her fate. Such **appalling**[8] thoughts destroyed her. She couldn't do that to her mum. She would call Cristy. Cristy was kind; she would help.

Unable to descend further into the claustrophobic pit, Claire gingerly removed the phone from her mouth and pushed it into her spare back pocket. As she **braced**[9] herself to climb back out into the cube, clinging on, something stopped her. She stilled, **riveted**[10], cocking an ear down towards the darkness, sure she'd heard something. She waited, but the ensuing silence was too loud. She must have imagined it – wished for it even. Perhaps it had been the

---

1 **gag** *(v)* retch or choke. *(s)* heave, suffocate, stifle, hyperventilate. *(ant)* breathe, swallow.

2 **manoeuvre** *(n)* one or several movements requiring care and skill. *(s)* action, procedure, exercise.

3 **limb** *(n)* arm, leg or wing. *(s)* appendage, member, offshoot.

4 **monstrous** *(adj)* completely evil or wrong. *(s)* grotesque, cruel, hideous, ghastly, horrendous. *(ant)* delightful.

5 **implode** *(v)* collapse inwardly. *(s)* cave in, fold, fall down, fold up. *(ant)* explode.

6 **rot** *(v)* decay. *(s)* decompose, disintegrate, crumble, fester. *(ant)* rejuvenate.

7 **conveniently** *(adv)* in a convenient (handy) way. *(s)* practically. *(ant)* inconveniently.

8 **appalling** *(adj)* very bad. *(s)* horrible, terrible, awful, shocking, horrific, ghastly. *(ant)* pleasant.

9 **brace** *(v)* prepare for something difficult or unpleasant. *(s)* steel, prime, fortify, steady, ready. *(ant)* weaken.

10 **riveted** *(adj)* completely engrossed so unable to move. *(s)* fascinated, enthralled, mesmerised. *(ant)* bored.

auditory[1] **equivalent**[2] of a **mirage**[3], vanishing along with her hopes.

Resigned[4], she tentatively moved one hand up the ladder, followed by her foot. She'd soon be on **terra firma**[5]. Then she heard the sound again. She froze, holding her breath. Her heart thumped. There it was, faint but there; she was sure of it. Her breaths now rapid and shallow, Claire waited.

Please! Please! she thought. *Please let it be ...*

Heartened[6], she fished the phone out of her pocket. She must not drop it. Clutching it, she shone it into the black **void**[7] but saw only ladder rungs until even they **petered**[8] out. She listened. Maybe she had imagined it or was hearing things. Despondent, Claire decided that once back in the cube, she would call Cristy. She listened for a few seconds more, then put the phone into her pocket and started the climb out.

She reached the top, stopped and, with her fingertips, felt the slate tiles above the rim. That final foot remained; she'd need to haul herself from the top rung up into the cube. Why had the ladder's **installer**[9] left such a gap between it and the opening?

She positioned a knee on the ladder and brought her other to join it, her hands holding on to the top rung. From here she would gain the **leverage**[10] to push from her bent knees, lift her hands over the top and flop her chest up and out onto the floor – but something stopped her.

Her heart **somersaulted**[11] – she hadn't imagined it. The sound was closer and louder. Checking the phone was secured in her pocket, she descended back towards the sound's **origin**[12]. It was a sound she knew well. It was the cry of a cat, and its **proximity**[13] was increasing with each mew.

---

1 **auditory** *(adj)* relating to hearing. *(s)* audible, aural, auditive.

2 **equivalent** *(n)* an equal in function, amount or meaning. *(s)* counterpart, parallel, analogue.

3 **mirage** *(n)* an optical illusion, especially in the desert. *(s)* vision, phantasmagoria, delusion, hallucination. *(ant)* reality.

4 **resigned** *(adj)* accepting what cannot be avoided. *(s)* compliant, acquiescent, unresisting. *(ant)* resistant.

5 **terra firma** *(n)* firm ground. *(s)* earth, terrain, dry land.

6 **hearten** *(v)* make confident or cheerful. *(s)* cheer, encourage, comfort, boost, reassure. *(ant)* dishearten.

7 **void** *(n)* an empty space. *(s)* hole, chasm, cavity, abyss, gulf, pit, gap.

8 **peter** *(v)* diminish or fade gradually to an end. *(s)* dwindle, decrease, decline, ease, ebb. *(ant)* increase, develop.

9 **installer** *(n)* a person who places or fixes something into position. *(s)* fitter, builder. *(ant)* remover.

10 **leverage** *(n)* the force applied to something by means of a lever.

11 **somersault** *(v)* perform a flip. *(s)* overturn.

12 **origin** *(n)* where something begins or comes from. *(s)* source, derivation, start, origination. *(ant)* conclusion.

13 **proximity** *(n)* nearness to. *(s)* closeness, immediacy, vicinity, adjacency. *(ant)* remoteness, distance.

*

Sipping sparkling water, the woman regarded the screen. Somewhat bemused, she smirked at Claire's struggles – her dithering at the mouth of the tunnel. It **bore**[1] little consequence to her which route the girl picked – the woman would **manipulate**[2] any tunnel Claire chose, to ensure her **bidding**[3]. No matter how hard this **intrepid**[4] child **strove**[5], the woman would pursue her to the gold.

Oddly, the woman thought of her firstborn. Why had this youngster **rekindled**[6] images of such bygone times? Although she thought the girl to be **banal**[7] and **predictable**[8], the woman conceded grudgingly that yesterday the girl had **exhibited**[9] unexpected **pluck**[10] and **gumption**[11], **mettle**[12] the woman had not foreseen. After months of observing, was she **fond of**[13] this one?

The woman drained the glass, placed it on the table next to her, and returned to the business in hand.

Once the girl was too deep in the underground network, the tracker would fail. Nevertheless, this tunnel had only one exit. The woman would know where the girl was – always. However, what she had not heard was the sound of a cat's covert calls …

---

1 **bear** *(v)* carry (past tense: bore). *(s)* convey, bring, deliver, present.

2 **manipulate** *(v)* alter, control or influence. *(s)* direct, affect, change, exploit, manoeuvre.

3 **bidding** *(n)* the asking or ordering of someone to do something. *(s)* request, command, behest.

4 **intrepid** *(adj)* fearless. *(s)* unafraid, dauntless, undaunted, daring, bold, audacious. *(ant)* fearful, cowardly.

5 **strive** *(v)* make huge efforts to acquire or accomplish something (past tense: strove). *(s)* endeavour, try. *(ant)* shirk, quit.

6 **rekindle** *(v)* bring to life again. *(s)* revive, renew, revitalise. *(ant)* extinguish.

7 **banal** *(adj)* boring or obvious from lack of originality. *(s)* trite, predictable, unimaginative. *(ant)* original.

8 **predictable** *(adj)* able to be predicted. *(s)* unsurprising, expected, unoriginal. *(ant)* unexpected, original.

9 **exhibit** *(v)* manifest (show) clearly, put on. *(s)* demonstrate, reveal, display, present. *(ant)* hide, conceal.

10 **pluck** *(n)* unwavering courage. *(s)* bravery, nerve, boldness, daring, spirit, mettle, valour. *(ant)* cowardice.

11 **gumption** *(n)* spirit and resourcefulness. *(s)* cleverness, enterprise, imagination, shrewdness. *(ant)* stupidity.

12 **mettle** *(n)* a person's ability to deal with problems. *(s)* tenacity, spirit, fortitude, steel, resolve, nerve. *(ant)* cowardice.

13 **fond of** *(adj)* having affection or liking of. *(s)* partial to, attached to. *(ant)* indifferent to.

10. Cat's Eyes

Claire shrieked down into the black **chasm**[1], 'Thomas, wait! I'm coming!'

She hoped it was him. She spat, pausing to rid her mouth of the tunnel's mouldy taste and **scold**[2] herself. Why had she put the phone in her pocket? The pit was too dark; the screen wouldn't ID her face, but she couldn't turn back. *Small mercies*, she thought, *the battery's alive.*

Thomas's calls urged her on, but she saw nothing. Claire's eyes had barely adjusted to the dense darkness. A **meagre**[3] haze of light glowed from the cube but dimmed with every downward step. Blindly she continued, recalling a **harrowing**[4] **documentary**[5] she'd once seen. A diver at the bottom of the North Sea had tangled and subsequently **severed**[6] his airline. Despite freezing temperatures, **thwarting**[7] all odds, the diver had survived. Was the oxygen thinner down here?

The temperature dropped with every rung she trod on. Earlier Claire had stuffed her coat into her backpack, the Gwalch Gem bracelet in the pocket. Claire hoped Ben still had her bag. Moreover, she hoped this rabbit hole might lead to them both. Despising being underground, Claire yearned for Gwilym and Jack. She prayed that Thomas was the cat creating the noise.

As the miaowing increased, Claire's confidence budded – it sounded just like Thomas. Gladys had said Thomas was a spy. It would make sense, particularly as Ben had told Claire cats had night vision.

---

1 **chasm** *(n)* a deep rift in the earth. *(s)* abyss, crevasse, cleft, crater, hole.

2 **scold** *(v)* tell someone off angrily. *(s)* reprimand, berate, rebuke, admonish, chastise. *(ant)* praise, commend.

3 **meagre** *(adj)* inadequate or scant amount. *(s)* small, measly, derisory, paltry, insufficient. *(ant)* plentiful.

4 **harrowing** *(adj)* distressing. *(s)* disturbing, shocking, troubling, traumatic, devastating. *(ant)* comforting.

5 **documentary** *(n)* a factual report or programme. *(s)* factual film, biopic.

6 **sever** *(v)* cut off. *(s)* remove, amputate, separate, detach, chop off, cleave. *(ant)* unite, attach, combine, join.

7 **thwart** *(v)* successfully oppose. *(s)* foil, counter, ruin, stop, impede, defeat, overpower. *(ant)* aid, facilitate.

Ben didn't read fiction; he devoured **obscure**[1] facts. Affectionately, and **ironically**[2], he had been dubbed 'Ben Bad Brain' at school. General knowledge was his forte. Claire **vividly**[3] remembered him saying, 'Cats can see using one-sixth of the light that people need.' Thomas would be her eyes and her **ally**[4].

Swamped[5] by the **unforgiving**[6] blackness, Claire squinted upwards. The cube's opening was now a pinprick – barely visible. Although she constantly moved, her teeth chattered, her hands ached, and her stomach groaned. She'd eaten nothing in the VIP restaurant and wished she'd drunk more water, something Ben **consistently**[7] **reprimanded**[8] her for. She longed to see him.

A sudden realisation jolted Claire back from her reverie. The darkness was silent. Claire struggled to grip the ladder. 'Thomas?' she shouted. 'Thomas, are you there? THOMAS!' she **bellowed**[9]. Fear crept up her legs.

'Breathe. Breathe,' she chanted. 'Breathe!' Her voice cracked. 'Thomas, are you there?' She listened, holding her breath. Panic **mushroomed**[10]. **Petrified**[11], Claire shrieked into the darkness, 'Thomas, where are you?'

Despairing thoughts **crippled**[12] her. What if it wasn't Thomas and was a trap? Or, even worse, what if they'd captured him? What would become of him? What if Drane or Dewi waited at the bottom?

For an insane moment, she pictured herself letting go of the ladder. Would it hurt? Would she feel anything?

'Oof!' Claire's body jerked, forcing an expelled breath. 'What the heck?' She grasped the ladder, her feet grappling for a rung, panic-stricken. Her head whirled. 'Eh! What?'

---

1 **obscure** *(adj)* not well known. *(s)* unfamous, little known, unheard of. *(ant)* famous, renowned.

2 **ironically** *(adv)* in a paradoxical, unexpected or coincidental way. *(s)* paradoxically, unexpectedly, coincidentally.

3 **vividly** *(adv)* in a vivid (strong and clear) way. *(s)* distinctly, lively, lucidly, plainly, acutely. *(ant)* vaguely.

4 **ally** *(n)* a person that helps another in a task. *(s)* friend, accomplice, supporter. *(ant)* opponent.

5 **swamp** *(v)* inundate. *(s)* overwhelm, flood, engulf, overload. *(ant)* drain.

6 **unforgiving** *(adj)* (of a place) difficult, harsh or hostile. *(s)* hard, demanding, taxing, challenging. *(ant)* easy.

7 **consistently** *(adv)* in a consistent (regular) manner. *(s)* reliably, dependably, constantly. *(ant)* inconsistently.

8 **reprimand** *(v)* address disapproval to (tell off). *(s)* rebuke, chastise, scold, reproach, chide. *(ant)* praise.

9 **bellow** *(v)* shout loudly and deeply. *(s)* holler, bark, roar, cry, yell. *(ant)* whisper.

10 **mushroom** *(v)* increase quickly. *(s)* bloom, spread, burgeon, sprout. *(ant)* contract, fail.

11 **petrified** *(adj)* made so frightened as to be unable to move. *(s)* terrified, scared, horrified, appalled. *(ant)* reassured.

12 **cripple** *(v)* cause to become unable to move properly. *(s)* immobilise, incapacitate, disable, paralyse.

Disorientated[1], Claire tapped the rung with her trainer's toe. Her foothold felt secure. 'Eh?' she said, realising the ladder felt different. She jabbed the rung with her toe and moved her foot down. She'd reached the bottom! Startled, Claire sprang sideways, colliding with the side of the pit. **Encapsulated**[2] by its constricting size, she could hardly move. Wherever she reached, she touched damp soil.

'Ouch!' Her **temple**[3] hit the ladder as she tilted her head. Already bruised from yesterday, it hurt even more.

Suddenly **exhausted**[4], Claire collapsed onto her **haunches**[5]. Spitting out **granules**[6] of grime, she blinked hard, wiping away **remnants**[7] of filthy tears. Then, out of the corner of her eye, she saw two **almond**[8]-shaped yellow-green **lanterns**[9] shining at her through the blackness.

'Thomas! Thomas!' she cried. 'It's really you.' His jet-black body had transformed him into an eerie **entity**[10] – just two glowing eyes.

Guided by the spooky glow, she scooped him up, **smothering**[11] his head with kisses.

'Thomas! Thomas! I'm so relieved to see you, or at least feel you.' She laughed, surprising herself. The cat's throat hummed, **emitting**[12] **joyful**[13] purrs.

'Why did you stop miaowing?' she asked, hoping he might answer. 'I thought you'd gone, or were caught or dead,' she gushed, gripping him tightly lest he vanish.

'Thomas, where's Jack and Gwilym?' She **kneaded**[14] his velvet fur between her fingers.

---

1 **disorientated** *(adj)* confused. *(s)* confounded, thrown, puzzled, baffled. *(ant)* clear, lucid.

2 **encapsulate** *(v)* enclose. *(s)* confine, encase, enfold, surround, cocoon.

3 **temple** *(n)* flat part of the head situated between the forehead and the ear.

4 **exhausted** *(adj)* extremely tired. *(s)* drained, shattered, fatigued, debilitated. *(ant)* refreshed, energised.

5 **haunches** *(n)* thighs and bottom together. *(s)* buttocks, hindquarters, rump, rear, backside, seat.

6 **granule** *(n)* a small particle. *(s)* grain, fragment, bit, scrap, morsel, mite, smidgen.

7 **remnant** *(n)* a part of something that is left over. *(s)* remainder, residue, leftover.

8 **almond** *(n)* the edible oval seed of an almond tree, the shape of an almond. *(s)* oval.

9 **lantern** *(n)* a portable (moveable) lamp with a handle. *(s)* light.

10 **entity** *(n)* a thing that exists. *(s)* object, unit, item, article, individual, being, creature. *(ant)* nonentity.

11 **smother** *(v)* cover completely. *(s)* smear, cake, plaster.

12 **emit** *(v)* produce and discharge (give off). *(s)* release, effuse, issue, vent, secrete, radiate. *(ant)* absorb.

13 **joyful** *(adj)* causing huge pleasure and happiness. *(s)* bright, enjoyable, pleasing. *(ant)* joyless, glum.

14 **knead** *(v)* squeeze and massage with the hands. *(s)* rub, stroke, manipulate, press.

He purred, pushing his face deeper into her **caresses**[1].

'How did you get here?' she asked, eventually plopping him onto the ground.

He miaowed, but his eyes moved **abnormally**[2]. Claire started and said, 'Are you OK, Tommy Boy?' She realised he was twirling in the same figure of eight as yesterday when he'd signalled Gladys's letter on the table.

'What is it, Tom? What are you trying to tell me?' she asked, watching his strangely glowing eyes. Ben had said cats see better than humans, but surely Thomas's eyes could only glow if reflecting light. Claire didn't care how they shone; she was just relieved they did. She felt sure he was beckoning her to follow him.

'Tom, I need to follow your eyes. I won't see you otherwise,' she said, still sitting on the ground and dreading her next move. 'How can we do this?' she asked. She knew full well whatever came next would involve being too near the soil.

Claire rubbed at her face. 'Yuck!' she yelped. Something with legs had tickled it. As Thomas's eyes seemed to pirouette in the dark, Claire struggled to follow them. Again something tickled her face. She batted it away, but it kept happening.

'Tommy, stop that!' she **chastised**[3] the cat, realising it was him.

Then the penny dropped.

'Of course!' she exclaimed, laughing in the gloom. 'Your tail! I can hold your tail.'

Thomas stilled. He miaowed, swished his tail again, and Claire dropped onto all fours. She checked the phone and glove were secure in her pocket, pulled up her hood and gently took the cat's tail.

Finding herself on all threes yet again, tail in hand, she scrabbled after Thomas, squeezing through a horribly tight opening into a narrow, dark tunnel.

---

1 **caress** *(n)* a gentle touch. *(s)* stroke, pat, skim, embrace. *(ant)* punch, hit, strike.

2 **abnormally** *(adv)* in an abnormal (unusual) way. *(s)* oddly, peculiarly, uncharacteristically. *(ant)* normally.

3 **chastise** *(v)* scold (tell off) in a harsh manner. *(s)* berate, reprimand, discipline, rebuke, censure. *(ant)* praise.

*

The woman's screen had blanked out before Claire reached the bottom of the shaft. It was **irrelevant**[1]; she'd expected it. Indeed, her **organisation**[2] **shunned**[3] technology in certain tunnels. Radio silence was their intention and **modus operandi**[4]. The woman had singled out this route, as it **terminated**[5] in one place. The place she required Claire to find.

---

1 **irrelevant** *(adj)* not relevant (important). *(s)* immaterial, trivial, insignificant, inconsequential. *(ant)* relevant.

2 **organisation** *(n)* an organised group of people with a shared purpose, such as a business. *(s)* firm, company, corporation.

3 **shun** *(v)* ignore, avoid or reject with persistence. *(s)* evade, eschew, reject, spurn. *(ant)* seek, accept, welcome.

4 **modus operandi** *(n)* a specific way of doing something. *(s)* technique, style, MO, manner.

5 **terminate** *(v)* come to an end. *(s)* conclude, stop, finish, discontinue. *(ant)* commence, begin, start.

11. The Compass

Crawling was killing Claire's knees. Thankful but barely able to stand in the confined space, she at least now unfolded to a stoop. Loyally Thomas sat at her feet. They'd reached a dead end. There seemed only one way out of this dugout – **retreat**[1].

Dumbfounded, Claire gawped through a thick glass panel. The interminable tunnel crawl had been hideous, but to hold Thomas's tail, a stroke of genius. However, nothing could have prepared her for this present **culmination**[2], for **glowering**[3] back at her from a stark white room was Robert Evans. The museum's curator, like a fish in an **aquarium**[4], was **captive**[5].

The light from Evans's cell illuminated Claire and Thomas, their silhouettes ghostly. The cat's eyes shone back at Evans, and Claire's filthy face remained frozen in disbelief. *Where the heck is Ben? Why is Evans here?*

She'd suspected Evans's **skulduggery**[6] from the moment she'd clapped eyes on him. His dead-fish eyes and **scaly**[7] skin **repelled**[8] her. *Apt for an aquarium.*

Determined[9] not to speak, Claire would hear *his* story first. She glowered back at him, resolute.

---

1 **retreat** *(n)* the act of withdrawing. *(s)* flight, withdrawal, escape. *(ant)* advance.

2 **culmination** *(n)* the highest or finishing point of something, especially after a long time. *(s)* zenith. *(ant)* nadir.

3 **glower** *(v)* scowl angrily or sullenly (glare daggers at). *(s)* stare, frown, gloom. *(ant)* beam, smile.

4 **aquarium** *(n)* a see-through tank containing fish, other water creatures and plants.

5 **captive** *(adj)* held, caged or locked up. *(s)* imprisoned, incarcerated, detained, confined. *(ant)* free.

6 **skulduggery** *(n)* bad behaviour. *(s)* trickery, swindling, machinations, shenanigans.

7 **scaly** *(adj)* flaking because of dryness. *(s)* peeling, crusty, scabby, encrusted, scaling. *(ant)* smooth.

8 **repel** *(v)* disgust or repulse. *(s)* revolt, offend, sicken, nauseate. *(ant)* appeal to, enchant, delight.

9 **determined** *(adj)* having or displaying resolve. *(s)* resolute, intent on, firm, unwavering. *(ant)* irresolute.

The **spartanly**[1] furnished cell **boasted**[2] only a thin bunk, a **modest**[3] desk and a hard-backed, upright chair. Evans perched on the bunk's edge, motionless and **mute**[4]. For what seemed like an age, their stand-off persisted. With Thomas by her side, Claire's confidence blossomed; she would not relent. She'd not come this far to be **fazed**[5] by the creepy curator guy. Claire crossed her arms and tilted her head, fixing her mouth in a thin line. She would wait or **withdraw**[6] – it was his choice.

With **laboured**[7] breathing and **fending off**[8] shivers, she repeated a *Calm, Claire* mantra in her head. Thomas neither budged nor **mewled**[9]. Evans said and did nothing. While desperate for a wee, both **famished**[10] and cold, Claire fidgeted.

From the dark **recesses**[11] of her mind, **defeatist**[12] thoughts **pestered**[13] Claire, nagging at her **resolve**[14]. *What if the Master has infiltrated the cube and followed? What should I do?* Claire's **determination**[15] began to crack. She ached to swoop up Thomas for a cuddle but remained silent. She must hold on.

Like a folded flag **unfurling**[16], Evans stood. His **frail**[17] **disposition**[18] and unsteady **stance**[19]

---

1 **spartanly** *(adv)* in a spartan (lacking comfort or luxury) way. *(s)* austerely, barely, starkly. *(ant)* luxuriously, opulently.

2 **boast** *(v)* possess a feature to be proud of. *(s)* have, own, enjoy.

3 **modest** *(adj)* not elaborate, large or expensive. *(s)* ordinary, humble, plain, simple. *(ant)* flashy, excessive.

4 **mute** *(adj)* remaining speechless. *(s)* silent, voiceless, taciturn, dumb, wordless, quiet. *(ant)* vocal, speaking.

5 **faze** *(v)* disconcert or disturb someone. *(s)* bother, deter, daunt, intimidate, discourage. *(ant)* encourage.

6 **withdraw** *(v)* leave. *(s)* quit, evacuate. (ant) enter.

7 **laboured** *(adj)* done with significant effort and strain. *(s)* heavy, difficult, strained, forced. *(ant)* easy.

8 **fend off** *(v)* defend oneself from something. *(s)* stop, block, repel, resist, parry, discourage. *(ant)* encourage.

9 **mewl** *(v)* make a high-pitched cry. *(s)* mew, miaow, yowl.

10 **famished** *(adj)* very hungry. *(s)* ravenous, starving, underfed, unfed, empty, hollow. *(ant)* full, sated, satiated.

11 **recess** *(n)* a remote or secret place. *(s)* dark corner, innermost part.

12 **defeatist** *(adj)* expecting or accepting failure. *(s)* pessimistic, negative, cynical, discouraged. *(ant)* optimistic, positive.

13 **pester** *(v)* annoy with continuing or regular interruptions. *(s)* bother, hound, badger, harass, torment.

14 **resolve** *(n)* firm determination. *(s)* firmness, resolution, steadfastness, tenacity, doggedness. *(ant)* indecision.

15 **determination** *(n)* the quality of being determined. *(s)* willpower, resolve, fortitude, grit. *(ant)* weakness.

16 **unfurl** *(v)* spread or roll out. *(s)* open out, unfold, expand, unroll. *(ant)* furl, fold up.

17 **frail** *(adj)* delicate and weak. *(s)* feeble, infirm, slight, unsound, puny, fragile. *(ant)* robust, sturdy, strong.

18 **disposition** *(n)* personal character. *(s)* temperament, nature, personality, temper, constitution.

19 **stance** *(n)* the way a person stands, especially when adopted on purpose. *(s)* pose, bearing, attitude, posture.

sparked Claire's **curiosity**[1]. Apart from the same **baleful**[2] look in his piggy eyes, everything about him had changed. Almost a shell of the **repugnant**[3] little man he already was, he now reminded her of Gollum from *The Lord of the Rings*.

How was this ***pitiable***[4] *pixie of a man ever a Knight Hawk?* she thought as he limped and **shuffled**[5] towards the glass **partition**[6], his **gait**[7] **unstable**[8].

Wobbling to a halt about half a metre from the glass, he tried to speak, but his voice emitted a mere croak. His **pallid**[9] skin sagged in grey folds beneath hollow, bloodshot eyes, and his barely visible lips no longer covered his crooked yellow teeth.

Claire was taken aback, and a pang of pity shook her. His form bore that of a dying man. Claire gasped, not because of her fleeting **compassion**[10] for Evans, not because she regretted her earlier **brutal**[11] **sentiments**[12], but because her **overwhelming**[13] devastation resulted from the realisation that this knight's impending death confirmed her worst fears – other knights, too, would be dying. She longed to ask Evans why he, and the other knights, had not turned into emerald and shattered into smithereens, but now wasn't the time.

The situation's fresh urgency **propelled**[14] her on. 'Speak up!' Claire barked in a new-found barbed tone. 'Tell me what you know!'

Evans's eyes widened, and the downturned corners of his mouth twitched.

'Gold,' he whispered, 'we need more gold.'

'Gold?' Claire hissed. 'What do you mean, *we* need more gold?'

---

1 **curiosity** *(n)* a desire to know or learn. *(s)* inquisitiveness, interest, nosiness. *(ant)* apathy, indifference.
2 **baleful** *(adj)* menacing or threatening harm. *(s)* unfriendly, hostile, vindictive, malevolent. *(ant)* benevolent.
3 **repugnant** *(adj)* unpleasant and unacceptable. *(s)* repulsive, abhorrent, revolting. *(ant)* pleasant, agreeable.
4 **pitiable** *(adj)* arousing disgust or scorn. *(s)* deplorable, pathetic, contemptible, wretched. *(ant)* estimable.
5 **shuffle** *(v)* move the feet along the ground without lifting them. *(s)* shamble, limp, scuffle. *(ant)* stride, strut.
6 **partition** *(n)* a structure splitting an area into two. *(s)* barrier, divider, screen, wall, panel.
7 **gait** *(n)* the way a person walks or strides. *(s)* step, manner, posture, bearing, style, carriage, movement.
8 **unstable** *(adj)* not stable. *(s)* unsteady, tottery, doddery, wobbly, rocky, shaky. *(ant)* stable, steady.
9 **pallid** *(adj)* pale. *(s)* wan, pasty, white, ashen, sallow, anaemic, blanched. *(ant)* rosy, healthy.
10 **compassion** *(n)* sympathy and concern for the sufferings of another. *(s)* care, empathy. *(ant)* indifference.
11 **brutal** *(adj)* cruel or unpleasant. *(s)* vicious, harsh, callous, ruthless, pitiless. *(ant)* gentle, humane.
12 **sentiment** *(n)* opinion or view held or given by another. *(s)* feeling, response, reaction, attitude. *(ant)* apathy.
13 **overwhelming** *(adj)* having a strong emotional effect. *(s)* forceful, profound, overpowering. *(ant)* underwhelming.
14 **propel** *(v)* drive or push into a specific direction. *(s)* move, boost, thrust, shoot, force, impel, launch. *(ant)* pull.

'You must find the gold,' he croaked. 'No other can help us now.'

'For goodness' sake! Stop the riddles and explain,' she yelled through the glass, remembering Ben's thoughts had **alluded**[1] to Evans and gold.

'Dewi – the Master, he has the Gwalch Gem bracelet. I am his prisoner.'

But that was not what Gladys had told her yesterday. Gladys had said Evans was missing with half of the Cutter.

'Go on!' she urged, trying to remember Gladys's exact words.

'I fled with half of the Cutter, but escaping the Master, even in tunnels I designed, proved impossible. He apprehended me and seized the precious half I had tried to conceal. He now possesses the Gwalch Gem bracelet, but **alas**[2], my current condition exposes an **unforeseen**[3] event – the **detachment**[4] of the gem from the Welsh gold. I know this, for I am dying.'

'Why would the Master pull the bracelet apart? It makes no sense,' said Claire, her voice hard and flat. 'Why should I trust you?'

'Why would I lie? I am about to die.'

Claire mulled over his words. She didn't trust him for a second, but what choice did she have?

As she glowered at him, he reminded her of a tortoise. Despite his tragic declaration, Claire's heart lifted. Had Evans just proved Jayne's innocence, rendering her dream nonsense? Was there a possibility Jayne had not put the bracelet into Claire's school bag after all? Could it have been Dewi or even Mrs Evans? ***Blackmail***[5]*?* thought Claire. *The Master has imprisoned her husband. Has he forced Mrs Evans to help?*

It was **feasible**[6]. The Master could have obtained both halves of the Cutter and stolen the bracelet. One of them must have pulled the bracelet apart, put it into her bag and left it outside her dad's flat. Did it make sense, or was Claire forcing the story to fit around the Master and not Jayne?

---

1 **allude** *(v)* call attention to indirectly, suggest. *(s)* hint at, imply, indicate, insinuate. *(ant)* announce, elucidate.

2 **alas** *(int)* used to express pity, regret, grief, disappointment or concern.

3 **unforeseen** *(adj)* not predicted, expected or anticipated. *(s)* surprising, unanticipated. *(ant)* foreseen.

4 **detachment** *(n)* the action of detaching. *(s)* separation, disconnection, parting. *(ant)* attachment.

5 **blackmail** *(n)* the manipulation of someone through threats. *(s)* extortion, intimidation.

6 **feasible** *(adj)* possible. *(s)* likely, probable, conceivable, imaginable. *(ant)* impossible.

Dewi was a **ruthless**[1], cold-hearted **maniac**[2] with a **volatile**[3] temper, and he held Mrs Evans's husband hostage. But why would the Master sabotage the bracelet? What would he gain from that? How and why the broken bracelet had found its way into her backpack, she was sure would be **apparent**[4] soon, but right now more **pressing**[5] issues prevailed.

Claire must prevent Gwilym's death. Ben's predicament paled in comparison. She must **prioritise**[6] the plight of the Knights Hawk.

'What do I do?' Claire snapped, despising asking Evans for help. Although he was captive and dying, **amenable**[7] was not how she felt towards this man.

'Take this. It will lead you to the gold. I have not the strength to retrieve it.'

'How do *you* know where it is?' asked Claire.

'I am a Knight Hawk,' he replied.

Evans held what looked like a gold pocket watch and chain in his hand. Claire had seen them before in books and films.

'How am I supposed to *take* that if you're in prison on the other side of that glass?' she asked, her **sardonic**[8] tone biting.

'The cat,' Evans **rasped**[9]. 'The cat can enter. There is a means. He will find it.'

Not pausing for thought, and pointing her finger at Evans, Claire commanded, 'Thomas, go!'

As silent as a shadow, Thomas turned and **sloped**[10] off into the darkness.

'Why should I believe your story?' Claire asked through the glass pane. 'What is that thing?' She pointed to the pocket watch.

'It is a compass,' replied Evans. 'It will lead you to the place that hides the unique Welsh gold.

---

1 **ruthless** *(adj)* showing no pity for others. *(s)* cruel, hard, merciless, pitiless. *(ant)* compassionate, merciful.

2 **maniac** *(n)* a person behaving wildly, violently and dangerously. *(s)* lunatic, psychopath. *(ant)* sane person.

3 **volatile** *(adj)* displaying random and quick changes of emotion. *(s)* explosive, impulsive. *(ant)* placid, stable.

4 **apparent** *(adj)* obvious, visible or understood. *(s)* clear, evident, plain, discernible, perceptible. *(ant)* unclear.

5 **pressing** *(adj)* needing urgent attention or action. *(s)* vital, critical, crucial, important. *(ant)* unimportant, non-urgent.

6 **prioritise** *(v)* make the most important. *(s)* prefer, put first, give precedence to. *(ant)* disregard.

7 **amenable** *(adj)* responsive and open. *(s)* agreeable, cooperative, willing, biddable. *(ant)* stubborn, unwilling.

8 **sardonic** *(adj)* cynical (bitter) or mocking. *(s)* scornful, ironic, sarcastic, derisive, scathing. *(ant)* sincere, kind.

9 **rasp** *(v)* say in a harsh, grating way. *(s)* croak, bark, snarl, growl. *(ant)* soothe.

10 **slope** *(v)* sneak away quietly. *(s)* leave, slip, creep, slink, steal.

Immediate rejuvenation of the gold in the Gwalch Gem bracelet is **imperative**[1]. Without it, all Knights Hawk will soon perish, and I will die first.'

'What do you mean, immediate rejuvenation?' Claire asked.

Evans cleared his throat. 'The bracelet lacks power. Centuries of use have depleted its energy. Once **revitalised**[2] by the Welsh gold, and stronger, we knights can ensure the emerald hawk and gold are paired once more. Then the Knights Hawk will live on.' Evans's eyes remained **downcast**[3] the entire time he spoke.

'Doesn't look like a compass to me,' retorted Claire, pointing to a **matt**[4] gemstone in the watch's centre. Then, digesting his words, she asked, 'Why will *you* die first?'

Evans **faltered**[5], labouring to stand. He spluttered something, coughing. With a **doleful**[6] look, he eventually said, 'I will die first because yesterday, Claire, I tangled time alone, for you.'

'What do you mean, you tangled time for me? And "alone", what's that supposed to mean?' Panic **hijacked**[7] her voice. Was she somehow to blame for the knights' plight? 'Answer me!' she demanded.

He cleared his throat again. Claire couldn't fathom why, but he seemed changed. *Does he look smug?* she wondered, but affording it **scant**[8] thought, she dismissed the question.

He paused as if about to **soliloquise**[9].

'When a Knight Hawk tangles time, they **forfeit**[10] power. How that sacrifice **manifests**[11] remains unknown, until **post**[12] the **deed**[13]. Tangling time alone, as I did for you, young Keeper,

---

1 **imperative** *(adj)* of vital (key) importance. *(s)* crucial, essential, urgent, critical. *(ant)* unimportant.

2 **revitalise** *(v)* bestow new life, strength or health. *(s)* reinvigorate, fortify, renew. *(ant)* depress.

3 **downcast** *(adj)* looking down. *(s)* lowered. *(ant)* raised, uplifted.

4 **matt** *(adj)* without shine. *(s)* dull, flat, unpolished. *(ant)* shiny, polished, glossy.

5 **falter** *(v)* lose momentum or strength. *(s)* hesitate, stall, delay, waver, pause, fade. *(ant)* rally, continue.

6 **doleful** *(adj)* expressing sadness and grief. *(s)* mournful, woeful, sorrowful. *(ant)* cheerful.

7 **hijack** *(v)* steal or take over. *(s)* seize, commandeer, capture, appropriate, kidnap, nick. *(ant)* give, bestow.

8 **scant** *(adj)* barely sufficient or adequate. *(s)* meagre, negligible, limited, scarce, inadequate. *(ant)* extensive.

9 **soliloquise** *(v)* speak one's thoughts aloud regardless of audience (speak a soliloquy).

10 **forfeit** *(v)* lose or give up something because of something else. *(s)* sacrifice, surrender, yield. *(ant)* retain.

11 **manifest** *(v)* appear. *(s)* show, display, present, exhibit. *(ant)* hide.

12 **post** *(prep)* after. *(s)* following, subsequent to. *(ant)* before, preceding.

13 **deed** *(n)* performance or action. *(s)* feat, act, endeavour, accomplishment, achievement, effort.

was uncharted territory. Thus, no knight foresaw its **fatal**[1] **aftermath**[2]. For you, Claire, I weakened my body thus, **accelerating**[3] my death.'

Claire gulped but almost expected him to take a bow. She **detested**[4] this man yet wanted no part in his death.

Then, stealthily, from beneath Evans's bunk, a furry black face appeared.

'Thomas!' cried Claire. 'You made it!'

However, Thomas had already pounced over to Evans, who bent and placed the compass into Thomas's mouth. Claire noticed Evans had removed its chain.

'Thomas, bring it!' she ordered.

The cat, compass in mouth, turned and departed beneath the bunk.

'How will that guide me to the gold?' Claire asked Evans.

'Hold it, and you will know.'

Claire rolled her eyes. 'What do you mean, I'll know? Can you be more **specific**[5]?'

'No, I cannot,' Evans replied.

'Where's my friend Ben?'

'Ben?' Evans **deliberated**[6], his **pondering**[7] creasing his **wizened**[8] face further. 'I do not know him,' he eventually replied.

Claire's heart sank.

Buoyed[9] by Thomas swirling around her legs, Claire bent and removed the object from his mouth. She polished it dry on her hoody, inspecting it. It wasn't a watch – it was faceless. Although it was less than five centimetres in diameter and about one centimetre thick, its unexpected heaviness surprised her. It appeared **antique**[10], and it was possibly real gold.

---

1 **fatal** *(adj)* causing death. *(s)* lethal, deadly, killing. *(ant)* harmless.

2 **aftermath** *(n)* the outcome of a terrible or significant event. *(s)* repercussions, fallout, upshot, wake.

3 **accelerate** *(v)* speed up. *(s)* quicken, hasten, escalate. *(ant)* decelerate, slow.

4 **detest** *(v)* dislike intensely. *(s)* abhor, despise, loathe, hate, abominate. *(ant)* love, adore.

5 **specific** *(adj)* exact and clear. *(s)* precise, correct, accurate, explicit. *(ant)* vague, unclear.

6 **deliberate** *(v)* engage in careful consideration. *(s)* think, consider, debate, contemplate, ponder. *(ant)* decide.

7 **pondering** *(n)* the act of thinking carefully. *(s)* contemplation, deliberation, musing, reflection. *(ant)* disregard.

8 **wizened** *(adj)* showing signs of old age. *(s)* wrinkled, shrivelled, creased, withered, wasted. *(ant)* smooth, young.

9 **buoy** *(v)* make optimistic and confident. *(s)* encourage, bolster, boost, cheer, hearten. *(ant)* depress.

10 **antique** *(adj)* belonging to former times. *(s)* old, collectable, vintage, historic. *(ant)* new.

Most **intriguing**[1] were the **intricate**[2] **engravings**[3] surrounding the dull stone. They resembled Chinese 'hanzi' – characters used to write the language. She had learned some Mandarin at school, and with Ben's mum being half Chinese, both Ben and Mr Brady were **fluent**[4]. At home, Jennifer Lee Brady had **mandated**[5] they **converse**[6] in Mandarin. It was almost Ben's mother tongue; he read and wrote it too.

Guilt crushed her, but saving the Knights Hawk was her priority now – Ben wasn't dying.

Gritting her teeth, she snapped at Evans, 'I'm holding this thing, but I can't feel anything.'

'Place your right thumb on the gem.'

'Gem?' asked Claire, curling her lip.

'The stone in the centre,' replied Evans. 'Hold your right thumb on it, and keep it there.'

Albeit[7] **reluctantly**[8], Claire obeyed, but nothing happened.

'Well?' scoffed Claire, scorn sharpening her voice. '*Really?*'

'You know what to do, young Keeper. You are just not doing it.'

Claire's eyes narrowed. She bit her lip, both physically and mentally. Internally **fuming**[9], she pressed the stone harder using her right thumb. Was it warming, or was that just **friction**[10]? She was so cold now, it was impossible to discern which it was. **Rotating**[11] her thumb was a natural progression as it moved in minuscule anticlockwise circles.

Flabbergasted[12], she withdrew her thumb. The stone was glowing, faintly but definitely glowing.

'OMG!' she blurted. 'It's a satnav!'

Her mum was hopeless with directions, so Dee's phone often sat in a holder stuck to the heater

---

1 **intriguing** *(adj)* arousing curiosity or interest. *(s)* captivating, attractive, enthralling. *(ant)* disenchanting.

2 **intricate** *(adj)* detailed and complicated. *(s)* complex, labyrinthine, elaborate, obscure. *(ant)* plain, simple.

3 **engraving** *(n)* a design cut into a hard surface. *(s)* inscription, scoring, etching, scratch.

4 **fluent** *(adj)* able to speak or write another language correctly and easily. *(s)* articulate, eloquent. *(ant)* inarticulate.

5 **mandate** *(v)* order or command with authority. *(s)* instruct, direct, decree.

6 **converse** *(v)* speak with others. *(s)* chat, discuss, talk, confer, parley, discourse.

7 **albeit** *(con)* although. *(s)* though, notwithstanding, even though, while.

8 **reluctantly** *(adv)* in a reluctant (hesitant or unwilling) way. *(s)* half-heartedly, grudgingly. *(ant)* willingly.

9 **fume** *(v)* feel or show great anger. *(s)* seethe, burn, smoulder, bristle, simmer, boil. *(ant)* beam, glow.

10 **friction** *(n)* resistance when two surfaces rub together. *(s)* scraping, chafing, rubbing, abrasion.

11 **rotate** *(v)* move in a circle. *(s)* turn, revolve, spin, swivel, pivot.

12 **flabbergasted** *(adj)* greatly surprised. *(s)* stunned, astonished, staggered, flummoxed, stupefied. *(ant)* sedate.

grille of their battered old car. The face was like the map on her phone. The stone displayed an arrow; it was rudimentary but visible.

'It will not talk to you,' said Evans, his tone matter-of-fact. 'However, it works underground.'

Claire stared, speechless.

'Your right thumb must maintain contact with the stone,' he added. 'Beware, however. Use it sparingly, as it will drain your power to **enable**[1] its own.'

She frowned. 'Eh?'

'In modern-day terms, it plugs into you,' replied Evans.

'Ah, I get it!' said Claire, mulling over the **magnitude**[2] of his response. 'So it could drain my battery?'

'Exactly,' replied Evans, who had crumpled into the hard-backed chair. He panted shallow breaths, looking **peaky**[3] and unwell; a blue hue tinged his lips.

'Hurry,' he whispered from across the **austere**[4] cell. 'Little time remains.'

'Hang on,' said Claire. 'There's only one way out of here: the way I came in.'

'Do not be **deceived**[5] by what you see,' **wheezed**[6] Evans.

'Thomas,' Claire said, falling onto all threes again. 'Let's go.' She gripped the compass in her hand, her right thumb pressed firmly on its glowing stone.

At the compass's mercy, and having no clue where she was headed, she crawled in the faint arrow's direction, Thomas following at her feet.

*

At the back of Evans's **sparse**[7] cell, a concealed door slid open. A woman entered.

'I have opened the tunnels you mentioned for the girl. If incorrect, then you die sooner,' said the woman. 'How long do you have left without more gold?' Her voice lacked emotion, a frost in its tone

---

1 **enable** *(v)* allow or make possible to do something. *(s)* empower, permit, facilitate. *(ant)* prevent.

2 **magnitude** *(n)* the large size or extent of something. *(s)* enormity, scale, degree, level. *(ant)* smallness.

3 **peaky** *(adj)* pale from being ill or tired. *(s)* pasty, wan, pallid, ashen. *(ant)* rosy, flushed.

4 **austere** *(adj)* having a plain appearance. *(s)* severe, simple, basic, sombre, unadorned. *(ant)* fussy, ornate.

5 **deceive** *(v)* give the wrong impression. *(s)* mislead, hoodwink, dupe, delude, trick. *(ant)* be honest.

6 **wheeze** *(v)* making a whistling or rattling sound in the chest. *(s)* gasp, rasp, cough, whisper.

7 **sparse** *(adj)* with few elements scattered about. *(s)* scarce, scant, paltry, bare, skimpy. *(ant)* crammed, packed.

'It is impossible to say,' rasped Evans, who sat in his chair, head in hands.

'The girl must reach the gold before you perish.' The woman plucked a piece of fluff from her jacket. 'If she thinks it is too late, she will lose her **motivation**[1]. To deliver the gold, she must believe the knights live on.'

Then, without another word, she turned and left, the door sliding closed behind her.

---

1 **motivation** *(n)* an incentive for acting or behaving in a certain way. *(s)* motive, stimulus, inspiration, reason. *(ant)* deterrent.

12. An Alternative Route

Claire despised the tunnels, vowing never to enter one again. Crawling while maintaining her thumb's pressure on the stone and following the dimly lit arrow proved **gruelling**[1]. As the compass palpably **debilitated**[2] Claire's energy, the **strenuous**[3] task tested her to the limit.

'I hope it's not much further, Tom. I don't know how long I'll last,' she mumbled, panic prickling again. *What if we die down here? What if it's a trap?*

With rapidly diminishing strength, she battled to expunge the negative thoughts gnawing at her. Her entire family flashed before her eyes; she prayed she'd see them again.

At least I have Thomas, she thought. He would bring help.

Who would rescue her though? The Knights Hawk were dying. **Anguish**[4] **consumed**[5] her. She was no longer able to contain her howl, but Thomas jumped onto Claire's back, purring, and pushed his furry face into her neck. Pausing to fight for breath in this oxygen-**deprived**[6] hellhole was **essential**[7]. With no idea of how long or how far they'd moved – both feeling like forever – Claire felt this level of exertion was **untenable**[8]. The compass now **incapacitated**[9] her.

Thomas hopped off Claire's back and moved around to her face.

---

1 **gruelling** *(adj)* extremely demanding and tiring. *(s)* exhausting, arduous, strenuous, harrowing. *(ant)* easy.
2 **debilitate** *(v)* make someone weak. *(s)* tire, drain, sap, exhaust, enfeeble, impair. *(ant)* strengthen, invigorate.
3 **strenuous** *(adj)* requiring huge effort. *(s)* difficult, arduous, hard, taxing, demanding. *(ant)* easy, effortless.
4 **anguish** *(n)* severe mental or physical pain. *(s)* suffering, agony, torment, torture. *(ant)* happiness, joy.
5 **consume** *(v)* strongly affect or overwhelm with a feeling. *(s)* dominate, overpower, control. *(ant)* abandon.
6 **deprived** *(adj)* prohibited from having or using something. *(s)* denied, stripped, starved. *(ant)* ridden, rich.
7 **essential** *(adj)* necessary. *(s)* needed, required, key, vital, critical, paramount. *(ant)* inessential, optional.
8 **untenable** *(adj)* unable to be maintained. *(s)* unsustainable, insupportable, implausible. *(ant)* tenable.
9 **incapacitate** *(v)* prevent from functioning normally. *(s)* debilitate, weaken, disable, undermine. *(ant)* enable.

'Thomas, my **saviour**[1],' she said weakly, looking into his eerie eyes. 'I know you're trying to **spur**[2] me on.'

Thomas mewed in response and gently pawed her face.

'Thanks, buddy,' she whispered, 'but we must keep moving. Ouch!' she suddenly yelped, dropping the compass into the soil. 'Why did you do that?' Claire cried, shocked.

Thomas had swiped her face, scratching it.

Claire reached down to pick up the compass, but Thomas pounced. Then, spitting a **fiendish**[3] hiss, he stole the compass away with his paw.

In an instant, sheer horror consumed Claire. Why was Thomas swiping at the compass, which was now out of her reach? He'd purposely struck it away from her. Why?

The stone's glow dimmed, but she saw the cat's outline. Thomas guarded the compass, hissing a warning, his back arched, his eyes evil. His **brandished**[4] tail waved in **vexed**[5] curls. Claire recoiled. Thomas had **morphed**[6] into an unrecognisable beast. Had he **betrayed**[7] her?

Warm tears soaked her cheeks. She had no energy for sound – the compass had **siphoned**[8] it. The diver in the harrowing film had said he'd felt no pain. In despair, she curled into a ball, rocking back and **forth**[9], waiting for the comfort of nothingness.

As she was silently sobbing, devastated by Thomas's **treachery**[10], a soft buzzing roused her – a faint droning sound.

'*Miaow! Miaow!*'

Afraid Thomas would strike again, Claire curled up tighter.

'*Miaow!*'

At that sound, Claire flinched in terror. Thomas had sprung onto her back, but now he purred

---

1 **saviour** *(n)* someone who saves someone else from peril or hardship. *(s)* rescuer, champion. *(ant)* condemner.

2 **spur** *(v)* encourage. *(s)* urge, stimulate, motivate, drive, inspire. *(ant)* discourage.

3 **fiendish** *(adj)* cruel and wicked. *(s)* evil, villainous, malicious, malevolent, cunning, devilish. *(ant)* pleasant.

4 **brandish** *(v)* wave as a threat or in excitement. *(s)* flourish, shake, wield, flash, display, flaunt. *(ant)* conceal.

5 **vexed** *(adj)* annoyed. *(s)* displeased, irked, riled, irritated, aggravated, exasperated. *(ant)* pacified, calm.

6 **morph** *(v)* undergo a gradual process of transformation. *(s)* convert, modify, transform. *(ant)* preserve, sustain.

7 **betray** *(v)* deceive someone. *(s)* mislead, trick, double-cross, cheat. *(ant)* be honest.

8 **siphon** *(v)* extract over a period. *(s)* draw off, bleed, drain, transfer, withdraw, deplete. *(ant)* enhance.

9 **forth** *(adv)* forward in direction (or time). *(s)* onwards, ahead. *(ant)* back.

10 **treachery** *(n)* a breach of trust. *(s)* betrayal, deceit, duplicity, disloyalty, dishonesty. *(ant)* loyalty, honesty.

and pawed, pulling her hood off her head. She peeped from her curled-up shell. The stone's light had almost extinguished, but it lay where Thomas had left it.

The cat jumped off her back, swooshing his tail repeatedly around her face and spinning in tight circles.

'Thomas?' whispered Claire.

How could she ever have doubted him? He was trying to win her attention again. Thomas was **diverting**[1] Claire away from the compass because it was **maiming**[2] her.

'Tommy, what is it?' she asked, a **tremendous**[3] relief lifting her. His sandpaper tongue licked her cheek.

The cat turned away from Claire's face, moved towards her upturned feet and spun in circles. In the compass's extinguishing light, Claire saw only his outline.

'What do you want?' she asked, turning around in the impossibly tight space to face him.

Thomas stilled, his glowing yellow-green eyes peering into hers.

'Show me, boy,' Claire said. 'Show me.'

Thomas let out the loudest, most **unnerving**[4] miaow she'd ever heard. He stood, swished his tail and walked away from her, heading back in the direction in which they'd come – towards Evans.

'Tommy, are you sure it's that way?' Claire asked, but Thomas didn't falter. Claire quickly reversed, grabbed the discarded compass, shoved it into her pocket with the glove and crawled as fast as she could after Thomas.

No longer powering the **parasitic**[5] compass, Claire's strength recovered somewhat, but she was cold, hungry and desperate to wee. No one would see her here, but this cramped hole **stymied**[6] all manoeuvrability. She'd have to hold on or wet herself – she quickly settled for the former.

As Claire trailed Thomas, grasping his tail in the pitch-blackness, thoughts of the ailing

---

1 **divert** *(v)* cause a change of course or direction. *(s)* distract, avert, deter, redirect, dissuade. *(ant)* focus.

2 **maim** *(v)* injure so as to be irreparably damaged. *(s)* hurt, disable, incapacitate. *(ant)* heal.

3 **tremendous** *(adj)* very great. *(s)* immense, massive, stupendous, huge. *(ant)* tiny, slight, small.

4 **unnerving** *(adj)* causing a loss in courage. *(s)* daunting, intimidating, perturbing, disconcerting. *(ant)* encouraging.

5 **parasitic** *(adj)* living off something or someone else as a parasite. *(s)* dependent, exploitative.

6 **stymie** *(v)* impede or stop the progress of. *(s)* hinder, obstruct, inhibit, stall, thwart, frustrate. *(ant)* help, assist.

knights, Ben and her family whirled cruelly around her head. Although she felt **horrendous**[1] guilt for doubting Thomas, she still longed for Jack.

Having drifted off into an uneasy reverie, she was caught unawares by Thomas stopping and abruptly sitting. He turned, purred and faced the tunnel's side. Claire knew immediately he was signalling something, but it was impossibly dark.

She patted the wall but felt only crumbling earth, recoiling in horror as something with numerous legs **scuttled**[2] across her hand. To see, she had to **reactivate**[3] the life-siphoning compass. Claire took it from her pocket. When she placed her right thumb in the centre, it immediately consumed her. As if dimming her internal fires to light its own, the gem glowed. **Inadequate**[4] as its light was, Claire surveyed the immediate locale. Thomas hadn't budged. She knew she was warm, even hot.

To shield her from bugs, Claire considered wearing her glove. **Wincing**[5], she ran her bare palm across the nearby surfaces but found nothing. She was **baffled**[6] and **infuriated**[7] at her failure and dug her thumb hard into the stone. Had the stone depressed? Had it yielded?

Nothing happened, so she pressed it harder. Suddenly a single beam of emerald-green light shot through her fingers. Like a laser pointer, it **projected**[8] a dot of green light onto the side of the tunnel.

Stunned, Claire stared at it. 'What the heck?' she muttered.

Trying to **ascertain**[9] its meaning, she turned quizzically to Thomas, but he didn't move.

She was afraid it might vanish, so Claire moved closer to inspect the dot and wiggled her hand. The beam seemed bent, but the dot remained **static**[10]. No matter where the compass faced

---

1 **horrendous** *(adj)* very unpleasant. *(s)* terrible, horrible, horrific, frightful, awful, vile, hideous. *(ant)* pleasant.

2 **scuttle** *(v)* run or scamper hurriedly or furtively (secretly). *(s)* dart, dash, rush, bustle, scurry. *(ant)* saunter.

3 **reactivate** *(v)* make active again. *(s)* restart, revive, reanimate.

4 **inadequate** *(adj)* lacking the required (needed) quantity or quality. *(s)* insufficient, deficient. *(ant)* adequate.

5 **wince** *(v)* grimace slightly in reaction to pain or distress. *(s)* flinch, blench, start, shrink. *(ant)* smile.

6 **baffled** *(adj)* totally confused. *(s)* bewildered, perplexed, puzzled, bemused, confused, confounded. *(ant)* enlightened.

7 **infuriated** *(adj)* very angry. *(s)* enraged, incensed, mad, inflamed, exasperated. *(ant)* soothed, calm.

8 **project** *(v)* cause light or shadow to fall onto a surface (sometimes creating an image). *(s)* cast.

9 **ascertain** *(v)* discover or make sure of something. *(s)* determine, verify, establish, identify. *(ant)* disprove, obscure.

10 **static** *(adj)* not moving or changing. *(s)* stationary, fixed, steady, unvarying. *(ant)* variable, mobile.

or its **altitude**[1], the dot remained in situ. 'Wow!' she said. 'That's cool.' She prodded the dot, turning the tip of her finger a spooky green. Then she let out a gasp and drew back – something **peculiar**[2] was happening.

Pouring like sand through a timer, a line of soil trickled from the centre of the green dot. 'What on earth?' she said, finding it oddly mesmerising. As the flowing earth began to **cascade**[3] down, the hole's **circumference**[4] expanded, its sides falling away like a fruit peeling to reveal its juicy interior.

She blinked, and blinked again, shaking her head in disbelief.

'No way!' she cried. 'It can't be!'

On the other side of the opening, shining and with all four tyres intact, sat Mr Brady's **slick**[5] black Tesla.

*

Incandescent[6] with rage, the woman stormed into Robert Evans's cell.

'What the hell happened to her?' she yelled at a **quailing**[7] Evans. 'Where the hell *is* she? How has she evaded *me*?'

Like a caged beast, the woman paced the cell, her heels **rapping**[8] out an infuriated rhythm on the glossy tiled floor.

'**Imbecile**[9]! How could you lose her?' she shrieked, her **livid**[10] features twisting into a **grotesque**[11] mask. 'THIS CANNOT HAPPEN!' she screamed, her face now centimetres from his.

---

1 **altitude** *(n)* height of something relating to sea or ground level. *(s)* elevation, highness.

2 **peculiar** *(adj)* different from normal or usual. *(s)* unusual, odd, bizarre, uncanny, queer, abnormal. *(ant)* normal.

3 **cascade** *(v)* pour or fall downwards. *(s)* descend, gush, flow, spill.

4 **circumference** *(n)* the curved line that forms the boundary of a circle. *(s)* edge, border. *(ant)* middle.

5 **slick** *(adj)* smooth and shiny. *(s)* sleek, glossy, shining. *(ant)* dull, rough.

6 **incandescent** *(adj)* very angry. *(s)* furious, enraged, seething, fuming. *(ant)* calm, content.

7 **quail** *(v)* show or feel fear. *(s)* quake, quaver, blench, cower, cringe, flinch, recoil, wince. *(ant)* confront.

8 **rap** *(v)* repeatedly strike a hard surface. *(s)* knock, tap, thump, thwack.

9 **imbecile** *(n)* a stupid person. *(s)* idiot, fool, halfwit, clod, ninny, chump, dunce. *(ant)* genius.

10 **livid** *(adj)* furiously angry. *(s)* seething, infuriated, incensed, enraged, outraged, fuming. *(ant)* pleased, calm.

11 **grotesque** *(adj)* ugly and distorted (out of shape). *(s)* malformed, deformed, misshapen. *(ant)* attractive.

Evans **cowered**[1], curling into the **fetal**[2] position, and quivered on the thin bunk.

'You **pathetic**[3], **craven**[4], **simpering**[5] mouse of a man. Call yourself a Knight Hawk?' she mocked. 'If it were not for your **looming**[6] death, I would see you **stripped**[7] of your undeserving honour. What greater shame could **befit**[8] one such as you?' she scoffed, her arms **flailing**[9] as she marched in manic circles.

She had **grossly**[10] **underestimated**[11] this girl's **tenacity**[12].

Most unaccustomed to this position, **floundering**[13], the woman straightened her jacket, tossed her hair over her shoulders and marched from the room.

---

1 **cower** *(v)* crouch or squat in fear. *(s)* shrink, recoil, grovel, flinch, quail, cringe, tremble. *(ant)* stand tall.

2 **fetal** *(adj)* denoting posture typical of a fetus (developing offspring, baby). *(s)* curled. *(ant)* straight.

3 **pathetic** *(adj)* arousing pity, inadequate. *(s)* pitiful, useless, laughable, weak. *(ant)* admirable, respectable.

4 **craven** *(adj)* completely lacking in courage. *(s)* cowardly, gutless, spineless, lily-livered. *(ant)* brave, bold.

5 **simpering** *(adj)* showing ingratiating (slimy, creepy, coy) behaviour. *(s)* demure, timid, sycophantic. *(ant)* brazen.

6 **looming** *(adj)* about to happen. *(s)* imminent, approaching, threatening, impending. *(ant)* remote.

7 **strip** *(v)* deprive someone of something. *(s)* deny, rob, relieve, dispossess, divest. *(ant)* award, give, bestow.

8 **befit** *(v)* be suitable for. *(s)* suit, fit, be in keeping with. *(ant)* be out of keeping with.

9 **flail** *(v)* swing or wave wildly. *(s)* thrash about, beat about, whirl, flap, flounder, lash.

10 **grossly** *(adv)* to an extreme extent. *(s)* excessively, vastly, hugely. *(ant)* moderately, slightly.

11 **underestimate** *(v)* regard to be less capable than really is. *(s)* undervalue, misjudge. *(ant)* overestimate.

12 **tenacity** *(n)* quality of being determined and persistent. *(s)* stubbornness, resolve, diligence. *(ant)* irresolution.

13 **flounder** *(v)* struggle physically or mentally. *(s)* falter, blunder, stumble, be flummoxed. *(ant)* succeed.

13. Noodles

Staggered, Claire pushed the compass into her pocket, scrabbled onto her knees and peeped through the expanding hole, Thomas by her side. Mr Brady's pristine Tesla sat sparkling in what appeared to be a **cluttered**[1] and chaotic workshop. A plethora of mucky tools lay strewn across the floor and surrounding surfaces. Oily rags adorned the worktops amid an array of filthy mugs. The **pungent**[2] **odour**[3] of oil and fumes **filtered**[4] through the hole. Claire sniffed.

Eh? Confused, Claire sniffed again. An unmistakable whiff of curry wafted through the hole. She suddenly screamed, **bowling**[5] sideways into Thomas, whacking her head again and landing face down in the dirt.

'You want this?' asked a flat voice.

Claire spat out soil, rubbed her grimy hands on her jeans and tried to regain her composure.

'Do you want this or not?' drawled the voice.

Speechless, Claire wriggled onto her knees and stared open-mouthed through the hole.

A baseball-capped Lily looked back at her and said, 'If *you* don't want it, I'll have it.'

Lily held a steaming curry-flavoured Pot Noodle, plastic cutlery poking out of the top. Before Claire could speak, Thomas, in one leap, pounced up and through the hole.

'Hungry, boy?' asked Lily, bending to stroke Thomas, who weaved contentedly between her

---

1 **cluttered** *(adj)* filled untidily with objects or mess. *(s)* littered, jumbled, messy, chaotic, disordered. *(ant)* austere, tidy.

2 **pungent** *(adj)* strong and sharp in taste or smell. *(s)* powerful, pervasive, overpowering. *(ant)* bland, plain.

3 **odour** *(n)* a distinctive, often unpleasant, smell. *(s)* scent, aroma, stink, stench, whiff.

4 **filter** *(v)* slowly enter. *(s)* trickle, flow, seep, permeate, ooze. *(ant)* flood, pour.

5 **bowl** *(v)* move rapidly in a certain direction. *(s)* speed, hurtle, roll, career, careen, streak. *(ant)* flounder.

shins. 'Do you want this or not?' she drawled in her **broad**[1] Welsh accent.

'I'm starving,' said Claire, 'but first, can I use your loo?'

'Come on through,' Lily answered, as if heads appearing via holes in solid walls was a **common**[2] occurrence. 'It's in the corner, over there.' She pointed, plonking the Pot Noodle on the bonnet of Mr Brady's prized **possession**[3].

'Come, Tommy. Welcome back. Let's get you some food.' And with that, Lily left the room.

She knows Thomas, and he clearly knows her! Claire was shocked. However, more pressing now was the hole. *How the heck do I get through it?* She was no Thomas.

Desperate not to embarrass herself further, she furtively scraped more soil from around the base of the hole until it reached below her midriff. She'd have to jump through it, land on her tummy and try the same see-saw balancing act she'd performed earlier to descend the ladder. She swore to get fitter.

In a single motion, Claire jumped up and forward. 'Oof!' she cried. She'd landed straight on her stomach, winding herself yet again, her legs stuck straight out behind her, **traversing**[4] the hole. See-sawing precariously, she slithered her weight forward towards the tipping point, which would propel her hands to the floor. To transfer her weight, Claire wriggled, swinging her feet up behind her. But instead of inching forward, she shot straight through, landing in an undignified heap on the garage floor. It wasn't pretty.

Crikey! she thought. *At least I made it.*

Claire sat brushing grime from her face and rubbing grit from her eyes, blinking hard. As her pupils adjusted to the light, she raised her head and saw four shins standing before her. She looked up to see Lily and another boy nonchalantly munching Pot Noodles, amused looks on their faces.

'Yours is gonna get cold,' said Lily, nodding towards the pot on Mr Brady's car.

As she struggled to stand, Claire's face burned in embarrassment.

'Thanks,' she muttered, finding her feet and **hobbling**[5] over to grab it. She'd crawled for so

---

1 **broad** *(adj)* (of an accent) noticeable and strong. *(s)* distinctive, heavy, pronounced. *(ant)* slight, unnoticeable.

2 **common** *(adj)* happening often. *(s)* usual, regular, frequent, familiar, customary, habitual. *(ant)* rare, unusual.

3 **possession** *(n)* an item that one owns. *(s)* property, asset, chattel, belonging.

4 **traverse** *(v)* move through or across. *(s)* negotiate, navigate, criss-cross, cross, cover.

5 **hobble** *(v)* walk in an awkward way. *(s)* limp, shuffle, falter, shamble, totter, stumble. *(ant)* stride, glide.

long her legs threatened to cramp, and her knees were raw. She prayed she could keep it at bay – cramp would be a killer embarrassment now. The loo could wait.

Today the predictable Pot Noodle tasted divine. Apart from the **revolting**[1] mouthful of cucumber sandwich, she'd eaten nothing since breakfast.

Still mortified by her **ungainly**[2] entrance, eyes aiming at the floor, Claire nibbled the noodles, hoping she wouldn't have to speak first. From a large plate by Lily's feet, Thomas lapped at his food, voraciously devouring it all.

A **toe-curling**[3] silence ensued. Claire was clearly the elephant in the room. Desperate to ask a million questions, she wanted to know everything about Lily and this mystery boy. Claire swallowed her pride, bracing herself to begin, but the only words that left her mouth were 'Any chance of some water, please?'

'Arjun, go fetch some water,' ordered Lily. 'I made the Pot Noodles.'

The boy tutted, threw his empty Pot Noodle onto the side and wandered off.

'I suppose you're wondering about stuff,' said Lily, peering up from beneath her cap.

Claire nodded, relieved Lily had **broached**[4] this first.

'I'm not one of *you lot*, if that's what you're thinking,' said Lily, sizing up Claire.

Claire shook her head, her mouth full of noodles. She didn't know what to think.

'But my dad is,' declared Lily, her icy eyes boring into Claire's, 'and right now, because of that damned bracelet, he's not too well at all.'

Claire almost choked on a noodle. Feeling herself becoming wide-eyed, she quickly rid her face of shock. *Geraint the Garage is a Knight Hawk? Was all that* ***bravado***[5] *earlier with Lily an act?* she thought, flabbergasted but nodding **gravely**[6] to hide it.

As if spoiling for a reaction, Lily just stared at Claire.

'Here's your water,' said the returning boy, interrupting the silence and handing over a plastic bottle.

---

1 **revolting** *(adj)* causing disgust. *(s)* sickening, repellent, repulsive, nauseating. *(ant)* delightful, enchanting.

2 **ungainly** *(adj)* clumsy. *(s)* awkward, graceless, inelegant, inept, lumbering. *(ant)* elegant, graceful.

3 **toe-curling** *(adj)* embarrassing. *(s)* awkward, humiliating, difficult, uncomfortable. *(ant)* comfortable.

4 **broach** *(v)* raise a difficult subject for discussion. *(s)* propose, approach, introduce, mention, open. *(ant)* close.

5 **bravado** *(n)* an intrepid manner meant to impress. *(s)* bluster, boldness, swagger, bombast. *(ant)* modesty.

6 **gravely** *(adv)* in a grave (serious) way. *(s)* urgently, profoundly, significantly. *(ant)* trivially.

'Thanks,' responded Claire, still in shock.

'This is Arjun. He's not like you either,' said Lily, introducing the boy.

'Hiya!' he said, smiling. 'Pleased to meet you.' His accent was Welsh, like Lily's.

'Pleased to meet you too,' said Claire, her tone formal.

'OK! **Niceties**[1] over,' snapped Lily. 'Someone is out to kill my dad and his knight mates. Seems I can't stop 'em, but you can,' said Lily, pointing at Claire.

'Me?' replied Claire.

'Yep, you. And we gotta get a move on,' said Lily, plonking her empty Pot Noodle onto the roof of Mr Brady's car.

'Open!' commanded Lily.

Claire glanced around, wondering who Lily was talking to, but then the driver's door of the Tesla opened.

'How did you do that?' said Claire, astonished. She'd travelled in the Tesla numerous times and never seen Mr Brady ask it to open.

'Get in!' ordered Lily.

'OK! Chill your beans, missus,' snapped Claire, forgetting her nerves as she headed for the rear door.

'No,' said Lily. 'Get in the front, the driver's seat.'

'What for?' asked Claire. 'I can't drive.'

'No need to drive this baby. She drives herself,' answered Lily in her usual monotone. 'Get in!'

'No!' Claire retorted. 'I can't drive!'

'As I said, she drives herself. Now get in, or do you want your friends to die? 'Cause I know *I* want my dad around for a bit longer,' said Lily.

'Go on, Claire, it's OK,' encouraged the boy in his heavy Welsh accent. 'I need to record your voice so she listens to you,' he added.

'What do you mean, so she listens to me?' asked Claire, her voice now at top note.

Arjun answered, his tone more **tolerant**[2] than Lily's. 'This is no ordinary car. I can programme her to listen to you, and she really *will* drive you where you ask her to go.'

---

1 **nicety** *(n)* nice or polite social behaviour. *(s)* courtesy, civility, grace, chit-chat, small talk. *(ant)* rudeness.

2 **tolerant** *(adj)* accepting or forbearing. *(s)* stoic, patient, lenient, passive. *(ant)* impatient.

'But what about the roads, and the police if they see me?'

'Along with a few *other* **tweaks**[1], we tinted the windows for you. No one will see you,' he answered, trying to reassure Claire.

'Look, quit moaning. Either get into the car or go,' barked Lily.

'Go where?' yelled Claire, her hands in the air.

'Exactly,' said Lily, her blue eyes frosty.

The garage fell silent.

Lily drummed her fingers on the car's roof. Nobody moved.

Claire's stomach swirled. She rubbed at her telltale twitching eye and shifted from foot to foot.

'OK. OK. I'll do it,' Claire answered eventually. 'But on one condition,' she added.

'Go on,' said Lily, stony-faced. 'What?'

'Can I use your toilet first?' said Claire.

*

Gwilym no longer saw Claire, and hearing her thoughts was sporadic. He rolled onto his side and stared **wistfully**[2] through the long picture window. His joints complained, his breaths were shallow, and his pulse was racing. His heart had been forced into **overdrive**[3] as his blood pressure plummeted.

The feather-light **eiderdown**[4] pressed his body, its silken **texture**[5] scratching his **tender**[6] skin. From the highest point of this magnificent castle, he surveyed his territory, the white-capped peaks of Snowdonia – the majestic jewels in the crown of North Wales.

He **reminisced**[7], recalling the years enjoyed before **heinous**[8] betrayal and loss. The highs and lows, family and friends, **acquaintances**[9] – both good and bad.

---

1 **tweak** *(n)* small adjustment to improve. *(s)* modification, alteration, refinement, adaptation. *(ant)* degradation.

2 **wistfully** *(adv)* done in a wistful (regretful, longing or yearning) manner. *(s)* sadly, pensively. *(ant)* contentedly.

3 **overdrive** *(n)* excessive or extreme activity. *(s)* hyperactivity. *(ant)* lethargy.

4 **eiderdown** *(n)* a quilt stuffed with down (originally from the eider duck) or a similar soft material.

5 **texture** *(n)* the way something feels or looks. *(s)* touch, structure, consistency, appearance, character.

6 **tender** *(adj)* (of the skin) sore. *(s)* sensitive, painful, raw, irritated. *(ant)* pain-free.

7 **reminisce** *(v)* think about enjoyable events from the past. *(s)* recall, remember, recollect, evoke. *(ant)* forget.

8 **heinous** *(adj)* wicked. *(s)* evil, monstrous, odious, atrocious, disgraceful, contemptible. *(ant)* admirable.

9 **acquaintance** *(n)* a person one knows but not a close friend. *(s)* connection, associate, colleague, ally. *(ant)* stranger.

He remembered the darkest times – Dewi controlling the bracelet, **spawning**[1] the quest to recover it and lock it away forever.

Now was his time to let go. Weary and **spent**[2], he closed his eyes and drifted away.

*

Beneath the silk-covered quilt, the wiry bundle curled tighter, pressing deeper into the small of his master's broad back.

He would not move. Unfaltering, he would stay there until the bitter end. Jack would never leave his master, Gwilym.

---

1 **spawn** *(v)* give rise to. *(s)* produce, create, generate, make, cause.

2 **spent** *(adj)* used up. *(s)* exhausted, consumed, depleted, drained, finished, emptied. *(ant)* replete.

14. Daisy

Claire snatched Lily's empty Pot Noodle from the Tesla's roof and, with a deft flick, tossed it into a nearby, overflowing bin.

'Go on,' Arjun urged. 'Get in. She won't bite.'

For the first time, Claire lowered herself into the driver's seat of a car. Although familiar with this awesome machine, its wow factor never failed.

'Not your usual learner driver's vehicle,' Arjun laughed, leaning in.

'You don't say,' replied Claire, her tone **caustic**[1].

'She's called Daisy,' Arjun announced with a proud grin.

'Daisy!' repeated Claire, pulling a questioning face.

'It was his nan's name,' **interjected**[2] Lily. 'Don't ask,' she added, shaking her head.

'I miss my nain. Talk to her,' Arjun enthused.

Nine? thought Claire.

'Go on, talk to Daisy. Earlier, when we shredded your tyres and jammed your seat belt to keep you in the car on your own, Daisy recorded a **snippet**[3] of your voice, but she didn't get quite enough,' said Arjun.

'*You* shredded our tyres,' shrieked Claire, rounding on Lily. '*You* jammed my seat belt!'

Lily raised her palm, batting Claire's words away like a cloud of **midges**[4]. 'Not now!' she ordered. 'No time. Arjun fixed it. Just talk to the car.'

---

1 **caustic** *(adj)* bitter, scathing and sarcastic. *(s)* cutting, biting, scornful, sharp, harsh, unkind. *(ant)* mild, kind.

2 **interject** *(v)* say brusquely as an aside or interruption. *(s)* intervene, remark, comment, cut in, butt in.

3 **snippet** *(n)* a short excerpt or small piece. *(s)* bit, extract, fragment, morsel.

4 **midge** *(n)* a tiny two-winged fly that lives near water and gathers into swarms.

Stumped and feeling preposterous and utterly self-conscious, Claire divulged her name, age and address to the car.

'That'll do,' said Arjun. 'Daisy recognises you now, but the more you two converse, the better she'll know you. Now, let me show you exactly what she can do,' he grinned.

'We two?' remarked Claire.

'AI. Machine learning,' Arjun replied. 'Treat her as a friend you're just getting to know, and she won't let you down.' Arjun's wide smile stretched as far as his voice, lifting Claire's mood. 'So, as she's pretty fast, best go easy on the **accelerator**[1],' Arjun laughed, 'although she'll limit your speed if needs be.'

'But I can't drive,' reiterated Claire.

'Just tell her where you wanna go,' **intervened**[2] a **terse**[3] Lily. 'She'll do the rest. Get on with it, Arjun. There's no time for a show-and-tell. Stick to the important stuff.'

Arjun sat in the front passenger seat alongside Claire. 'I stealth programmed her, and I wrote new code for her Thought Comms. They won't kick in until you're better acquainted though,' he added, as though discussing the weather.

Arjun was clearly to Lily what Q was to James Bond.

'Thought Comms?' questioned Claire, her face screwed up in consternation.

'Remember, AI. Artificial intelligence,' said Arjun. 'I programmed new—'

Lily interrupted, poking her head over the passenger seat. 'Time's up!' She focused her laser-like gaze at Claire. 'You're just gonna have to use your Instinct stuff, like Luke Skywalker in *Star Wars*.'

'I've never seen *Star Wars*,' snapped Claire, her tone barbed.

'Your loss!' Lily said. 'Great films.'

Then, lowering her cap over her eyes, Lily nodded at Arjun and walked away.

'Don't worry. Daisy will look after you,' he said, comforting an angst-ridden Claire.

'Oh, and you can talk to us any time, once the Thought Comms' **synapses**[4] fire up.'

---

1 **accelerator** *(n)* a device, such as a foot pedal, for controlling the speed of a vehicle's engine.

2 **intervene** *(v)* interrupt. *(s)* interfere, intercede, intrude.

3 **terse** *(adj)* using few words. *(s)* snappy, abrupt, curt, brusque, short, brief. *(ant)* verbose, rambling.

4 **synapse** *(n)* a connection between nerve cells (neurons).

Claire raised her hands, then flopped them onto her thighs in despair. 'How do I even *start* the thing?'

'Daisy is no ordinary Tesla. Just ask her,' Arjun reassured her. 'Oh, and one other thing,' he added.

'What?' said Claire, perturbed.

'Wear your seat belt,' Arjun replied with a nod in its direction.

'I can't even see through the windscreen. I'm too short!' she said, bouncing up and down.

'Claire ...' Arjun gently reprimanded her as he **clambered**[1] out of the car.

'OK! OK! I hear you!' Claire said, shutting down the conversation.

Feeling ridiculous, she buckled up. Lily sauntered over and stood by Arjun.

Without emotion, Lily asked, 'You forgetting something?'

Claire glanced about the Tesla's minimalistic interior.

'I've got water,' she replied. Then suddenly Thomas sprang from nowhere and, like an Egyptian **sphinx**[2], lay beside her on the passenger seat, his lemon-shaped eyes flashing.

'Cats don't need seat belts,' drawled Lily. 'Nine lives.'

For the first time, Claire suspected a hint of **mirth**[3] had sneaked across Lily's face.

'Now go!' ordered Lily. 'Before it's too late.'

Dumbstruck[4], Claire gawped at the Tesla's blank dashboard. Embarrassed, she muttered, 'Start,' and the car's **ample**[5] display lit up. She glanced out around the cluttered garage. 'Duh! How do I get out?' she said, seeing no visible exit.

'Ask Daisy,' said Arjun.

'Thomas, this better work,' Claire said. Then, in an overly polite voice, she muttered, 'Daisy, please exit.'

'No need to say please,' replied a kind, elderly sounding voice.

Claire reeled. 'What the ...?' she blurted through the car's open window.

'That's my nain's voice,' boasted Arjun.

---

1 **clamber** *(v)* climb or move awkwardly. *(s)* scale, mount, crawl, scramble, ascend.

2 **sphinx** *(n)* a creature from Greek mythology with a woman's head, a lion's body and wings.

3 **mirth** *(n)* amusement. *(s)* laughter, cheerfulness, merriment, cheer, glee, joy, levity. *(ant)* misery, gloom.

4 **dumbstruck** *(adj)* speechless due to shock. *(s)* dumbfounded, flabbergasted, amazed, astonished.

5 **ample** *(adj)* enough or more than enough. *(s)* plentiful, abundant, generous. *(ant)* insufficient, meagre.

'What?' said Claire. 'What do you mean, your nine's voice?'

'I told you, don't ask,' drawled Lily, rolling her eyes at a beaming Arjun. 'Nain is the Welsh word for 'nan', or 'granny', or whatever you wanna call it.'

'Really?' said Claire, stifling a chuckle. Daisy's name and voice were most unsuitable for a customised high-tech car, but she loved it. Claire forgot her dilemma and said, 'OK, Daisy, we can leave now.'

'Where would you like to go, Claire?' asked the lady's voice.

'Oh no!' Claire answered, blushing. 'Daisy, open the window fully.' Claire popped her head out, and to an expectant Lily, she said, 'Um, where *am* I going?'

'Wondered when you'd get around to asking that,' drawled Lily. 'You're going to mine some gold.'

*

In his private rooms, the **groggy**[1] man **prised**[2] open his gunk-filled eyes. They were sticky and refused to focus in the dark. Unaware of his whereabouts, he **fumbled**[3] under his pillow and located his phone. He saw the time, remembering. She was right; he had been exhausted and had slept for hours.

Rousing himself, he pushed down on his hands and propped his back against his plush velvet headboard. Something was **amiss**[4]. As though being crushed in a **vice**[5], oscillating waves of pain gripped his forehead. His mouth tasted like an **exhumed**[6] body. He waved at his bedside lamp, its brightening glow settling on an **unobtrusive**[7] shade of gold.

The man smacked his lips together and ran his fur-coated tongue around the inside of his **fetid**[8] mouth. He leaned over and snatched an ice-cold bottle of water from the discreet fridge adjacent to his bed. In one, he drained it and tossed it onto the floor. He dug the sleep from his eyes, casually flicking it into the air, and farted.

---

1 **groggy** *(adj)* dazed. *(s)* fuddled, muzzy, disorientated, bewildered, shaky, discombobulated. *(ant)* sharp.

2 **prise** *(v)* use force to pull or move apart. *(s)* wrench, lever, yank, tug, heave, haul. *(ant)* push, clamp.

3 **fumble** *(v)* move the hands about clumsily. *(s)* scrabble, feel, search, root, dig, rummage.

4 **amiss** *(adj)* out of place or not right. *(s)* wrong, awry, incorrect, untoward. *(ant)* right, in order.

5 **vice** *(n)* a metal tool with jaws for holding an object securely in place. *(s)* clamp, brace, press, clasp.

6 **exhume** *(v)* dig out from the earth. *(s)* unearth, disinter. *(ant)* bury.

7 **unobtrusive** *(adj)* not intruding or attracting attention. *(s)* inconspicuous, tasteful, discreet. *(ant)* obtrusive.

8 **fetid** *(adj)* smelling extremely unpleasant. *(s)* stinking, putrid, rotten, rank, fusty, malodorous. *(ant)* fresh.

He **revelled**[1] in being **uncouth**[2] and **coarse**[3]; he preferred this David Lewis – the one his adoring employees were not **privy to**[4].

Throwing back his luxurious quilt, he grunted, swinging his legs to stand. The room swam before him. He could not blame champagne **consumption**[5]. Last night he had purposely **abstained**[6], bar the one glass in the Bentley, yet his demeanour portrayed otherwise. Dizziness and nausea **pitched**[7] him sideways, and with a deep retch, he lurched onto his bed and vomited. It was rapid, **projectile**[8] and spattered everywhere. He **belched**[9], spitting remnants of food onto the quilt.

He **evaluated**[10] the situation, pondering his **symptoms**[11]: no fever met his touch; no overwhelming weakness plagued his muscles or joints; and after lying still for several minutes, his violent nausea passed.

Eventually sitting, he swung his legs around, planting his feet on the floor. He sat with his fingers **interlocked**[12] on his lap, contemplating. It would be a **rarity**[13], but had he **contracted**[14] an illness? He believed not. Had he **consumed**[15] **rogue**[16] food? If so, it would have **contaminated**[17] his taster, an alarm would have been raised, and he would have been alerted.

---

1 **revel** *(v)* gain pleasure from. *(s)* delight, bask, luxuriate, wallow, glory, enjoy, savour, relish. *(ant)* dislike, hate.

2 **uncouth** *(adj)* lacking manners. *(s)* impolite, crude, gross, unrefined, rough, coarse, offensive. *(ant)* polite, refined.

3 **coarse** *(adj)* rude. *(s)* vulgar, uncouth, crude, crass, rough, obscene. *(ant)* decent, polite, refined.

4 **privy to** *(adj)* aware of something private or secret. *(s)* conscious of, acquainted with, informed of. *(ant)* ignorant of.

5 **consumption** *(n)* the act of eating or drinking. *(s)* devouring, ingestion, swallowing, imbibing.

6 **abstain** *(v)* stop oneself from doing or enjoying something. *(s)* cease, forgo, refrain. *(ant)* continue, accept.

7 **pitch** *(v)* throw. *(s)* toss, fling, hurl, cast, propel. *(ant)* catch.

8 **projectile** *(adj)* propelled with force through the air. *(s)* projected, impelled.

9 **belch** *(v)* burp. *(s)* eruct, emit, vent.

10 **evaluate** *(v)* form an idea of. *(s)* assess, judge, work out, calculate, rate, gauge, weigh up. *(ant)* misjudge.

11 **symptom** *(n)* a mental or physical manifestation of a health issue. *(s)* sign, feature, indication.

12 **interlock** *(v)* overlap or fit things together. *(s)* interconnect, mesh, engage, interlink. *(ant)* disengage.

13 **rarity** *(n)* something that is rare or unusual. *(s)* oddity, curiosity, rareness, anomaly. *(ant)* regularity.

14 **contract** *(v)* develop or catch a disease or illness. *(s)* get, pick up, come down with.

15 **consume** *(v)* eat or drink. *(s)* ingest, devour, swallow, gobble, imbibe.

16 **rogue** *(adj)* inferior or damaging. *(s)* shady, dodgy, shifty, harmful. *(ant)* beneficial.

17 **contaminate** *(v)* make sick by exposure to a poisonous substance. *(s)* poison, harm. *(adj)* cure.

No stranger to such **tactics**[1], he recognised **foul play**[2]. Someone had drugged him. Yet there existed a more **sinister**[3] and **audacious**[4] aspect to this **malicious**[5] **subterfuge**[6]. The **perpetrator**[7], and he guessed who, had intended to kill him, for the **odious**[8] pool of **putrid**[9] vomit, which now stained his quilt, was an ominous jet-black. Before him lay evidence of a deadly poison. He recognised it because he often **administered**[10] it to others. He threw back his head, cackling. His poisoner had underestimated his prodigious **constitution**[11]. It would require more than a suitably skilled **apothecary**[12] to **dispose of**[13] the mighty Master – Dewi.

---

1 **tactic** *(n)* an action to achieve something specific. *(s)* plan, strategy, ploy.

2 **foul play** *(n)* immoral or wicked behaviour. *(s)* wrongdoing, crime, villainy, misconduct. *(ant)* righteousness.

3 **sinister** *(adj)* wicked or criminal. *(s)* evil, nefarious, malicious, malign. *(ant)* innocent.

4 **audacious** *(adj)* daring and bold or showing a lack of respect. *(s)* brave, overconfident. *(ant)* reticent, respectful.

5 **malicious** *(adj)* having malice, intending harm. *(s)* malevolent, spiteful, mean, cruel, wicked. *(ant)* kind.

6 **subterfuge** *(n)* deceit. *(s)* trickery, deception, duplicity, guile, cunning, dishonesty. *(ant)* honesty.

7 **perpetrator** *(n)* someone who does something wrong or illegal. *(s)* culprit, offender, criminal.

8 **odious** *(adj)* extremely unpleasant. *(s)* abominable, revolting, repulsive, offensive, abhorrent. *(ant)* delightful.

9 **putrid** *(adj)* repulsive. *(s)* rancid, foul, bad, rotten, stinking. *(ant)* fresh, perfumed.

10 **administer** *(v)* dispense (give out) or apply. *(s)* deliver, issue, deal, distribute. *(ant)* withhold, deny.

11 **constitution** *(n)* physical make-up and health. *(s)* structure, build, nature, physique, fettle.

12 **apothecary** *(n)* a person who prepares drugs and medicines. *(s)* druggist, pharmacist, chemist.

13 **dispose of** *(v)* get rid of, do away with. *(s)* banish, discard, throw away, ditch. *(ant)* retain.

15. The Predator

'You're going to Cadwaladr Castle,' said Lily. 'Now get a move on.'

'Just keep talking to Daisy,' Arjun reminded Claire. 'My nain will help get you there. Don't forget, keep chatting, and once the Thought Comms are up, we're in your head.'

'How will I know?'

'You'll know!' snapped Lily. Then, with the tiniest hint of warmth, she added, 'Now get lost.'

More familiar with Lily's killer tongue, Claire nodded and smiled a faint goodbye at Arjun.

She looked ahead, still **reticent**[1], but in a more buoyant tone, she said, 'Daisy, Cadwaladr Castle.'

Like a scene from an old Batman movie, the worktops in Geraint's garage shuddered, scattering oily **debris**[2] onto the floor. Then slowly they creaked apart, revealing the gaping mouth of a tunnel.

Not again! What's wrong with roads? thought Claire, her heart sinking. 'At least we don't have to crawl through this tunnel, Thomas.'

'Indeed, you don't.'

Claire let go of the steering wheel and shot upright. 'No **offence**[3], Daisy,' she said, gasping, 'but I'm gonna take a while to get used to you.'

'None taken, dear. Hold tight, not onto the steering wheel though – no need,' replied Arjun's nain's voice. 'I will drive.'

---

1 **reticent** *(adj)* reluctant to disclose one's feelings or thoughts. *(s)* restrained, reserved, shy. *(ant)* garrulous.

2 **debris** *(n)* the remains of anything broken down or destroyed. *(s)* waste, rubbish, detritus.

3 **offence** *(n)* the act of hurting someone's feelings. *(s)* insult, affront, slight. *(ant)* compliment.

Claire glanced sideways at Thomas curled up like a doughnut on the passenger seat. Clearly unfazed, he was fast asleep.

She hoisted up her bum and prised the phone, glove and compass from her back pocket. She realised she mustn't crush them.

Cristy – should I call her?

She hesitated, flipping the phone in her hand. Then, along with the compass, she wedged it between her thighs, leaving the glove and tattered plastic on her lap.

No matter how often she travelled in this car, unless music played or Ben **wittered**[1] in her ear, its silence always stunned her. As the Tesla glided into the tunnel, its headlights cutting through the dark, she swore Arjun and Lily might hear her heartbeat.

As the car accelerated, its sides almost brushed the walls. It reminded her of the confined London Tube trains – she'd only travelled on them once, but she'd loathed it.

She glanced at Thomas; he didn't stir. Sitting behind the wheel of the Tesla was **bizarre**[2], but in a cramped tunnel, it felt freaky. The Tesla's display showed only dull, earthy blackness up ahead. Yet it **navigated**[3] the dense darkness with ease.

Not one for silence, Claire blurted, 'Are we nearly there yet, Daisy?' Then, turning pink, she said, 'I can't believe I asked that!'

'You sound like my grandson, Arjun,' replied the car. 'ETA is twelve minutes.'

Claire caught sight of their speed and gulped.

That's gotta be wrong, she thought, gripping the sides of the seat. Even though the digital speedometer displayed over one hundred miles per hour, it felt like thirty. The car swept through the tunnel as if on rails. If they **exceeded**[4] thirty in her mum's car, it **quaked**[5].

'Daisy?' asked Claire, a question in her tone.

'Yes?'

'What happens if you need charging?'

'To charge is unnecessary, cariad.'

---

1 **witter** *(v)* speak at length about unimportant things. *(s)* chatter, prattle, babble, gabble, jabber, go on, blather, waffle.

2 **bizarre** *(adj)* unusual or strange. *(s)* peculiar, odd, remarkable, abnormal. *(ant)* normal, ordinary.

3 **navigate** *(v)* find the way, guide or steer. *(s)* cross, traverse, direct, journey.

4 **exceed** *(v)* be greater in number or size, surpass a limit. *(s)* transcend, pass, top, go over, eclipse. *(ant)* fall short of.

5 **quake** *(v)* tremble or shake. *(s)* shudder, wobble, vibrate, rock.

Tears pricked Claire's eyes. *Cariad*. That was what Gladys called her. She flung her hand to her mouth, but half the sob escaped.

Daisy said nothing.

'Why did you call me cariad?' Claire asked eventually, a **hitch**[1] in her voice.

'My grandson programmed me this way. He was *my* cariad.'

'Oh!' whispered Claire, choking up again.

Thoughts of her family flooded back. A tear ran down her face. She hoped she'd see her mum again.

'What's that?' asked Claire, pointing to the screen.

A red dot beeped, flashing and **pulsating**[2] behind the image that depicted the Tesla on the display.

'What do you mean?' asked Daisy. 'I hear you but I cannot see you.'

'The red dot chasing us, on the screen,' said Claire, pointing furiously. 'What is it?'

Thomas was now sitting upright.

'It seems the radar has **detected**[3] another entity.'

'Another entity?' cried Claire. 'Living or not?'

'I detect heat but cannot confirm life.'

As the beep grew louder, the dot drew closer.

'Daisy!' yelled Claire. 'GO FASTER!'

The Tesla's screen suddenly flashed that it was in 'Ludicrous+' mode, and as if **hurtling**[4] down the runway in a departing jet, Claire's head jolted back into the Tesla's leather headrest. Claire gripped her seat, and Thomas hopped down into the footwell. The tunnel's walls, now indistinguishable, flew by in a blur of black. With a yelp, Claire ducked, bracing herself as the Tesla shot forth into the **onyx**[5]-coloured void. Her body quivered like jelly.

After several minutes of riding this roller coaster, they slowed to a stop. Claire lifted her head and peeped at the Tesla's screen. What should have taken twelve minutes had taken three. She

1 **hitch** *(n)* an instability in the voice. *(s)* catch, stammer, stutter, tremor, wobble.

2 **pulsate** *(v)* expand and contract regularly. *(s)* beat, throb, pulse, palpitate, pound.

3 **detect** *(v)* discern the presence of something. *(s)* notice, sense, perceive. *(ant)* miss, overlook.

4 **hurtle** *(v)* move at speed, typically in an uncontrolled way. *(s)* career, bolt, bowl, dash, careen. *(ant)* dawdle.

5 **onyx** *(n)* a semi-precious black agate (stone).

stared at the persistent dot; it was further behind but **closing**[1].

'What *is* that thing, Daisy?'

'I am unsure. It is **sophisticated**[2]. It is **subverting**[3] my radar.'

'How long before it's on us?'

'**Impact**[4] in four minutes.'

'Impact!' cried Claire.

In one agile leap, Thomas sprang up from the footwell onto Claire's lap.

'Mind the glove, Tommy!'

Claire rescued it from underneath him, grabbed the compass and phone, lifted her **buttocks**[5] and squeezed all three into her back pockets.

Thomas's **sulphur**[6]-coloured eyes bored into Claire's.

'What is it, Tom?'

He spun on her lap, his claws snagging her jeans. The red dot's proximity increased, its pulsating circumference growing as it neared the Tesla's **icon**[7] on the screen.

'Daisy, help me! What does Thomas want?'

'I cannot see the animal,' she replied, 'but I can hear you both.'

The Tesla remained stationary. Thomas clawed at Claire's jeans.

'Daisy, help!' cried Claire again. 'That dot's almost on us.'

'How may I help?' asked Daisy.

Claire realised her error.

'I'm such an idiot!' she yelled. 'Daisy, enter the castle!'

Thomas stilled, then, like an **uncoiling**[8] spring, sprang onto the passenger seat.

Realisation dawned on Claire. Unless explicitly commanded, Daisy couldn't help – she wasn't

---

1 **close** *(v)* slowly get nearer. *(s)* approach, catch up, draw near. *(ant)* diverge, deviate, digress.

2 **sophisticated** *(adj)* developed to a great degree of complexity. *(s)* smart, clever, advanced, complex. (ant) crude.

3 **subvert** *(v)* undermine (weaken). *(s)* unsettle, disrupt, upset, destabilise, suppress. *(ant)* aid, strengthen.

4 **impact** *(n)* an instance of one object hitting another. *(s)* collision, crash, bang, blow, contact. *(ant)* avoidance.

5 **buttocks** *(n)* bottom. *(s)* backside, behind, seat, rump, rear, haunches.

6 **sulphur** *(n)* a yellow chemical.

7 **icon** *(n)* a symbol on a screen. *(s)* image, logo, emblem, representation, sign, badge, motif, insignia, design.

8 **uncoil** *(v)* straighten from a curled position. *(s)* unfurl, unwind, unravel. *(ant)* coil, curl.

entirely **autonomous**[1]. Although she sounded like Arjun's nan, Daisy was a program, made to emulate a boy's **late**[2] grandma.

Claire glanced at the screen. Like Pac-Man about to gobble up his **prey**[3], the red dot loomed larger, throbbing like an angry **boil**[4]. Claire's stomach somersaulted as her bottom lifted from the seat. Thomas leaped down, crouching in the footwell. Claire shrieked. As if consumed by a giant **sinkhole**[5], the Tesla was dropping like a stone. It plummeted, free-falling through the air like a theme park ride.

'Mum! Mum!' she screamed, **anticipating**[6] a **lethal**[7] impact.

Then a calm elderly voice said, 'You have reached your **destination**[8].'

Dumbfounded, Claire lowered her hands from her eyes. Those were the exact words her mum's satnav used.

I'm alive, she thought. *I'm alive.*

Thomas sat beside her in the passenger seat, the Tesla stationary.

'Your grandson has a sick sense of humour,' exclaimed Claire, referring to the satnav's comment.

'I am sorry for that,' Daisy replied.

Claire checked the screen; the dot was gone. 'Thank goodness for that!' she said.

'Thank goodness for what?' Daisy asked.

'Sorry,' replied Claire, remembering Daisy couldn't see her. 'The dot, it's gone.'

'That does not mean it has ceased its **pursuit**[9],' said Daisy.

'What do you mean?' asked Claire.

---

1 **autonomous** *(adj)* able to act independently (alone). *(s)* free, uncontrolled, self-governing. *(ant)* dependent.

2 **late** *(adj)* no longer alive. *(s)* dead, deceased, departed, passed, gone. *(ant)* alive, existing.

3 **prey** *(n)* an animal that is hunted and killed by another for food. *(s)* quarry, game, kill. *(ant)* predator, hunter.

4 **boil** *(n)* a large spot filled with puss. *(s)* abscess, sore, pimple, pustule, carbuncle.

5 **sinkhole** *(n)* a hollow in the earth caused by water erosion. *(s)* crater, excavation, cavity, pit, void, sinkage.

6 **anticipate** *(v)* see as being possible. *(s)* predict, expect, foresee, forecast, foretell.

7 **lethal** *(adj)* able to cause death, hugely harmful or destructive. *(s)* deadly, fatal, mortal. *(ant)* life-giving.

8 **destination** *(n)* the place where someone or something is going to. *(s)* objective, target. *(ant)* starting point.

9 **pursuit** *(n)* action of pursuing (search, chase, follow). *(s)* quest, hunt, detection, pursual, stalking. *(ant)* retreat.

'Do not underestimate this **predator**[1]. My systems failed to **classify**[2] it,' finished Daisy, sounding **sombre**[3].

'I'm not with you,' said Claire.

'Whatever hunts you is swift, sophisticated and **unidentifiable**[4],' answered Daisy.

*

In his palatial rooms, Dewi paced, his bony hands raking through his dark hair. He must think. The game had changed. Should he allow his poisoner to know they had failed, or would his position strengthen if he was thought dead? There was little time. Dewi drained his champagne glass and threw it at the wall, **quelling**[5] his **ire**[6].

He must **outwit**[7] the traitor and their **conspirators**[8]. He must deploy his spies. He must locate Evans and seize the other half of the Cutter from the **wily**[9] knight who had somehow vanished with it in the tunnels yesterday.

After showering quickly, he **slicked**[10] back his **sodden**[11] hair, donned a clean suit and tied up the laces on his crocodile skin shoes. After **spritzing**[12] himself with his custom-made cologne, he snatched two phones and the tiny **oblong**[13] box containing the other half of the Cutter. Placing all three into the breast pocket of his suit, he turned and left, his face, gait and demeanour now that of David Lewis again.

---

1 **predator** *(n)* an animal or person that hunts others. *(s)* hunter.
2 **classify** *(v)* identify something as a member of a class or category. *(s)* recognise, label, discern.
3 **sombre** *(adj)* deeply serious or sad (feeling or looking). *(s)* melancholy, solemn, grave, sober. *(ant)* cheerful.
4 **unidentifiable** *(adj)* unable to be identified (recognised). *(s)* unrecognisable, unknown. *(ant)* identifiable.
5 **quell** *(v)* suppress (put an end to) and silence. *(s)* subdue, quash, crush, repress, control. *(ant)* incite, intensify.
6 **ire** *(n)* anger. *(s)* annoyance, fury, rage, temper, wrath, outrage, vexation, exasperation. *(ant)* calmness, joy.
7 **outwit** *(v)* deceive by greater ingenuity. *(s)* outsmart, outmanoeuvre, outfox, defeat, beat. *(ant)* lose.
8 **conspirator** *(n)* someone who conspires and assists in a conspiracy. *(s)* collaborator, accomplice.
9 **wily** *(adj)* clever and sharp, sometimes deceitfully so. *(s)* shrewd, astute, sly, crafty, cunning. *(ant)* guileless.
10 **slick** *(v)* make smooth and glossy. *(s)* sleek, flatten, plaster, gel. *(ant)* roughen, rumple, tousle.
11 **sodden** *(adj)* soaked through with liquid. *(s)* saturated, soaking, sopping, drenched, wringing. *(ant)* dry.
12 **spritz** *(v)* spray liquid in brief bursts. *(s)* squirt, scatter, atomise.
13 **oblong** *(adj)* rectangular in shape. *(s)* quadrilateral, four-sided.

16. Stranded

Claire stared through the Tesla's windscreen. Apart from the headlight beams, blackness enveloped them.

'Daisy, are you sure this is Cadwaladr Castle?'

'We have reached our destination,' replied Daisy.

'Doesn't look like a castle to me, more like a **dungeon**[1],' said Claire, peering through the windscreen into darkness.

She glanced at Thomas. He sat unperturbed on the passenger seat.

'What happens now?' Claire asked.

'I do not know,' replied Daisy.

'Tommy?' questioned Claire, but he didn't move a muscle.

Claire bit her lip, contemplating, then unbuckled her seat belt.

Lily had said she was going to mine some gold. Had Lily meant that **literally**[2]? Was that why Claire was here, in a supposed castle? Was she supposed to find a gold mine and dig with her bare hands?

'Daisy, open the door,' ordered Claire, but the red dot reappeared on the perimeter of the screen. Thomas pounced into the footwell.

'ETA?' cried Claire.

'Two minutes,' said Daisy.

'Drive!' yelled Claire.

---

1 **dungeon** *(n)* an underground prison cell, particularly in a castle. *(s)* jail, lock-up, vault.

2 **literally** *(adv)* in a literal manner or sense. *(s)* exactly, precisely, really, truly. *(ant)* figuratively, indirectly.

'Destination?' replied Daisy.

'I don't care. Just lose that dot.'

Within seconds the Tesla had reached Ludicrous Plus mode, but this time the dot didn't vanish; it closed on them.

'Faster!' bellowed Claire, pinned to her seat.

'The tunnel's confines **prohibit**[1] higher speeds. We have reached upper limits,' said Daisy.

'I don't care!' shrieked Claire as the dot almost reached them.

Suddenly the picture on the Tesla's screen split, and a girl's face appeared.

'Thought Comms are up,' said a Welsh voice. 'I'll be in your head in thirty seconds. Then I help guide you.'

Speechless, Claire gripped her seat and stared at the screen.

'What the …?' she said.

'Quiet!' ordered the girl. 'I cannot enter your thoughts if you speak.'

Claire's eyes widened, but reluctantly her mouth stayed shut.

'Twenty seconds,' announced the girl. 'Ten seconds … five … We're in.'

The girl's face vanished from the screen.

Claire blinked, rubbing her eyes. 'What? What!' she said, blinking hard.

Before her eyes, but in her head, she saw the girl's face and heard her voice. The girl who had been speaking from the screen, who'd just 'entered her head', was Felicity, the police officer-paramedic from yesterday.

Claire, don't think. Don't question. There's no time. Empty your mind. You know how to do it, said Felicity's voice. *I will guide Daisy.*

The dot grew on the screen and was closing fast. Claire heard Felicity's commands: *Daisy, bear left; bear right; reduce speed; sharp left; sharp right. Now prepare: three, two, one, stealth mode.*

Claire's bum left her seat half a second before her head hit the Tesla's roof.

'Ouch!' she yelled before landing hard, sideways, in her seat. The Tesla had dropped again, then stopped. The dot had vanished.

Always wear your seat belt, said Felicity.

---

1 **prohibit** *(v)* make something impossible. *(s)* stop, prevent, preclude, hinder, impede, hamper. *(ant)* allow, facilitate.

Claire rubbed her head. She'd caught the spot already bruised and sore.

'I need to ask you questions,' said Claire.

Yes, replied Felicity, *but little time remains.*

'Are Jack and Gwilym … alive?' Claire's voice caught.

Yes, replied Felicity, *but Gwilym, not for much longer.*

'All the knights?' asked Claire.

All the knights, replied Felicity.

'Can you help me find the gold?' asked Claire in a hopeful whisper.

I can help, but you must try, said Felicity.

'So, you're not a Knight Hawk?' Claire asked.

I am as you are, a niece of Gwilym Cadwaladr, not yet knighted, said Felicity, her voice sounding formal.

Daisy suddenly spoke. The Tesla's passenger door popped open, and Thomas sprang out.

'Thomas?' cried Claire, but all she saw was his soot-black tail disappearing around the Tesla's door. 'Where's he going?' shouted Claire.

Patience, replied Felicity. *And remember, Claire, I'm now in your thoughts. Speaking aloud is unnecessary. Think, and I will hear you.*

'Oh yeah,' said Claire. 'I forgot.'

Put your seat belt on, said Felicity.

'What about Thomas?' implored Claire.

Patience, said Felicity.

The passenger door closed. Claire looked ahead, but it was pitch-black.

Daisy began to move, not forward but backwards, a beam of light slicing through the blackness. So far, no dot had appeared on her screen.

The Tesla's got headlights in the rear, thought Claire, marvelling at its **burgeoning**[1] speed as they reached an excess of one hundred miles per hour – backwards.

Felicity was silent, perhaps **communicating**[2] with Daisy. Claire dared not think. She studied the screen's speed readout, almost disappointed when it decreased, bringing them to a

---

1 **burgeoning** *(adj)* growing or increasing rapidly. *(s)* accelerating, mounting, ballooning. *(ant)* dwindling.

2 **communicate** *(v)* exchange information. *(s)* converse, talk, speak, interface, commune.

standstill again. Then everything turned black. Claire saw nothing, not even her finger before her nose. A ringing silence fell.

Claire waited, desperate to speak, her heartbeat increasing with each **elapsing**[1] second. Minutes passed. She recalled Felicity's words: *Patience, Claire.* She felt an empty sensation in her stomach. Felicity was silent. Alone, underground and in the dark, without Daisy, Claire didn't even know how to start the Tesla.

'Felicity,' she whispered. 'Felicity? Daisy?' Her cries became frantic, her rising **dismay**[2] no longer **suppressed**[3]. 'I can't even turn on the stupid phone – it's too dark,' she yelled, both palms pounding the steering wheel. She fumbled and felt her way, her quaking hands struggling to unbuckle her seat belt.

'Daisy!' she **hollered**[4] into the silence.

Patting the panel beside her, pulling and pushing at whatever she could, she opened the door. 'Thomas! Thomas!' she screamed. 'Thomas!'

The car was dead. It was starkly **evident**[5] that no one was coming. Shutting the door, she wriggled her hips up, working Cristy's phone from her pocket. In the dark, discerning its front from its back proved impossible. No way would it boot up.

Wrestling with despair, she lifted her bum, removed the compass and pushed the phone back into her pocket. Patting the other, she felt the glove, relieved it was still there. While **cradling**[6] the compass in her right palm, Claire's thumb found the fine engravings and the stone in its centre. Bracing herself, she pressed her thumb hard onto the cool gem. It yielded a **mite**[7]. She pushed harder. The moment its **nucleus**[8] sparked into life, Claire bore the **instantaneous**[9] drain on her own. Trembling, she waited for the green laser to shoot and point its dot and reveal her

---

1 **elapse** *(v)* (of time) pass. *(s)* advance, proceed, progress, lapse, go by.

2 **dismay** *(n)* anxiety or distress. *(s)* alarm, consternation, disquiet, trepidation. *(ant)* relief.

3 **suppressed** *(adj)* inhibited. *(s)* restrained, smothered, concealed, stifled, controlled, checked. *(ant)* allowed, unleashed.

4 **holler** *(v)* shout or cry loudly. *(s)* bellow, bawl, roar, shriek, yell, howl, vociferate. *(ant)* whisper.

5 **evident** *(adj)* clearly understood or visible. *(s)* apparent, obvious, noticeable, perceptible. *(ant)* unnoticeable.

6 **cradle** *(v)* hold gently and protectively. *(s)* support, embrace, clasp, nestle, lull, tend, rock. *(ant)* drop, abandon.

7 **mite** *(n)* a small amount. *(s)* tiny bit, little, dash, touch, tad, smidgen, mote. *(ant)* lot, loads, tons, heaps.

8 **nucleus** *(n)* the central and most important part. *(s)* centre, heart, core, nub, kernel. *(ant)* outside, edge.

9 **instantaneous** *(adj)* done or happening instantly. *(s)* instant, immediate, prompt, speedy, rapid. *(ant)* delayed.

exit. Nothing. The gem just glowed, sucking away her energy, and what felt like her **soul**[1].

'What an idiot!' she blurted. 'The satnav! I don't want the laser; it's the satnav I need.'

Dredging[2] her mind for Evans's words, she released a tad of pressure and rotated her right thumb in tiny anticlockwise circles. With each increasing movement, the gem glowed brighter, until the small arrow appeared. She removed her thumb, and there it was: a rudimentary map of what lay before her. As it was almost impossible to follow while maintaining pressure on the gem, progress would be a struggle.

Loath[3] to leave the stricken Tesla behind, she **groped**[4] around the driver's door again and popped it open.

I wonder if Daisy has *run out of charge*, she thought, stepping out of the car and stooping into a **hunch**[5]. As she was about to drop onto all threes for the inevitable crawl, the faint glow from beneath her aching right thumb revealed an unexpected but welcome surprise. This tunnel provided enough height to stand. In sweeping circular motions, using the compass's dim light, she surveyed her murky surroundings.

Apart from its height, albeit vague, something about this tunnel struck her as different.

What is it? she thought, blinking **intensely**[6], willing her pupils to adjust to the scant light.

She sniffed. Odd. It was the smell. The tunnel's odour was unlike the others. Sniffing continuously, as Jack would, she stepped away from the Tesla.

What is that smell?

Fleetingly, as it rose above the **must**[7], she caught a **transitory**[8] sweet waft before losing it again.

Practically snorting, she took **cagey**[9] steps in the arrow's direction, and the smell registered with her nostrils and brain.

---

1 **soul** *(n)* the spiritual essence of a human or animal. *(s)* spirit, life force.

2 **dredge** *(v)* search deeply. *(s)* explore, delve, probe, comb, scrutinise. *(ant)* overlook.

3 **loath** *(adj)* unwilling or reluctant (not wanting to do something). *(s)* opposed, disinclined, averse. *(ant)* eager.

4 **grope** *(v)* feel or search about for blindly with the hands. *(s)* fumble, scrabble, finger, fish. *(ant)* withdraw.

5 **hunch** *(n)* a humped posture. *(s)* bend, bow, crouch, curve, stoop, hump.

6 **intensely** *(adv)* in an intense (strong) manner. *(s)* fiercely, vehemently, strongly. *(ant)* mildly, apathetically.

7 **must** *(n)* dampness. *(s)* mould, mustiness, decay, mildew. *(ant)* dryness.

8 **transitory** *(adj)* not permanent. *(s)* brief, temporary, transient, short. *(ant)* permanent, perpetual.

9 **cagey** *(adj)* reluctant. *(s)* cautious, circumspect, wary, careful. *(ant)* willing.

'No way!' she blurted. 'What took me so long? It's lilies! I can smell lilies.'

Claire's heart **soared**[1]. Yesterday the scent of lilies had led her nose to the narrow fissure in the case's **crazed**[2] glass. Yes, she had seen the horrid depiction of Gwilym shattering into smithereens, but the smell had directed her successfully. Little shoots of hope provided much-desired **solace**[3].

Trapped between the horns of decision, she pressed her thumb into the compass, stuck her nose into the air and followed the flickering arrow. If Thomas were here, she wondered, would he claw it from her hand? Her predicament offered no choices. At least this tall tunnel afforded her **unhindered**[4] movement. Shivering, Claire placed her left hand against the damp, crumbling wall. She inched forward, hoping nothing would slither across the back of her hand.

Claire sucked in a much-needed breath. As her energy **leached**[5] into the stone, she prayed the pursuing red dot wasn't too close.

*

The woman was closing on Claire. Jamming the castle's communications had crippled the car, but how long she could continue to ***intercept***[6] the Castle's messages was the unknown **variable**[7].

Although the Knights Hawk were dying, their allies were **influential**[8]. **Associates**[9] would soon **rally**[10] to thwart the woman's plans. Her covert spies now operated in the knights' subterranean territory, but it was a landscape at odds with Via-Corp's HQ2, from where she conducted her command and control.

It was known and hitherto accepted that, to the uninvited, Cadwaladr Castle was only **accessible**[11] by air. Her one **prior**[12] attempt had failed but taught her well. In this field, the

---

1 **soar** *(v)* climb or fly rapidly above usual levels. *(s)* ascend, escalate, rise. *(ant)* decline, descend, plummet.

2 **crazed** *(adj)* having lots of fine cracks. *(s)* flawed, damaged, shattered, splintered, split. *(ant)* unblemished.

3 **solace** *(n)* comfort in a bad situation. *(s)* condolence, consolation, support, relief, help. *(ant)* aggravation.

4 **unhindered** *(adj)* not hindered (obstructed). *(s)* unimpeded, unobstructed, unhampered. *(ant)* hindered.

5 **leach** *(v)* drain or pass through slowly. *(s)* empty, leak, trickle, seep, filter, discharge. *(ant)* pour, gush, fill.

6 **intercept** *(v)* obstruct to prevent from continuing. *(s)* stop, interrupt, block, catch, divert. *(ant)* help, allow.

7 **variable** *(n)* something that is likely to change. *(ant)* constant.

8 **influential** *(adj)* having influence. *(s)* strong, powerful, dominant, important, authoritative. *(ant)* unimportant.

9 **associate** *(n)* a business partner or companion. *(s)* colleague, ally, comrade, supporter, connection.

10 **rally** *(v)* come together to fight after a defeat. *(s)* regroup, reassemble, reunite. *(ant)* disperse.

11 **accessible** *(adj)* able to be entered or reached. *(s)* approachable, reachable, attainable. *(ant)* inaccessible.

12 **prior** *(adj)* coming or existing before. *(s)* previous, earlier, preceding, initial. *(ant)* subsequent, later.

knights' skills and **resources**[1] exceeded hers. A second attempt would be **cumbersome**[2], and undoubtedly, the knights' defences would **obliterate**[3] her.

The woman must access the fortress from beneath the mountain, but she did not know how. No maps existed for these tunnels. Rumours suggested they were locked away in the castle's **vaults**[4]. Fortuitously, she knew of one place she would **garner**[5] this information, and that was from the tunnels' creator, the creator who she now had full access to, Robert Evans.

Extracting[6] information from the **feeble**[7] knight had been easier than even she could have imagined. Threats to his wife and family were unnecessary, his craven **capitulation**[8] coming in seconds. He had **snitched**[9], divulging his **sacred**[10] secrets like a squealing rat. Despite his traitorous **collaboration**[11], the woman neither desired nor was able to help him. She doubted even the gold could save him; he would soon be **deceased**[12]. She didn't care. She had all she needed from him; he was **expendable**[13].

Critically, the woman must ensure Claire located the gold before the knights' demise, or the girl's motivation would be lost. Without replenishing the Welsh gold, the Gwalch Gem bracelet was **redundant**[14] – no longer a priceless, **unparalleled**[15] and powerful tool, but a worthless **trinket**[16].

She observed the hawk-shaped emerald sitting in the centre of her palm. It was **lacklustre**[17]

---

1 **resources** *(n)* items or capabilities that enable effectiveness. *(s)* materials, supplies, people, assets, money.

2 **cumbersome** *(adj)* inefficiently complex or slow. *(s)* unwieldy, wasteful, unmanageable. *(ant)* efficient, straightforward.

3 **obliterate** *(v)* wipe out. *(s)* destroy, annihilate, exterminate, kill, eliminate, eradicate. *(ant)* create, establish.

4 **vault** *(n)* a secure room used for storage, usually underground. *(s)* basement, cellar, safe, strongroom

5 **garner** *(v)* collect or gather. *(s)* extract, glean, harvest, gain. *(ant)* distribute.

6 **extract** *(v)* remove or take out, often with huge effort or force. *(s)* obtain, extricate, unearth. *(ant)* insert.

7 **feeble** *(adj)* weak or lacking strength of character. *(s)* craven, cowardly, spineless, timid. *(ant)* brave, forceful.

8 **capitulation** *(n)* the act of ceasing to resist. *(s)* surrender, defeat, fall, submission, yielding. *(ant)* resistance.

9 **snitch** *(v)* disclose facts about something or someone. *(s)* betray, confess, blab, squeal, tell, tip. *(ant)* conceal.

10 **sacred** *(adj)* regarded with respect and reverence (admiration). *(s)* venerable, protected. *(ant)* profane.

11 **collaboration** *(n)* the act of working with someone. *(s)* collusion, cooperation, alliance, association. *(ant)* separation.

12 **deceased** *(adj)* recently dead. *(s)* gone, departed, no more, late, lost. *(ant)* alive.

13 **expendable** *(adj)* not worth keeping or maintaining. *(s)* disposable, unimportant, superfluous. *(ant)* indispensable.

14 **redundant** *(adj)* no longer useful. *(s)* dispensable, useless, unnecessary. *(ant)* essential.

15 **unparalleled** *(adj)* having no equal. *(s)* unique, rare, exceptional, unprecedented. *(ant)* ordinary, unexceptional.

16 **trinket** *(n)* a small ornament or item of jewellery. *(s)* knick-knack, bauble, charm, trifle.

17 **lacklustre** *(adj)* not shining. *(s)* flat, dull, dim, drab. *(ant)* shiny, bright, brilliant.

without the gold's power, and its allure was lost and **unappealing**[1].

Last night, when she'd stolen the other half of the Cutter from its purpose-built box in Dewi's jacket pocket, she had risked everything.

She had been **outraged**[2] when she had realised the bracelet's power would no longer deliver, and in a fit of **fury**[3], she had plucked the gem from the gold. Only when the snivelling knight Evans had fallen ill and begged her for the rejuvenating Welsh gold had she realised there remained a chance to **reinstate**[4] the Gwalch Gem bracelet's full potential.

The woman glanced at the bag. One of her thugs held the boy Ben captive. A lethal threat to her friend would cripple Claire, **enticing**[5] her back. The girl would return to rescue Ben, her backpack and the incomplete chain mail bracelet. For now, the bracelet would stay in Claire's school backpack – the backpack that sat on the floor by the woman's well-shod feet.

---

1 **unappealing** *(adj)* not attractive. *(s)* uninviting, dreary, unattractive, plain. *(ant)* appealing, attractive.

2 **outraged** *(adj)* very indignant, shocked or angered. *(s)* incensed, enraged, offended, affronted. *(ant)* placated.

3 **fury** *(n)* wild anger. *(s)* rage, passion, wrath, outrage, temper, frenzy. *(ant)* calmness.

4 **reinstate** *(v)* restore. *(s)* renew, revive, return.

5 **entice** *(v)* tempt or attract. *(s)* lure, cajole, invite, persuade, seduce, inveigle. *(ant)* dissuade, deter.

17. The Prisoner

No matter how hard she tried, maintaining pressure on the soul-sucking gem while following the faint arrow crippled Claire. The **transient**[1] lilies eluded her. Their guiding scent, so successful yesterday, today failed to increase in **intensity**[2], leading her nowhere.

Clueless as to her location, Claire prayed that she **trudged**[3] somewhere beneath Cadwaladr Castle and that she might now be near the gold.

Exhausted, she squinted at the arrow, but her hand shook so vigorously the image blurred. Claire pulled up her hood and drew its strings beneath her chin. She hoped Ben had her backpack. Even if she found the gold here, how would she get it to Ben? The bracelet remained in her bag, and she knew where neither were.

She'd **slogged**[4] on for what felt like hours but what she feared was only minutes. Her right thumb and arm became so numb that if she weren't staring at that arrow, she wouldn't have felt the compass. **Foolhardy**[5], not having drunk a drop, she'd left her water in the Tesla. Oddly for Claire, hunger eluded her, but she struggled for breath.

Neither fear nor **cowardice**[6] claimed victory in this battle. Loath to stop, she now ran on empty. Claire's **torpid**[7], depleted body surrendered, and her brain jammed. No longer fazed by the ubiquitous beetles and bugs, she slumped down the side of the tunnel. The compass rolled

---

1 **transient** *(adj)* lasting for only a short while. *(s)* fleeting, passing, temporary, momentary. *(ant)* permanent.

2 **intensity** *(n)* strength or brightness. *(s)* power, potency, vigour, force, magnitude. *(ant)* weakness.

3 **trudge** *(v)* walk slowly. *(s)* lumber, plod, trail, trek, tramp, traipse, slog. *(ant)* run, sprint, tiptoe.

4 **slog** *(v)* work or move with difficulty for a time. *(s)* labour, toil, grind, slave, trudge. *(ant)* skive, hurtle.

5 **foolhardy** *(adj)* carelessly silly or bold. *(s)* reckless, heedless, rash, incautious, imprudent. *(ant)* wise, cautious.

6 **cowardice** *(n)* lack of bravery or valour. *(s)* weakness, fear, spinelessness, timidity, cravenness. *(ant)* courage.

7 **torpid** *(adj)* inactive. *(s)* slow, sluggish, lethargic, inert, lifeless, listless, fatigued. *(ant)* lively, energetic.

from her open palm, resting on the floor beside her.

Forced into **resignation**[1] by her now-feeble body, Claire stared, mesmerised, as the gemstone's glow dwindled. In peace, she rolled onto her side, her face almost touching it. She blinked, **inexplicably**[2] comforted by the stone's diminishing light, which faded **in tandem**[3] with her.

As the gem's life extinguished, Claire's eyes closed, picturing the diver who, in those final few seconds, had said he'd felt no pain, just nothingness.

*

Buried deep beneath HQ2, like a lonely caged animal, Ben paced his grey cell. With **ferocious**[4] and sporadic blows, he kicked and punched its padded sides, as if intending to kill with kung fu.

Having been imprisoned for what felt like an **eternity**[5], Ben screamed and yelled for his father until his voice became **hoarse**[6]. Josh Drane had ripped Claire's bag from him and, with sharp cable ties, another youth bound both wrists behind his back. The younger thug had then dragged him down the stairs that had appeared below the glass cube's floor.

Josh Drane, the **apparent**[7] **ringleader**[8] and stronger of the two, had descended via an adjacent, smaller opening, into what looked like a deep shaft with a flimsy ladder attached to its side. It had relieved Ben when they hadn't hauled him down there.

Enraged[9], Ben now howled and booted his bottle of water across his cell. The boy had thrown it in after cutting the cable ties and leaving. Were Ben's hands not numbed for lack of blood supply, he'd have had more chance. He had aimed a high kick at the boy, but he'd danced away. Ben recognised another martial artist when he saw one. Although small, the boy was **wiry**[10]

---

1 **resignation** *(n)* acceptance of something undesirable yet inevitable. *(s)* tolerance, sufferance. *(ant)* defiance.

2 **inexplicably** *(adv)* in an unexplainable way. *(s)* mysteriously, unaccountably, puzzlingly. *(ant)* explicably.

3 **in tandem** (adv) in the manner of one following or behind the others.

4 **ferocious** *(adj)* great and extreme. *(s)* strong, vicious, aggressive, brutal, savage, barbarous. *(ant)* gentle, mild.

5 **eternity** *(n)* infinite or unending time. *(s)* perpetuity, forever, endlessness, aeon. *(ant)* instant, jiffy.

6 **hoarse** *(adj)* harsh and rough. *(s)* husky, croaking, croaky, gruff, gravelly. *(ant)* soft, mellow.

7 **apparent** *(adj)* appearing true or real, but unconfirmed. *(s)* supposed, purported, presumed. (ant) genuine.

8 **ringleader** *(n)* a person who leads bad or illicit activity. *(s)* leader, boss, brains, instigator. *(ant)* follower.

9 **enraged** *(adj)* extremely angry. *(s)* furious, incensed, infuriated, fuming, irate, exasperated. *(ant)* calm.

10 **wiry** *(adj)* lean and strong. *(s)* tough, agile, athletic, sinewy, muscular, slim, thin. *(ant)* fat, frail, flabby.

and his moves nimble. Ben knew his type and tactics; they were deceptive – lightning-quick manoeuvrability **trumping**[1] strength.

Pounding the cell's door bruised Ben's fists. He hollered for his dad again. **Searing**[2] pain sliced through his temples. He must calm down. He must engage his Shaolin skills and cast off his enemy – anger. Fury would drain his energy and worsen his dire situation. His captors would return, and he must prepare for their imminent arrival.

---

1 **trump** *(v)* surpass (better). *(s)* beat, outdo, upstage, outshine, outclass, eclipse, outperform. *(ant)* lose to.

2 **searing** *(adj)* intense. *(s)* excruciating, agonising, severe, extreme. *(ant)* mild.

18. Special Delivery

A sting of intense **scorching**[1] streaked across her cheek. Remnants of what might have been a dream swirled around her fog-filled head. She was unable to feel her limbs, as cold enveloped her, rendering her body a prisoner.

Was she dead or alive?

For a moment, Claire forgot her whereabouts, but it didn't take long to recall them.

She lay curled up, motionless apart from her **uppermost**[2] side, which was oddly heavy and warm. Her weary eyes battled against opening; she let them win.

Claire's fuzzy head buzzed with a steady hum. Something strange touched her cheek. She no longer cared what, but it happened again and again. She tried to bat the invading insect away, but her arm refused to **comply**[3]. The incessant drone in her ears filled her head. Reluctantly she forced her fused eyelids apart, but they met with the familiar and **impenetrable**[4] blackness.

Compelled[5] into eventual action by the insect's **relentless**[6] pestering, Claire stretched out an arm, forcing her numb fingers to her cheek. Her feeble hand brushed against the tenacious culprit. Whatever touched her face was big and hairy. Still not worried by what it was, she just wanted it off. She swiped a weak wave at her cheek and finally batted it away.

---

1 **scorching** *(n)* extreme heat. *(s)* burning, blazing, blistering, searing, fire. *(ant)* chill.

2 **uppermost** *(adj)* highest or most important. *(s)* top, topmost, most elevated. *(ant)* lowest, lowermost.

3 **comply** *(v)* obey a wish or command. *(s)* abide by, observe, conform, yield, respect, submit. *(ant)* disobey.

4 **impenetrable** *(adj)* impossible to pass through or enter. *(s)* dense, solid, impermeable, thick. *(ant)* penetrable.

5 **compel** *(v)* force or oblige someone to do something. *(s)* impel, make, drive, obligate.

6 **relentless** *(adj)* not relenting (giving up). *(s)* non-stop, incessant, persistent, tenacious, constant. *(ant)* irresolute.

Relieved, Claire wished she could **curb**[1] the persistent buzz plaguing her ears. Then a faint glow caught her eye. She remembered the compass had been in her hand. Surely it would be dead by now, **inert**[2] without her **donated**[3] energy to power it. She tried to focus. Maybe she'd lain here mere minutes. Seeing double, she reached towards the glow with her hand. As if touching a flame, she recoiled. She realised she wasn't looking at the compass and hadn't batted away a bug. The **vibrating**[4] noise in her ears was not a pain in her head.

'Thomas?' she mouthed, not forming the word. 'Thomas?' she whispered.

The incessant **thrum**[5] stopped. The cat's yellow-green eyes bored into hers.

'Tommy, you came back,' she croaked. 'You came back.'

Thomas sat in **absolute**[6] silence.

'Thomas,' she whispered again, her voice dry and **reedy**[7].

He moved closer, his nose against hers. Claire tried to touch him but couldn't. At least she would not be alone.

As if to comfort her more, Thomas moved even closer, purring his soft tune. She stared at him. He didn't blink. Her tired eyes fought to close. Mustering her last **joule**[8] of energy, she lifted her hand to touch his head, resting it there, comforted by his velvet fur.

Heartened, she caressed his neck. He miaowed. He was wearing a collar. Thomas *never* wore a collar. Claire's fingers followed the **choker**[9]. Something hung beneath Thomas's chin. His eyes suddenly vanished, then faced her. He miaowed again, louder. She knew the **drill**[10], but could she manage it?

Whatever swung from Thomas's neck, Claire needed it. The cat hadn't returned empty-pawed. He'd delivered something to her. Her friend had come to help her.

---

1 **curb** *(v)* keep in check. *(s)* control, restrain, suppress, silence, gag. *(ant)* release, increase.

2 **inert** *(adj)* unable to work or move. *(s)* dormant, lifeless, inanimate, inactive, still, immobile. *(ant)* active, moving.

3 **donate** *(v)* give without payment. *(s)* grant, provide, contribute, supply, gift. *(ant)* receive, keep.

4 **vibrate** *(v)* shake. *(s)* tremble, quiver, quaver, shudder, jiggle.

5 **thrum** *(n)* continuous humming sound. *(s)* hum, vibration, drone, whirr, whine, buzz.

6 **absolute** *(adj)* complete, total. *(s)* utter, outright, entire, pure, sheer, downright. *(ant)* partial, uncertain.

7 **reedy** *(adj)* feeble and high in tone. *(s)* quiet, low, thin, small, meagre. *(ant)* loud, deep, strong.

8 **joule** *(n)* a unit of energy.

9 **choker** *(n)* a tightly fitted necklace. *(s)* collar, neckband.

10 **drill** *(n)* the correct or established procedure. *(s)* routine, practice, system, method.

With one hand, she found what dangled beneath his chin and called on all her strength to tug it. She was desperate not to drop it, so she precariously clasped the object in her shaky hand. Barely able to hold it, she wondered what to do next.

'Tommy?' she whispered.

He twirled again. Then his paw brushed Claire's lips.

'My mouth?'

Thomas pawed her lips again.

'You want me to eat it, boy?'

Using her fingertips, Claire rolled the object from her palm until she pinched it between her forefinger and thumb. It felt the size and shape of a butter bean, but it was rough, hard and heavy. She bit it, sure it was metal.

'I can't eat this, Tommy …' Her voice trailed off.

Thomas pawed at her mouth again but harder. He glared, his eerie eyes vanishing each time he blinked.

Claire now realised the searing pain across her cheek earlier had been Thomas's claw, and with **trepidation**[1], she placed the object into her mouth. Just as her mum had taught her to take medication, she pushed it along her tongue until she gagged, then swallowed. It was like **ingesting**[2] a stone. She coughed, **heaving**[3] for air. Whatever she'd consumed was stuck. Intense pain **radiated**[4] from her spine, consuming her ribcage and back. But like after devouring a hunk of baguette in **haste**[5], the **penetrating**[6] pain began to fade.

Over and over, Claire swallowed, hoping to force the object further down. As the excruciating pain eased, she looked into Thomas's eyes one last time and smiled. Then hers gently closed.

---

1 **trepidation** *(n)* anxiety or fear about what may happen. *(s)* dread, foreboding, apprehension. *(ant)* assurance.

2 **ingest** *(v)* swallow or absorb into the body. *(s)* consume, eat, drink, down, devour.

3 **heave** *(v)* breathe deeply or with effort. *(s)* pant, gasp, wheeze.

4 **radiate** *(v)* emanate (give off) a feeling or quality. *(s)* transmit, exude, emit, circulate, shine. *(ant)* absorb.

5 **haste** *(n)* speed or urgency, hurry. *(s)* swiftness, briskness, dash, alacrity, rapidity. *(ant)* slowness, delay.

6 **penetrating** *(adj)* piercing or sharp. *(s)* stinging, acute, harsh, fierce, cutting. *(ant)* blunt, dull.

*

Rattled[1], David Lewis **prowled**[2] his circular office, his fingers pressed together in a **steeple**[3], his lips fixed in a **grim**[4] line.

He had summoned her. He had waited. She had not come.

'She is currently unavailable,' one of her minions had reported, as if he, David Lewis, were a **lowlife**[5]. He would deal with them later. His suppressed rage burned in his chest. She was never unavailable to him.

'NEVER!' he screeched, swiping the contents of his desk onto the floor. The act of violence soothed him, and his fingers drummed an ugly rhythm on the desk's glass top.

What was she doing? She must know her **malignant**[6] poisoning **machination**[7] had failed. Had she fled? He doubted it. She was no **poltroon**[8]; cowardice was an attribute not possessed by her. Where there was a will there was a plan, and he knew she had **hatched**[9] one. He would wait no longer.

*

The woman stared at the black screen, the tracker still dead, evidence that Claire was deep in the **labyrinth**[10]. The castle's communications remained jammed, and having located the stricken vehicle, her boy was now in the same tunnel network as Claire. The girl must be nearing the gold, and the boy's heat-seeking device would detect her. The woman smirked. The gold would soon be hers, and the superpowered Gwalch Gem bracelet, reborn.

---

1 **rattled** *(adj)* nervous or irritated. *(s)* perturbed, disconcerted, disturbed, flustered, agitated. *(ant)* comforted.

2 **prowl** *(v)* move about stealthily, often in search of prey. *(s)* lurk, patrol, sneak, skulk, steal, stalk. *(ant)* parade.

3 **steeple** *(n)* a shape resembling a church spire.

4 **grim** *(adj)* serious or gloomy. *(s)* stern, dour, severe, surly, morose, unkind. *(ant)* kind, pleasant, cheerful.

5 **lowlife** *(n)* someone considered to be lowly or criminal. *(s)* beggar, wretch, rascal, bum, pauper. *(ant)* altruist, noble.

6 **malignant** *(adj)* evil. *(s)* malicious, malevolent, spiteful, baleful, vicious. *(ant)* benevolent.

7 **machination** *(n)* a scheme or plot. *(s)* intrigue, conspiracy, ploy, ruse, design. *(ant)* honesty, frankness.

8 **poltroon** *(n)* a total coward. *(s)* wimp, chicken, craven, weakling. *(ant)* hero.

9 **hatch** *(v)* bring into being. *(s)* create, concoct, devise, conceive, invent, spawn, originate. *(ant)* destroy, kill.

10 **labyrinth** *(n)* a complicated network of passages. *(s)* maze, warren, tangle, web, jumble, muddle.

19. A Familiar Face

Claire's eyes fluttered open. Burning through the blackness, Thomas's peered into hers. He purred and gently pawed her face.

'Tommy,' she whispered, 'you're still here.'

The cat miaowed.

Something had changed. From the pit of Claire's stomach, heat radiated outwards. As the soothing sensation swept through Claire's body, she let her eyes close. Akin to hot cocoa on a cold day, it comforted and revived, warming her torso.

Behind Claire's closed lids, a peaceful hue settled.

I'm dreaming!

She opened her eyes, but Thomas's stared back.

Strength drawn from her stomach gradually reached each **organ**[1], each limb, each **extremity**[2], until she bathed in a golden glow of new life. Whatever she'd swallowed had replenished what had been **pilfered**[3] by the parasitic compass.

Claire rolled onto her stomach, pushed onto all fours and slowly unfurled, standing in the pitch-blackness. Upright, she blinked, allowing her pupils to adjust. Afraid they wouldn't move, she looked down and **splayed**[4] her fingers, lifting her arms. Staggered, she wiggled them again. They worked fine; the difference was she could see them. The tunnel was deathly black, yet the outline of Claire's fingers was visible.

---

1 **organ** *(n)* part of the body that has a specific function.

2 **extremity** *(n)* hands and feet.

3 **pilfer** *(v)* steal. *(s)* take, rob, thieve, snatch, purloin, loot, rifle, pillage. *(ant)* give.

4 **splay** *(v)* spread or thrust apart. *(s)* spread out, expand, extend, drape, stretch, strew, span. *(ant)* huddle.

'Thomas!' Her voice was urgent. Claire caught his eyes, and sure enough, she saw him. A silhouette and faint, but his outline existed. Claire patted what she thought was the tunnel's side. It was – she could see that too.

'What did you give me, Tommy Boy?' she asked, but Thomas didn't budge. 'I can see in the dark.'

Whatever he'd fed her had worked. She was no longer cold, thirsty or even hungry, and her body responded with **vigour**[1]. **Energised**[2] and unhindered, Claire removed her hood, looking left and right.

'Tommy?' she asked, a question in her voice.

Thomas turned a tight circle, miaowed and headed left, to what Claire hoped was Cadwaladr Castle.

'Thomas, wait!'

Claire dropped onto all fours, patting the ground. Without **contrast**[3], the floor **merged**[4] into a black carpet. As Claire crawled in circles, groping for what she **sought**[5], her hand brushed a solid object. She grabbed it. It wasn't a stone; she'd found the compass. Claire sprang to her feet. The cold, lifeless item sat in her right palm. She stared at its shape, running her thumb around the edge's engravings.

'I wonder what you mean,' Claire whispered as her fingers explored the minuscule **etchings**[5]. 'Has Evans **conned**[7] me, or is my **inability**[8] to power you down to my Instinctive inexperience?'

Amongst all her rhetorical questions, a decision loomed. She glanced at Thomas. **Formerly**[9] Claire had been no risk-taker, but she must now trust her Instinct. She jabbed her right thumb onto the gem. She prayed Thomas had swiped it from her earlier because he knew it was killing her, and not because Evans had deceived her. Trust and Evans were not things she would readily

---

1 **vigour** *(n)* strength and energy. *(s)* robustness, hardiness, stamina, sturdiness, toughness. *(ant)* weakness, lethargy.

2 **energise** *(v)* give vitality (life). *(s)* boost, invigorate, strengthen, revitalise. *(ant)* drain, enervate.

3 **contrast** *(n)* differences in light or colour that create visual variation.

4 **merge** *(v)* blend or mingle into something else. *(s)* meld, mix, combine, unify, conflate. *(ant)* separate, diverge.

5 **seek** *(v)* try to find (past tense: *sought*). *(s)* look for, hunt for, search for, pursue. *(ant)* lose.

6 **etching** *(n)* engraving or carving on a surface. *(s)* mark, impression, imprint, inscription, score, scratch.

7 **con** *(v)* trick someone by lying. *(s)* dupe, deceive, fool, mislead, bluff, swindle, hoodwink. *(ant)* be honest.

8 **inability** *(n)* the state of being unable to do something. *(s)* incompetence, incapacity, incapability. *(ant)* ability.

9 **formerly** *(adv)* in the past. *(s)* previously, earlier, before, hitherto. *(ant)* subsequently, henceforth.

associate[1], but Claire knew the worm had given her the compass as a guide to the gold. His **chivalrous**[2] actions, neither **noble**[3] nor born of a sense of **duty**[4], had fooled Claire. His **motive**[5] was entirely selfish: Evans would die without the Welsh gold. Claire would **gamble**[6].

Claire increased her thumb's pressure, anticipating the inevitable bleed of life from her body. The stone sank millimetres. If an exit existed in this **godforsaken**[7] place, she knew it would show itself.

As Claire waited, the hammering of her heart intensified. Thomas stayed statue-still. The compass remained cold – dead. Her spirits sank. Stubbornly Claire drove her right thumb further into its centre, and without warning, the emerald-green laser shot out through her fingers. Again it projected its single dot onto the tunnel wall.

'Yes!' she said.

Claire wiggled her hand. As before, the beam bent, but the pointer remained static. No matter how she moved the compass, it revealed an exit.

'Tommy, this way.' Claire shuffled closer to the dot hovering on the tunnel wall. As before, she poked it with her left index finger. Stepping back, she waited, Thomas at her feet. Claire watched as the rocky wall yielded a trickle of pouring soil and grit, quickly opening out to a hole and widening all the time. Her face shining in anticipation, she pushed the compass into her back pocket, half expecting Lily's face to emerge from the other side. Appalled, Claire staggered back as a shock wave streaked through her.

Maybe that's why I didn't hear his voice again. Claire clawed at the hole with her hands, grabbing at the rock and soil. He didn't move. He lay in the fetal position, his head tucked into his chest. His hood hid his face.

'Ben?' she whispered, excavating the hole with frantic hands. The compass had led her to him. *Ben, what have I done to you?*

---

1 **associate** *(v)* connect in the mind. *(s)* relate, link, correlate, join, pair. *(ant)* detach.

2 **chivalrous** *(adj)* polite and respectful. *(s)* gallant, honourable, thoughtful, considerate. *(ant)* rude, boorish.

3 **noble** *(adj)* having fine qualities and good morals. *(s)* honest, honourable, righteous, virtuous. *(ant)* dishonourable.

4 **duty** *(n)* responsibility. *(s)* obligation, commitment, loyalty, respect.

5 **motive** *(n)* an incentive for acting or behaving in a certain way. *(s)* motivation, grounds, basis, reason. *(ant)* deterrent.

6 **gamble** *(v)* take a risky action. *(s)* chance, brave, dare, risk. *(ant)* safeguard.

7 **godforsaken** *(adj)* lacking any attraction. *(s)* miserable, wretched, grim, dismal, depressing. *(ant)* charming.

'Thomas,' she commanded, pointing at the hole. In one pounce, the cat leaped through, landing on the floor of Ben's padded cell. Claire tore at the gap, ripping her nails and slicing her skin.

Thomas circled Ben's head. He purred; his tail swirled like drifting smoke. He miaowed as his face disappeared beneath Ben's hood.

Claire thought she'd known fear yesterday, but that paled in comparison. A vice-like grasp gripped her chest. With both fists clutching earth, she stilled, **beseeching**[1] him to move. She let out a heart-wrenching sob, and tears blinded her.

'Ben!' she screamed. 'Ben!'

She took five steps back, then shot forward, and springing from both feet, she dived **headlong**[2] through the hole.

'Oof!' she grunted, landing flat on her face and stomach.

'Ben! Ben! I thought you were dead. Have they hurt you?' Her words poured out in a **torrent**[3]. 'Thank goodness you're alive.'

Ben sat up, blinking. He gawped open-mouthed at Claire, his eyes shifting from her to the hole and back again.

'Are you OK?' she asked, scrambling to her feet. At least this landing had been soft.

'Claire?' he whispered, his face screwed into a question mark.

'Yes, it's me,' she reassured him.

Ben looked at Thomas, then pointed at the hole, shaking his head, his mouth still open.

'You can shut your trap now,' Claire said, disposing of the niceties, her face **deadpan**[4].

'What the heck?' Ben pointed to the hole. 'What's Thomas doing here?' He looked utterly bewildered.

'Later,' she replied. 'No time now. Were you asleep?' she asked, confused.

'Deep meditation,' he answered, stroking a purring Thomas. 'I got too mad. Had to contain my fury.' He **slugged**[5] water from a plastic bottle. 'Want some?'

---

1 **beseech** *(v)* ask someone urgently or fervently. *(s)* implore, beg, request, entreat, plead, supplicate. *(ant)* offer.

2 **headlong** *(adv)* head first. *(s)* head foremost. *(ant)* feet first.

3 **torrent** *(n)* an overwhelming outburst (often of emotion). *(s)* flood, gush, rush, surge, deluge. *(ant)* trickle.

4 **deadpan** *(adj)* without expression. *(s)* impassive, stony, blank, serious, inscrutable. *(ant)* animated.

5 **slug** *(v)* drink in one draught. *(s)* swig, gulp, guzzle. *(ant)* sip.

'No, thanks. You drink it.' Claire waved it away. 'I'm not thirsty.'

Ben drained the bottle and threw it across the cell.

'Tell me what happened,' urged Claire.

'Josh Drane and his boy dragged me into one of those glass cells. What's *Josh Drane* even doing here?'

'Not now,' said Claire, shutting him down, 'I'll tell you later.'

'I could see you, but you couldn't see me. I used one of your pens to write a C, but they snatched it from me.'

'Yeah, I get that bit. I found the C, but what else? Where are we now?'

'I dunno. They snatched your bag from me, then strapped my wrists together.' He flashed his purple skin at Claire.

'I'm so sorry, Ben,' responded Claire, feeling **accountable**[1] and **blameworthy**[2].

'A hole appeared in the cell floor, and the younger one dragged me down the stairs and chucked me in here.'

'What about Drane?' she asked. 'Where did he go?'

'There was another opening in the floor. It looked grim.'

'Go on.' Claire nodded her chin at him.

'Drane went down that hole. It was deep and dark, and the ladder attached to the side looked flimsy to me.'

Claire gulped. 'You sure Drane went down that hole?' she asked, her mind racing.

'Yup. He climbed right in and vanished,' said Ben. 'Why?'

''Cause Rat-Boy Drane might just find *this* hole.' Claire pointed to the hole **whence**[3] she'd appeared.

'And if there's only one way out, through *that* hole, then we'll bump straight into him,' said Claire.

'Well, we need to do something, because that other boy will be here soon,' said Ben.

'Which boy?' said Claire, glancing at the hole.

'The younger lad, he checks on me regularly. He'll throw in a bottle of water, make some

---

1 **accountable** *(adj)* responsible for one's actions. *(s)* answerable, liable, culpable, chargeable. *(ant)* unaccountable.

2 **blameworthy** *(adj)* deserving of blame. *(s)* guilty, responsible, condemnable, culpable. *(ant)* innocent, blameless.

3 **whence** *(adv)* from where. *(s)* wherefrom, from what place.

snide[1] comment, then slam the door.'

'I reckon the two of us could **deck**[2] him,' said Claire.

'It's risky,' said Ben. 'What if Rat-Boy's face shows up at that hole first?'

'What choice do we have?' said Claire.

'None,' said Ben, jumping to his feet. 'He's fast, but so am I. If you stand next to the door, flush against the wall, I'll surprise him. Then you jump him and pin him down. I'll finish him off,' said Ben. 'If I've gauged it right, he'll be here soon.'

'How soon?' asked Claire.

'Couple of minutes,' said Ben.

'You're kidding.' Claire lowered her voice.

'No,' he replied.

'OK. I'll scooch along the wall away from the door, or he'll clock me,' said Claire. 'I'll keep Thomas quiet and out of the way. Once he opens the door and leans in, BAM! **Ambush**[3]!'

'What if he has **cronies**[4] behind him?' said Ben.

'What if? It can't be worse than now,' said Claire, **shimmying**[5] along the padded wall and squeezing herself into it.

'Tommy, come,' she ordered, pointing to her feet. He followed, then sat.

Ben sat on the floor crossed-legged, pretending to meditate.

Claire pressed her back further into the cell's padded wall.

They waited for what felt like ages, afraid to speak lest the door open mid-word.

As if reading Claire's thoughts, Ben whispered, 'He'll be here, trust me.'

Then the door clunked ajar an inch. The boy pushed it half-open and threw in a bottle of water. 'You can pee in the empties,' he **sniggered**[6], reversing.

Before Ben had leaped to his feet, Thomas sprang, pouncing on his startled prey, his claws clinging to the boy's face.

---

1 **snide** *(adj)* slyly mocking. *(s)* ridiculing, disparaging, scornful, spiteful. *(ant)* complimentary.

2 **deck** *(v)* knock to the ground with a strike. *(s)* floor, punch, thump, hit.

3 **ambush** *(n)* a surprise attack. *(s)* assault, trap, ensnarement, deception, trick, ambuscade.

4 **crony** *(n)* a companion or close friend. *(s)* associate, comrade, colleague, mate.

5 **shimmy** *(v)* move hastily or irregularly. *(s)* hustle, jostle.

6 **snigger** *(v)* laugh in a half-suppressed, typically scornful way. *(s)* snicker, sneer, smirk. *(ant)* admire, applaud.

The boy screamed, clutching the fur on Thomas's back.

With lightning speed, Ben's foot caught the side of the boy's head, knocking him to the ground.

Claire threw herself onto the boy's chest, her knees pinning down his arms. Thomas leaped off his face.

The boy howled, struggling.

'Shut up!' ordered Claire. 'Now! Ben, check outside.'

Thomas sat beside the **wailing**[1] boy.

'Shut it now, or the cat comes back,' hissed Claire.

The boy quietened to a whine, blood streaming down his cheeks.

'You're lucky you still have eyes,' said Claire with a **flinty**[2] **glint**[3] in hers. 'Now, matey boy, cough and tell us who you're working for, or I call the cat back.'

Thomas purred a prompt and malicious warning.

The boy **whimpered**[4], shaking his head.

'**Confess**[5], or the cat attacks.'

Thomas moved closer, his tail twitching like a rattlesnake's.

'I can't,' he whispered, shaking his head.

'Oh, yes, you can, and you will. Thomas.' She gestured to the cat. Thomas mewed, arched his back and stood as if on tiptoe, spitting a hiss at the boy's face.

'I work for Siân,' he squealed. 'I work for Siân.' He let out a sob. 'Call off the cat.'

'Thomas!' Claire lifted her nose in an 'Off' signal.

'Siân?' Claire's eyes narrowed. 'Siân who?' The name rang no bells. 'Siân who?' she repeated.

'Siân Cadwaladr,' spluttered the boy. 'I work for Siân Cadwaladr.'

Claire's heart sputtered against her ribs. She gasped, fighting for words.

Struggling to maintain a closed expression, battling her way back, Claire repeated, 'Siân Cadwaladr, I see …' She allowed her voice to trail off, hoping the boy would say more.

Who was this woman Siân, with the same surname as hers and Gwilym's, and why hadn't

---

1 **wail** *(v)* make a prolonged, high-pitched sound. *(s)* bawl, yowl, cry, scream, moan, screech. *(ant)* laugh, giggle.

2 **flinty** *(adj)* hard. *(s)* tough, unyielding, steely, stony, inflexible, rigid. *(ant)* soft, gentle, flexible.

3 **glint** *(n)* small gleam or flash of light. *(s)* glimmer, shimmer, flicker, sparkle, glance, trace. *(ant)* dullness.

4 **whimper** *(v)* make low, feeble sounds expressing displeasure. *(s)* whine, mewl, snivel, bleat. *(ant)* rejoice.

5 **confess** *(v)* admit or make known. *(s)* tell, reveal, divulge, disclose, assert, affirm. *(ant)* deny, hide, conceal.

she heard her mentioned yesterday?

Ben poked his head around the door. 'It's all clear. Just an empty space leading to stairs. Here,' he said, hurling a bunch of plastic cable ties towards Claire. 'They're his. Bind his wrists and ankles, and make sure they're tight like mine were.' Ben threw a satisfying smirk of **revenge**[1] the boy's way, then left.

With one knee, Claire applied brutal pressure. She lifted her other off the boy's arm and hauled him over. Standing by the boy's head, Thomas arched his back. Claire grabbed his other wrist, wrenching his arm up his back like they had done to Ben earlier. She held the cable tie around it, threaded it and tugged it with her teeth.

'Tommy, guard him,' Claire ordered, and moving to the boy's ankles, she yanked off his trainers and, with the cable ties, did the same. Then she peeled off his socks, tied them together and pulled until the knot she'd made tightened and shrank. To finish, she pushed the fabric into his mouth, wrapped it around the back of his head and tied it, gagging him.

'Hope you like the taste and the stink of your sweat.'

'Come on, Claire,' said Ben, popping his head around the door. 'It's all clear. We should go.'

'He's taken care of.' Claire nodded. 'Tommy, come,' she said, heading towards the exit.

'One minute,' said Ben to a bemused Claire.

Ben strode to the back of the cell and picked up a plastic bottle. He walked nonchalantly over to the boy, slowly unscrewed the cap, poured its straw-coloured contents over the boy's head and said, 'If you need to pee, you can use the empties.' Hurling the empty bottle, Ben turned to Claire and said, 'On my way.'

All three friends, one **feline**[2], left the grey padded cell, slamming the door behind them.

*

With his heat-seeker locked on to its source, Josh Drane peered through the hole into the grey padded cell. It was not the girl but Drane's **inept**[3] accomplice who lay bound and gagged on the cell floor, its door locked. Both Mal-Instinctives had failed. How had this supposedly unremarkable girl escaped with the boy Ben? What powers enabled her to navigate and exit the tunnels through earth and rock walls?

---

1 **revenge** *(n)* retaliation for a wrong suffered. *(s)* vengeance, retribution, redress, payback.

2 **feline** *(n)* a cat. *(s)* moggie, mog, pussy cat, mouser.

3 **inept** *(adj)* showing or having no skill. *(s)* amateurish, maladroit, bungling, incompetent. *(ant)* competent.

Siân Cadwaladr's **fuse**[1] would be spent, her **tolerance**[2] wiped out. Doomed, he had but one chance. He must find the Master and switch **allegiance**[3], **defect**[4] *back* to his camp and work with him. Drane suspected Siân Cadwaladr had not yet revealed him as a **turncoat**[5] to the Master. She had **staked**[6] too much to risk that. Her entire plan **hinged**[7] on the Master trusting Drane. He must now **discredit**[8] her to **bolster**[9] his position with Dewi. Drane prayed *he* could locate the Master before Siân Cadwaladr found and captured *him*, Drane.

---

1 **fuse** *(n)* a device used to control the timing of a bomb, used figuratively to indicate a person's patience.

2 **tolerance** *(n)* the ability to endure something undesirable. *(s)* endurance, forbearance, restraint. *(ant)* intolerance.

3 **allegiance** *(n)* devotion or loyalty to a superior person, a group or a cause. *(s)* commitment, dedication. *(ant)* disloyalty.

4 **defect** *(v)* abandon a cause in favour of a rival cause. *(s)* desert, rebel, renounce. *(ant)* commit.

5 **turncoat** *(n)* someone who abandons one cause in order to join a rival cause. *(s)* traitor, renegade. *(ant)* follower, supporter.

6 **stake** *(v)* risk. *(s)* wager, bet, chance, venture, pledge, hazard.

7 **hinge** *(v)* depend completely on. *(s)* rest, centre, turn, pivot.

8 **discredit** *(v)* spoil the good reputation of. *(s)* compromise, disgrace, dishonour, disparage. *(ant)* praise.

9 **bolster** *(v)* support or strengthen. *(s)* boost, fortify, sustain, assist, prop, shore up. *(ant)* weaken, hinder.

20. Scuppered

Claire and Ben slammed the cell door shut and, with Thomas, crept up the cramped stone stairs to a dead end.

'We can't go back,' said Claire, glancing around the space, her fingers tugging at her lips. She ran her hand along the rock. An exit existed; it must. How else had the boy entered and subsequently left? No apparent security jumped out at her, no eye or hand scanner. Claire eased her glove from her back pocket. The plastic hung from it in tatters.

'Will that thing still work?' Ben pointed, pulling a defeatist face. 'It's wrecked!'

'Worth a try,' said Claire, smoothing the ragged plastic over her gloved hand. 'She's not failed me yet. Scour around for a receptacle, a hidden panel, anything.'

Ben ran his hands over the walls. 'I can't see anything.'

Claire waved the glove over the surfaces. It was **tenuous**[1], but a slim chance remained that Cristy's print might reveal an exit.

'Ben, check the floor.'

From his knees, Ben peered up at Claire, who was waving at the walls like a lunatic. 'Nothing down here. We've got to go back. Ouch!' he shrieked.

Thomas had **vaulted**[2] onto Ben and pounced onto his lap, then his head and then up onto Claire's shoulder.

'What's up, pal?' Claire winced as Thomas **flexed**[3] his claws, gripping her hoody and skin. 'Tell me, buddy,' she said, steadying him with her left hand.

---

1 **tenuous** *(adj)* (of a situation or concept) weak or slight. *(s)* vague, flimsy, hazy, sketchy. *(ant)* substantial.

2 **vault** *(v)* leap or spring by supporting or propelling oneself with one's hands (or paws). *(s)* jump, bound.

3 **flex** *(v)* move or extend through muscle contraction. *(s)* activate, stretch, protrude. *(ant)* relax, retract.

He stood wobbling on her shoulder, pawing at the low, sloped ceiling. He clawed at the rock and earth above them, mewing. Claire reached up, scraping with her filthy fingers.

'Ugh!' She shuddered as her nails scratched metal. Like an **acrobat**[1], Thomas sprang to the floor and stilled. 'Tom's found something.' Claire dug at the edges of a flush metal plate.

Ben bounced to his feet.

On tiptoe, Claire hooked her fingertips around the edge of the plate and pulled. 'Ouch!' she yelped as her fingernails bent back. She sucked a grubby finger.

'Let me try,' said Ben.

'Nope. I'll do it.' Claire removed the redundant plastic and glove from her right hand and pushed them into her back pocket. On tiptoe again, with her fingertips forced into the scant gap between the plate and the rock, Claire pulled hard, levering it open. 'Gotcha!' She looked at Ben and pointed at a yellow button.

Ben nodded.

As if launching a nuclear missile, Claire pressed it. Nothing happened.

'Press again,' urged Ben.

Claire depressed the button, holding it for a few seconds this time. In the ceiling, a **trapdoor**[2] opened out to a ninety-degree angle.

'Great, but how the heck do we climb from floor to ceiling? They don't make things easy,' moaned Claire.

'I can pull myself up,' said Ben.

Claire glowered at him. 'Well, Beefy-Bones here can't,' she **sniped**[3], rolling her eyes.

'You could try,' said Ben.

Claire's face didn't move.

'Press it again,' said Ben, pointing.

'No, it'll just close.' Claire crossed her arms.

Ignoring her, Ben stretched and planted his finger on the button. From the rim of the hole, a **lightweight**[4] ladder appeared and unfurled, its feet landing gently on the floor.

---

1 **acrobat** *(n)* an entertainer who performs gymnastic feats. *(s)* gymnast, tumbler, aerialist.

2 **trapdoor** *(n)* a small door (often hidden) in a floor, ceiling or roof. *(s)* escape hatch.

3 **snipe** *(v)* make a sly or petty verbal attack. *(s)* criticise, scoff, taunt, ridicule, jeer, dig. *(ant)* praise, applaud.

4 **lightweight** *(adj)* thin, flimsy or weighing less than average. *(s)* insubstantial, light, frail. *(ant)* heavy, sturdy.

'Just like our loft ladder at home.' Ben grinned, clearly **chuffed**[1] at his ingenuity.

'OK, smuglet. Lose the Cheshire cat face. But hey, nice one!' Claire heard herself sounding just like her brother, Pete. Reality struck her hard. 'Let's get out of here and find my backpack.'

Although she was confident that Thomas could **negotiate**[2] the short ladder, Claire nevertheless bent down and scooped him up. With Thomas in her arms, she climbed up, Ben on her tail.

'Out you go.' Claire popped Thomas through the opening and scrambled out onto her knees into the cube. 'It's still opaque,' she informed Ben, who'd exited with a tad more grace than her.

'Ben, the **hatch**[3].' Claire pointed at the opening.

Ben gave it a gentle push, and it floated closed.

'Oh no!' Claire's face fell.

'What's wrong?' asked Ben.

'We're scuppered.' Claire removed the plastic shreds from her back pocket. 'Without this, we're locked in.'

'Try it. Go on.' Ben nodded towards the palm scanner.

Claire wiggled the damp glove onto her right hand and **draped**[4] the torn plastic over it, holding the **slivers**[5] in place with her left.

'Here goes,' she said, her tone unconvinced. Claire's hand **lingered**[6] on the palm reader. With sad eyes aimed at her feet, she shook her head. 'We're trapped.'

Ben stared at her. Thomas sat at her feet, neither of them offering any help.

I wonder if the compass will work in here. Claire peeled off her plastic invention, and although it was now useless, she stuffed it back into her pocket. She worked the compass from the other pocket and jabbed her right thumb into its centre.

'What the heck's that?' Ben's face was a picture.

---

1 **chuffed** *(adj)* extremely pleased. *(s)* happy, delighted, glad, thrilled, overjoyed. *(ant)* disappointed, gutted.

2 **negotiate** *(v)* find a way through, round or over a difficult obstacle or route. *(s)* surmount, clear. *(ant)* fumble.

3 **hatch** *(n)* a small opening for access in a floor, wall or roof. *(s)* flap, entrance, doorway.

4 **drape** *(v)* cover loosely or casually. *(s)* wrap, swathe, shroud, envelop, hang.

5 **sliver** *(n)* a small, thin, narrow piece. *(s)* splinter, slice, shaving, fragment, shard, flake. *(ant)* whole.

6 **linger** *(v)* take or stay longer than necessary due to reluctance. *(s)* delay, dawdle, dither, dally. *(ant)* rush.

Claire put a finger to her lips. She pressed harder, willing its emerald beam to appear. **Frigid**[1], the compass remained dormant.

Maybe the laser pointer only works in the tunnels. 'Later,' said Claire, putting it back into her pocket.

'We've gotta go back down,' said Ben, his colour **wan**[2].

'Look, we're in deep doo-doo, and we need a cover story,' said Claire, 'but we're not turning back now.'

Ben wore his blank face.

'We're out of options, Ben. I'm calling Cristy.'

'My dad's not gonna like this.' Ben's pallid face turned greyer.

Claire reached for Cristy's mobile and stared at the screen. It booted up within seconds. What yarn could she spin for Cristy? They had wandered off and got lost? How had they even left the rec area without the **pertinent**[3] ID? Claire couldn't tell Cristy she'd **duplicated**[4] her palm print. No matter which way Claire sliced it, they were **kippered**[5]. Unless she blew her cover, there *was* no **credible**[6] story.

'I'm gonna call Cristy. When she arrives, I do the talking. OK?'

'Got it,' said Ben.

Press any key. Claire recalled Cristy's instructions as her finger hovered over the keypad.

She closed her eyes, inhaled and pressed a key. 'Ben, prepare for a **roasting**[7].' She put the phone to her ear and opened her eyes. It rang once.

'Claire! Hi! Having a great day?' Cristy's **sugary**[8] voice sang down the line.

'Um, sort of. Somehow, Ben and me, we got a bit lost.'

'Oh no!' Cristy's tone revealed her concern. 'You guys are safe though, right?'

'Yeah, yeah. We're two proper turkeys. So sorry. Could you, or perhaps Ben's dad, come to

---

1 **frigid** *(adj)* lacking in enthusiasm. *(s)* apathetic, cold, indifferent. *(ant)* eager, enthusiastic.

2 **wan** *(adj)* pale-faced and giving the impression of illness or exhaustion. *(s)* pallid, ashen, drawn. *(ant)* glowing.

3 **pertinent** *(adj)* appropriate, applicable or relevant. *(s)* apposite, apt, suitable, fitting. *(ant)* irrelevant.

4 **duplicate** *(v)* make an accurate copy of something. *(s)* clone, reproduce, replicate, repeat.

5 **kippered** *(adj)* (slang) done for. *(s)* unsuccessful, beaten, broken, dashed, defeated, finished, foiled. *(ant)* successful.

6 **credible** *(adj)* able to be believed. *(s)* believable, convincing, plausible, realistic. (ant) unbelievable.

7 **roasting** *(n)* (slang) a telling-off. *(s)* scolding, chiding, reproach, rebuke, reprimand. *(ant)* commendation.

8 **sugary** *(adj)* excessively sweet. *(s)* honeyed, sickly, oversweet. *(ant)* sour.

find us, please?' **Contrition**[1] **oozed**[2] from Claire's voice.

'Of course. I'll track my cell phone and **rally**[3] a search party.'

'Will you tell Ben's dad?' Claire's voice faded to a whisper.

'No, not right now,' Cristy chirped. 'John wasn't feeling too well, so he retired to his executive suite.'

'Really?' said Claire. 'I hope he's OK.' She turned away from Ben.

'I'm sure John will be fine. He need not know about your **escapade**[4]. Our little secret.' Cristy chuckled.

'Phew! Thanks, Cristy.' Claire exhaled, relieved.

'Search party deployed,' said Cristy with a **chortle**[5]. 'See you soon.'

'Everything OK?' Ben asked as Claire put the phone in her pocket.

It was Claire's turn to **blanch**[6].

'My dad's gonna kill me, right?'

Claire avoided Ben's question. 'I'm fine. Let me do the talking when they turn up.' Claire's face was ashen. Did Mr Brady's illness mean anything? 'I don't think your dad will show. Cristy said he wasn't feeling too well, so went for a lie-down. Small mercies,' she laughed, her voice **artificially**[7] breezy.

'Really?' Ben looked alarmed.

'Cristy said it's nothing. He was off-colour, that's all.'

'Oh! OK. I'm kinda glad he can't come.' Ben sounded American. 'At least his roasting will wait. Claire ...?' Ben's eyes narrowed, his voice petering out, hanging in a question.

'What?' asked Claire, suspecting the inevitable.

'What's gonna happen? What are you going to say to Cristy? It's totally nuts!'

'I know. I know. I'm on it. If we tell the truth, they'll think we've made it up, so perhaps that's

---

1 **contrition** *(n)* a feeling of remorse and penitence (sorry). *(s)* apology, regret, repentance. *(ant)* impenitence.

2 **ooze** *(v)* gently flow, trickle or seep. *(s)* bleed, exude, emerge, leak, creep, drip, leach, issue. *(ant)* gush, pour.

3 **rally** *(v)* assemble. *(s)* collect, accumulate, gather, muster, organise, marshal. *(ant)* disband.

4 **escapade** *(n)* a daring, adventurous or exciting act or incident. *(s)* caper, stunt, romp, exploit, antic, venture.

5 **chortle** *(n)* a loud or gleeful laugh. *(s)* snigger, titter, cackle, snort, guffaw. *(ant)* wail, lamentation.

6 **blanch** *(v)* become white or pale. *(s)* whiten, lighten, grey, blench, bleach, drain, fade. *(ant)* blush, colour.

7 **artificially** *(adj)* in an affected or insincere manner. *(s)* unnaturally, insincerely, spuriously. *(ant)* genuinely, sincerely.

the best route anyway.' Claire didn't believe herself for a second.

Claire had travelled in circles to achieve one thing: finding Ben. She didn't know the whereabouts of her backpack, containing the bracelet, and the knights were fading with each ticking second. The elation of finding Ben **fizzled**[1] to zero.

'Claire?' Ben's eyes searched hers.

Wrestling back tears, Claire gulped down the lump in her throat, but a sob broke free. 'I'm rubbish. I can't even keep hold of my school bag.'

Ben wrapped her in a hug.

'My friends are dying, Ben, *dying*. They need help, and I've failed.'

Ben squeezed her. 'Maybe there's time yet. You've done great. You found me. Let's get out of this glass hellhole. Your head will clear.'

Thomas mewed a quiet, **sympathetic**[2] mew.

Claire broke free, her tears drying up.

'Buddy! I forgot about you. I'm so sorry.' Claire bent to pet Thomas.

Thomas swirled around her legs, his tail following his nose, which rubbed with affection against her **calves**[3].

For a moment, Claire's **woes**[4] vanished. Then the cell's glass panel slid sideways.

'Cristy!' both kids **chorused**[5] in **unison**[6].

'Hey, turkeys!' Cristy was laughing.

Much to Claire's surprise, she found her arms hugging Cristy.

'We're so sorry,' said Claire, letting go. 'We've been a right pair of wallies.'

Cristy interrupted, waving Claire's words away and smiling. 'No need to apologise. No worries. The security breach blew our internal settings. It's no wonder you guys wandered off – most doors have failed at some point. It's been catastrophic. All fixed now though.' Cristy beamed at them both.

---

1 **fizzle** *(v)* fade or weaken. *(s)* peter, taper, ebb, wane, wilt. *(ant)* flourish.

2 **sympathetic** *(adj)* showing or feeling sympathy (pity). *(s)* consoling, compassionate. *(ant)* unsympathetic, indifferent.

3 **calf** *(n)* the fleshy part at the back of a person's legs below the knee (plural: *calves*).

4 **woe** *(n)* great distress, misery or sorrow. *(s)* anguish, burden, despair, gloom, misfortune. *(ant)* happiness, joy.

5 **chorus** *(v)* say or sing the same thing at the same time.

6 **unison** *(n)* harmonious and simultaneous performance. *(s)* chorus, harmony, unity, union. *(ant)* discord.

'Really?' remarked Claire, relieved. Then her stomach lurched. *Thomas!* she thought, her eyes swivelling to look around the cube, but he had vanished. *Good lad.* He'd not blown their cover. How in heaven would Claire have explained a black cat?

Ben was silent.

'Cat got your tongue, Ben?' joked Cristy, her comment **serendipitously**[1] apt.

'Is my dad OK?' Ben murmured, his face sheepish.

'I'm sure he's fine. He's **toiled**[2] real hard to patch this security breach. I think he's exhausted and making the most of the amazing facilities here. Don't worry, I won't snitch.' Cristy winked. 'Come on, you guys. Let's get out of here.'

Claire raised her brows and threw Ben a look that said, 'Phew.' She wondered if Cristy worked for Jayne. She certainly emulated Jayne's style. They looked quite similar.

Claire and Ben had dodged that bullet but changed **zilch**[3] for the knights. As she followed Cristy, that dragging, familiar fear resurfaced.

Then Cristy stopped so abruptly Claire collided with her.

'Oops! Sorry, Claire,' said Cristy, pointing into a corner of the glass cube. 'Isn't that your backpack?'

Claire's eyes followed the end of Cristy's finger.

'You might need that,' said Cristy, winking.

Claire gulped. She shot a stumped glance Ben's way and forced a smile.

'Oh, thanks, Cristy. Good job you noticed it.'

Claire cringed at her artificial voice. **Confounded**[4], and with another portentous sense of doom, she grabbed her backpack and followed Cristy and Ben from the cube.

*

Siân Cadwaladr folded her arms, smiling at the **animated**[5] screen. Claire's live image proved she had surfaced from the tunnels. The cell phone's covert tracker and camera were back online.

---

1 **serendipitously** *(adv)* in a serendipitous (happening by chance) way. *(s)* fortuitously, coincidentally. *(ant)* deliberately.

2 **toil** *(v)* work incessantly (non-stop) or extremely hard. *(s)* labour, slog, strive, slave. *(ant)* laze, idle, relax.

3 **zilch** *(n)* nothing. *(s)* zero, nada, naught, nought, diddly-squat, zip.

4 **confounded** *(adj)* surprised or confused. *(s)* muddled, puzzled, baffled, perplexed, bemused. *(ant)* clear.

5 **animated** *(adj)* lively. *(s)* vivid, activated, active, animate. *(ant)* inanimate, lifeless, inert.

Conceit[1] comforted Siân. As planned, the girl was reunited with her bag – the bag that contained half of the Gwalch Gem bracelet.

The large screen flickered, then blanked out. The phone must be back in Claire's pocket. It didn't matter; the tracking function continued. All that remained was to recover the **regenerated**[2] bracelet from the girl's bag. That part would be easy.

The surprising girl had somehow replenished the gold. She must have, because with a glint of greed tinting her eyes a deeper green, Siân Cadwaladr stared at the twinkling object in her palm. A shiver of **adrenaline**[3] surprised her. The alluring piece glowed, its life still **embryonic**[4] but blossoming as its saviour neared – proof that the unique gold was in this building.

She cared not how or whence Claire had retrieved the gold. As the gem glowed, her prize neared. Once she had the girl's backpack again, she could marry both pieces of the bracelet together once more. Then she would **wrest**[5] all power from him and never stoop to call him sir again. Her interminable wait was almost over. Soon she would be rid of him forever.

Her eyes fell to the emerald glow radiating through her palm.

'Such beauty,' she **cooed**[6], as if admiring a child.

Siân Cadwaladr marvelled as the exquisite Gwalch Gem twinkled against her skin. She rocked her hand, **hypnotised**[7] as its power shone. The gem, the all-powerful emerald hawk, glittered. At last its heart was beating to the rhythm of new-found life. Once reunited with the **recharged**[8] Welsh gold bracelet, its stupendous power would prevail.

*

As he marched to his private walkway, David Lewis dropped his **dashing**[9] demeanour and stormed from his circular office. The after-effects of the poison still polluted his head. She would

---

1 **conceit** *(n)* excessive pride. *(s)* self-importance, big-headiness, vanity, smugness, arrogance. *(ant)* modesty.

2 **regenerated** *(adj)* newly energised or brought to life. *(s)* revived, replenished, revitalised, invigorated. *(ant)* damaged.

3 **adrenaline** *(n)* a hormone (naturally produced chemical) that increases reaction times in the body.

4 **embryonic** *(adj)* in an early stage of development (like an embryo).

5 **wrest** *(v)* forcefully pull something from someone's grasp. *(s)* snatch, seize, wrench, grab. *(ant)* give.

6 **coo** *(v)* make soft murmuring sounds. *(s)* fuss, cluck, murmur.

7 **hypnotise** *(v)* completely capture the attention of someone. *(s)* fascinate, captivate, mesmerise, stupefy. *(ant)* bore.

8 **recharge** *(v)* return to normal strength. *(s)* revitalise, rejuvenate, re-energise, reinvigorate. *(ant)* drain, empty.

9 **dashing** *(adj)* fashionable and stylish. *(s)* dapper, spruce, fancy, groomed, debonair. *(ant)* unfashionable, dowdy.

not see him coming; he would **blindside**[1] her. His trusted boy Drane had located her operations room and reported back. Drane had also uncovered and disclosed her plans.

Fury **fuelled**[2] him, now as Dewi. Forgiveness was no option, not this time. He had **overlooked**[3] her **unscrupulous**[4] machinations before. To aim her guns at him was foolhardy. He would **smite**[5] her without mercy, inflicting on her what she had attempted on him. His iron constitution had thwarted her deadly, poisonous **plotting**[6]. Dewi, the Master, would prevail. His strength **surpassed**[7] hers. He snorted, sniffing the air, then spat. He would seize the Gwalch Gem bracelet, then crush her.

---

1 **blindside** *(v)* attack unexpectedly. *(s)* ambush, trap, surprise. *(ant)* forewarn.

2 **fuel** *(v)* power. *(s)* feed, charge, fire. *(ant)* deplete.

3 **overlook** *(v)* disregard or ignore. *(s)* neglect, omit, forget. *(ant)* consider.

4 **unscrupulous** *(adj)* not fair or honest, having poor morals. *(s)* dishonest, corrupt, immoral. *(ant)* honest.

5 **smite** *(v)* conquer or defeat. *(s)* beat, destroy, overthrow, kill, quash, crush. *(ant)* lose to.

6 **plotting** *(n)* the act of devising harmful or secret plans. *(s)* conspiring, conniving, contriving, scheming.

7 **surpass** *(v)* be better or greater than. *(s)* beat, eclipse, exceed, overshadow, transcend. *(ant)* follow, fail.

21. Blackout

Ben didn't yet know the Gwalch Gem bracelet was in Claire's backpack. She'd not told him; no apt **occasion**[1] had arisen. Claire wished it had, because to whisper here would be too chancy – Cristy was within earshot. Her spotting Claire's bag in the glass cube had felt way too convenient.

Claire had scoured that very cube earlier, looking for clues of Ben, before the tunnel hole had opened up. She would have seen her backpack then. It hadn't been in that cube before Claire had climbed down and found Thomas. Someone had put it there afterwards – probably the boy who had been checking on Ben, but Claire wasn't trusting anyone now. She glanced at Cristy.

'Cristy, could we go back to the skate park, please?' asked Ben.

Claire rolled her eyes, but she couldn't blame Ben. He needed speed to escape the insanity of their plight. Claire got that.

'Is there a cafe in there?' asked Ben.

'Sure,' said Cristy. 'Let's head there. You guys can skate, and I'll check on your dad, Ben. How does that sound?'

'Coolio,' said Ben.

Claire's stomach didn't grumble, and thirst hadn't called. Even though she'd not eaten or drunk for hours, **fatigue**[2] didn't dog her. *Maybe I* am *getting fitter.*

As she trudged beside Cristy, unexpected tears flooded Claire's eyes.

'You OK?' Cristy cocked a concerned half smile at Claire.

'Mortified,' said Claire. 'Just relieved you found us.'

---

1 **occasion** *(n)* an opportune time. *(s)* opportunity, opening, moment, chance, possibility.

2 **fatigue** *(n)* extreme tiredness. *(s)* exhaustion, weariness, lethargy, lassitude, weakness. *(ant)* refreshment.

Claire's tears fell for Gwilym and Gladys, for Anwen and Owen and the Knights Hawk she'd not yet met. Claire **pined**[1] for Jack, and eating bread and drinking tea in Gladys's cosy kitchen, for seeing Gwilym's stern face and weird **tattoos**[2]. She needed her mum, Pete and **scatty**[3] Rebecca, her dad and Jayne. Jayne could help.

'Cristy, do you work with Jayne Lewis?'

'Sorry, I didn't catch that,' said Cristy, slowing and frowning.

'Do you work with Jayne Lewis?'

'Sometimes. I don't report in to her. Ben's dad was with Jayne today. He's more senior.' Cristy smiled, speeding up and striding off.

Claire tugged the straps of her backpack until they dug into her shoulders. No way was she losing it again. *I need to check it's still there*, she thought.

'Cristy, sorry to pester,' said Claire, catching up with her, 'but I'm desperate for the loo. Can I pop in there?' Claire nodded to a 'Ladies' sign. 'I'll be super quick.'

'Go ahead,' said Cristy. 'Take your time. Ben and I will wait right here.'

'Thanks!'

Claire shot in, found an empty cubicle and locked it. She sat, yanked her bag onto her lap and dug out her crumpled coat. 'Please be there. Please be there,' she whispered. Her hands jigged so much she fought to unzip the pocket. Claire lifted the toilet paper from her pocket. Weighing the packet in her palm helped quell her trembling.

'Eh?' she said as furrows appeared, creasing her forehead. Her bushy brows met. As Claire unwrapped the paper, her mouth **slackened**[4], and her eyes widened.

'No way!' she gasped, too loudly. One hand flew to her mouth as she gawped at the bracelet in the other. 'What the heck?'

With dancing hands, Claire removed the loo roll, discarding it. It wasn't her imagination; her left hand detected the same warmth as her right. Captivated by its **transformation**[5], Claire

---

1 **pine** *(v)* miss and long for. *(s)* ache, yearn, crave, hanker, languish. *(ant)* dislike.

2 **tattoo** *(n)* an indelible (permanent) mark on the skin from injecting pigment (colour). *(s)* brand, mark.

3 **scatty** *(adj)* absent-minded. *(s)* airheaded, silly, scatterbrained, feather-brained. *(ant)* astute, alert.

4 **slacken** *(v)* become slack (loose). *(s)* ease, release, relax, weaken, relent, soften. *(ant)* tighten, strengthen.

5 **transformation** *(n)* a noticeable change in form, nature or appearance. *(s)* alteration, metamorphosis. *(ant)* preservation.

marvelled. As if **injected**[1] with life, the links of the bracelet shimmered as they had yesterday when she'd put her eye to the cracked exhibition case in the museum and seen the legendary artefact. A rush of elation raised the **downy**[2] hairs on her arms as goosebumps crept across her skin.

'How?' she whispered, though not caring. If the bracelet was alive, hope remained for the knights. In **awe**[3], she gazed, mesmerised by its allure. A warm tingle flowed through her entire being.

Thomas leaped to her mind.

Tommy, what did you give me to swallow in that tunnel? I've not been hungry since then. I've not drunk since this morning, and I'm not thirsty. I'm not even tired.

'What did you feed me, Tommy Boy? What was it?' But she knew. Claire pulled back her grubby cuff and slipped the bracelet onto her wrist, closing its clasp. Somehow, it was a perfect fit. A shiver shot up her arm.

'No way!' she blurted, sharing its power. 'Tommy, you fed me the Welsh gold …'

The Gwalch Gem bracelet, albeit minus the emerald hawk and its full power, lived and breathed on Claire's wrist.

Will I need the emerald to save the knights? Can I help them without it? she asked herself, pulling her cuff down over her wrist. With new-found **alacrity**[4], she took the now-**obsolete**[5] glove and plastic from her back pocket and shoved it into her backpack. Claire stuffed her coat on top, fastened her bag, hauled it onto her shoulders and left the loos.

'Sorry about the wait,' Claire apologised. 'Number two,' she announced, her face deadpan.

'Ugh, really?' cried Ben, his face **distorted**[6] in disgust.

Cristy giggled. 'Come on, guys. There's a neat shortcut through to the rec area.'

Drawn by the gold's warmth, Claire clutched her cuff again. She glanced at an **oblivious**[7] Ben.

---

1 **inject** *(v)* introduce into something. *(s)* instil, infuse, imbue, impregnate. *(ant)* drain.

2 **downy** *(adj)* soft and light (like down feathers). *(s)* fluffy, silky, velvety, fuzzy. *(ant)* coarse, wiry.

3 **awe** *(n)* respect and wonderment. *(s)* admiration, amazement, surprise. *(ant)* contempt, indifference.

4 **alacrity** *(n)* cheerful enthusiasm. *(s)* readiness, eagerness, fervour, willingness. *(ant)* apathy, indifference.

5 **obsolete** *(adj)* no longer useful. *(s)* defunct, disused, outmoded. *(ant)* functional, useful.

6 **distorted** *(adj)* pulled or twisted out of shape. *(s)* awry, contorted, deformed, disfigured, warped. *(ant)* straight.

7 **oblivious** *(adj)* unaware or unconcerned about what is happening. *(s)* ignorant, unconscious. *(ant)* conscious.

She'd show him the bracelet as soon as possible.

Cristy navigated the glass cubes with ease. Not following any flashing floor guides, she led Claire and Ben past the glittering staircase. 'Wow!' said Claire, pretending it was the first time she'd seen it up close, all the while her eyes imploring Ben to keep his mouth shut.

'Boss's office. Pretty darn cool, hey?' said Cristy.

Just as she was about to answer, Claire tripped, grabbing at Cristy's back for support. Bowled sideways but staying on her feet, she cried, 'What's happening?' The entire massive workspace had blacked out, **plunging**[1] it into darkness. In the **mayhem**[2], someone grabbed at Claire's back, pulling her to the floor. 'Ben!' she shrieked, her hands flailing behind to break her fall. 'Ouch! Ben?' she cried as her backside hit the floor.

'I'm OK. Are you?' said Ben, but his voice drifted over from a distance.

'Ben? Ben?' Panic consumed her.

A loud clunk, followed by a hum, **preceded**[3] a **reinstatement**[4] of power. The vast workspace flickered back to life.

Claire struggled to her feet, her **dilated**[5] pupils **readjusting**[6].

'You OK, guys?' said a terrified-looking Cristy as she wobbled to her feet. 'I'm so sorry. I don't know what happened there.'

Claire nodded, tugging her cuff over her wrist.

'This place is **flaky**[7] today,' said Cristy.

Several metres away from Claire, Ben sat crossed-legged on the floor, multicoloured guide lights flashing beneath his backside.

'Ben?' Claire asked, her hand shooting round to her empty back.

'Yeah?' he replied, seeming unfazed.

Claire's legs numbed with shock. 'Phew! Just glad you're OK,' she fibbed, thinking quickly and

---

1 **plunge** *(v)* suddenly bring into a specified condition or state. *(s)* thrust, force, throw.

2 **mayhem** *(n)* extreme disorder. *(s)* confusion, chaos, havoc, bedlam, pandemonium, tumult. *(ant)* order, peace.

3 **precede** *(v)* come before in order, position or time. *(s)* introduce, foreshadow, lead. *(ant)* follow, succeed.

4 **reinstatement** *(n)* the restoration of something. *(s)* recovery, reinstitution, reappearance. *(ant)* removal.

5 **dilated** *(adj)* expanded. *(s)* enlarged, widened, swollen. *(ant)* contracted.

6 **readjust** *(v)* adjust to a change. *(s)* adapt, acclimatise, accommodate.

7 **flaky** *(adj)* likely to behave in an odd or eccentric way. *(s)* unconventional, irregular, peculiar. *(ant)* conventional, ordinary.

facing both Ben and Cristy. Scared of what her face exposed, she cracked a false smile. 'To the skate park, then,' she said, nodding but hanging back a tad. Her bag was gone. Whoever had just decked her and swiped it from her back must have assumed the bracelet was in it. Claire touched her cuff and glanced at Cristy. The bracelet adorned Claire's wrist, and she must rescue it from this compound. Swallowing the gold had saved her. Every part of Claire now prayed its magic might work without the Gwalch Gem and she wasn't too late to save the knights.

*

Dazed, John Brady stared at the ceiling. How long he had lain **unconscious**[1], he did not know. His symptoms had niggled early on, from the moment he'd left home. Attributing it to fatigue, he had dismissed them as minor. He wasn't getting any younger. The unavoidable drive had challenged him, but he had pushed on regardless.

After leaving Ben and Claire, a rapid **deterioration**[2] had forced him to retire to his suite. Now, as his long legs stretched the length of his sofa, his condition improved.

John Brady pushed down with his hands, easing himself upwards. He wriggled his bottom into a sitting position, but his body fought back. His stomach swirled, his head hammered, and his limbs seized. Defeated and frustrated, he flopped back onto the couch and reached for his phone. He pressed one key, waited, then closed his eyes.

---

1 **unconscious** *(adj)* not awake or aware of one's environment. *(s)* asleep, comatose. *(ant)* conscious.

2 **deterioration** *(n)* a progressive worsening. *(s)* decline, decay, downturn. *(ant)* improvement.

22. No Skateboarding Allowed

'Are you OK hitting the skate park for a while?' Ben whispered to Claire. Via the shortcut, they both followed a shaken Cristy to the rec area.

'Yeah, it's the best bet,' said Claire, a **vehement**[1] tone in her voice. 'I need some time.'

Swallowing the Welsh gold, regardless of the lack of emerald in the bracelet, had saved and rejuvenated her. Somehow *she* now powered the bracelet with the gold in her belly. Would the gold alone save the knights? Not knowing the emerald's whereabouts, she'd have to run that risk. Besides, if the Master had the Gwalch Gem, she didn't fancy facing him alone.

Ben had not yet seen what glowed around her wrist; Claire hadn't shown him. Her Instinct screamed to get the bracelet out of the compound, emerald or not. How, she must figure out. She'd buy time in the skate park.

'Cristy,' said Ben, walking beside her. 'Could you let me know how my dad is, please?'

'Sure. I'll call the moment I have news. Please don't fret. He'll be fine. I'm sure of it.' Cristy flashed a reassuring smile at him.

Claire touched Ben's arm. 'Don't worry, buddy,' she said, feigning **sincerity**[2] but worrying about why Mr Brady had become ill on today of all days.

'Cristy, you OK?' said Claire, perturbed and glancing sideways at Ben. Cristy had halted and was peering up at one of the glass walkways suspended above their heads. Her face had drained to a wan **pallor**[3].

---

1 **vehement** *(adj)* showing strong feeling. *(s)* fervent, vigorous, forceful, ardent, emphatic. *(ant)* apathetic.

2 **sincerity** *(n)* honesty. *(s)* truthfulness, candour, integrity. *(ant)* insincerity.

3 **pallor** *(n)* a pale and unhealthy appearance. *(s)* whiteness, paleness, sallowness, pastiness. *(ant)* rosiness.

'I'm fine. It's nothing. I just remembered something *real* important,' Cristy replied, then continued walking, her pace now urgent.

'Come on, slowcoach,' said Ben, beckoning to Claire, who was staring up at the same glass walkway.

'I'm coming,' murmured Claire, replying as normally as shock would allow.

Claire had seen the back of what had caused Cristy's face to fall. Her astute eyes had caught the flash of fear disclosed by Cristy's.

Yesterday had **branded**[1] Dewi's image, forever burning it as a scar, on Claire's brain. She'd recognise him anywhere: his **muscular**[2] but lithe **physique**[3], the arrogant gait, his **coiffured**[4] hair and those overly **dapper**[5], dashing clothes.

Cristy had blanched at the sight of her boss – David Lewis. Why would a happy and **competent**[6] high-ranking employee baulk at seeing her boss? Even *she* knew that bosses shouldn't bully workers in the twenty-first century, and not in a company this large.

She was now certain Dewi was masquerading as David Lewis, and like a piercing alarm, the truth rang clearly in Claire's head. Cristy's eyes had **unwittingly**[7] revealed terror. Cristy didn't fear David Lewis; she feared Dewi, the Master – Cristy knew who he was.

With disbelief, Claire's eyes tracked Cristy. She toyed with trying to read Cristy's thoughts, but there was no time; she needed quiet to do that. No proof existed against Cristy, bar the look she'd seen in her eyes. Until she knew who had stolen her backpack, and which side Cristy was on, Claire was trusting no one.

'CLAIRE!' Ben shouted, walking over, his shoulders up by his ears, his palms turned upwards in frustration. '*Come on!*' He gesticulated towards Cristy, who now strode metres ahead of them.

'Sorry,' she said, clutching her cuff and breaking into a half trot.

Cristy reached the exit and turned to face the approaching kids.

---

1 **brand** *(v)* mark indelibly (unable to remove). *(s)* stamp, imprint, tattoo, burn, scar.

2 **muscular** *(adj)* having well-developed muscles. *(s)* strong, muscly, sinewy, brawny. *(ant)* weedy, weak.

3 **physique** *(n)* the form of a person's body. *(s)* figure, frame, anatomy, shape, build.

4 **coiffured** *(adj)* (of hair) styled. *(s)* fashioned, combed, brushed, arranged. *(ant)* messy.

5 **dapper** *(adj)* smart and stylish in dress or appearance. *(s)* dashing, classy, neat, spruce, tidy, chic. *(ant)* scruffy.

6 **competent** *(adj)* capable, able and efficient (good at something). *(s)* proficient, adept. *(ant)* incompetent.

7 **unwittingly** *(adv)* in an unwitting (unintentional) way. *(s)* accidentally, inadvertently. *(ant)* wittingly, deliberately.

Claire caught up, gushing a 'Sorry, sorry. My fault, too easily distracted.' Claire wore her most **earnest**[1] and apologetic face, but beneath **lurked**[2] a **distrusting**[3] scowl.

Cristy performed the palm–eye security manoeuvres, and the door opened. All three stepped into the corridor lined with rec doors.

'OK, guys,' Cristy chirped, opening the skate park door, but Claire saw the shadows that flitted across her face.

A deep bass sound boomed as Cristy held open the door and beckoned them through.

'Please, come in for a minute. We'll miss you,' Claire begged, flashing her sweetest fake smile.

'I'm *really* sorry, but a pressing issue calls,' said Cristy, her movements **skittish**[4] and **birdlike**[5].

'Can you open the locker, please?' Claire blurted.

'Oh yes, sorry, I forgot – your gear,' said Cristy, pressing one hand against the metal locker and lining up its **combination**[6] with the other. 'There you go,' she said as the door clicked open. 'Ben, I'll call when I have news. No wandering off this time, you two.' Her face was stern.

'Thanks, Cristy!' said Ben, hugging her.

'Yeah, thanks,' said Claire, forcing a grin.

Cristy turned and left.

'Fab, it's not too busy in here,' said Ben, scanning the room.

Claire was on her knees, **rummaging**[7] through her school bag. 'You're not gonna be skating in here,' she said, her voice raised above the bass.

'What?' Ben screwed up his face in confusion.

'Find the cafe. Order a cucumber sandwich, no butter.' Claire held the five-pound note Dee had given her this morning.

Ben stared at her, his mouth open.

'They *must* wrap it in cling film. Ben, do it now! I need to wait here. Be *super* quick.'

---

1 **earnest** *(adj)* serious and sincere. *(s)* solemn, deep, heartfelt, devoted. *(ant)* insincere, superficial.

2 **lurk** *(v)* be or remain hidden, hang about. *(s)* prowl, loiter, skulk, creep, steal, slink. *(ant)* appear, materialise.

3 **distrust** *(v)* doubt the honesty of. *(s)* mistrust, suspect, disbelieve, question. *(ant)* trust, believe.

4 **skittish** *(adj)* nervous. *(s)* jumpy, fidgety, edgy. *(ant)* calm, collected, composed.

5 **birdlike** *(adj)* like a bird in movement or appearance. *(s)* flighty, erratic. *(ant)* steady, predictable.

6 **combination** *(n)* a sequence or numbers or letters that unlocks a combination lock.

7 **rummage** *(v)* search untidily through something. *(s)* hunt, dig, ransack, forage, delve.

Ben took one look at Claire's face, grabbed the fiver and left.

With a **deliberate**[1] lack of urgency, Claire unpacked Ben's skateboarding gear from the locker. She fiddled around with the helmet straps, plonking the pink one onto her head, then pretending to fit it. Her neck prickled with sweat. She dug out the sweaty glove and put it on her hand.

Her eyes scoured the room for Ben's return.

Come on, Ben. Come on.

'Thank goodness,' she muttered as Ben's head popped into view.

She beckoned him with a 'Hurry' motion with her left hand and widened her eyes, urging him to move more quickly.

'Got it,' said Ben, proffering the wrapped sandwich, but Claire snatched it from him.

'**Faff**[2] around here getting your gear on for a minute,' she said. 'Shield me from view.'

Claire unwrapped the sandwich, throwing the bread and cucumber into the locker. She closed its door and pressed the plastic flat onto the spot where Cristy's hand had been.

'That should do it,' she said, peeling it off and wrapping it around her right glove. 'Ben, tighten it up and finish the top bit. Same as last time.'

'Where are we going?' asked Ben, putting on his helmet and picking up his board.

'No idea yet,' said Claire, 'but we're getting out of here.'

Using the glove, Claire **bypassed**[3] security. 'Bingo!' she said as they left the booming bass behind and stepped out into the corridor lined with doors.

'We know that one's the VIP restaurant,' Claire said, pointing, 'and that's the Hive.' The pink helmet wobbled on her head, and the board protruded from under her armpit.

'Claire, this is **barmy**[4],' said Ben.

His **pasty**[5] face and dark-ringed eyes concerned Claire.

'Just call Cristy again. We'll go stay with my dad.'

'We can't.' Claire shook her head.

'Why not?' asked Ben, his brow creasing.

---

1 **deliberate** *(adj)* done on purpose. *(s)* intentional, knowing, wilful, conscious, intended. *(ant)* unintentional.

2 **faff** *(v)* spend time in an unproductive way. *(s)* mess about, fiddle, hang around.

3 **bypass** *(v)* avoid. *(s)* get around, circumvent, elude, sidestep, evade. *(ant)* confront.

4 **barmy** *(adj)* very foolish. *(s)* stupid, silly, idiotic, witless, imprudent, absurd, rash. *(ant)* wise, judicious.

5 **pasty** *(adj)* pale in complexion. *(s)* sallow, ashen, pallid, wan, waxen, chalky, drained. *(ant)* flushed, healthy.

'Because I reckon she's **dodgy**[1].'

'What?' said Ben, his face incredulous.

Claire glanced around the corridor. No way would she show the sparkling bracelet to Ben here – too many prying digital eyes and ears.

Claire put the board onto the floor and moved closer to Ben. 'Take your helmet off so I can see your ear,' she whispered.

'What?' he asked.

'Ben, just do it!' she hissed.

He removed his helmet, and Claire sidled up to him as if to kiss his ear.

'Don't look down when I speak. Don't react. Nothing. You hear me?'

'Got it,' whispered Ben.

'Remember that magical gold bracelet I told you about earlier? The one that can change time and stuff.'

'Yeah,' said Ben.

'Half of it is around my wrist. Don't react!' she urged. 'They're watching us. I have something they need. That's why we're here.'

She wrapped her arms around him.

'Pretend to blub,' she said. Ben pulled away. She yanked him back. 'Just do it.'

Sobbing a fake cry, Ben's shoulders heaved up and down.

'I saw David Lewis–Dewi–the Master in action yesterday at that museum. No way he'd let us wander around here like this. He could crush us within seconds if he wanted to. He needs us,' Claire whispered.

Ben looked at her.

'Keep crying,' she mouthed. 'I was nearly done for in that tunnel. I was dying of cold and thirst, totally lost. Tommy turned up, fed me something, and now I'm not hungry or thirsty, and my energy is back. He gave me gold to swallow, Ben, the Welsh gold the knights need. The bracelet is glowing. The gold inside me is giving *it* life.'

Ben wiped his eyes, pulling away from her, his mouth moving to speak.

Claire shook her head, her eyes widening, saying a silent no. 'The Master's letting us roam

---

1 **dodgy** *(adj)* dishonest. *(s)* dubious, deceitful, traitorous, duplicitous, unscrupulous. *(ant)* trustworthy, honourable.

because he needs what's in my stomach. Well, I'm not going to let him have it.'

Confident no one would stop them, because they needed her, and not even convinced the jury-rigged glove was working, or ever had, she picked up the skateboard. 'This way.' Claire nodded, heading towards the door that led to the Hive.

Ben followed in silence.

Suddenly Claire stopped, dropping the skateboard.

'What is it?' said Ben, alarm ringing in his voice.

'Er, nothing. **Butterfingers**[1],' replied Claire, bending to pick up the board.

The now-familiar Welsh voice had just said, *Thought Comms are up.*

Claire straightened, her face concealing her thoughts.

Felicity's face flashed before Claire's eyes; she was in her head. Thought Comms were back up and running.

Don't speak, urged Felicity's voice. *Just listen.*

Claire wanted to scream but she nodded instead.

Ben turned to see what Claire was nodding at. She shushed him with a finger to her lips. Her eyes begging him to stay quiet.

You must reach Daisy, said Felicity. *I will help to guide you. Forget your glove. Until they realise you have outside help, they will maintain your all-areas access.*

Claire nodded again. Ben looked baffled.

From where you stand, count five doors along to your right, said Felicity.

Walking sideways, Claire counted the doors.

We don't know how long you have before they lock down the compound, said Felicity.

Wait! thought Claire to Felicity in her head.

With a sudden nod, Claire beckoned Ben closer. '**Low-key**[2] take this to the rec room and stick it back into the locker we just used.' With a surreptitious **sleight of hand**[3], Claire slipped him Cristy's phone. 'I reckon it's been tracking us; we need Cristy to think we're still in there, at least for a few minutes.'

'What? How will I get in there?' Ben asked.

---

1 **butterfingers** *(n)* a clumsy person who drops things. *(s)* bungler, clod, duffer, klutz, fumbler.

2 **low-key** *(adv)* in a subtle manner. *(s)* quietly, discreetly, unobtrusively. *(ant)* obviously, obtrusively.

3 **sleight of hand** *(n)* a dexterous trick. *(s)* deception, deceit.

'Use your palm; the door should open if we've got access, regardless of security. Go now. We have no time. Hurry back.'

'OK,' replied Ben, putting his skateboard down and rushing off.

Felicity, said Claire in her head. *The phone. I think it's tracking me.*

They have ears and eyes everywhere, as do we, but yes, most likely, replied Felicity.

Ben reappeared in the corridor and hurried back to Claire.

The fifth door, said Felicity. *Enter now.*

'Come on,' said Claire, 'and don't forget your skateboard.'

*

Demented[1] with rage, David Lewis trashed the **vacated**[2] operations room.

He threw objects, kicking leftover kit, smashing all in his wake. Siân had been here; he could smell her. Who had informed her? Who had known he was coming?

He stilled as realisation dawned, then snatched the slim, unbranded phone from his breast pocket. He glared at it and pressed one key. A familiar face flashed onto its screen. Her forced smile revealed her obvious guilt – she looked just like her mother. He paused, torturing her a few seconds more. For her, lying to him was **unattainable**[3], and always had been.

'Where is she?' he asked, an edge of **malice**[4] sharpening his voice.

1 **demented** *(adj)* behaving irrationally (crazily). *(s)* deranged, unhinged, insane, lunatic, frenzied. *(ant)* rational.

2 **vacate** *(v)* leave empty. *(s)* abandon, evacuate, quit, desert, empty, forsake. *(ant)* occupy, inhabit.

3 **unattainable** *(adj)* not achievable. *(s)* impossible, unrealistic, unachievable. *(ant)* attainable.

4 **malice** *(n)* the desire to hurt or harm someone. *(s)* spite, animosity, malevolence, evil, hate. *(ant)* kindness.

23. A Hero's Last Stand

Open the door, said Felicity's voice. *If you still have access to all areas, your palm should* ***suffice***[1].

Claire placed her hand onto the scanner, expecting the opening door to reveal blackness. Instead, an empty glass walkway stretched out before them.

Hurry, said Felicity. *If we are to save the knights without the emerald, you and the bracelet must reach the castle soon.*

Claire nodded at Ben and marched into the glass tube. The flat surface beneath their feet was opaque, everywhere else transparent. Other walkways ran beside, above and below them, tangled like spaghetti. A steady stream of Via-Corp employees moved through them, eyes fixed on devices as they walked.

'What's happening?' asked Ben.

'I'm not sure,' said Claire, wishing she could tell Ben about Felicity, but knowing she must **unclutter**[2] her thoughts while Felicity was still in her head.

Claire, increase your speed. Felicity's voice rang with a new urgency.

Claire's pace picked up, breaking into a trot. Ben followed.

Felicity? questioned Claire.

We may have seen a problem, said Felicity. *Keep moving – fast!*

Claire stopped. Ben almost crashed into her. She plopped her skateboard onto the walkway's opaque base. 'We're skating,' she said to an astonished Ben.

'What?' said Ben.

---

1 **suffice** *(v)* be enough. *(s)* serve, do, work, satisfy, avail, suit. *(ant)* be inadequate.

2 **unclutter** *(v)* make orderly. *(s)* order, tidy, neaten, straighten up, arrange. *(ant)* clutter.

'You go first. I'll copy you,' said Claire.

Open-mouthed, Ben hesitated, took one look at Claire, dropped his deck on the floor and hopped on, **punting**[1] forward.

'Not too fast,' she said, placing her left foot on the front of her board and pushing off with her right. 'Whoa!' she cried, wobbling onto the board. It shot out from under her foot and hit the back of Ben's.

Ben stopped. 'You OK? Look, watch for a second. Then follow. You can't fall far in this tube. Just go for it.' Ben punted along, shouting instructions.

Claire inhaled deeply, put her foot on the board and pushed away again. 'Whoa!' she said again, her arms flailing for balance.

'Don't stare at your feet. Head up,' shouted Ben, looking backwards.

Within two minutes, Claire was **tailing**[2] him and picking up speed.

That's better, said Felicity. *Keep pushing at this pace.*

Claire struggled to think her answer – she was concentrating too much.

'Wow,' said Ben, glancing at her. 'Get you! You're a natural.'

For a moment, Claire forgot everything and revelled in her new-found talent. She was flying.

Claire, said Felicity, *we have a problem.*

With a jolt, Claire stopped her board. 'Ben, wait!' she shouted. *What problem?* she asked, tuning in to Felicity, her toe on her board.

This tube terminates at the compound's exit. Daisy will be on the other side. However, we fear you may no longer have clearance.

You fear? said Claire.

We won't know until you try to leave, answered Felicity.

Why? asked Claire. *What's changed?*

We're not yet sure, said Felicity.

Ben waited a few metres ahead, his face asking a question.

'I'm coming,' she said. 'I fell off. Just finding my feet.' There was no time to explain about Felicity. 'Let me go in front,' she said, pushing her board forward. 'You follow me.'

---

1 **punt** *(v)* propel using a punt (a pole) or as if using a punt.

2 **tail** *(v)* follow. *(s)* track, shadow, trail, pursue, chase. *(ant)* lead, guide.

Ben's eyebrows shot up. 'Wow! Look at you, Miss Confident!'

With their roles reversed, Claire jumped onto her board and sped ahead, Ben in her wake.

Your ***estimated***[1] *exit time, maintaining this pace, is two minutes,* said Felicity.

For the first time in a while, Claire noticed the warmth **issuing**[2] from the bracelet. Its power **circulated**[3], **diffusing**[4] its generous energy to her mind and body. She bent her left knee and punted hard with her right foot, aiming to reach her destination faster, Ben in hot pursuit.

Claire, your exit is approaching, said Felicity.

In the distance, Claire saw a rock face preceded by a metal platform. She braked with her right toe, slowing her board to a controllable speed.

Your palm should *suffice*, said Felicity.

I hope so, said Claire.

As she approached the walkway's end, she stopped her board, jumped off and, with a deft kick, flipped it into the air and caught it.

Ben pulled up beside her, his face full of respect. '**Kudos**[5],' he said, doing the same. 'You're **rad**[6] on that board.'

Claire ignored him, bit her lip and slapped her palm onto the scanner. Nothing happened.

Your eye, said Felicity. *Try your eye.*

Claire focused her right eye towards the **iris**[7] scanner and, although she didn't realise it, held her breath.

The exit, identical in colour and texture to the rock, slid sideways to reveal a thick pane of glass. Beyond the glass lay a snow-covered road. Daisy, shrouded in a coat of falling white flakes, waited.

Claire peered into the scanner again, and the glass pane slid sideways. She ran over to Daisy, her trainers crunching deep prints into the snow.

---

1 **estimated** *(adj)* roughly calculated. *(s)* approximate, general, guessed, vague. *(ant)* precise, exact.

2 **issue** *(v)* flow out from. *(s)* emanate, exude, discharge, emerge, radiate, release. *(ant)* withdraw.

3 **circulate** *(v)* move freely in a closed area or system. *(s)* flow, travel, distribute, spread.

4 **diffuse** *(v)* spread out. *(s)* circulate, disperse, distribute, radiate, disseminate. *(ant)* concentrate, collect.

5 **kudos** *(n)* compliments or congratulations. *(s)* respect, praise, credit, prestige, cachet. *(ant)* infamy.

6 **rad** *(adj)* (slang) impressive, outstanding. *(s)* sublime, fabulous, sensational, amazing, astounding. *(ant)* poor.

7 **iris** *(n)* the coloured part of the eye.

'Open!' she cried.

Daisy's door opened. Claire threw the skateboard into the back and jumped into the driver's seat.

'Ben?' she called, assuming he'd followed her. 'Ben!' Her voice became a scream.

Claire leaped out of the Tesla. Scrabbling for purchase in the snow, she bolted towards the exit. 'No!' she screamed. 'No! Get your hands off him!'

Drane gripped Ben in a **headlock**[1] and was **lugging**[2] him backwards towards the compound. Ben's feet attempted to **parry**[3] but left only a useless trail in the snow.

Claire sprinted through the snow and launched herself at Drane, pummelling his head with her fists. Drane **tottered**[4] sideways but recovered and thrust her away. She landed hard in the snow. Claire vaulted to her feet and sprang at him again. She wrapped her legs around his waist, grabbing at his eyes and toppling them all over into the snow. Claire hit the ground so hard she yelled, gasping in pain, as Drane and Ben now lay on top of her.

Ben soon got to his feet, **squaring up**[5] to Drane, who was also standing. Winded, Claire nursed what felt like an awful **stitch**[6] in her side. She rolled onto all fours, trying to catch her breath. The bracelet slid down her wrist into view. To shield it from Drane, she yanked her cuff down.

Suddenly, from the opening in the rock behind them, Cristy ran out. 'What on earth?' she shouted. 'Claire! Ben! Are you OK?'

Claire whirled around, stunned to see Cristy hobbling over, her high heels disappearing in the snow.

Drane seemed to back away from Ben, who stood positioned to defend himself.

'Claire, Claire, are you OK?' said Cristy. She knelt beside Claire in the snow. Felicity said nothing.

As Claire's pain subsided, her brain caught up, and she sat up in the snow. 'Cristy?' she muttered.

---

1 **headlock** *(n)* a way of restraining someone by holding an arm around their head.

2 **lug** *(v)* drag with great effort. *(s)* heave, haul, manhandle, tug, tow. *(ant)* push.

3 **parry** *(v)* ward (fight) off an attack with a countermove. *(s)* deflect, block, dodge, prevent. *(ant)* take, allow.

4 **totter** *(v)* move in a feeble or unsteady way. *(s)* falter, wobble, stagger, teeter, dodder. *(ant)* balance, stabilise.

5 **square up** *(v)* assume a position ready to fight. *(s)* confront, face. *(ant)* retreat, shy away.

6 **stitch** *(n)* a sudden and intense pain in the side of the body, caused by exercise.

'Who is this boy?' asked Cristy, her face frowning in consternation.

'I don't know,' Claire lied. 'He attacked Ben.'

'What are you two doing out here? It's freezing! And John's car?' Cristy pointed, looking bewildered.

Ben shifted away from Drane and approached them.

'Oh my! What will your father say?' said Cristy with a worried look.

Then her face changed. Claire tensed, startled by Cristy's sudden switch of expression. Cristy was staring at something. Claire's eyes tracked Cristy's gaze, to her own wrist. Poking out from beneath the cuff of Claire's hoody was the bracelet. Ben stared too. A strange silence smothered the group; the falling flakes seemed loud. Claire wriggled to her feet, brushing snow off her backside. As she tugged down her cuff, Claire's face fought to hide her feelings, but its colour betrayed her.

With a languid **flourish**[1], Cristy brushed snow from her hair and shoulders, then smiled. Claire heaved a silent sigh of relief, turning towards Ben, but before she could open her mouth, as swift as a seasoned **pickpocket**[2], Cristy wrenched the bracelet from Claire. As it left Claire's wrist, like flicking a switch, a life force in Claire extinguished, gushing away like rain down a storm drain.

Cristy clutched the bracelet with an evil look targeting Claire. Ben crouched as if ready to pounce. Claire squatted too, ready to **lunge**[3], but her legs complained and her head was hazy as her body adjusted to the gold vanishing from her wrist.

'Drane!' commanded Cristy. '**Inform**[4] my father NOW!' She pivoted on her heel and marched towards the compound.

Claire's knees **buckled**[5]. Ben knelt beside her. 'Claire? Claire?' he whispered. She didn't answer.

'Claire?' said Felicity. Claire ignored her.

One question burned in Claire's mind, to which she already knew the answer: *Who is Cristy's father?* Claire remembered the look she'd seen on Cristy's face, the look of absolute terror when

---

1 **flourish** *(n)* a bold or extravagant gesture or action. *(s)* display, wave, shake, gesture, brandish.

2 **pickpocket** *(n)* a thief who steals from people's pockets. *(s)* cutpurse, bag snatcher, dipper, finger.

3 **lunge** *(v)* thrust forward. *(s)* pounce, rush, leap, spring, jump, charge.

4 **inform** *(v)* give someone information or facts. *(s)* tell, notify, advise, brief, update, warn. *(ant)* hide, conceal.

5 **buckle** *(v)* bend and give way under strain or pressure. *(s)* crumple, collapse, fold, warp. *(ant)* straighten.

Cristy had spotted David Lewis in the walkway above their heads. *Surely not*, Claire thought, shaking her head. *Surely she's not the Master's daughter.*

A **blood-curdling**[1] screech suddenly pierced the silence. Claire whirled around as Ben sprang to his feet. Over by the compound's entrance, Cristy **thrashed**[2] wildly, screaming and spinning, her hands clutched to a black object covering her face.

'Thomas?' screamed Claire, struggling to her feet. 'Thomas!'

Drane, as fast as the snow allowed, was sprinting towards Cristy.

As if in slow motion, Claire watched as Drane grabbed Thomas with both hands, clasping the cat's midriff. Thomas seemed so small. His claws gripped Cristy's head, but Drane was strong. He prised Thomas from Cristy's slashed face. Then, like a **trophy**[3], Drane lifted Thomas above his head and, with a mighty roar, hurled him against the side of the solid-rock compound. Ben dived at Drane to stop him, but too late, Ben suffered a sturdy blow to his cheek from Drane.

Thomas lay in the snow. Claire ran, skidding to a halt by the still black bundle. 'Thomas?' She dared not touch him. 'Thomas?' Despite the devastating blow, she still expected him to spring to his feet. 'Thomas?' She stroked him now, then prodded him. 'Thomas!' she screamed, her heart breaking.

'Claire, Claire, come,' said Ben. 'Come now.'

Ben knelt, scooping up Thomas's **limp**[4] body, cradling him in his arms. Claire turned towards a whimpering Cristy. Drane was holding her, trying to guide her as blood dripped from her eyes and face.

'I will GET YOU BOTH!' screamed Claire, her muscles taut, tensed to attack.

'CLAIRE, HERE, NOW!' Ben kicked her – his arms were full. 'Now!' he yelled, running towards the Tesla.

Claire! Felicity's voice cut through the mayhem. *Follow Ben. Go now.*

White with rage and despair, Claire ran to the Tesla. Ben was sitting in the front passenger seat. Thomas lay deathly still on his lap.

'Put this on!' said Ben. He held the Gwalch Gem bracelet in his hand. 'Cristy dropped it. When

---

1 **blood-curdling** *(adj)* expressing or causing terror. *(s)* frightening, chilling, fearsome. *(ant)* comforting.

2 **thrash** *(v)* flail or jerk about. *(s)* toss, writhe, wriggle, squirm, flounder.

3 **trophy** *(n)* an object given as a prize for a success or victory. *(s)* cup, medal, award.

4 **limp** *(adj)* lacking internal strength or structure, not stiff or firm. *(s)* bendy, droopy, floppy. *(ant)* stiff, rigid.

Tom attacked her, she dropped it.' Tears rolled down Ben's cheeks, and Claire's eyes **brimmed**[1] over. She looked at Ben, pleading for a sign that Thomas was alive. He shook his head. Claire let out a heart-wrenching sob.

Claire, said Felicity's voice, *get in, fasten your seat belt, and make Ben do the same. I will guide Daisy.*

Too **choked**[2] to speak, she got in, pulled on her seat belt and nodded at Ben to follow suit.

And leave those helmets on, said Felicity.

*

Siân Cadwaladr had escaped seconds before Dewi had stormed into her operations room. Only when in public did she think of or refer to him as David Lewis. Her source had warned her in the nick of time; she must now flee with only **essentials**[3]. No one, not even this most trusted **informant**[4], would find her. She must **take stock**[5], stealing the Gwalch Gem away with her. The stunning stone no longer glowed like earlier, its warmth having **dissipated**[6]. The newly found Welsh gold must now be distant. Where was the girl?

Suffering neither anger nor disappointment, Siân Cadwaladr held the trump card in her palm. She slipped the emerald hawk into a velvet pouch, then into her breast pocket, and picked up her slim, unbranded phone. That would be her one means of communication with her trusted ally; any others would prove too perilous. Dewi would not stop. She had underestimated his physical resolve; he was robust, more so than she had **bargained for**[7]. The poison had killed its earlier, **unwitting**[8] hosts.

It was a most out-of-character **trait**[9] for her, but Siân Cadwaladr had grossly **underrated**[10] the

---

1 **brim** *(v)* become full to the point of overflowing. *(s)* flood, spill.

2 **choked** *(adj)* emotional. *(s)* affected, touched, upset, distressed. *(ant)* unfeeling, cold.

3 **essential** *(n)* a necessary item. *(s)* necessity, basic, fundamental, must, requirement. *(ant)* non-essential.

4 **informant** *(n)* someone who gives information to another. *(s)* spy, informer, grass, sneak, snitch, mole.

5 **take stock** *(v)* make an assessment of a certain situation before deciding something. *(s)* review, assess, evaluate.

6 **dissipate** *(v)* disperse (discharge) or scatter. *(s)* disappear, evaporate, dissolve, vanish. *(ant)* grow, develop.

7 **bargain for** *(v)* expect or be ready for. *(s)* anticipate, predict, foresee, envisage.

8 **unwitting** *(adj)* not aware. *(s)* unknowing, unconscious, oblivious, ignorant. *(ant)* knowing, conscious.

9 **trait** *(n)* a quality or characteristic. *(s)* attribute, feature, property, quirk, foible, habit, custom.

10 **underrate** *(v)* underestimate (misjudge) something. *(s)* undervalue, miscalculate, devalue. *(ant)* overrate.

girl Claire. A forced **exile**[1] would afford Siân the opportunity to ponder that **blunder**[2] and allow her time to plot again. She headed towards her secret tunnel, then paused. The traitorous knight Evans remained in his cell. No matter – thanks to her separating the gem from the bracelet, that craven fool would soon die.

Siân Cadwaladr flicked her blonde waves over her shoulders, smoothed her suit jacket and marched towards the exit, her heels stabbing hard at the floor.

1 **exile** *(n)* deportation or banishment from a place. *(s)* eviction, expulsion, exclusion. *(ant)* inclusion.

2 **blunder** *(n)* a careless or foolish mistake. *(s)* oversight, fault, slip, error, lapse. *(ant)* accuracy, correctness.

24. Boards versus Bentley

The moment Claire had put the bracelet back on, her energy had **resurged**[1], but she sat hunched in the Tesla. Thomas lay lifeless on Ben's lap. Claire couldn't look at him.

Felicity's voice said, *Claire, we must leave now.*

Claire didn't care. Josh Drane had killed her beloved Thomas. Thomas had saved *her* life. It would devastate Gladys. It would devastate Jack. It devastated *her*.

The Tesla pulled away, autonomously gliding through the falling snow.

You won't hear me as I help guide Daisy to the castle, said Felicity, *but if I* ***address***[2] *you, Claire, please listen to me. Claire?* Felicity's voice was pleading.

Claire didn't answer. She was thinking.

The Tesla navigated the mountain road with the **expertise**[3] of a **snowmobile**[4].

Ben, oblivious to Felicity's existence, said, 'Claire, I know you're distraught – I am too – but who the heck is driving this car?'

Claire buried her face in her hands, not accepting that Thomas was dead.

Ben touched the display, switching on the heated seats and increasing the temperature. Both kids were shivering, soaked by the snow. He stared at the display as it depicted the Tesla tracking the road. Shaking his head in bewilderment, Ben frowned at the ghostly steering wheel as it turned automatically. The Tesla didn't slide at all; it stuck to the road like glue.

The temperature rose rapidly. Ben unbuckled his seat belt and removed his hoody. Replacing

---

1 **resurge** *(v)* come back. *(s)* return, resume, rebound, reappear. *(ant)* depart, leave.

2 **address** *(v)* speak to. *(s)* lecture, talk to, discuss with, make a speech to.

3 **expertise** *(n)* expert knowledge or skill. *(s)* ability, prowess, capability, proficiency. *(ant)* inability.

4 **snowmobile** *(n)* a vehicle for travelling over snow.

his restraint, he glanced at Claire. Ben lifted Thomas and placed his hoody beneath him. To cover Thomas, and shroud him from Claire's view, Ben **cocooned**[1] him in the hoody, laying him in his arms.

Ben glanced around the Tesla. Claire's wet skateboard dripped onto the back seat. 'Oh no,' he muttered. 'I left my best deck back there.'

'You'll get over it,' whispered Claire.

Ben looked at her, his expression **contrite**[2] for having uttered such a **shallow**[3] comment. 'Claire,' he whispered, 'you can't see Tommy. I've wrapped him up.'

Claire glanced at Ben's lap, then looked away. **Incensed**[4] at the sight of the **morbid**[5] parcel lying motionless, she thought of Jack. He would miss his pal – his constant **companion**[6]. If Gladys survived, she might never forgive Claire. How could Claire have let this **tragedy**[7] happen on her watch? Claire adored Thomas and Jack, and they were no ordinary cat and dog. Drane wouldn't get away with this.

She lifted her head and looked straight at Ben. 'Please, put Thomas in the back. Rest him in the footwell. He'll be safe there.'

Looking flabbergasted, Ben unclipped his belt again, gathered Thomas up and turned, scrabbling onto his knees to face the back. 'I can't reach the footwell,' he said, stretching over.

'Try harder,' said Claire, a chill in her voice.

At full stretch, Ben placed Thomas on the floor and tucked him into the footwell. He flopped back into his seat, buckled up and looked at Claire. She stared out of the windscreen at the falling snow as the wipers swooshed a hypnotic rhythm. The warmth from the bracelet radiated through her as the gold in her belly **sustained**[8] the bracelet's life. Thomas's sacrifice would save the Knights Hawk; she would not permit that to have been in vain. She would pursue Josh Drane until he wished he had never existed.

---

1 **cocoon** *(v)* envelop (wrap in) in a protective or comforting way. *(s)* surround, swathe, cosset. *(ant)* expose.

2 **contrite** *(adj)* expressing or feeling sorry for a wrongdoing. *(s)* remorseful, penitent, repentant. *(ant)* unrepentant, defiant.

3 **shallow** *(adj)* showing a lack of serious thought. *(s)* superficial, facile, simplistic, ignorant, foolish. *(ant)* deep, profound.

4 **incensed** *(adj)* incredibly angry. *(s)* enraged, infuriated, exasperated, riled, annoyed. *(ant)* placated, calm.

5 **morbid** *(adj)* gloomy and miserable. *(s)* depressing, solemn, wretched, forlorn. *(ant)* festive, cheerful.

6 **companion** *(n)* someone one spends time with. *(s)* friend, acquaintance, ally, buddy, chum. *(ant)* foe, enemy.

7 **tragedy** (n) a terrible event. *(s)* disaster, calamity, catastrophe, mishap, blow, misfortune. *(ant)* fortune, windfall.

8 **sustain** *(v)* provide nourishment or support. *(s)* maintain, preserve, nourish, nurture. *(ant)* sap, undermine.

Claire turned to Ben. He stared at her, wide-eyed. Claire's face was closed. 'Cristy, if that's even her name, is a Mal-Instinctive. Not just any baddy though, she's the Master's daughter. She has used your dad and us.'

Ben was silent.

'Once Dewi sees his daughter's now-not-so-pretty face and realises she **squandered**[1] his prize, the bracelet, he'll be on us. And believe me, when he's mad, he's not pretty either,' said Claire.

Ben looked nervous. 'Claire,' he said, his voice quiet, 'who is driving my dad's car right now?'

'Felicity,' replied Claire.

Ben's face screwed up.

'And your dad's car is called Daisy.'

'What? Have you gone nuts?'

Claire glared at him. His expression changed.

'It's complicated,' said Claire. 'Not now though – I'm thinking.'

Ben didn't argue.

Cristy, the imposter, had conned her. Sweet, **swindling**[2] Cristy, masquerading as **decent**[3], friendly and innocent. The blonde witch whose every action had concealed a threat and a lie. Claire's mind jumped to Jayne Lewis; her surname now rankled even more.

Claire. Felicity's voice popped into Claire's head.

Claire straightened, her body tensing. *Yes?* she replied in her head.

Ben noticed. He straightened too.

We detect a ***hostile***[4] *in pursuit. Transmitting to your screen now.* Felicity's voice possessed a note of urgency.

A red dot beeped, flashing and pulsating behind the Tesla's image on the display.

'What's that?' exclaimed Ben.

'The Master,' replied Claire. 'Shush!'

Claire looked out through the windscreen. The grey sky promised more snow.

How long before he's on us? Claire asked Felicity.

---

1 **squander** *(v)* waste an opportunity or money. *(s)* blow, lose, misuse, misspend, frivol, trifle. *(ant)* save, hoard.

2 **swindle** *(v)* cheat. *(s)* deceive, dupe, con, fool, trick. *(ant)* be honest.

3 **decent** *(adj)* conforming to respectable or moral behaviour. *(s)* honest, honourable, virtuous, upright. *(ant)* dishonest.

4 **hostile** *(n)* an enemy. *(s)* adversary, opponent, antagonist, foe, rival. *(ant)* friend, ally.

ETA, ten minutes, but the vehicle is gaining. It is better **adapted**[1] *for snow than Daisy*, warned Felicity.

Ludicrous Plus mode? asked Claire.

We believe it to be risky – the snow, said Felicity.

How risky? asked Claire.

There was a pause.

Felicity? prompted Claire.

Perilous, said Felicity.

Claire glanced at the rear-view mirror; visibility was dire.

How long before we reach Cadwaladr Castle? asked Claire.

At this speed, replied Felicity, *thirty minutes.*

Drive faster, said Claire.

It's too risky, reiterated Felicity.

If you don't speed this car up, I'll *drive it, and* that *will be very risky*, said Claire.

The Tesla shot forward.

Ben's hands gripped his seat, his face ashen. 'Claire?' he asked.

'Shush!' she snapped.

Ben shushed.

Suddenly the Tesla's rear slid sideways. Ben's head hit the window with a loud clonk, his helmet protecting his skull.

The Tesla **compensated**[2] but was travelling with such fast, precarious movements, their heads wobbled like **rally**[3] drivers' heads.

The red dot's proximity increased, its pulsating circumference growing as it neared the Tesla's icon on the screen.

Felicity, he's still gaining on us.

Claire glanced in the rear-view mirror. The faintest glow of headlights shone through the snow.

Felicity, Ludicrous Plus mode, said Claire, but Felicity didn't answer. *Felicity*, urged Claire.

---

1 **adapted** *(adj)* suited to a specific purpose or use. *(s)* modified, altered, adjusted, attuned. *(ant)* maladapted.

2 **compensate** *(v)* neutralise an effect. *(s)* rectify, balance, counteract, offset. *(ant)* exaggerate.

3 **rally** *(n)* a long race for motor vehicles using public roads or rough terrain, usually in several stages.

I cannot, and neither must you, said Felicity, her voice flat and **severe**[1].

Stealth mode? asked Claire.

Impossible, said Felicity.

Then speed up, said Claire.

The faster the car moved, the more they slid, their descent steepening with every twist and turn.

Ben stared at Claire.

The dot, in hot pursuit, still gained ground, albeit more slowly.

Claire spotted the headlights again.

Felicity, how far to the castle? said Claire.

Fifteen minutes. We will reach the tunnel entrance in five. We must arrive unseen, said Felicity. *If he sees the castle's secret tunnel, we are doomed.*

All downhill? asked Claire, glancing in the mirror. The headlights had gone. The snow had eased.

Yes, downhill, said Felicity.

How long before that dot hits us? asked Claire.

Five minutes, said Felicity.

'DAISY, STOP!' yelled Claire.

Ben screamed. The Tesla skidded, spinning a three-hundred-and-sixty-degree turn. It spun again and, with a hideous crunch of collapsing metal, jerked as its front collided with the mountain. Claire knew the Tesla could have skidded the other way and over the cliff's edge.

The airbags deployed.

'Ben!' Claire yelled. 'Get out now!'

She was already out of the car and on her feet in the snow. She ran around to Ben and dragged him out of the car. The crash had hurt neither of them.

'Daisy, open the boot,' cried Claire.

Ben looked dazed. Claire shook him.

'Get your snowboarding gear on now,' she ordered. 'And please tell me you have two of everything.'

---

1 **severe** *(adj)* harsh and stern. *(s)* strict, hard, austere, unsympathetic, cruel, ruthless, hard-hearted. *(ant)* mild.

Ben spluttered.

'JUST DO IT!' she yelled in his face.

She had grabbed gear from the boot and was rummaging through the leftovers. 'We've no time. Get it on,' she said.

'That stuff is my dad's.' Ben pointed at it.

'I'm fatter than you,' she said, throwing on Mr Brady's jacket and stepping into his snowboarding boots – they were huge. She pulled the **fastenings**[1] as tight as she could. Ben grabbed his helmet.

'You're already wearing one,' said Claire.

Ben threw it back.

'It can't be much different from skateboarding,' said Claire, hoping she was right.

'We'll need gloves,' said Ben.

'No time,' said Claire, 'and besides, I need to keep my thumb on this.' She showed Ben the compass.

'What's that?' he asked.

'Our satnav,' she replied.

Ben said nothing. He threw a board into the snow and then grabbed another, throwing that down for Claire.

'Stamp your foot into the front **binding**[2],' Ben said. 'Your left foot, like when you were skateboarding.'

She stamped her left foot hard on the board, engaging the binding.

'You're gonna punt like skateboarding. Then, when you're ready, stamp that back foot down, hard. Once your boots are in, they're in. This stuff's powder. Lean back, look down the mountain, and keep momentum. If you stop, you sink; you're stranded.'

'Got it,' said Claire. 'Now get Thomas – you're carrying him. You can snowboard; I can't,' she said, punting away from the Tesla, towards the cliff edge. No way was Claire leaving Thomas for the Master to find.

The compass's arrow shone but brighter than before. All she'd done was take it from her

---

1 **fastening** *(n)* a device used to close or secure something. *(s)* fastener, clasp, lock, catch, lace, binding. *(ant)* opener.

2 **binding** *(n)* a device fixed to a snowboard or ski to grip and hold a boot in place.

pocket; it just worked. *The gold*, she thought as the bracelet **thawed**[1] her wrist and the **nugget**[2] warmed her stomach. *If the gold helped me, then, just maybe, it could help Thomas*, thought Claire. Bringing Thomas was not an act of **sentimentality**[3]. If the gold saved her, and the knights could tangle time, then maybe there was a chance for Thomas.

Ben trudged through the snow, a bundle in his arms.

Claire didn't look.

Ben stamped one foot in his binding and punted his board over to her.

Claire clocked the throaty growl of the powerful car before it rounded the bend and came into view.

Teetering on the **brink**[4] of the steep, snow-covered drop was hairy. Claire held the compass and shimmied her board's nose to the edge.

Ben stood behind her, board on, ready to go.

The supercar's growl was nearing.

'Thanks, buddy,' Claire said to Ben, unable to look at the bundle beneath his arm.

With that, she held the compass up before her face and edged forward until a third of the board stuck out over the drop. She pictured Gwilym, and Thomas's yellow-green eyes, leaned forward until her weight tipped her board over into the snow, and with a slight lurch, she was off.

Ben waited until she was at a safe distance, then ollied over the edge and followed her.

*

David Lewis jumped out of his Bentley and peered inside the Tesla. It was empty. He kicked it, hard. He would catch the young fools. They were on foot, wearing inadequate clothing. He'd survived the deadliest of poisons; a little snow wouldn't **hinder**[5] him.

He saw the airbags and cackled a hubristic crow. To catch them would be easy. Did they not realise snow left tracks? He might let them run, enjoy the **illusion**[6] of escaping, before he swooped on them. Or maybe he would leave them longer, until they froze to death. Either way,

---

1 **thaw** *(v)* warm enough to soften or melt. *(s)* unfreeze, defrost, liquefy. *(ant)* freeze, harden, solidify.

2 **nugget** *(n)* a small chunk of precious metal found in the earth. *(s)* lump, hunk, clump.

3 **sentimentality** *(n)* feelings of pity or love, especially for past things. *(s)* mawkishness, nostalgia.

4 **brink** *(n)* the edge of something. *(s)* verge, margin, rim, lip.

5 **hinder** *(v)* make difficult, hamper, obstruct or slow down. *(s)* delay, inhibit, thwart, impede. *(ant)* help.

6 **illusion** *(n)* a deceptive image or false idea. *(s)* delusion, deception, misconception, fantasy. *(ant)* fact, reality.

the **clod**[1] of a girl had the bracelet, and it would soon be his.

Curious[2], he moved to the car's open trunk. He froze. Then, like a wounded wolf, he let out an **almighty**[3] blood-curdling howl. Two pairs of trainers, helmets, gloves and various snowboarding **paraphernalia**[4] lay scattered – discarded. Now as Dewi, he **cursed**[5] and swore, snatching the gear and hurling it into the snow.

He slammed the boot shut, thumping it hard.

There was no chance he would catch them on snowboards. A straight line down the rock face would beat his Bentley via the mountain pass. He had no skiing gear. To follow on foot, futile. He hollered, walked over to his Bentley and kicked it hard, making a **considerable**[6] dent. The only way to that castle was by air.

---

1 **clod** *(n)* a stupid person. *(s)* idiot, fool, halfwit, blockhead, buffoon, imbecile, dunce, dope. *(ant)* genius.

2 **curious** *(adj)* eager to learn or know something. *(s)* inquisitive, snooping, prying. *(ant)* apathetic, indifferent.

3 **almighty** *(adj)* great or enormous. *(s)* massive, supreme, mighty. *(ant)* weak, insignificant, feeble.

4 **paraphernalia** *(n)* assorted articles, typically required for an activity. *(s)* kit, gear, apparatus, equipment.

5 **curse** *(v)* use offensive (crude) words. *(s)* swear, cuss, damn, blaspheme.

6 **considerable** *(adj)* large in size, extent or amount. *(s)* big, substantial, great, sizable, extensive. *(ant)* little, insignificant.

25. A Dicey Crossing

Claire could snowboard well. Was it because of swallowing the gold, or the bracelet around her wrist helping her? She didn't care. Claire flew down the snow-covered mountain on Mr Brady's snowboard; it was easier than skateboarding. With both feet fixed to this plank, she must just stay upright, avoiding rocks and trees. Claire glanced behind. Ben followed at a safe distance, making it look even easier. Had she seen him jump something just then?

Holding the compass in front helped Claire's balance. Her other arm stuck out behind her back, acting as a rudder steering the board. A merciful decrease in the falling snow meant good navigation without goggles, but visibility was fading along with the daylight. *The castle can't be far now.* The compass's satnav had no ETA, but they were boarding in a straightish line.

Keep going, Claire. She remembered Ben's words. If she stopped, she'd sink. This was deep powder snow. Claire leaned back on the board, lifting its nose a safe distance out of the snow, so as not to dig in and stop. She floated on the surface, shifting her weight from side to side, edging the board to control its speed. She loved it. She soon **sobered**[1] though, remembering the bundle tucked under Ben's arm. Determined not to lose a second, Claire picked up pace, following the arrow in front of her nose.

In the distance, Claire spotted a twinkling red light, the kind used on the top of high structures to warn low-flying aircraft to keep clear. It was the castle; there would be aircraft flying in there all the time. Claire turned to Ben and shouted, 'I see it. We're almost there.'

Ben **saluted**[2] in acknowledgement.

---

1 **sober** *(v)* become or make more serious or glum. *(s)* subdue, calm down, steady. *(ant)* enliven, arouse.

2 **salute** *(v)* raise the hand to the head formally in recognition. *(s)* acknowledge, greet, wave. *(ant)* shun.

Claire dodged trees and rocks, boarding in as straight a line as possible until the red light grew bigger and brighter. Then she saw the castle.

Hogwarts, she thought, *but less pointy*.

The snow beneath the board seemed to change. It was harder, more **compacted**[1]. To **accommodate**[2] the terrain in natural moves, Claire shifted her stance as needed. The trees grew denser than before.

'Claire,' Ben shouted. 'Stop here. You won't sink. The snow's older and harder.'

Claire swooshed the back of the board around to a stop, a spray of snow flying off in its wake. Ben did the same but showered Claire with snow. He grinned. Then his face fell. He'd noticed Claire's eyes fixed on the bundle beneath his arm.

'I'm so sorry,' said Ben.

'Me too,' said Claire, turning towards the castle. 'Can you lead us down there?'

'Sure.' He nodded.

'This snow's trickier. I nearly flipped out just then,' said Claire. 'You'll pick a better route. You read the snow better than me.'

'You seem to do a pretty good job.' Ben smiled.

'We don't need the compass now we can see the castle.' Claire put it in her back pocket.

Ben surveyed the run down to the castle. 'I see an easyish route,' he said, 'but it's still a black run.'

'Black?' Claire's brows met in a question.

'Don't worry,' said Ben. 'What you rode down just now took me years to **accomplish**[3].'

Claire shrugged. She noticed Ben tuck Thomas's body further under his arm. He flipped his board around, popped an ollie and headed off. 'I'll keep it steady,' he shouted.

The compacted snow challenged Claire. It was **arduous**[4], more strenuous. With constant twitches, the edge of the board threatened to catch in the snow, determined to flip her over.

'You're not getting the better of me,' she said, bending her knees harder to regain control. Her thighs burned. Now the compass was back in her pocket, Claire concentrated on looking ahead.

---

1 **compacted** *(adj)* packed or pressed together firmly. *(s)* compressed, solidified, dense. *(ant)* loosened.

2 **accommodate** *(v)* allow for. *(s)* factor in, consider, provide for. *(ant)* disregard.

3 **accomplish** *(v)* complete or achieve. *(s)* succeed in, realise, execute, manage, attain. *(ant)* fail.

4 **arduous** *(adj)* difficult and tiring. *(s)* strenuous, onerous, taxing, laborious, gruelling, toilsome. *(ant)* easy.

From this distance, the castle was grey, austere and uninviting.

Well camouflaged in this snow, thought Claire, and she wondered how trees grew up here, but then, these were the Knights Hawk.

Ben's 'steady' was fast. He read the terrain like a pro, dodging and weaving, avoiding gullies and rocks, all the while holding Thomas. At least he'd had the common sense not to jump anything again. Despite her **prowess**[1], she wasn't up to that yet.

Claire traced Ben's line, driving her knees into the snow on toe turns, and then her backside on heel turns. She nailed it; she'd never worked so hard in her life. Regardless of the gold's power issuing from inside her, it felt good.

The castle loomed; they'd arrive in minutes. Ben slowed as the terrain levelled, then dropped again. His board caught some **unintended**[2] air. **Airborne**[3] for seconds, Ben landed with ease. Claire followed. As the board hit the **lip**[4], her knees bent, the front left the ground, and she flew, her arms floating outwards for balance. When the board hit the ground again, her knees softened into **shock absorbers**[5] – a perfect landing.

As she straightened up and followed Ben, she couldn't contain the loud 'Woo-hoo!' that escaped her mouth.

Ben slowed his board to a stop. Patches of brown rock showed through the **slush**[6] on the ground. Claire's board scraped over the bare rock; she braked hard.

'We're gonna have to climb down from here,' said Ben. 'It doesn't look too bad. I've clambered down worse in the snow.'

'OK,' said Claire, releasing her feet from the bindings. 'Let's leave the boards here. We can get them later.'

Ben looked as if he was about to **contest**[7] this, but Claire threw him a 'Don't argue with me' look. Ben removed his board and, with one hand, lifted it out of the snow. His gear cost a

---

1 **prowess** *(n)* remarkable ability in a specific activity or area. *(s)* talent, skill, aptitude, mastery, expertise. *(ant)* ineptitude.

2 **unintended** *(adj)* not deliberate or planned. *(s)* unintentional, unplanned, unforeseen. *(ant)* planned, intentional.

3 **airborne** *(adj)* in the air. *(s)* gliding, flying, soaring, aerial, floating. *(ant)* grounded.

4 **lip** *(n)* the edge of something. *(s)* brim, rim, verge, brink.

5 **shock absorber** *(n)* a device for absorbing vibrations and jolts, often found on vehicles. *(s)* cushion, suspension system.

6 **slush** *(n)* partly melted ice or snow. *(s)* mush, sludge.

7 **contest** *(v)* disagree with something. *(s)* challenge, dispute, oppose, question. *(ant)* agree.

fortune[1], but that didn't matter now. She'd deal with that later if needs be.

'Keep the helmet on,' said Claire. 'Might come in handy.'

Ben leaned his board against a substantial tree trunk and repositioned Thomas under his arm. Claire inhaled the crisp mountain air and propped her board against the same tree. Her body was cooling quickly. Even with wearing Mr Brady's snowboarding jacket, it was freezing out here. Claire brushed the snow from her palms and pulled the jacket's cuff lower over the glowing bracelet. 'Let's go,' she said, leading.

Close up, the castle was magnificent and surrounded by a towering wall. Curtain walls – Claire had learned that at school. Four round towers topped with **battlements**[2] provided the **cornerstones**[3]; smaller towers marked the centre of each curtain wall. **Ramparts**[4] didn't protect this castle; it sat nestled in a valley, its **sentinels**[5], mountains. Claire marvelled. How could roads access this? She remembered Felicity's words, *secret tunnel*. No roads existed; this castle was accessible via a rock face, tunnel or air.

Claire and Ben slid down the mountain, bouncing off their bottoms. Claire had moved the compass from her jeans to the jacket. Ben's job was gruelling, having only one hand with which to steady himself. Neither spoke.

Panting and sweating, relief written on their faces, they finally reached the bottom. A wide **moat**[6] surrounded the castle.

'What now?' said Ben. 'I'm not swimming across that.'

'It's frozen in parts,' said Claire, wondering if the moat would hold her hefty weight. The ice looked precarious, too thin. 'Let's walk around,' she said, heading off to the right. 'It might be more accessible this way.'

Ben followed. The ground was a treacherous mixture of snow, ice-covered rock and loose stones. Claire's feet sloshed around in Mr Brady's oversized boots; she slipped often. The light

---

1 **fortune** *(n)* a large amount of money or assets (things of value). *(s)* packet, bundle, bomb. *(ant)* pittance.

2 **battlement** *(n)* a low wall at the top of a fort or castle, with evenly spaced openings for shooting through. *(s)* bulwark.

3 **cornerstone** *(n)* a stone forming the corner of a building.

4 **rampart** *(n)* a defensive wall or embankment topped by a parapet. *(s)* earthwork, battlement, bulwark.

5 **sentinel** *(n)* a guard or soldier who keeps watch. *(s)* sentry, lookout, watchperson, protector.

6 **moat** *(n)* a defensive, water-filled trench surrounding a castle or town.

was fading fast, and none **emanated**[1] from the castle. On a high **spire**[2], marking the tower's **summit**[3], a lone flag fluttered. *Gwilym*, thought Claire, *beneath that flag.*

'See that tower,' she said, pointing, 'the one with the flag. We're heading there.' It was the furthest away. They trudged on.

'Do you have any idea what you're doing?' asked Ben.

'Not really,' she replied. 'Just following my Instinct.'

Ben nodded.

Claire breathed onto her hands, wrapping one around the warm bracelet.

'Mine are freezing too,' said Ben, breathing on his.

'Hold on to this for a few seconds.' Claire pulled back her cuff to reveal the bracelet.

Ben hesitated.

'It's keeping me *more than* going,' said Claire. 'It won't bite.'

Ben placed his right hand around Claire's wrist, enveloping the glowing gold in his palm. His face melted into a smile.

'I can feel that!' Ben exclaimed, looking at Claire, who smiled back. 'It's like drinking hot chocolate,' he laughed.

'Exactly,' said Claire. 'Finish your mug and let's get moving. You can have another later.'

She pulled her cuff down and glanced at Thomas, the *Keep going* mantra chanting in her head.

Claire studied the moat. If needs be, she would swim across and leave Ben, but she didn't plan on getting Thomas wet.

They scrabbled around to the far side of the castle. Claire wasn't tired, but Ben complained.

The tower flying the flag, unbeknown to them, faced north. The moat looked frozen. They glanced at each other with grim faces.

'I'll go first,' said Claire. 'If it cracks and I sink, grab a rock and smash the ice. I'll struggle back.'

'Ice can be lethal. I don't like the look of it,' said Ben, shaking his head.

'Me neither,' said Claire.

Ben watched as Claire got to her knees, removed the compass from the jacket and put it into

---

1 **emanate** *(v)* come or spread out from. *(s)* arise, derive, issue, emerge, rise, proceed. *(ant)* absorb, withdraw.

2 **spire** *(n)* a conical or pyramidal tower. *(s)* steeple, belfry.

3 **summit** *(n)* the highest point. *(s)* peak, top, apex, brow. *(ant)* bottom, base.

her back pocket. Face down, she lay on the ground in a starfish shape, rendering herself flat and wide. Claire wriggled out onto the ice, limbs splayed, her chin and hands burning with cold. Damp **seeped**[1] through her jeans. At least the jacket was **waterproof**[2]. Her toes touched the front of Mr Brady's boots, leaving a two-inch gap at both heels.

With subtle and slow movements, holding her breath lest it melt the ice, Claire manoeuvred across the moat, expecting to hear an ominous crack at any moment.

'You're halfway,' encouraged Ben.

'I know,' said Claire, her eyes on the bank opposite. She prayed the jacket would **stave off**[3] the warmth from her body. Her body heat would **expedite**[4] the melting of the ice beneath her. Claire wished she'd grabbed gloves from Daisy's boot. Her fingertips touched the bank, but she couldn't feel it. She grasped against the rock, snapping her nails, but they didn't hurt. As Claire slid closer, she maintained an even weight spread and heaved herself further, her arm muscles burning. The skin beneath her chin was **grazed**[5] as it scraped along a jutting rock. She didn't feel that either, but her blood stained the snow. Finally Claire hauled herself up and onto the bank; she'd made it. She flipped over, looked up at the dusky sky and breathed again.

Claire sat and peered across at Ben. He didn't look happy. It was his turn.

'Be sure to wrap Thomas well in that hoody,' called Claire. 'One push, Ben. Thomas needs to reach me in one push. If he doesn't, you're gonna have to rescue him,' she said.

Ben placed the bundle onto the ground and tightened up the arms of his hoody, which held the package together. Claire watched, gutted. Ben was accurate; he'd slide Thomas across the moat. She waited, letting Ben take his time.

That was when Claire heard the helicopter.

---

1 **seep** *(v)* slowly leak through porous (absorbent) material or small holes. *(s)* ooze, bleed, trickle, permeate. *(ant)* pour.

2 **waterproof** *(adj)* not allowing water through. *(s)* impervious, impermeable, watertight, weatherproof. *(ant)* leaky, porous.

3 **stave off** *(v)* delay or prevent something. *(s)* stop, avert, inhibit, hinder, thwart. *(ant)* embrace, encourage.

4 **expedite** *(v)* make something happen more quickly. *(s)* hurry, accelerate, quicken, hasten. *(ant)* hinder, delay.

5 **graze** *(v)* scrape. *(s)* abrade, scratch, chafe, scuff.

*

His guard down, Dewi had dropped the David Lewis **persona**[1] before **rampaging**[2] through Via-Corp's walkways. His private lift had stopped at his helipad. He would fly his prized machine himself. He was Dewi; he needed no co-pilot. He would handle the aircraft alone – from the gunner's position at the front.

---

1 **persona** *(n)* a personality portrayed to others. *(s)* character, face, facade, image, guise.

2 **rampage** *(v)* rush wildly. *(s)* storm, charge, tear, steam, riot. *(ant)* saunter.

26. The Monster from Above

It didn't sound like a normal helicopter.

Ben gaped across the moat at Claire; he'd heard it too.

'Ben, hurry. Send Thomas across in the most **dignified**[1] way possible, but he must reach me.'

If Ben didn't make it across, so be it – he could hide – but Claire wanted Thomas. There was no way she was letting him rot out here without trying to do something for him.

Ben glanced across the moat again, then in one deft movement, as if curling, slid Thomas out across the ice. Thomas's little body skated across, gently slowing as it reached Claire's waiting hands. Forcing back a choke, Claire scooped Thomas up. He was wet and stiff, but she made sure his shroud didn't **unravel**[2], and tucked Thomas under her arm.

'Come on, Ben,' she shouted. The helicopter was nearing. It didn't sound like the Sea King Claire had flown in yesterday.

Ben hesitated, then dropped to the floor, copying Claire's earlier movements.

'Scooch a tad to the right,' Claire advised. 'The ice might be stronger where I didn't cross.'

Ben moved to the right, then gently launched himself onto the ice. He pushed away with his feet, and like a newly hatched turtle making its urgent dash to the sea, he wriggled across the moat.

Claire watched, her eyes urging Ben onwards. The *whomp-whomp-whomp-whomp* sound of approaching **rotor**[3] blades chopped through the silence. It sounded more like a machine gun than a helicopter.

---

1 **dignified** *(adj)* having a serious, respectful manner. *(s)* gracious, formal, noble, proper. *(ant)* undignified.

2 **unravel** *(v)* fall apart or unwind. *(s)* collapse, crumble, break down, fail. *(ant)* interlace, entwine.

3 **rotor** *(n)* a rotary part of a machine (part that turns). *(s)* blade, propeller, turbine. *(ant)* stator.

Suddenly a sickening sound **superseded**[1] that of the helicopter. Claire and Ben froze. A **zigzag**[2] appeared behind Ben, weaving back to the bank. Neither spoke.

Claire scanned the crack; it ran only behind Ben. 'Keep going,' she shouted, looking at the sky, not yet seeing the **chopper**[3].

Ben slid along, reaching the bank. Claire grabbed his hand, revealing the glowing bracelet around her wrist. With one almighty yank, she pulled Ben onto the bank and off the ice, just as it shattered, breaking into floating **fragments**[4] on the surface of the water.

'Thanks,' said Ben, shaking. 'That was close.'

'Quick!' said Claire, dragging Ben behind a lonely shrub by the castle wall. Claire had seen the nose of the Apache enter the valley.

Fond of documentaries, Claire recognised the laser-guided Hellfire missiles and deadly rockets that hung from the **pylons**[5] beneath each wing. The United States Army had dubbed the Apache 'the Monster' because just the sight of it silenced enemy guns. Claire pulled Ben out of view.

'If the Master wants us out of the way, we're **goners**[6],' she said as the metal killing machine swooped past. 'That thing can see us,' she added. 'Dewi needs me around for a reason.'

Ben stared at her. 'I know it's not the right time,' he said, 'but that thing is awesome.'

'American,' Claire said. 'We gotta run. He'll be back, and I don't want to see him.'

'How do we get into this place?' asked Ben.

'Satnav,' said Claire, holding the bright compass in her right hand. Claire still held Thomas; she wasn't about to let go.

The helicopter sounded distant but was approaching again.

'We've got to get in before he comes back. If Dewi sees us enter, he'll land that thing and follow us,' said Claire. 'Apaches fly fast. We don't have long.'

Claire and Ben followed the satnav's arrow.

'That can't be right,' said Ben.

---

1 **supersede** *(v)* take the place of. *(s)* replace, overthrow, supplant, overtake. *(ant)* submit to.

2 **zigzag** *(n)* course with alternate right and left turns. *(s)* wiggle, squiggle. *(ant)* straight.

3 **chopper** *(n)* an informal name for a helicopter.

4 **fragment** *(n)* a part broken or detached from a whole. *(s)* piece, scrap, portion, bit, sliver, chip. *(ant)* whole.

5 **pylon** *(n)* a structure attached to an aircraft to support something, such as an engine, weapon or fuel tank.

6 **goner** *(n)* someone or something that cannot be saved.

They were facing part of the castle's curtain wall, close to the round tower. The arrow refused to move. Claire wiggled her hand, but the arrow's **orientation**[1] didn't change.

'We're missing something,' said Claire, 'like when we escaped from your padded cell.' Claire realised what she'd said, and that Thomas couldn't help them now. 'Look closer,' she said. 'I can't – my hands are full.'

Ben ran his palms along the wall, stretching on tiptoe and bending low. Claire scoured every inch closely.

Whomp-whomp-whomp-whomp ... The Apache was swooping for a second pass through the valley. Should they hide again? It was futile, but Claire didn't want that fiend Dewi to **eyeball**[2] her.

'Quick, back behind the bush,' Claire snapped to Ben.

The Apache's nose, angled menacingly downwards, entered the valley, its guns **trained**[3] on Claire and Ben. As its nose dipped further, like a hungry black shark, the petrified friends gulped in unison.

Suddenly, from nowhere, a fleeting shadow darted across the ground beneath them, followed by an ear-splitting boom.

The Tornado screamed through the centre of the valley, heading straight for the Apache. Claire's and Ben's insides vibrated. Both aircraft flew at each other head-on.

'They're gonna crash!' yelled Claire.

With barely one second to spare, the Tornado's nose lifted, its lowered **landing gear**[4] skimming and obliterating the Apache's radar, which protruded quite incongruously, like a hat, from its roof.

'Yes!' the kids shouted, fist-pumping and jumping to their feet.

The Tornado was gone. The Apache flew by, minus its radar.

'He'll be back,' said Claire. 'We've got to find that entrance.'

With the valley now on the brink of darkness, they ran to the wall, but the compass pointed to the same place.

---

1 **orientation** *(n)* direction or position in relation to something. *(s)* placement, bearing. *(ant)* disorientation.

2 **eyeball** *(v)* look at closely. *(s)* see, regard, eye, observe, view. *(ant)* ignore, disregard.

3 **train** *(v)* aim or point at something. *(s)* direct, level, position, focus, sight.

4 **landing gear** *(n)* the wheels and supporting structure for the wheels on an aircraft.

With **tender**[1] care, Claire placed Thomas's body on the ground and put the compass into her pocket. She knew the entrance existed; they just had to find it.

'You move right, and I'll move left,' Claire instructed. 'Press every stone, and stick your finger in every crack. The opening is here; we just can't see it.'

In almost darkness, Claire and Ben moved outwards, leaving Thomas's body on the ground. The temperature was plummeting. Their hands were numb, but they carried on.

After several minutes, Ben called over, 'I can't find anything. I'm getting scared.'

Loath to admit it, Claire was too. 'Let's work our way back and **regroup**[2]. I'll try the compass again once I have Thomas.'

They both inched back to where they'd started, meticulously checking the wall for clues. Claire worried. It was cold and wet, and although she could cope, she wasn't sure Ben could. She wasn't hungry or thirsty, but he must be. She stopped. 'Wait a second.'

'What is it?' he asked.

'I dunno. A rabbit or something?' Claire cocked her head to one side. 'Stay still for a sec.'

It was dark now. Claire took the compass from her pocket.

There it is again, she thought as the compass glowed, affording her a glimmer of light.

Claire heard an animal's whimper, one that sounded pained. As quickly as she could in the poor light, Claire moved towards Thomas. Something stood over Thomas's body, sniffing it. Falling to her knees, Claire burst into tears.

Ben came flying over to her. 'What is it? What's wrong?' he yelled, wrapping his arms around Claire.

No words came. Claire just gulped in air and pointed towards Thomas. Tears flooded her cheeks.

Ben stared but said nothing. He turned back to Claire, his face looking broken.

Next to Thomas stood a little black, tan and white bundle, its nose prodding Ben's hoody. Jack's tail hid between his legs, and he whined over his dead friend.

Claire shook, **racked**[3] with guilt, pain and anguish.

Ben stepped in, leaving Claire to weep, but gently took the compass and turned towards Jack.

---

1 **tender** *(adj)* showing kindness and affection. *(s)* kindly, caring, compassionate, gentle. *(ant)* callous.

2 **regroup** *(v)* reassemble, especially after a defeat. *(s)* rally, reconvene, reunite. *(ant)* disperse.

3 **rack** *(v)* cause extreme anguish or pain. *(s)* beset, agonise, torment, torture, harrow, crucify. *(ant)* comfort, relieve.

A tear ran down Ben's face. It was the saddest thing he'd ever seen. Today was the strangest day of his life – a **whirlwind**[1], a **tempest**[2]. His best friend was magic and had transformed into an athlete overnight; he'd been held prisoner; and his dad's car was called Daisy. It was also such a tragic day.

'Jacky Boy,' Ben whispered, bending to stroke the Jack Russell. Jack always greeted Ben with a whirring tail and sloppy, wet kisses, but this time, he didn't even look at Ben. Ben's heart broke.

Jack pawed at Ben's hoody, sniffing it and whimpering. Ben knelt beside Jack and sobbed too.

'I'm so sorry, Jacky,' he muttered. 'I'm so sorry.'

Jack continued to prod the hoody with his nose.

Claire dropped down next to Ben. She wanted to swoop Jack up into her arms, **console**[3] him, but for once, Claire wasn't sure how to handle Jack. She looked at Ben. 'Unwrap him.'

Horrified, Ben glared at Claire.

'Unwrap Thomas, please, Ben. Jack knows; he just needs to see him. I'm sorry, but I can't do it. Please, Ben,' she pleaded.

Ben hesitated, his hand hovering above the hoody. Jack whimpered, pawing the bundle.

'Come here, Jacky Boy,' said Claire, gently moving Jack out of Ben's way. Jack **resisted**[4], but she held him back. 'One minute, lad.'

Ben unwrapped Thomas's body. Claire let out a massive sob and released Jack.

Jack approached his friend, hanging back at first, his nose twitching. Then Jack stepped closer and sniffed Thomas, seeming confused. He pawed Thomas and let out the tiniest of whines. Ben looked at Claire.

'Leave him for a minute,' she said.

Claire and Ben sat huddled, arms **entwined**[5], in silence as they waited for Jack to come to terms with his loss.

Jack sat beside Thomas. He didn't paw, sniff or whine. He just gazed at his friend. Claire and Ben waited. When he was ready, Jack turned away from Thomas and shuffled over to Claire and

---

1 **whirlwind** *(n)* a chaotic rush. *(s)* bedlam, mayhem, pandemonium. *(ant)* tranquillity.

2 **tempest** *(n)* an uproar. *(s)* turmoil, tumult, disorder, commotion. *(ant)* tranquillity.

3 **console** *(v)* give comfort and reduce grief. *(s)* soothe, assuage, relieve, cheer. *(ant)* upset, distress.

4 **resist** *(v)* withstand, combat or counter an action or effect. *(s)* refuse, defy, refrain from. *(ant)* succumb to.

5 **entwine** *(v)* twist, wind or weave together. *(s)* intertwine, interlace, interweave, interlink. *(ant)* unravel.

Ben, his tail tucked away, his body small.

'Jacky,' said Claire, pulling him closer. Claire didn't smother Jack; she just wanted him to know she was there. 'Ben,' she said, nodding towards Thomas.

Ben passed the compass back to Claire, got up and gently rewrapped Thomas in the hoody. 'What now?' he asked, cradling Thomas in his arms.

'We go back to the wall and find that entrance. I know it's there somewhere,' said Claire.

Jack wriggled away from Claire. Starting from his head, he shook his little body down to his tail, spraying Claire and Ben with a fine mist of water and grit. He finished with a shudder, then turned a small circle, accompanied by a light bark. Claire looked at Ben.

'Jack,' she said, 'what is it, boy?'

Jack yapped, spinning in circles and chasing his tail. Claire vaulted to her feet. Ben followed suit.

'What is it? Show us, boy,' Claire urged, shining the compass down on him.

Jack trotted ahead, stopped, then looked back at them.

'Follow him,' said Claire.

*

Gwilym Cadwaladr sensed the gold was close.

Jack was gone. He would not leave his master without good reason.

Gwilym's agony had eased, and from time to time, he thought he heard Claire, but Gwilym knew the Knights Hawk were not yet safe. Claire was not in the castle – he would hear her.

Unless the replenished gold bracelet found a way to Gwilym Cadwaladr's wrist soon, the Knights Hawk would die.

27. Cadwaladr Castle

Claire and Ben followed Jack over to the wall.

'It's the same place as before,' Ben said.

'Give him a chance,' said Claire, shining the compass on Jack.

Jack **snuffled**[1] along the wall, his tail a little lifted, but it didn't wag.

He ran back and forth, sniffing and grunting, his busy little legs trotting up and down. Then he stopped, inhaled with a considerable snort, exhaled with a woof and pawed at a spot on the wall. Claire bent and shone the compass at it. Nothing visible jumped out at her. She gently moved Jack to one side and inspected it closer.

'I'm such an idiot!' she shrieked.

Confounded, Ben stared.

'The compass!' she cried. 'The pointer!'

Ben shook his head perplexedly.

'Jack, clever lad,' she said, bending to pat him.

Claire held the compass and pressed her right thumb into its centre. Although nothing happened, she got the drill now. She pushed it harder. Suddenly the single beam of green light shot through her fingers, projecting an emerald dot onto the wall.

'Bingo!' she said.

She prodded the dot, and her fingertip glowed green. As the hole manifested, Ben stared again, mouth open. He hadn't seen this before – he'd been on the other side of his padded cell's wall, meditating.

---

1 **snuffle** *(v)* make repeated sniffing and breathing sounds as though smelling at something. *(s)* snort, pant, inhale.

'Mad, isn't it?' said Claire.

'Mind-boggling,' he muttered as the hole's circumference grew. Claire put the compass into her back pocket. Her jeans were damp and so tight now, it was safe there.

'I'll go through first,' she said, peering through the **extending**[1] hole into a dimly lit **courtyard**[2], 'after Jack, that is.'

Claire scooped up Jack and plopped him through the hole. He landed on the other side, sat and stared up at her, but his tail still didn't wag.

'I'll go now,' she said to Ben. 'Then you pass Thomas through to me and follow him. Beware, the landing isn't soft,' she said, glancing at the stone floor on the other side. 'I'll help you though.'

Once the bottom of the hole reached her waist, she pushed her torso through, see-sawing and balancing on her hips. She brought her heels up and tipped forward. Her hands reached the floor, and she slithered through to the other side. She was getting better at this. She jumped to her feet.

'Pass Thomas to me,' she said to Ben.

Ben passed him through the hole. Claire placed Thomas on the floor by Jack. Jack's nose twitched towards the hoody and lingered for a second. Then he sat upright again, watching Claire.

'Your turn,' Claire said. 'Aim to get your hips onto the wall. It'll hurt. Then pivot your hands onto the floor. I'll stop you from shooting through it.'

Ben was fit and agile, and before Claire could help, he was through the hole and on his feet beside her.

'Where next?' he asked, a little grin creeping onto his face.

'Jack,' said Claire as she picked up Thomas, 'where to, buddy?' Jack barked a **livelier**[3] woof and turned away, his tail held slightly higher. Ben walked straight after him, and Claire went to follow, but something caught her eye. She turned towards the hole.

As if in reverse, bit by bit, centimetre by centimetre, the hole's circumference shrank from the outside in, until no trace of it existed. Dewi would never find this entrance. Claire smiled and turned to follow Ben and Jack. They both waited. After he saw the hole close, Ben's chin

---

1 **extend** *(v)* expand. *(s)* enlarge, widen, stretch, broaden. *(ant)* reduce, shrink.

2 **courtyard** *(n)* an area completely or partly surrounded by walls but with no roof.

3 **lively** *(adj)* energetic. *(s)* animated, bright, cheerful, buoyant, peppy, spirited. *(ant)* apathetic, depressed.

comically[1] almost rested against his neck. He marvelled at the now-complete wall.

'Catching flies?' asked Claire. 'Come on.' She touched the bracelet on her wrist.

They stood inside a courtyard surrounded by interior walls. Ahead of them loomed the tower. Its only light came from a single flame that burned in a rock bowl in the courtyard's centre. The dish was enormous. Its flame seemed too small, lost in comparison, but it emitted enough light for them to see Jack's wiry white coat.

Jack stopped at a massive oak-and-iron door that curved around the tower's round base. In one leap, Jack sprang, depressed the handle, and the door clicked open.

'How did he do that?' Ben was agog. 'That thing must weigh a ton.'

'He's special,' said Claire, remembering how special Thomas had been.

Once inside, they faced a stone spiral staircase. It was lit by burning torches, equally spaced and fixed to the walls.

'I never believed those things existed,' said Ben. 'I thought they were just for the movies.'

'Watch your hair near those flames,' said Claire as they followed Jack.

Ben's hand shot to his head, only to touch his helmet. Claire smiled at her **prank**[2], feeling easier. She glanced behind, but no one followed. Fortified by the bracelet's power and warmth, and the gold in her stomach, she held Thomas tighter.

'Cor!' said Ben. 'I thought I was fit, but these stairs are steep.'

'Yes,' said Claire, not at all tired. She moved like an athlete, strengthening with each gruelling step. Her goal was nearing; Claire had sensed Gwilym's presence from the moment she'd entered the castle.

She looked upwards. Jack's claws click-clacked on the stone steps, his white tail waving as he ascended, but it didn't wag. Claire looked at the bundle beneath her arm, took a deep breath and continued.

At the top of the stairs, Jack waited on a wood-panelled landing. The ceiling towered above him. Once Claire and Ben arrived, Jack trotted off to the other end and stopped at an **imposing**[3] oak-and-iron door. As Claire approached, she realised two doors met in the middle. A heavy

---

1 **comically** *(adv)* in a funny or amusing way. *(s)* hilariously, entertainingly. *(ant)* seriously, solemnly.

2 **prank** *(n)* mischievous act or practical joke. *(s)* trick, stunt, caper, jape, lark, hoax, antic.

3 **imposing** *(adj)* impressive, striking and grand in appearance. *(s)* commanding, monumental. *(ant)* modest.

latch[1] lay in place, holding the doors together.

'I'll get this, Jack,' said Claire.

With two hands, Claire heaved it up and open, and pulled both doors towards her.

Claire and Ben stared, agog.

They stood at the entrance to what was clearly the great hall. The polished floor shone a **vibrant**[2], rich oak, as did the lower walls. Above the wood **panelling**[3], **interspersed**[4] between long, arched picture windows, hung vast, intricately woven **tapestries**[5]. Claire and Ben followed Jack, who trotted in as if he owned the place. Two enormous **chandeliers**[6] holding hundreds of burning candles hung from the exposed beams.

'I wonder who keeps those lit,' said Ben, gawping skywards.

Claire held Thomas, gazing at a tapestry that depicted a familiar scene. Claire had no doubt as to the **participants**[7]' identities: a **nobly**[8] countenanced young man, daubed with blood, sobbing and cradling a baby. Next to him rested the massive head of a **shaggy**[9] grey hound, a final stillness about it.

'Llywelyn,' she whispered, 'and Gelert.'

'What?' asked Ben.

'Nothing,' said Claire. 'Come on, Jack.'

Claire touched her wrist. Was the bracelet getting hotter? She pulled back her cuff. The gold was brighter than earlier. Her heart skipped a beat. 'Jack, which way?'

Jack's claws tapped along the wooden floor towards a stage. Two **regal**[10] wooden thrones sat empty. Claire studied them. *Llywelyn's and his wife's?*

Jack hopped onto the stage and turned to look at Claire and Ben. They both climbed up. Jack

---

1 **latch** *(n)* a metal bar with a catch and lever used to fasten a door or gate. *(s)* fastening, clasp, hook, bar.

2 **vibrant** *(adj)* (of a colour) vivid and bright. *(s)* striking, brilliant, intense, strong, rich. *(ant)* pale, washed out.

3 **panelling** *(n)* panels (usually wood) that cover a wall.

4 **intersperse** *(v)* distribute among or between other things. *(s)* spread, strew, scatter. *(ant)* gather, collect.

5 **tapestry** *(n)* a wall hanging with designs made from woven threads.

6 **chandelier** *(n)* a decorative hanging light with branches for light bulbs or candles.

7 **participant** *(n)* something or someone who takes part in something. *(s)* contributor, member. *(ant)* observer.

8 **nobly** *(abv)* in a noble (grand) way. *(s)* splendidly, majestically, magnificently, stately. *(ant)* humbly.

9 **shaggy** *(adj)* having long, thick, messy hair or fur. *(s)* hairy, ragged, tousled, ruffled, unkempt. *(ant)* sleek, smooth.

10 **regal** *(adj)* fit for a ruler. *(s)* royal, grand, majestic, noble, impressive, splendid. *(ant)* plebeian.

ran up and down the length of the platform, his nose working **overtime**[1]. He stilled, prodding what appeared to be part of the stage, but then an opening appeared. On her knees, Claire peered inside it.

'I knew there'd be another tunnel! Ben, prepare to crawl.'

Jack scuttled in, Claire following, and Ben behind them. Mercifully, the crawl was a **cinch**[2]. Within two minutes, they were out the other side and facing yet another stone staircase.

'Prepare to climb!' said Ben.

Jack led, followed by Ben and Claire, who checked behind them. At the top of the staircase was another, identical wood-panelled landing.

'I think we've come full circle,' said Ben, looking around, **circumspect**[3].

Claire shook her head.

She approached the oak door and looked down at Jack. His tail was wagging. Claire knew where they were. She lifted the solid latch, heaving it over, and pulled open the doors. Candles cast shadows. Jack sprinted in and jumped straight up onto a **four-poster bed**[4]. Claire stood at the doorway with Ben. She swallowed. Thomas suddenly felt heavy.

'Ben, stay here for a moment, please,' she said.

Carrying Thomas, Claire walked as quietly as Mr Brady's boots allowed, her mouth dry. Tied-back **drapes**[5] revealed the outline of a person lying beneath a silk-covered quilt. It didn't move.

'Gwilym?' she whispered, praying he was still alive.

Claire laid Thomas on the bed next to Jack. She trembled as she moved closer and pulled back the quilt to reveal his face. Gwilym lay motionless, his eyes closed.

'Gwilym?' Claire said again, but nothing, no response. That familiar panic rose. She knelt, resting her wrist on the bed, and released the bracelet's clasp. Claire removed it and found Gwilym's arm, afraid to touch his wrist in case it was cold, like Thomas. It was barely warm. She placed the bracelet around Gwilym's wrist and fastened the clasp. It was tight, but she closed it.

Claire glanced at Ben, who still stood at the threshold. She looked at Jack, who sat by Thomas,

---

1 **overtime** *(adv)* more diligently than normal. *(s)* rigorously, industriously, painstakingly. *(ant)* lazily.

2 **cinch** *(n)* an easy task. *(s)* breeze, nothing, doddle, gift, snap, cakewalk. *(ant)* difficulty, nightmare, hardship.

3 **circumspect** *(adj)* reluctant to take risks. *(s)* wary, careful, cautious, guarded, watchful. *(ant)* unguarded.

4 **four-poster bed** *(n)* a type of bed with a canopy held up by four corner posts.

5 **drape** *(n)* a long curtain. *(s)* drapery, screen, shroud, veil, hanging.

and waited in silence, aware of her breathing – hoping.

Whomp-whomp-whomp-whomp … It was distant, but those things flew fast. Claire looked at Ben. He went white and seemed small; he heard it too. Claire understood how the weapons on an Apache worked – she hoped Ben didn't.

Claire jumped to her feet. Jack's **hackles**[1] shot up. He growled.

'Gwilym! Gwilym!' she shouted. 'Wake up! Wake up!' Her voice was desperate.

Whomp-whomp-whomp-whomp … The sickening sound, louder now, chopped through the air.

Claire grabbed Gwilym's wrist, covering the bracelet with both hands. Suddenly a golden beam of light shot from Claire's midriff out to the bracelet, dazzling her and forcing her head away.

'Claire?' whispered a quiet, hoarse voice.

Claire's head whirled around. 'Gwilym,' she whispered, 'you're alive.'

'Hold the bracelet just as you are,' he murmured. 'Maintain the light.'

His eyes closed.

Whomp-whomp-whomp-whomp …

Claire looked at Ben. He hadn't moved. Claire *couldn't* move. She clasped the bracelet, squinting at the light beaming from the swallowed gold.

Whomp-whomp-whomp-whomp …

Her family's faces flashed before her. Fat tears rolled down each cheek. She couldn't wipe them away.

Whomp-whomp-whomp-whomp … It was so loud now.

'BEN, RUN!' she screamed. 'RUN!'

He didn't move.

'BEN!' she screamed again.

She'd seen those documentaries. Claire knew the Master would spot them with his night-flying infrared systems. She knew he could use his target acquisition designation system to obliterate the tower.

Whomp-whomp-whomp-whomp …

---

1 **hackles** *(n)* erectile (upright) hairs on an animal's back, risen when it is alarmed. *(s)* spikes, spines, bristles.

The glass in the long picture window vibrated.

Claire turned. Outside the window, the Apache monster hovered like a hungry **vulture**[1], its red light flashing an ominous warning. She couldn't see Dewi's eyes – lenses covered them, like the kid from *Star Wars* who flew in the pod race. Claire hadn't seen the whole film, but Pete had made her watch that scene over and over. Her heart ached – she'd never see her brother again.

Whomp-whomp-whomp-whomp …

Two alien-like night-vision goggles peered out from the cockpit. The Master could trigger the guns using the helmet-mounted display before his eyes. He didn't need hands to fire, so she wouldn't see the end coming. Claire blinked – had he smiled?

She glanced at Ben, who stood petrified, his **vacant**[2] eyes peering straight through her.

Whomp-whomp-whomp-whomp …

The Master hovered outside the window. Claire dared to look at him again. His goggles stared back, trained straight on her. Sickened, Claire saw he was enjoying his **reign**[3] of terror – he could have annihilated them by now.

Claire continued to hold Gwilym's wrist with her right hand and leaped to her feet. Using her left, she grappled with her back pocket, tugging at the compass constricted by the damp denim. The golden beam transmitting to Gwilym had died; Claire prayed Gwilym wouldn't. With a quaking hand, she dislodged the compass and jammed her thumb into its middle.

Whomp-whomp-whomp-whomp …

'Work, you stupid thing, work!' Claire screamed, pressing her thumb into the matt stone. Nothing happened. She pressed harder.

Whomp-whomp-whomp-whomp …

'You idiot!' she shouted, letting go of Gwilym's wrist completely and pushing her right thumb hard into the stone's centre. It sprang to life. Claire shone the piercing emerald laser straight through the window and into the Master's right lens. She **banked on**[4] that being his strongest eye – his target-seeking eye.

Whomp-whomp-whomp-whomp …

---

1 **vulture** *(n)* a scavenger bird of prey that circles above sick or injured animals, waiting for them to die.

2 **vacant** *(adj)* lacking expression or intelligence. *(s)* empty, blank, deadpan, expressionless, inexpressive. *(ant)* expressive.

3 **reign** *(n)* a period of supremacy. *(s)* rule, dominion, tenancy. *(ant)* impotence.

4 **bank on** *(v)* rely or depend upon. *(s)* count on, reckon on, bargain on. *(ant)* doubt, distrust.

But the engine noise changed, sounding not quite so vehement. The Apache's nose turned away from the window, and the rotors' **din**[1] faded, a little.

'BEN, PLEASE, RUN!' she screamed again, torn between Gwilym and her friend. She knew the Apache's missiles could hit a target from around a corner. She knew she was buying time.

'BEN, PLEASE!' she pleaded, but it was as if he'd turned to stone.

Whomp-whomp-whomp-whomp ...

The Master was circling back.

Claire knelt, placing the compass on the floor beside her. She took Gwilym's wrist in both hands, wrapping them around the bracelet. The beam returned, shining from her midriff into the ailing knight.

Whomp-whomp-whomp-whomp ... It was louder.

Looking at Ben was heartbreaking. Claire glanced at Jack and Thomas, and thought of her mum. She closed her eyes, **compressing**[2] Gwilym's wrist more – she would not let go.

Whomp-whomp-whomp-whomp ...

Claire would not give Dewi the **satisfaction**[3] of eye contact again.

Resolute, and squeezing Gwilym's wrist harder, she winced as an ear-splitting sound pierced the air, followed by a strange whining noise. The Master had launched a Hellfire missile. Claire gripped the bracelet, and like the deep-sea diver, she felt only peace.

BOOM!

Claire screamed but didn't let go.

The missile hit, obliterating its target.

Shrapnel[4] showered her from the **splintered**[5] window, the hot shards **indiscriminately**[6] embedding in her skin. Blood poured from her, but she held on to Gwilym.

After several seconds, Claire realised there had been no Hellfire launch. The Tornado's

---

1 **din** *(n)* a loud, often unpleasant noise. *(s)* racket, uproar, commotion. *(ant)* silence, peace.

2 **compress** *(v)* squeeze or press. *(s)* squash, crush, constrict, squidge. *(ant)* release, ease off.

3 **satisfaction** *(n)* enjoyment. *(s)* fulfilment, pleasure, delight, gratification. *(ant)* dissatisfaction.

4 **shrapnel** *(n)* fragments of debris from an explosion.

5 **splinter** *(v)* break into pieces. *(s)* smash, shatter, crack, split, fracture. *(ant)* fix, mend, combine.

6 **indiscriminately** *(adv)* in an indiscriminate (random) manner. *(s)* aimlessly, haphazardly. *(ant)* selectively.

Advanced Short Range Air-to-Air Missile had **decimated**[1] the Apache, **reducing**[2] it to a fireball. The Master was toast. Claire knew the helicopter didn't have an **ejection seat**[3]. Not the Apache. She liked documentaries.

What little remained of the Apache dropped like a stone, landing with a sickening sound of crunching crushed metal.

'Ben?' Claire yelled.

Ben hadn't budged. He stood glued to the spot, helmet on, ghostly white, eyes wide.

'Ben!' she shrieked. 'He's gone! He's done for! He's toast!'

Ben didn't move, but Claire held on to Gwilym's wrist, unsure whether the light emanating from her belly or the fireball had traumatised Ben. Maybe it was because she now sat on the bed like a **pincushion**[4], adorned with glass shards and dripping blood. She was glad of Ben's pink helmet, and she still held the bracelet.

'Claire,' Gwilym whispered, his eyes opening.

Jack barked, jumping onto his master and licking his face.

Claire smiled – she'd done her job. Gwilym's face softened. His eyes closed again, but his mouth rested in almost a smile. He was being rejuvenated.

Claire glanced at Thomas. That **soured**[5] the moment.

'Ben,' she said. 'Come on over. He didn't move. IT'S AN ORDER!' she yelled.

That seemed to work. Ben hobbled across, looking utterly **shell-shocked**[6]. Claire nodded her chin towards the bed. 'Sit,' she said. 'We did it, Ben. We made it!'

Ben looked at her, his eyes distant and **glassy**[7].

'I'm glad this castle is built from stone and not wood,' he eventually said, sniffing hard and inhaling the **acrid**[8] smell of burning helicopter.

---

1 **decimate** *(v)* destroy. *(s)* annihilate, obliterate, exterminate, finish. *(ant)* create, preserve.

2 **reduce** *(v)* bring something to a worse condition. *(s)* diminish, weaken. *(ant)* strengthen.

3 **ejection seat** *(n)* a device that propels the pilot away from an aircraft in an emergency.

4 **pincushion** *(n)* a pad for holding and storing pins safely.

5 **sour** *(v)* make or become bitter or unpleasant. *(s)* embitter, spoil, tarnish, mar, disenchant. *(ant)* sweeten, improve.

6 **shell-shocked** *(adj)* confused or shocked after a distressing or unexpected experience. *(s)* disturbed. *(ant)* carefree.

7 **glassy** *(adj)* (of a person's expression or eyes) dull or without animation. *(s)* vacant, glazed, lifeless. *(ant)* alert, expressive.

8 **acrid** *(adj)* unpleasantly pungent or bitter. *(s)* choking, harsh, acidic, sharp. *(ant)* pleasant, sweet.

*

Josh Drane assumed his end was **nigh**[1]. The Master would see his daughter's face and, at best, **oust**[2] him forever, taking away his longevity, or at worst, he would finish him now.

On accompanying his daughter back to Dewi's private **apartments**[3], her face shredded, Drane was both astounded and relieved to find the Master **absent**[4]. That would afford Drane the fortuitous opportunity to **tend**[5] to the Master's daughter's wounds before he returned. Thankfully, he had so far evaded Siân Cadwaladr. How he had managed that, he was not sure.

He was playing a **dicey**[6], **duplicitous**[7] game in hoodwinking both into believing he was on their side. They were not a pair to cross.

Away from prying eyes, he dressed the daughter's wounds and, with her **consent**[8], administered **intravenous**[9] painkillers and a **sedative**[10]. She would benefit from sleep and recuperation. He prayed scars would not **disfigure**[11] her too much. The cutting-edge medical technologies at Via-Corp would help with that.

When Drane heard that the Master had perished at Cadwaladr Castle, he was elated. He hoped for two things: that Siân Cadwaladr had not yet realised he had switched allegiances and helped the Master, and that Claire Cadwallader still had the Gwalch Gem bracelet.

He would retrieve the incomplete piece and return it to Siân, as she was, and always had been, the true **mastermind**[12] behind the power of the Mal-Instinctives. With Dewi deceased, *he*, Josh Drane, could prove *his* **invaluable**[13] worth, and she, Siân, would **elect**[14] to have him by her side.

---

1 **nigh** *(adj)* near. *(s)* close, nearby. *(ant)* distant, remote.

2 **oust** *(v)* remove from a position or place. *(s)* expel, depose, dislodge, eject, overthrow, topple. *(ant)* accept, crown.

3 **apartments** *(n)* a suite of private rooms within a larger building. *(s)* quarters, penthouse, flat.

4 **absent** *(adj)* not present. *(s)* away, out, missing, gone, vanished. *(ant)* present.

5 **tend** *(v)* look after, care for. *(s)* attend to, minister to, nurse. *(ant)* neglect.

6 **dicey** *(adj)* potentially dangerous and risky. *(s)* unpredictable, precarious, uncertain, perilous. *(ant)* certain, safe.

7 **duplicitous** *(adj)* deceitful. *(s)* dishonest, deceptive, underhanded, untrustworthy. *(ant)* honest, trustworthy.

8 **consent** *(n)* permission or agreement. *(s)* approval, assent, clearance, sanction. *(ant)* dissent.

9 **intravenous** *(adj)* within or into the veins.

10 **sedative** *(n)* a drug that helps to calm or induce sleep. *(s)* tranquiliser, calmative, soporific, depressant.

11 **disfigure** *(v)* ruin the appearance of. *(s)* spoil, deform, maim, deface, blemish, scar, mar. *(ant)* beautify, enhance.

12 **mastermind** *(n)* a creator or director of ingenious plans or schemes. *(s)* genius, architect, intellect.

13 **invaluable** *(adj)* extremely useful. *(s)* indispensable, crucial, irreplaceable, vital, important. *(ant)* worthless.

14 **elect** *(v)* choose. *(s)* pick, decide, opt, select, appoint. *(ant)* reject, decline.

28. Bedside Manner

'Do you realise you could have died out there? Do you realise they could **fire**[1] me for this? What will your mother say, Claire?'

Mr Brady paced like a **Bengal tiger**[2]. His voice had reached the **zenith**[3] of its **crescendo**[4] when he had yelled the word *mother*.

Claire hung her head in feigned shame. A waft of lingering smoke **molecules**[5] hit her nostrils. She hoped Mr Brady couldn't smell it. How would they explain the burning Apache?

'Benjamin Lee Brady, what in heaven's name possessed you to think snow hiking and rock climbing was a good move?' Mr Brady's **tirade**[6] continued, his face puce and not so handsome now. 'Were you trying to kill your friend here? Look at the state of her. She's cut to ribbons after her fall. All I can say is thank goodness you were wearing helmets.'

Ben's head also hung in suitable shame.

Both kids eyeballed each other sideways, then **resumed**[7] their humiliated stance.

'What a dreadful day!' he ranted, still pacing. 'I get food poisoning; that **buffoon**[8] Geraint crashes my Tesla in the snow while bringing it back with new tyres; someone steals the boarding gear; and you've lost your best skateboard!' He pointed at Ben, who took a step back. But Mr

---

1 **fire** *(v)* dismiss someone from a position or job. *(s)* sack, axe, discharge. *(ant)* hire, employ, appoint.

2 **Bengal tiger** *(n)* a species of tiger that lives in parts of India, Bangladesh and other places in South Asia.

3 **zenith** *(n)* the highest point or state. *(s)* top, apex, peak, summit, pinnacle, acme. *(ant)* nadir, bottom, pit.

4 **crescendo** *(n)* a gradually increasing sound. *(ant)* diminuendo.

5 **molecule** *(n)* the tiniest particle of a substance. *(s)* atom.

6 **tirade** *(n)* a lengthy, angry speech, criticism or accusation. *(s)* outburst, rant, diatribe, harangue. *(ant)* praise.

7 **resume** *(v)* continue or begin again (after pausing or an interruption). *(s)* restart, recommence. *(ant)* stop.

8 **buffoon** *(n)* an absurd person. *(s)* clown, idiot, fool, nincompoop, wally. *(ant)* sage, genius.

Brady hadn't finished. 'And the RAF Search and Rescue were called to find you! I'm mortified, just mortified! You'll **recompense**[1] the **taxpayer**[2] for that, Ben Lee Brady, from your pocket money!'

Claire hoped Mr Brady would never realise that the RAF no longer conducted mountain rescues and that the iconic yellow Sea King helicopter that Felicity had appeared in to fly them back to Via-Corp was long retired. She also worried Mr Brady might have a heart attack. If he didn't have one now, just wait until he saw her mother's face. Dee would flip.

Sorry, Mr Brady, she thought, *on both counts: for doubting you in the first place and for believing, even for a second, you could be a Mal-Instinctive.* But the fact that Mr Brady had been ill at the same time as Gwilym and Geraint still niggled Claire.

'Claire, I do not **relish**[3] calling your mother about your injuries or the idea that we must stay overnight. I have a good mind to make you call her yourself.'

Claire didn't fancy that. 'I'm so sorry, Mr Brady,' she whispered, her eyes watching her feet.

He still paced the floor.

'I'm so sorry, Dad,' said Ben, equally contrite.

'Your mother will be furious,' scolded Mr Brady, but in Mandarin.

Claire glanced at Ben, who'd told her his dad never spoke Mandarin away from home unless he was *really* mad.

'At least we don't have to find a hotel at this ridiculously late hour,' he said, his tone a tad calmer. 'You guys can use Cristy's executive quarters – she's been called away.'

Claire's and Ben's eyes met.

'We lost a Via-Corp chopper in this appalling snowstorm, which is still **unaccounted for**[4]. The storm YOU TWO got lost in and then wasted the RAF's time over. You're lucky to be ALIVE.' Mr Brady resumed his shouting and pacing.

The children said nothing; there was nothing to say.

'Let's tend to those cuts, young lady.' Mr Brady lifted his chin; his colour was calming down. 'The rescue team did a great job of cleaning you up, but those wounds need proper medical

---

1 **recompense** *(v)* pay back. *(s)* repay, reimburse, compensate. *(ant)* take, penalise, fine.

2 **taxpayer** *(n)* a person who pays taxes.

3 **relish** *(v)* enjoy greatly and savour. *(s)* admire, revel, like, appreciate, delight in. *(ant)* detest, dislike, loathe.

4 **unaccounted for** *(adj)* unexplained. *(s)* unknown, undiscovered, unfound, lost, mysterious. *(ant)* known, explained.

attention. What will your mother say?' he said again, shaking his head.

Claire dismissed Dee's potential reaction. It paled compared to Gwilym's revelation, when she'd broken down, weeping over Thomas's cold body. Only he and the knights mattered now, and she'd stop at nothing until she found the gem. Claire hadn't eaten since swallowing the gold, and sleep would elude her tonight. Due to leave for Manchester first thing, assuming the now-raging storm eased, she had only hours left to find what she needed.

Thomas had located the Welsh gold in the **bowels**[1] of Cadwaladr Castle and brought it to Claire. It had saved the Knights Hawk – it was enough – and for now, it remained in her belly. She hadn't needed to eat or drink anything since swallowing it. She just hoped that the gold would stay there.

Claire toyed with telling Ben her plans, but she feared his tiredness. Although fitter than most, he had no energising gold inside him to rejuvenate him. To involve Ben would jeopardise him more. Claire decided she would hunt for the Gwalch Gem alone.

If she found the emerald hawk and placed it back into the gold bracelet, the knights would live, but there also remained a chance that Thomas might live again. The **caveat**[2]: there wasn't much time.

Gwilym had said the bracelet did not possess the power to **reanimate**[3] humans, but animals, yes. The knights were reinvigorated and had longer, but a potential reanimation for Thomas must be attempted within twenty-four hours of his death. After that, there was no hope.

'Hungry?' asked Mr Brady.

'Starving,' replied Ben. His dad rolled his eyes.

'Yes, I am Mr Brady. Thank you,' said Claire, fibbing.

'Oh, Claire, by the way, someone handed your backpack in to lost property. You guys seem to be losing everything today.' He tutted, then passed it over to an abashed-looking Claire, who hung it on her shoulder.

Claire held her bare wrist, missing the bracelet's warmth. Tonight she must find the Gwalch Gem – the emerald hawk. The bracelet must become whole once more. The clock ticked. Claire prayed the emerald hadn't evaporated with the Master and his Apache, and wondered if Via-

---

1 **bowels** *(n)* the depths, the deepest part. *(s)* core, belly, heart, interior, middle. *(ant)* peak, summit.

2 **caveat** *(n)* a detail that modifies a situation. *(s)* condition, limitation, proviso, stipulation.

3 **reanimate** *(v)* bring back to life or consciousness. *(s)* revive, resurrect, resuscitate. *(ant)* destroy.

Corp yet knew of the demise of David Lewis – the Master.

Cristy would be her starting point – the Master's daughter. Sweet, swindling Cristy, the blonde witch. Claire would make her pay for the agonies inflicted on her friends.

'Right, let's have your face looked at,' said Mr Brady. 'Then we'll get you some food and a bed.'

'Claire?' whispered Ben.

'Yeah?'

'Who do you reckon flew the Tornado?'

Until now Claire hadn't thought about that, but if the Knights Hawk had been dying, then who *had* flown the GR4?

'Good question,' she whispered back.

'Come on, follow me,' said Mr Brady, heading towards the security panel of his private suite.

Claire secured her backpack over both shoulders and turned to follow.

'Er, excuse me, Mr Brady,' said Claire.

'Yes?' he replied, removing his hand from the panel as the door slid sideways.

'Have you seen Jayne Lewis today? My dad's friend?'

Mr Brady paused, a **pensive**[1] look on his face. 'Not in a while.' His voice was **airy**[2].

'Oh, OK,' said Claire, concealing her disappointment.

Claire and Ben followed Mr Brady out into a plush, carpeted corridor.

'We have great Via-Corp doctors,' said Mr Brady. 'You'll need butterfly stitches and an antibiotic shot.' He frowned at Claire.

They arrived at the lifts. Mr Brady did the palm–eye routine, and they stepped in to the sounds of cheesy music.

Claire wondered where Felicity was now. *Felicity, a pilot!* Maybe *she* had flown the Tornado, but Claire doubted that. She thought of Lily and Arjun, and hoped Geraint was on the mend. *Geraint*, marvelled Claire, picturing the **brusque**[3] barrel of a man, *a Knight Hawk*. He and Lily had hidden that well with **banter**[4] when they had come to tow the Tesla away. *Never judge a book by its cover*, Claire admonished herself.

---

1 **pensive** *(adj)* thoughtful. *(s)* reflective, contemplative, preoccupied, meditative. *(ant)* thoughtless.

2 **airy** *(adj)* not serious. *(s)* light, casual, nonchalant, breezy, jaunty, blithe, cheerful. *(ant)* serious.

3 **brusque** *(adj)* blunt and abrupt in manner. *(s)* curt, direct, outspoken, tactless, offhand. *(ant)* evasive, verbose.

4 **banter** *(n)* a friendly exchange of teasing. *(s)* repartee, raillery, ribbing, quips, joking, wisecracks.

'Here we are,' said Mr Brady as the lift opened. 'We're **privileged**[1] to have a mini hospital on the compound,' he said. 'It's so isolated up here it's necessary.'

Wafts of **disinfectant**[2] and **antiseptic**[3] pinched Claire's nostrils – she hated those smells. The corridor gleamed, the floor, shiny tiles, the walls, all a brilliant white.

They marched along, reaching a large door with a red cross in its centre.

'In here,' said Mr Brady, his palm on the panel. The door clicked open.

Claire wondered why certain doors slid sideways and others just opened.

A smiling young woman wearing a nurse's uniform greeted them. 'Come through,' she beckoned. 'The on-duty doctor is expecting you.'

The nurse led them past various **booths**[4], beeping machines and banks of screens. Staff tended patients. Claire didn't think any of her cuts needed attention, but what could she say to Mr Brady? She'd have to go along with it. Claire knew the gold in her stomach would heal her wounds.

'The doctor will see you now,' said the nurse, smiling.

'In you go, kids,' said Mr Brady, turning to thank the nurse.

They entered a **swish**[5] examination room. Claire's one experience of hospital was at her local A & E when she'd tripped and hurt her ankle. Although the staff had been friendly, A & E had spilled over with drunks and vomit, and the examination rooms had been **poky**[6]. It hadn't been pleasant.

'Take a seat,' said the doctor. 'I'll be with you in two ticks.'

The doctor's back faced them; he was **prepping**[7] something on the worktop. Rows of screens covered one wall, and space-aged monitors another.

'Patient up on the bed,' he said, snapping on a thin plastic glove. 'Our security **footage**[8] showed

---

1 **privileged** *(adj)* having special benefits or rights. *(s)* advantaged, fortunate. *(ant)* underprivileged, disadvantaged.

2 **disinfectant** *(n)* a chemical that kills bacteria. *(s)* antiseptic, germicide, sanitiser, cleanser.

3 **antiseptic** *(n)* a substance that prevents the growth of bacteria. *(s)* disinfectant, germicide, bactericide.

4 **booth** *(n)* an enclosed area that allows privacy. *(s)* cubicle, compartment, enclosure, recess.

5 **swish** *(adj)* impressively modern or smart. *(s)* plush, fancy, swanky, posh. *(ant)* scruffy, downmarket.

6 **poky** *(adj)* (of a place) uncomfortably small and cramped. *(s)* tiny, restricted, tight, boxy. *(ant)* spacious.

7 **prep** *(v)* prepare. *(s)* ready, prime, organise. *(ant)* disorganise.

8 **footage** *(n)* video. *(s)* recording, tape, film.

me enough to know you require an antibiotic shot and local **anaesthetic**[1] to fix those cuts,' he said.

A couple of **piddling**[2] injections didn't faze Claire any more.

Distracted, Mr Brady swiped his phone, and Ben gazed around, admiring the technology.

Claire lay back on the bed, blinking at the dazzling light in the ceiling, the compass in her back pocket pressing into her bottom. She glanced at the borrowed trainers on her feet, they were pretty cool. Claire closed her eyes and thought of Dewi being another form of the name David. She wondered what Gwilym might mean in English.

Claire's eyes snapped wide open. Her limbs weakened, and her insides turned watery. Barely able to muster her voice, she muttered, 'Mr Brady, you're good at languages. Do you know what the name Siân means in English?'

Mr Brady glanced up from his phone, a pensive look on his face. 'Mmm, it's a **traditional**[3] Welsh name. I'm pretty sure it means Jane,' he said, then went back to his phone.

Even with the fortifying Welsh gold in her belly, **in one fell swoop**[4], shock sucked all strength from Claire. Sweat pricked her body. She wanted to scream but retched instead. Siân Cadwaladr, if translated into English, meant Jane Cadwaladr. Was Jayne Lewis Siân Cadwaladr?

The doctor's second glove snapped on, and he turned around to face Claire, a **syringe**[5] in his hand. Incapacitated by shock, her eyes swivelled towards him.

'OK,' he said, smiling. 'Let's start with the anaesthetic.'

Claire felt as though the ground beneath her was **receding**[6]. She looked at Ben. He'd turned as white as the walls. Engrossed, Mr Brady studied his phone.

The young doctor approached, the long needle glistening in the **clinical**[7] light.

'Sharp scratch,' said the cheery doctor as he neared, his smile twisting into a smirk.

---

1 **anaesthetic** *(n)* a substance that reduces or blocks sensitivity to pain. *(s)* painkiller, anodyne, analgesic.

2 **piddling** *(adj)* of no importance or significance. *(s)* trivial, trifling, insignificant, unimportant. *(ant)* significant.

3 **traditional** *(adj)* long-established in a particular place. *(s)* conventional, customary, classic. *(ant)* novel, unconventional.

4 **in one fell swoop** *(adv)* in one go. *(s)* all at once.

5 **syringe** *(n)* a tube with a hollow needle used to inject or withdraw fluids. *(s)* injection, jab.

6 **recede** *(v)* move back or diminish. *(s)* withdraw, retreat, ebb, fade. *(ant)* advance, grow.

7 **clinical** *(adj)* stark and functional. *(s)* cold, plain, unadorned, simple, austere, practical. *(ant)* ornate, warm.

Mr Brady still didn't look up. Ben's eyes pleaded with Claire's. She had seconds to decide: reveal everything to Mr Brady and scupper her chances of saving the Knights Hawk and Thomas, or let Josh Drane stab her with a three-inch needle.

THE END

Learn With *The Cadwaladr Quests* Series

Your *The Cadwaladr Quests: Book 2 - Race For The Gold* forms part of *The Cadwaladr Quests* integrated education series.

Read Book 1 in the series - the vocabulary novel *Tangled Time* - then consolidate your comprehension, creative writing and vocabulary skills with the *Tangled Time Workbook*.

Finally, further test your knowledge with the *Vocabulary Revision Notebook*.

Find all the available *The Cadwaladr Quests Series* books online via your local Amazon store.

The Cadwaladr Quests - Book 1: Tangled Time

The Cadwaladr Quests - Book 1: Tangled Time Workbook

The Cadwaladr Quests - Book 1: Tangled Time Vocabulary Revision Notebook

PS: Need *The Cadwaladr Quests* in US English? Please visit your local Amazon site for the USA version!

Reviews, please!

If you've enjoyed *The Cadwaladr Quests: Book 2 - Race For The Gold* please feel free to leave a review online at the book's Amazon page.

Errata & Information

To report any **errata**[1], please email: **errata@slager.co.uk**
If you would like information about new books in *The Cadwaladr Quests* series, please visit:

SLAGER.CO.UK

You can stay up to date with S. L. Ager, author of *The Cadwaladr Quests* series, on social media:

facebook.com/SLAgerAuthor
instagram.com/SLAgerAuthor
linkedin.com/in/SLAgerAuthor
pinterest.com/SLAgerAuthor
twitter.com/SLAgerAuthor

1 **erratum** *(n)* an error in writing or publishing (plural: *errata*).

Printed in Great Britain
by Amazon

41347055R00149